A Guidebook to
Virginia's Historical Markers

THE UNIVERSITY PRESS OF VIRGINIA
Copyright © 1985 by the Virginia Historic Landmarks Commission
First published 1985

Library of Congress Cataloging in Publication Data

Peters, Margaret T.
  A guidebook to Virginia's historical markers.

  Includes index.
    1. Historical markers—Virginia—Guide-books.
  2. Virginia—History, Local. 3. Virginia—Description
  and travel—1981-   —Guide-books. I. Virginia
  Historic Landmarks Commission. II. Title.
  F227.P48   1985   917.55   84-20914
  ISBN 0-8139-1047-1

Cover photo of Burke's Garden by David Edwards

Printed in the United States of America

CONTENTS

COMMONWEALTH of VIRGINIA

Office of the Governor

Richmond 23219

Ladies and Gentlemen:

It is indeed a pleasure to present this guidebook to Virginia's highway historical markers. This volume has been prepared by the Virginia Historic Landmarks Commission and is the first update published by the Commonwealth since 1948.

Virginia's highway historical marker program, which began in 1926, is among the oldest in the nation. Our predecessors felt strongly that Virginia's illustrious history should be put forward on roadside markers. Today we continue to hope that the travelling public will use the markers and this guidebook as a means to learn more about this place which we cherish so deeply.

I hope that you will find this book both enjoyable and an educational enhancement to your travels in Virginia.

Sincerely,

Charles S. Robb

INTRODUCTION

VIRGINIA HISTORIC LANDMARKS COMMISSION

The primary role of the Virginia Historic Landmarks Commission is to identify and to encourage the preservation of Virginia's great wealth of historic, architectural, and archaeological resources. Prior to the creation of the VHLC by the General Assembly in 1966, Virginia had no governmental apparatus for safeguarding its heritage of historic buildings and sites, for coordinating historic preservation activity in the state, or for fitting the surviving components of this resource into the pattern of planning for the future. In response to mounting evidence that this heritage was being exploited or destroyed, and that this destruction was not inevitable, the General Assembly established the Commission upon the principle that it is the state's basic responsibility to promote the conservation of irreplaceable man-made as well as natural resources, and that the state should assume a leadership role in providing overall coordination in the field of historic preservation.

The Commission is composed of nine members; seven are appointed by the governor, and two—the state librarian and the director of the Department of Conservation and Economic Development—are ex-officio members. Serving the Commission is a professional staff consisting of an executive director assisted by architectural historians, archaeologists, historians, architects, and other specialists.

The main office of the VHLC is located in Richmond, and its Research Center for Archaeology is in Yorktown. The Commission is mandated to survey, evaluate, and plan for the proper protection of historic sites and structures. This includes publication of a Virginia Landmarks Register that recognizes Virginia's most significant sites and buildings and the nomination of outstanding properties to the National Register of Historic Places. The VHLC is an important link in the federal historic preservation program as well. Under the federal mandate, in addition to the preparation of National Register nominations, the VHLC evaluates appropriateness of rehabilitation of historic properties in Virginia under the terms of the Economic Recovery Tax Act of 1981, reviews and comments upon any federally funded, licensed, or sponsored project that may threaten a historic building or site, and prepares a comprehensive statewide preservation plan to provide a framework for preservation activities and a guide to land-use planners. The Virginia Historic Landmarks Commission is committed to providing public education in the field of historic preservation and is available to assist in an advisory capacity to local governments, preservation groups, and owners of historic properties. The Commission publishes a periodic report of its activities, *Notes on Virginia*, as well as a series of research reports on the most significant archaeological findings of its staff.

HISTORY OF THE MARKER PROGRAM IN VIRGINIA

The highway historical marker program in Virginia has its roots in legislation enacted by Virginia's General Assembly in 1926. The 1926 law created the Conservation and Economic Development Commission and provided funds for advertising the advantages and resources of the state to a growing traveling public. The state's leaders concluded that a state as rich in history as Virginia, the scene of two major wars, needed to explain that rich history to visitors to the Commonwealth. Soon thereafter, Dr. H. C. Eckenrode was selected by the Conservation and Economic Development Commission to direct a program to ascertain the historic sites in Virginia and to mark them appropriately. Highlights of the activities of the American Revolution and the Civil War that took place in Virginia proved to be among the most popular sites selected for recognition; also included were historic homes, churches, and sites of other major events in Virginia's past. Prominent Virginia historians such as Douglas Southall Freeman, H. R. McIlwaine, and Lyon G. Tyler served on a History Advisory Committee to assist Dr. Eckenrode in the selection of sites to be marked as well as in the preparation of texts for those markers.

Markers were identified by a letter/numeral code. The letter indicated the highway, since at that time highways were only designated by letter. The numeral assigned served to distinguish the markers on any one highway and were assigned as each marker was erected. This system has been followed to some degree throughout the years; however, changes in highway routes, along with the addition of many markers, have made strict adherence to the original system all but impossible.

Markers were to be placed along major travel routes in order to reach the largest number of travelers. Care was taken to place markers so that they would not impede safe travel, but so that they could be easily read by motorists as they passed by. As automobile speeds increased, Dr. Eckenrode realized the need for a guidebook containing the inscriptions on the markers, so in 1930 the first highway marker guidebook was published.

The number of markers increased steadily. By 1934, 1,200 markers were in place, with plans for an additional 400 as funds became available. During the depression years, efforts were made to provide "pull-offs" for the markers, so the motorist could stop safely and read the text of each marker.

The marker program was suspended during World War II and did not resume until 1946. The last official marker guidebook was published in 1948 by the Department of Conservation and Economic Development's Division of History and Archaeology. Responsibility for the erection and maintenance of markers was subsequently transferred to the Virginia Department of Highways, while the responsibility for researching and approving new markers was assigned to the Virginia State Library. The State Library continued to have jurisdiction over the marker program until 1966, when the General Assembly transferred the program to the newly created Virginia Historic Landmarks Commission.

Between 1948 and 1976, some one hundred new markers were erected, and efforts were made to broaden and diversify the subjects included on them. Although a number of the new markers continued to identify sites associated with the Civil War, many explained some important events in Virginia's twentieth-century history, as well as lesser known sites associated with colonial and antebellum Virginia. In 1976, the Virginia General Assembly curtailed state funding for new or replacement markers.

Today all funds for new markers come from private sources or local governments. Approximately twenty to twenty-five new markers are approved by the Virginia Historic Landmarks Commission each year. The Virginia Department of Highways and Transportation retains responsibility for the erection of new markers and the maintenance of existing ones.

The original intent of the marker program was to foster interest nationwide in Virginia's history and to encourage tourism in Virginia. While subsequent research may have cast doubt on the complete accuracy of some very early markers, the markers remain a valuable source of information that enhances the appeal to those using Virginia's highways. This updated guide to the markers in the state system as of December 1983 is intended to make that information even more readily available to today's traveler.

HOW TO USE THE GUIDEBOOK

The marker guidebook has been arranged to accommodate contemporary travel patterns and to facilitate finding a specific marker. The texts of the markers are arranged by symbol and number, beginning with A-1 and continuing through XP-5. This arrangement generally follows the location of primary highways. Markers with no accompanying letter/numeral symbols are arranged alphabetically by title at the end of the listings.

Three separate indexing systems have been developed. The first is alphabetical by marker title. The second is arranged by subject, so that a reader may refer to all markers displaying information on a particular subject or marking buildings of a specific type. The large group of markers pertaining to the Civil War are arranged regionally in that index to assist the traveler in a particular area of the state. The final index is arranged alphabetically by county and independent city, with the text (if any) for each jurisdiction marker followed by the location of all markers in that particular jurisdiction.

Markers with an asterisk are no longer in place, but their inscriptions have been included together with their original locations. Distances have been measured from the closest village, town, or major intersection; all locations were verified by the district offices of the Virginia Department of Highways and Transportation in 1982–83. The text of each marker has been reproduced as it appears on the face of the marker itself. The traveler should be aware that, while there may be other historical markers that resemble the state's in shape and design, only markers formally approved by the state are included in this book.

ACKNOWLEDGMENTS

The district offices of the Virginia Department of Highways and Transportation who inventoried all standing markers in 1982–83.

Boyd Cassell and Cindy Denton of the Operations and Maintenance Section of the Virginia Department of Highways and Transportation.

Aubrey Shelton, who with his staff at the Virginia Department of Highways and Transportation prepared the map.

The Virginia State Travel Service and the Virginia Department of State Parks, who also provided information for this guidebook.

The clerical staff of the Virginia Historic Landmarks Commission, who helped in preparation of the manuscript.

David Edwards, Architectural Historian, the Virginia Historic Landmarks Commission, for the cover photograph.

A-1*   ACTION AT STEPHENSON'S DEPOT

Near this place, Ewell, on June 15, 1863, captured wagon trains, cannon and several thousand men of Milroy's army, which had been driven from Winchester by Early. *Frederick County: Route 11, 4 miles n. of Winchester.*

A-2*   ACTION OF CARTER'S FARM

Near here the Confederate General Ramseur was attacked by Averell and pushed back toward Winchester, July 20, 1864. *Frederick County: Route 11, 2.75 miles n. of Winchester.*

A-3   CAPTURE OF STAR FORT

The fort on the hilltop to the southwest, known as Star Fort, was taken by Colonel Schoonmaker of Sheridan's army in the battle of September 19, 1864. *Frederick County: Route 11, .8 mile n. of Winchester.*

A-4*   FORT COLLIER

Just to the south was built by Joseph E. Johnston, 1861. Early's left rested here, Third Battle of Winchester, September 19, 1864. *Frederick County: Route 11, .4 mile n. of Winchester.*

A-6*   FIRST BATTLE OF WINCHESTER

On the morning of May 25, 1862, New England troops in Bank's army held this position, facing Jackson, who was advancing from the south. *Frederick County: Route 11, s. of Winchester.*

A-7   FIRST BATTLE OF WINCHESTER

Here Stonewall Jackson, in the early morning of May 25, 1862, halted his advance guard and observed the Union position. *Frederick County: Route 11, .6 mile s. of Winchester.*

A-8*   SECOND BATTLE OF WINCHESTER

Here Ewell, on June 14, 1863, detached Early to move around Milroy's flank and attack the works west of Winchester. *Frederick County: Route 11, .6 mile s. of Winchester.*

A-9   BATTLE OF KERNSTOWN

On the hill to the west, Stonewall Jackson, late in the afternoon of March 23, 1862, attacked the Union force under Shields holding Winchester. After a fierce action, Jackson, who was greatly outnumbered, withdrew southward, leaving his dead on the field. These were buried next day by citizens of Winchester. *Frederick County: Route 11, 5.3 miles n. of Stephens City.*

A-10   EARLY AND CROOK

Here Early, just returned from his raid to Washington, attacked a pursuing force under Crook and drove it back, July 24, 1864. *Frederick County: Route 11, 1 mile n. of Kernstown.*

A-11   FIRST BATTLE OF WINCHESTER

The main body of Stonewall Jackson's army halted here to rest in the early morning of May 25, 1862. *Frederick County: Route 11, 3.2 miles n. of Stephens City.*

A-12   HOUSE OF FIRST SETTLER

Springdale, home of Colonel John Hite, son of Joist Hite, leader of the first settlers in this section, was built in 1753. Just to the south are the ruins of Hite's Fort, built about 1734. *Frederick County: Route 11, 2.3 miles n. of Stephens City.*

A-13*   STEPHENS CITY

General David Hunter ordered the burning of this town, on May 30, 1864; but Major Stearns, First New York cavalry, prevented it. *Frederick County: Route 11, center of Stephens City.*

A-14   END OF SHERIDAN'S RIDE

This knoll marks the position of the Union Army when Sheridan rejoined it at 10:30 A.M., October 19, 1864, in the battle of Cedar Creek. His arrival, with Wright's efforts, checked the Union retreat. *Frederick County: Route 11, 3.2 miles s. of Stephens City.*

A-15   BATTLE OF CEDAR CREEK

Near this point General Early, on the morning of October 19, 1864, stopped his advance, and from this position he was driven by Sheridan in the afternoon. *Frederick County: Route 11, .2 mile n. of Middletown.*

A-16   ENGAGEMENT OF MIDDLETOWN

Here Stonewall Jackson, on May 24, 1862, attacked Banks, retreating from Strasburg, and forced him to divide his army. *Frederick County: Route 11, at Middletown.*

A-17   TOMB OF AN UNKNOWN SOLDIER

On the highest mountain top to the southeast is the grave of an unknown soldier. The mountain top was used as a signal station by both armies, 1861–1865. *Frederick County: Route 11, 1 mile s. of Middletown.*

A-18   ABRAHAM LINCOLN'S FATHER

Four miles west, Thomas Lincoln, father of the President, was born about 1778. He was taken to Kentucky by his father about 1781. Beside the road here was Lincoln Inn, long kept by a member of the family. *Rockingham County: Route 11, at Lacey Spring.*

A-19   TRENCHES ON HUPP'S HILL

These trenches were constructed by Sheridan in the autumn of 1864 while campaigning against Early. *Shenandoah County: Route 11, .8 mile n. of Strasburg.*

A-20   FRONTIER FORT

This house, built about 1755, is the old Hupp homestead. It was used as a fort in Indian attacks. *Shenandoah County: Route 11, at Strasburg.*

A-21   BATTLE OF CEDAR CREEK

The breaking of this bridge in the evening of October 19, 1864, permitted Sheridan to retake most of the material captured in the morning by Early. *Shenandoah County: Route 11, at Strasburg.*

A-22* BATTLE OF FISHER'S HILL

Early took position here after the battle of Winchester, and here he was attacked by Sheridan, September 22, 1864, and forced to retire. *Shenandoah County: Route 11, 1.9 miles s. of Strasburg.*

A-23 BATTLE OF FISHER'S HILL

Here Early's Adjutant-General, A. S. Pendleton, while attempting to check Sheridan's attack, was mortally wounded, September 22, 1864. *Shenandoah County: Route 11, 3.1 miles s. of Strasburg.*

A-24 BANKS' FORT

The earthworks on the hilltop to the southwest were constructed by General Banks in the campaign of 1862. *Shenandoah County: Route 11, at Strasburg.*

A-25 ACTION OF TOM'S BROOK

Here Early's cavalry under Rosser and Lomax was driven back by Sheridan's cavalry under Torbert, October 9, 1864. *Shenandoah County: Route 11, .1 mile s. of Tom's Brook.*

A-26* CAVALRY ENGAGEMENT

Near this point the First Virginia Cavalry and the First New York Cavalry fought an engagement, November 17, 1863. *Shenandoah County: Route 11, 1 mile s. of Mount Jackson.*

A-27 RUDE'S HILL ACTION

Rude's Hill was reached by two divisions of Sheridan's Union cavalry following the Confederate General Jubal A. Early, on November 22, 1864. Early promptly took position on the hill to oppose them. The cavalry, charging across the flats, were repulsed in a sharp action and fell back northward. *Shenandoah County: Route 11, 3.7 miles n. of New Market.*

A-28 BATTLE OF NEW MARKET

On the hills to the north took place the battle of New Market, May 15, 1864. The Union Army, under General Franz Sigel, faced southwest. John C. Breckinridge, once Vice-President of the United States, commanded the Confederates. General Scott Shipp commanded the cadet corps of the Virginia Military Institute, which distinguished itself, capturing a battery. The battle ended in Sigel's retreat northward. *Shenandoah County: Route 11, .6 mile n. of New Market.*

A-29 CAVALRY ENGAGEMENT

Here, at Lacey's Springs, Rosser's Confederate cavalry attacked Custer's camp, December 20, 1864. Rosser and Custer (of Indian fame) had been roommates at West Point. *Rockingham County: Route 11, 7.5 miles n. of Harrisonburg.*

A-30 WHERE ASHBY FELL

A mile and a half east of this point, Turner Ashby, Stonewall Jackson's cavalry commander, was killed, June 6, 1862, while opposing Fremont's advance. *Rockingham County: Route 11, 1.5 miles s. of Harrisonburg.*

A-31   OLD PROVIDENCE CHURCH

Two and a half miles northwest. As early as 1748, a log meeting house stood there. In 1793 a stone church (still standing) was built. In 1859 it was succeeded by a brick church, which gave way to the present building in 1918. In the graveyard rest ancestors of Cyrus McCormick, inventor of the reaper, and fourteen Revolutionary soldiers. *Augusta County: Route 340, 1.4 miles n. of Steeles Tavern.*

A-32   SHERIDAN'S LAST RAID

Here was fought the engagement of Mount Crawford, March 1, 1865, in Sheridan's last raid. *Rockingham County: Route 11, .3 mile s. of Mount Crawford.*

A-33   HARRISONBURG

Here Thomas Harrison and wife deeded land for the Rockingham County public buildings, August 5, 1779. The same act established both Louisville, Ky., and Harrisonburg, May, 1780. Named for its founder, the town was also known as Rocktown. It was incorporated in 1849. In its vicinity battles were fought in 1862 and 1864. The present courthouse was built in 1897. Harrisonburg became a city in 1916. *Rockingham County: Route 11, at Harrisonburg.*

A-34   SEVIER'S BIRTHPLACE

Near here was born John Sevier, pioneer and soldier, September 23, 1745. He was a leader in the Indian wars and at the battle of King's Mountain, 1780. He was the only governor of the short-lived state of Franklin and the first governor of Tennessee. Sevier died in Georgia, September 24, 1815. *Shenandoah County: Route 11, .7 mile s. of New Market.*

A-35   END OF THE CAMPAIGN

Here Stonewall Jackson, retreating up the Valley before the converging columns of Fremont and Shields, turned at bay, June, 1862. A mile southeast Jackson's cavalry commander, Ashby, was killed, June 6. At Cross Keys, six miles southeast, Ewell of Jackson's army defeated Fremont, June 8. Near Port Republic, ten miles southeast, Jackson defeated Shields, June 9. This was the end of Jackson's Valley Campaign. *Rockingham County: Route 11, at Harrisonburg.*

A-36   FAIRFAX LINE

Here ran the southwestern boundary of Lord Fairfax's vast land grant, the Northern Neck. It was surveyed by Peter Jefferson, Thomas Jefferson's father, and others in 1746. *Shenandoah County: Route 11, .7 mile s. of New Market.*

A-37   OLD STONE FORT

One mile west is the Old Stone Fort, built about 1755. The northern end is loopholed for defense against Indians. *Frederick County: Route 11, at Middletown.*

A-38* HACKWOOD PARK

One mile east is Hackwood Park House, built in 1777 by General John Smith. It was used by Union troops as a hospital, September 19, 1864. *Frederick County: Route 11, 1.7 miles n. of Winchester.*

A-39 NEW PROVIDENCE CHURCH

This church, seven and a half miles west, was organized by John Blair in 1746. Five successive church buildings have been erected. The first pastor was John Brown. Samuel Brown, second pastor, had as wife Mary Moore, captured in youth by Indians and known as "The Captive of Abb's Valley." The synod of Virginia was organized here, 1788. *Augusta County: Route 340, at Steeles Tavern.*

A-40* FIRST SETTLER'S CAMP

Near here the first settler of Rockbridge County, John McDowell, pitched his first camp in the county, October, 1737. *Augusta County: Route 340, at Steeles Tavern.*

A-41 LAST INDIAN OUTRAGE

Here, in 1766, took place the last Indian outrage in Shenandoah County. Five Indians attacked two settler families fleeing to Woodstock. Two men were killed; the women and children escaped. *Shenandoah County: Route 11, 1.9 miles s. of Woodstock.*

A-42* RUFFNER'S HOME

Just to the west is Tribrook, home of W. H. Ruffner, first superintendent of public instruction of Virginia. He began, in 1870, the state's public school system. *Rockbridge County: Route 11, at Lexington.*

A-42* CHRISMAN'S SPRING

Four hundred yards northeast of this spring is the home of Jacob Chrisman, son-in-law of Joist Hite, built about 1753. *Frederick County: Route 11, 2 miles s. of Stephens City.*

A-43 MCDOWELL'S GRAVE

In this cemetery are the graves of Captain John McDowell and seven companions, who were killed by Indians near Balcony Falls, December 14, 1742. This fight began a war that lasted until 1744. *Rockbridge County: Route 11, 1.1 miles s. of Fairfield.*

A-44 LIBERTY HALL ACADEMY

This school, which was founded in 1777 and finally grew into Washington and Lee University, stood a short distance to the southwest of this point. *Rockbridge County: Route 11, 5.3 miles n. of Lexington.*

A-45* RED HOUSE ESTATE

This was the site of the home of Captain John McDowell, killed by the Indians in 1742, and the birthplace of Doctor Ephraim McDowell, pioneer in abdominal surgery. *Rockbridge County: Route 11, 1.1 miles s. of Fairfield.*

A-46 TIMBER RIDGE CHURCH

This Presbyterian Church was built in 1756, nineteen years after the first settlement in Rockbridge County. *Rockbridge County: Route 11, 5.3 miles n. of Lexington (at Sam Houston Wayside).*

A-47   CHERRY GROVE ESTATE

Here was born James McDowell, Governor of Virginia, 1843–46. *Rockbridge County: Route 11, .3 mile s. of Fairfield.*

A-48   AUDLEY PAUL'S FORT

Near here stood the stockade fort of Captain Audley Paul, noted colonial frontier soldier. He served in the Sandy Creek expedition against the Shawnees, 1756, at the battle of Point Pleasant, 1774, and in repelling Indian raids. In 1761, the fort was crowded with settlers' families seeking protection against marauding Shawnees. *Botetourt County: Route 11, 4.5 miles s. of Natural Bridge.*

A-49   THORN HILL ESTATE

Home of Colonel John Bowyer, an officer in the Revolutionary War, and of General E. F. Paxton, commander of the Stonewall Brigade, killed at Chancellorsville, May 3, 1863. *Rockbridge County: Route 251, .6 mile n. of Lexington.*

A-50   INDIAN MASSACRE

Near here was the Renick settlement, raided by the Shawnee Indians in 1757. Five settlers were killed and nine taken captive. *Botetourt County: Route 11, .9 mile n. of Buchanan.*

A-51   VIRGINIA INVENTORS

A mile and a half northwest, Cyrus H. McCormick perfected, in 1831, the grain reaper. In that vicinity, in 1856, J.A.E. Gibbs devised the chainstitch sewing machine. *Augusta County: Route 340, at Steeles Tavern.*

A-52   BIRTHPLACE OF SAM HOUSTON

In a cabin on the hilltop to the east Sam Houston was born, March 2, 1793. As commander-in-chief of the Texas army, he won the battle of San Jacinto, which secured Texan independence, April 21, 1836. He was President of Texas, 1836–1838, 1841–1844; United States Senator, 1846–1859; Governor, 1860–1861. He died, July, 1863. *Rockbridge County: Route 11, 5.3 miles n. of Lexington.*

A-53   BETHEL CHURCH

Two miles west. The first church was built by Colonel Robert Doak in 1779. Captain James Tate, an elder, led in the battles of Cowpens and Guilford Courthouse (1781) a company drawn mainly from this church. In the churchyard 23 Revolutionary soldiers are buried. The present building was erected in 1888. *Augusta County: Route 340, 2.1 miles n. of Greenville.*

A-54   FORT TRIAL

Near here stood Fort Trial, one of a chain of forts built in 1756, in the French and Indian War, as places of refuge in Indian attacks. Washington visited it soon after its erection. *Henry County: Route 57, 6 miles n. of Martinsville.*

A-55*   FORT BOWMAN

The stone house to the south is Fort Bowman, or Harmony Hall, built about 1753. Here was born Major Joseph Bowman, second in command in George Rogers Clark's expedition for the conquest of the Northwest. *Shenandoah County: Route 11, 1.9 miles n. of Strasburg.*

A-56 BATTLE OF CEDAR CREEK

Here the Union army lay in an entrenched camp, October 19, 1864. Crook was in the valley to the east; the Nineteenth Corps on the hillside facing south. At dawn the Confederates attacked from the east and south, capturing the camp and driving the Unionists northward two miles and a half. Wright finally halted the retreat. *Frederick County: Route 11, 1.3 miles s. of Middletown.*

A-57 WILLIAM BYRD'S CAMP

Near here, on Matrimony Creek, William Byrd pitched his camp, November, 1728, while determining the Virginia–North Carolina boundary line. *Henry County: Route 220, 3.5 miles s.w. of Ridgeway.*

A-58 BUCHANAN

The town was established in 1811 and named for Colonel John Buchanan, pioneer and soldier. It was incorporated in 1833. Its importance consisted in its being the western terminus of the James River and Kanawha Canal, which reached the town in 1851. Hunter passed here moving to Lynchburg, June, 1864. The town was reincorporated in 1892. *Botetourt County: Route 11, at Buchanan.*

A-59 DR. JESSEE BENNETT (1769–1842)

Near Edom, Virginia, on January 14, 1794, in a heroic effort to save his wife, Elizabeth, and child, Dr. Jessee Bennett performed the first successful Caesarian section and oophorectomy to be done in America. *Rockingham County: Route 42, at Edom.*

A-60 ROCKY MOUNT

This place was established as the county seat when Franklin County was formed. The first court was held in March, 1786. The first (log) courthouse was replaced in 1831. In 1836 the town consisted of 30 dwellings and a number of business houses. General Jubal A. Early practiced law here. The town was incorporated in 1873. The present courthouse was built in 1909. *Franklin County: Route 220, at Rocky Mount.*

A-62* BELLEFONT

The house on the hill to the north is Bellefont, home of John Lewis, first settler in this region, who came here from Pennsylvania in 1732. The building, which was half dwelling, half fort, is thought to be the oldest occupied in the Shenandoah Valley. *Augusta County: Route 254, 1 mile w. of Route 11.*

A-61, A-62 BIRTHPLACE OF WOODROW WILSON, U.S. PRESIDENT 1913–21

Three and one half miles south, on Coalter Street in Staunton, is the birthplace of Thomas Woodrow Wilson, 8th Virginia-born president of the U.S., Princeton University president, New Jersey governor, 28th President (World War I), he was chief author and sponsor of the League of Nations. Born December 28, 1856, died in Washington, February 3, 1924. The birthplace is maintained as an historic shrine. *Route 11, 1.5 miles n. of Staunton.*

A-72   NATURAL BRIDGE OF VIRGINIA

Legend says the Monocan Indians called it "The Bridge of God" and worshipped it. Thomas Jefferson was the first American owner, patenting it with 157 acres on July 5, 1774, "for twenty shillings of good and lawful money." Millions of years old, Natural Bridge is considered one of the seven natural wonders of the world. *Rockbridge County: Route 11, at Natural Bridge.*

A-79   HOLLINS COLLEGE

First chartered college for women in Virginia, established 1842. The estate was the pioneer home of William Carvin, who settled here before 1746. *Roanoke County: Route 11, 5.8 miles n. of Roanoke.*

A-80   COMING OF THE RAILROAD

Near here took place the historic meeting of John C. Moonmaw and C. M. Thomas that led to the termination of the Shenandoah Valley Railroad at Big Lick (now Roanoke), April, 1881. This was the beginning of the city of Roanoke. *Botetourt County: Route 11, 4.2 miles n. of Troutville.*

A-81   OLD CAROLINA ROAD

This is the old road from Pennsylvania to the Yadkin Valley, over which in early times settlers passed going south. On it were the Black Horse Tavern and the Tinker Creek Presbyterian Church. *Botetourt County: Route 11, 8 miles n. of Roanoke.*

A-82   CLOVERDALE FURNACE

Here was situated Cloverdale Furnace, an early iron industry, developed by Carter Beverly, in 1808. *Botetourt County: Route 11, 8.2 miles n. of Roanoke.*

A-91   LOONEY'S FERRY

Looney's Ferry, established in 1742, was the first crossing over the James River in this region. On the other side of the river was Cherry Tree Bottom, home of Colonel John Buchanan, and above the mouth of this creek stood Fort Fauquier, 1758–1763. *Botetourt County: Route 11, .7 mile s. of Buchanan.*

A-92   CARTMILL'S GAP

Indian raiders going west passed through this gap after massacring settlers on Cedar Creek near Natural Bridge, 1757. *Botetourt County: Route 11, 1.4 miles n. of Buchanan.*

A-93   FORT BLACKWATER

Near here stood a stockade erected by Capt. Nathaniel Terry and garrisoned by men under his command. Washington made "Terry's Fort" a link in his chain of forts and inspected it in the fall of 1756. *Franklin County: Route 220, 3 miles n. of Rocky Mount.*

A-94   MARTINSVILLE

Named for Joseph Martin, pioneer, who settled here in 1773. In 1793 the courthouse of Henry County was moved here and the town was established. Patrick Henry, for whom the county was named, lived near here once. In 1865, Stoneman, moving south to join Sherman, captured Martinsville. It was incorporated as a town in 1873 and as a city in 1929. *Henry County: Route 220 at Martinsville.*

A-135   BELLEVIEW

Three miles southwest is Belleview, home of Major John Redd, a pioneer in this section. Redd served in the Indian wars and in the Revolution, being present at the siege of Yorktown in 1781. *Henry County: Route 220, 4 miles s. of Martinsville.*

AL-5   GLEBE BURYING GROUND

On the hill to the west is the oldest burying ground in this vicinity. It contains the grave of Colonel John Wilson, member of the House of Burgesses, 1748–1773; graves of colonial and Revolutionary soldiers, and those of victims of early Indian massacres. *Augusta County: Route 876, 12 miles s.w. of Staunton.*

AS-1   FAIRY STONE STATE PARK

This park was developed by the National Park Service, Interior Department, through the Civilian Conservation Corps, in conjunction with the Virginia Conservation Commission. It covers 5,000 acres and was opened, June 15, 1936. It takes its name from the fairy, or lucky, stones found everywhere in this area. *Patrick County: Route 623, 6 miles s. of Franklin County line.*

B-2*   THE BRIARS

One mile to the north is the home of John Esten Cooke, soldier, historian and novelist. Born in 1830, he died here in 1886. Cooke moved to the place in 1869. *Clarke County: Route 50, 3 miles n.w. of Boyce.*

B-4*   SARATOGA

Built in 1782 by General Daniel Morgan and named for the battle of Saratoga, 1777. Hessian prisoners did the construction work. Lee had his headquarters here in June, 1863, on the way to Gettysburg. *Clarke County: Route 50, at Boyce.*

B-7   SIGNAL STATION

On the hilltop to the south stood an important signal station used by both armies, 1861–1865. *Clarke County: Route 50, .7 mile w. of Paris.*

B-11 CAMPAIGN OF SECOND
MANASSAS

Stonewall Jackson, sent by Lee to move around Pope's retreating army at Centreville and cut it off from Alexandria, reached this place August 31, 1862. Here Jackson turned east toward Fairfax. *Fairfax County: Route 50, 2.8 miles w. of Fairfax.*

B-13* ACTION OF OX HILL

Stonewall Jackson reached Ox Hill (Chantilly) on September 1, 1862, attempting to prevent Pope, at Centreville, from retreating to Alexandria. The Confederates came into contact with Union troops and there followed a fierce action, ended by storm and darkness. General Philip Kearny was killed. Pope fell back to Alexandria. *Fairfax County: Route 50, 6.9 miles w. of Fairfax.*

B-18 WILLA CATHER BIRTHPLACE

Here Willa Sibert Cather, the novelist, was born December 7, 1873. This community was her home until 1883 when her family moved to Nebraska. Nearby on Back Creek stands the old mill described in her novel "Sapphira and the Slave Girl." *Frederick County: Route 50, at Gore.*

B-19 SECOND BATTLE OF WINCHESTER

Here Jubal A. Early, detached to attack the rear of Milroy, holding Winchester, crossed this road and moved eastward in the afternoon of June 15, 1863. *Frederick County: Route 50, 2.5 miles w. of Winchester.*

B-20 JACKSON'S BIVOUAC

Near here Jackson's men, going to First Manassas, sank down to rest, July 19, 1861, without placing pickets. Jackson said: "Let the poor fellows sleep, I will guard the camp myself." *Fauquier County: Routes 50 and 17, at Paris.*

B-21 DELAPLANE

On July 19, 1861, Stonewall Jackson's brigade of General Joseph E. Johnston's corps marched to this station from Winchester. They crowded into freight and cattle cars and travelled to the 1st Battle of Manassas. The use of a railroad to carry more than ten thousand troops to the Manassas battlefield gave striking demonstration of the arrival of a new era in military transport and contributed significantly to the Confederate victory there. *Fauquier County: Route 17, 6.5 miles s. of Paris.*

B-22* MILITARY MOVEMENTS

This road was used by both armies, 1861–1864. Cavalry engagements took place near Middleburg on March 28, 1862, and June 19, 1863. *Loudoun County: Route 50, at Middleburg.*

B-23* ASHBY'S TAVERN

The old house to the north was Ashby's Tavern. As early as 1753, Thomas Watts had a license to keep a tavern here. He was succeeded by the Ashbys. In October, 1781, British prisoners from Yorktown rested here on their way to Winchester. *Clarke County: Route 50, 2 miles n.w. of Paris.*

B-24*   ANCIENT HIGHWAY

The road to the south is the road from Dumfries, on the Potomac, to the Shenandoah Valley. It was traveled in March, 1748, by George Washington, then a lad of sixteen on his way to Greenway Court to survey Lord Fairfax's land beyond the Blue Ridge. *Fauquier County: Route 17, 1 mile s. of Paris.*

B-25   MOSBY'S RANGERS

Here at Atoka (Rector's Crossroads), on June 10, 1863, Company "A," 43rd Battalion of Partisan Rangers, known as "Mosby's Rangers," was formally organized. James William Foster was elected captain; Thomas Turner, first lieutenant; W. L. Hunter, second lieutenant; and G. H. Whitescarver, third lieutenant. Shortly after, Brawner's company of Prince William cavalry joined the command. *Fauquier County: Route 50, 4 miles w. of Middleburg.*

B-26   MOSBY'S MIDNIGHT RAID

Mosby, entering the town in the night of March 8, 1863, captured the Union General Stoughton. *Fairfax City: Route 123, .34 mile s. of Route 236.*

B-27*   BRADDOCK ROAD

Here the wagon trains of General Braddock, in his expedition against the French, turned northeast to Snicker's Gap, June, 1755. Braddock was waiting for the wagons in Winchester before moving west to Fort Duquesne. [Removed as inaccurate, May 1939.] *Loudoun County: Route 50, at Aldie.*

B-28   MERCER'S HOME

Aldie was the home of Charles Fenton Mercer (born 1778, died 1858), liberal statesman. Mercer was a Congressman and member of the Virginia convention of 1829–30, in which he advocated manhood suffrage. His attempt to establish a free school system in Virginia nearly succeeded, 1817. He was a leading advocate of the colonization of free negroes in Liberia. *Loudoun County: Route 50, at Aldie.*

B-29   SHARPSBURG (ANTIETAM) CAMPAIGN

Here Lee turned north, on the Ox Road, and moved toward Dranesville and Leesburg, September 3, 1862. The army entered Maryland, September 5–6, 1862. *Fairfax City: Route 50, at w. city limits.*

B-30*   STUART AND BAYARD

Near here Stuart attacked the Union cavalry under Bayard, October 31, 1862. Bayard withdrew in the night to Chantilly. *Loudoun County: Route 50, at Aldie.*

B-31   STUART AND GREGG

Near here the Union cavalry general Gregg attacked Stuart and forced him to retire, June 19, 1863. *Fauquier County: Route 50, .4 mile e. of Upperville.*

B-32*   GETTYSBURG CAMPAIGN

Here Stuart, screening Lee's movement into Pennsylvania, was surprised by Duffie of Hooker's cavalry and driven out of Middleburg, June 17, 1863. That night Stuart returned and drove Duffie out. *Loudoun County: Route 50, at limits of Middleburg.*

B-33   A REVOLUTIONARY WAR HERO

Near here stood the home of Sergeant Major John Champe (1752–1798), Continental soldier. Champe faked desertion and enlisted in Benedict Arnold's British command for the purpose of capturing the traitor. Failing in his attempt, Champe rejoined the American army. His meritorious service was attested to by such patriots as General Henry (Light Horse Harry) Lee. *Loudoun County: Route 50, 1.1 miles w. of Aldie.*

B-36   STUART AND MOSBY

Here on the evening of August 22, 1862, General J.E.B. Stuart raided General Pope's headquarters. Unable to burn the railroad bridge because of a heavy thunderstorm, Stuart withdrew his troops as well as 300 federal prisoners and Pope's dispatch case. At nearby Warrenton Junction (Calverton) on May 3, 1863, Colonel John S. Mosby attacked the Federal 1st West Virginia Regiment, but was forced to flee when surprised by 1st Vermont and 5th New York Cavalry. *Fauquier County: Route 28, 3.10 miles w. of Prince William County line.*

BW-2   BURKE'S STATION RAID

Burke's Station, four miles south, was raided by Stuart's cavalry, December, 1862. Stuart telegraphed to Washington complaining of the bad quality of the mules he had captured—a famous joke. *Fairfax City: Route 236, 1 mile e. of Route 123.*

BX-2*   BRENT TOWN

Here the first blockhouse in this part of Virginia for protection against the Indians was built about 1688. The town was named for George Brent, engaged in a scheme for bringing Hugenots [sic] here to settle. *Fauquier County: Route 806, 5 miles s. of Catlett.*

BX-7   NEAVIL'S ORDINARY

Near here stood George Neavil's Ordinary, built at an early date and in existence as late as 1792. George Washington and George William Fairfax on their way to the Shenandoah Valley stopped here in 1748. *Fauquier County: Route 670, 6.1 miles e. of Warrenton.*

C-1*   CLAY AND RANDOLPH DUEL

Near here Henry Clay and John Randolph of Roanoke fought a duel April 8, 1826. Randolph had called Clay a "blackleg" in a speech. Both men were unhurt, but Randolph's coat was pierced by a bullet. *Arlington County: Route 123, near Fairfax County line.*

C-2   WORLD'S FIRST PUBLIC PASSENGER FLIGHT

On September 9, 1908, near this site, Orville Wright carried aloft in public his first passenger, Lt. Frank P. Lahm, for a flight lasting 6 minutes and 24 seconds. Three days later, he took Major George O. Squier on a flight of 9 minutes and 6 seconds duration. From this primitive beginning has evolved an air transportation system that today spans the globe. *Arlington County: Route 50 and Pershing Drive at Fort Myer.*

C-3*   CAVALRY ENGAGEMENT

Robertson, shielding Stonewall Jackson's rear, fought an engagement here with Union cavalry, June 30, 1862. *Page County: Route 211, at Luray.*

C-4   CAVALRY ENGAGEMENT

Near this place an engagement took place between Robertson's brigade and the First Maine Cavalry, July 5, 1862. *Rappahannock County: Route 211, at Sperryville.*

C-5   WASHINGTON, VIRGINIA, THE FIRST OF THEM ALL

Of the 28 Washingtons in the United States, the "records very conclusively disclosed" that this town, "the first Washington of all," was surveyed and platted by George Washington on the 24th day of July (old style) 1749. He was assisted by John Lonem and Edward Corder as chairmen. By the General Assembly of Virginia it was officially established as a town in 1796 and incorported in 1894. *Rappahannock County: Route 211, at Washington.*

C-5*   MCCLELLAN'S FAREWELL

Half a mile north of this spot General McClellan issued his farewell order to the Army of the Potomac, November 7, 1862. *Fauquier County: Route 211, 3 miles w. of Buckland.*

C-6   CAMPAIGN OF SECOND MANASSAS

Here Stonewall Jackson, on his march around Pope's army by way of Jeffersonton to Bristoe Station, turned north, August 25, 1862. *Rappahannock County: Route 211, 7.2 miles e. of Massies Corner.*

C-7   FIRST HEAVIER-THAN-AIR FLIGHT IN VIRGINIA

The first heavier-than-air flight in Virginia was made by Orville Wright at Fort Myers on 4 September, 1908. A United States Signal Corps log noted the flight spanned three miles at a height of 40 feet. The engine's condition following the flight of four minutes and fifteen seconds was described as "good." The engine ran a total of six minutes. *Arlington County: Route 50, at entrance to Fort Myer.*

C-8   STUART'S RIDE AROUND POPE

Stuart, starting here with his cavalry on August 22, 1862, rode around Pope's army to Catlett's Station. He destroyed supplies and army material and captured Pope's headquarters wagons. *Culpeper County: Route 613, 6 miles w. of Warrenton.*

C-19 BULL RUN BATTLEFIELDS

Ten miles west were fought the two battles of Manasses or Bull Run. *Fairfax City: at Fairfax, e. of Route 236.*

C-20 FIRST BATTLE OF MANASSAS

McDowell gathered his forces here, July 18, 1861, to attack Beauregard, who lay west of Bull Run. From here a part of the Union army moved north to cross Bull Run and turn the Confederate left wing, July 21, 1861. This movement brought on the battle. *Fairfax County: Route 211, at Centreville.*

C-21 CONFEDERATE DEFENSES

Here Joseph E. Early built fortifications in the winter of 1861–62 while the Confederate army was camped at Centreville. These strong works led McClellan in the spring of 1862 to attack Richmond from the York-James peninsula instead of from the north. *Fairfax County: Route 211, at Centreville.*

C-22 SECOND BATTLE OF MANASSAS

Here Pope gathered his forces, August 30–31, 1862. From this point he detached troops to check Jackson at Ox Hill while the Union army retreated to the defenses at Alexandria. *Fairfax County: Route 211, at Centreville.*

C-23 THE STONE BRIDGE

The old stone bridge, just to the north, played a part in the battles of Manassas. Here rested the Confederate left in the early morning of July 21, 1861; over the bridge Pope's retreating army passed, August 30, 1862. *Prince William County: Route 211, 6 miles e. of Gainesville.*

C-26* BATTLE OF GROVETON

Stonewall Jackson, to prevent a junction of Pope and McClellan while he was awaiting Longstreet, brought on an action here with Gibbon, August 28, 1862. Jackson's position was a short distance north of this road and facing it. Gibbon retired after a fierce fight. *Prince William County: Route 211, 3.5 miles e. of Gainesville.*

C-27 SECOND BATTLE OF MANASSAS

The center of Lee's army rested here on August 30, 1862; Jackson was to the north of this road, Longstreet to the south. Late in the afternoon, after Jackson had repulsed Pope's assaults, Longstreet moved eastward, driving the Union forces facing him toward Henry Hill. Jackson advanced southward at the same time. *Prince William County: Route 211, 1.6 miles e. of Gainesville.*

C-28* CAMPAIGN OF SECOND MANASSAS

Stonewall Jackson, moving southward on his march around Pope, was here joined by Stuart with his cavalry, August 26, 1862. From Gainesville, Jackson moved on to Bristoe Station. *Prince William County: Route 211, at Gainesville.*

C-29 COLONIAL ROAD

This crossroad is the ancient Dumfries-Winchester highway. Over it William Fairfax accompanied George Washington, then a lad of sixteen, on his first visit to Lord Fairfax at Greenway Court. It was on this occasion that Washington assisted in surveying the Fairfax grant. *Fauquier County: Route 211, 2.6 miles e. of Warrenton.*

C-30 WHITE HOUSE

The old building just north of the road was built for a fort in 1760. It has long been a landmark in this valley. *Page County: Route 211, 4 miles w. of Luray.*

C-31 BULL RUN BATTLEFIELDS

Just to the east were fought the two battles of Manassas or Bull Run. *Prince William County: Route 211, .4 mile e. of Gainesville.*

C-31* FORT LONG

Six miles south, near Alma, is Fort Long, built about 1740. *Page County: Route 211, 2 miles w. of Luray.*

C-33* SECOND BATTLE OF MANASSAS

Half a mile north, along a railway cut, Stonewall Jackson held position, August 29–30, 1862, repulsing all of Pope's assaults. When ammunition gave out on a section of the Confederate line, the soldiers used stones as missiles. Late in the afternoon of August 30, when Longstreet attacked, Jackson swept southward, completing the victory. *Prince William County: Route 211, 3 miles e. of Gainesville.*

C-34 FIRST BATTLE OF MANASSAS

Henry Hill lies just to the south. Here the Confederates repulsed the repeated attacks of the Union army under McDowell, July 21, 1861. Here Jackson won the name "Stonewall," and from here began McDowell's retreat that ended at Washington. *Prince William County: Route 211, 4.7 miles e. of Gainesville.*

C-40 CAMPAIGN OF SECOND MANASSAS

Seven miles south is Manassas, where Jackson, on his turning movement around Pope, destroyed vast quantities of supplies, August 26–27, 1862. Hill and Ewell of Jackson's force, coming from Manassas, reached Centreville on their way to Jackson's position north of Groveton, August 28, 1862. *Fairfax County: Route 211, at Centreville.*

C-42* FIRST BATTLE OF MANASSAS

In the afternoon of July 21, 1861, the bridge over Cub Run was jammed by the upsetting of a wagon. This turned the retreat of the Union forces into disorder; carriages, cannon and caissons were abandoned as civilians and soldiers escaped across the stream on foot on their way to Alexandria. *Fairfax County: Route 211, 1.8 miles w. of Centreville.*

C-44   FIRST BATTLE OF MANASSAS

On the Matthews Hill, just to the north, the Confederates repulsed the attack of the Unionists, coming from the north, in the forenoon of July 21, 1861. The Union force, reinforced, drove the Confederates to the Henry Hill, just to the south. There the latter reformed under cover of Stonewall Jackson. In the afternoon, McDowell vainly attempted to rally his retreating troops on the Matthews Hill after they had been driven down the Henry Hill. *Prince William County: Route 211, 4.7 miles e. of Gainesville.*

C-46   SECOND BATTLE OF MANASSAS

On the Henry Hill, Pope's rear guard, in the late afternoon of August 30, 1862, repulsed the attacks of Longstreet coming from the west. If the hill had been taken, Pope's army would have been doomed; but the Unionists held it while the rest of their troops retreated across Bull Run on the way to Centreville. *Prince William County: Route 211, 4.7 miles e. of Gainesville.*

C-48   CAMPAIGN OF SECOND MANASSAS

Here Taliaferro, of Jackson's force, came into the highway in the late night of August 27, 1862. He was marching from Manassas to the position about a mile and a half to the north held by Jackson in the Second Battle of Manassas. *Prince William County: Route 211, 4.7 miles e. of Gainesville.*

C-50   THOROUGHFARE GAP

Five miles northwest is Thoroughfare Gap in the Bull Run Mountains. Through this gap J. E. Johnston and Jackson came, July 19, 1861, on their way to the First Battle of Manassas. Through it Lee sent Jackson, August 26, 1862, and followed with Longstreet to take part in the Second Battle of Manassas. *Prince William County: Route 55, at Gainesville.*

C-54*   CAMPAIGN OF SECOND MANASSAS

Eight miles southeast, near Bristoe, Stonewall Jackson destroyed a railroad bridge over this stream as he moved to the rear of Pope's army, August 26, 1862. Reaching Manassas, Pope's supply depot, he destroyed vast quantities of stores. *Fauquier County: Route 211, 4.5 miles w. of Gainesville.*

C-56   WILLIAM RANDOLPH BARBEE

Here stood "Hawburg" birthplace of the eminent sculptor William R. Barbee (1818–1868). He studied in Florence, Italy where he carved his famed "Coquette" and "The Fisher Girl." Returning to the United States in 1858 he was at work on a design for the pediment of the U.S. House of Representatives when the outbreak of the war brought his career to an end. He died at "The Bower" which stood not far away. *Rappahannock County: Route 211 and Skyline Drive, at Panoramo.*

C-56*   FREDERICKSBURG CAMPAIGN

In this vicinity Burnside took command of the Army of the Potomac, November 7, 1862. He reorganized the army and turned it southward to the Rappahannock River at Fredericksburg. On November 19, his headquarters were near Falmouth. On December 13, the battle of Fredericksburg was fought. *Fauquier County: Route 211, 2.6 miles e. of Warrenton.*

C-58*   CAMPAIGN OF SECOND MANASSAS

By this road Stuart came on his raid to Catlett's Station, August 22, 1862. At that time most of the Union troops were guarding the passages of the Rappahannock River. Crossing at Waterloo Bridge, Stuart moved around the right of Pope's army to its rear. This raid should have awakened Pope to his dangerous position. *Fauquier County: Route 211, 4 miles w. of Warrenton.*

C-60   CAMPAIGN OF SECOND MANASSAS

About two miles north is Waterloo Bridge, where J.E.B. Stuart began his raid to Catlett's Station in the rear of Pope's army, August 22, 1862. Some miles farther north is Hinton's Mill, where Stonewall Jackson crossed this river, August 25, 1862, on the march around Pope that resulted in the Second Battle of Manassas. *Fauquier County: Route 211, 5.1 miles w. of Warrenton.*

C-61   CAMPAIGN OF SECOND MANASSAS

Here J.E.B. Stuart, raiding around Pope's army, turned northeast, August 22, 1862. He passed through Warrenton and went on to Catlett's Station, where he captured some of Pope's wagons, in one of which were found Pope's order book and uniform. *Rappahannock County: Route 211, 9.5 miles e. of Massies Corner.*

C-90   THE FALLS CHURCH

The first church on this site was built in 1734 and was in Truro Parish. George Washington was elected a vestryman, October 3, 1763. In 1765 the church fell within the newly-created Fairfax Parish, of which Washington was chosen a vestryman. The present church was built in 1768. It was used as a recruiting station in the Revolution and as a stable by the Union troops, 1862–64. *Fairfax County: at Falls Church, s. of Route 7.*

CB-1   CAMPAIGN OF SECOND MANASSAS

Here Lee and Longstreet, on their way to join Jackson then at Bristoe Station, camped on August 26, 1862. *Fauquier County: Route 688, 12 miles w. of Warrenton.*

CL-2   RUFFNER PUBLIC SCHOOL NUMBER 1

Named for Wm. H. Ruffner, Virginia's First Superintendent of Public Instruction, and opened as a public school on this date. Before free public schools were established by the Virginia Constitution of 1869, a one room free school was in operation with voluntary gifts. *In Manassas: Route 28, .1 mile s. of route 334.*

CL-3   JOHN MARSHALL'S BIRTHPLACE

About one half mile southeast, just across the railroad, a stone marks the site of the birthplace, September 24, 1755. He died at Philadelphia, July 6, 1835. Revolutionary officer, congressman, Secretary of State, he is immortal as Chief Justice of the United States Supreme Court. During his long term of office his wise interpretation of the U.S. Constitution gave it enduring life. *Fauquier County: Route 28, .8 mile e. of Midland.*

D-6   BATTLE OF CROSS KEYS

Three miles south, on Mill Creek, Jackson's rearguard, under Ewell, was attacked by Fremont, June 8, 1862. Trimble, of Ewell's command, counterattacked, driving the Unionists back. Jackson, with the rest of his army, was near Port Republic awaiting the advance of Shields up the east bank of the Shenandoah River. *Rockingham County: Route 33, 5 miles e. of Harrisonburg.*

D-10   KNIGHTS OF THE GOLDEN HORSESHOE

Here, it is believed, Governor Alexander Spotswood and his party crossed the mountains into the Shenandoah Valley, September 5, 1716. This expedition paved the way for the settlement of the West. On the return east, Spotswood gave his companions small golden horseshoes because their shoeless horses had to be shod for the mountain journey. *Rockingham County: Route 33, 7 miles s.e. of Elkton.*

D-20   MONTEBELLO

Here was born Zachary Taylor, twelfth president of the United States, November 24, 1784. Taylor, commanding the American army, won the notable battle of Buena Vista in Mexico, 1847. *Orange County: Route 33, 3 miles w. of Gordonsville.*

D-22   BARBOURSVILLE

A short distance south are the ruins of Barboursville, built, 1814–1822, by James Barbour partly after plans made by Jefferson. It was burned, December 25, 1884. James Barbour, buried here, was Governor of Virginia, 1812–1815, United States Senator, Secretary of War, Minister to England. *Orange County: Route 33, at Barboursville.*

D-24   FORT LEWIS

Seven miles east stood a small stockade known first as Wilson's Fort. It was garrisoned in the fall of 1756 by a force under the command of Lt. Charles Lewis, younger brother of the famous Indian fighter, Andrew Lewis. *Bath County: Route 220, 11 miles n. of Warm Springs.*

D-26 FORT BRECKENRIDGE

Three miles west at the mouth of Falling Spring Creek was a post garrisoned by militia under Capt. Robert Breckenridge. Washington inspected it in 1756. It survived an attack by Shawnees under Cornstalk during Pontiac's war in 1763. *Alleghany County: Route 220, 3 miles n. of Covington.*

D-27 FORT YOUNG

George Washington, Commander of Virginia Defense Forces in the French and Indian War, inspected this post near here in 1756. A relief force from here, sent to the aid of Fort Breckenridge in 1763, was ambushed by Indians. *City of Covington: Route 154, on Durant Road, n. of Jackson River.*

D-28 FINCASTLE

Miller's place here was selected as the county seat of Botetourt in 1770. In 1772 the town of Fincastle was established on land donated by Israel Christian and named for Lord Fincastle, eldest son of Governor Lord Dunmore. It was incorporated in 1828. In 1845 it had a population of 700. The present courthouse was erected about 1850. *Botetourt County: Route 220, at Fincastle.*

D-29 FORT WILLIAM

Captain William Preston built this post near here, and it was inspected by Colonel George Washington in 1756. It was attacked by Indians that October. Settlers in the area "forted up" here during Pontiac's War, 1763. *Botetourt County: Route 220, 3 miles s. of Fincastle.*

D-30* GREENFIELD

One mile west is Greenfield, home of William Preston, built before the Revolution. Preston was a member of the House of Burgesses for Augusta County, 1765–1768, and for Botetourt County, 1769–1771. He was an officer in the Indian wars and the Revolution, dying in 1783. *Botetourt County: Route 220, 5 miles s. of Fincastle.*

E-1* BACON'S PLANTATION

In 1676 this region was Bacon's "Quarter," or Plantation, the property of Nathaniel Bacon, who headed a rebellion that was a forerunner of the Revolution. *Richmond: Chamberlayne Avenue.*

E-2* INTERMEDIATE DEFENSES

Here ran, east and west, the intermediate line of Richmond defenses, 1862–65. Kilpatrick on his raid came, March 1, 1864, nearly to this spot. *Richmond: Laburnum and Chamberlayne avenues.*

E-3* WHERE SHERIDAN MOVED EAST

Sheridan, in his raid to Richmond on May 11, 1864, entered the outer defenses on the Brook Road. At this point he turned east to Mechanicsville. *Henrico County: Chamberlayne and Azalia avenues.*

E-4* BROOK ROAD

By this road Lafayette came to Richmond, on April 29, 1781, to oppose the British invasion, and he retreated before Cornwallis on the same road on May 27, 1781. *Richmond: intersection of Brook Road and Route 1.*

E-5   FORK CHURCH

Fork Church was first housed in a 1722 frame building near the present church site. It was known as "The Chapel in the Forks" and derived its name from the nearby confluence of the North and South Anna rivers and the Little and Newfound rivers. The present building was erected between 1736 and 1740. Erected in Memory of Stuart Anderson Oliver, 1982. *Hanover County: Route 738, 4.5 miles w. of Route 1.*

E-6   OUTER FORTIFICATIONS

Here, east and west, ran the outer line of Richmond defenses, 1862–65. At this point Sheridan's cavalry, raiding to Richmond, broke through the line on May 11, 1864, after the fight at Yellow Tavern. *Henrico County: Route 1, .7 mile n. of Richmond.*

E-7   YELLOW TAVERN

This is the site of Yellow Tavern, an old inn of the Richmond road. In this vicinity a cavalry engagement took place, on May 11, 1864, between Sheridan raiding to Richmond and J.E.B. Stuart defending the city. Sheridan penetrated the outer defenses of Richmond but then turned off. *Henrico County: Route 1, 2.5 miles n. of Richmond.*

E-8   STUART

At this point J.E.B. Stuart had his headquarters and cavalry camp in December, 1862. *Spotsylvania County: Route 1, 5.4 miles s. of Falmouth.*

E-9   STUART'S MORTAL WOUND

One half mile to the east, on the Old Telegraph Road, is a monument marking the field where General J.E.B. Stuart was mortally wounded on May 11, 1864. The monument was erected by veterans of Stuart's Cavalry in 1888. *Henrico County: Route 1, at Route 677 (Francis Road).*

E-9*   CAVALRY ENGAGEMENT

In this vicinity was fought the engagement of Yellow Tavern between Sheridan's cavalry raiding to Richmond and the confederates, May 11, 1864. *Henrico County: Route 1, 6.25 miles n. of Richmond.*

E-11*   BATTLES ON THE
        CHICKAHOMINY

Near this river and some miles to the east were fought the battles of Seven Pines, May 31–June 1, 1862; Mechanicsville, June 26, 1862; Gaines's Mill, June 27, 1862; Savage's Station, June 29, 1862; and Cold Harbor, June 3, 1864. *Hanover County: Route 1, 4.9 miles s. of Ashland.*

E-12*   SMITH AND LAFAYETTE

On this stream some miles to the east, Captain John Smith was captured by the Indians in December, 1607. On it Lafayette and Cornwallis camped in 1781. *Hanover County: Route 1, 4.9 miles s. of Ashland.*

E-13 LEE'S TURN TO COLD HARBOR

Lee had his headquarters near here, May 27, 1864, while moving south from the North Anna River. Here Longstreet's (Anderson's) and Hill's corps of his army turned east to meet Grant at Cold Harbor, where a great battle was fought, June 3, 1864. *Hanover County: Route 1, 4.5 miles s. of Ashland.*

E-14* CAVALRY SKIRMISH

On this spot, on June 25, 1862, the Fourth Virginia Cavalry fought a skirmish with the Eighth Illinois Cavalry. *Hanover County: Route 1, 1 mile s. of Ashland.*

E-14* JACKSON'S MARCH TO GAINES'S MILL

Stonewall Jackson, coming from the Shenandoah Valley, moved east over the Ashcake Road to join Lee, confronting McClellan at Mechanicsville, June 26, 1862. Owing to many obstacles, Jackson did not join Lee until the next day, June 27, 1862, while the battle of Gaines's Mill was raging. His attack won the battle. *Hanover County: Route 1, .4 mile s. of Ashland.*

E-15 HENRY AT HANOVER COURTHOUSE

Six miles east still stands Hanover Courthouse, in which, December, 1763, Patrick Henry delivered his great speech in the "Parsons' Cause," when he denounced the British government for vetoing an act of the Virginia General Assembly. *Hanover County: Route 1, at Ashland.*

E-16* ASHLAND

Henry Clay was born a few miles to the east, and as a boy brought grain to a mill here. This place was raided by Stoneman, on May 3, 1863; by Kilpatrick, on March 1, 1864; and by Sheridan, on May 11, 1864. *Hanover County: Route 1, at Ashland.*

E-17* ELLETT'S BRIDGE

The wagon trains of Lee's army crossed the South Anna here on May 27, 1864. On the railroad bridge just to the east Longstreet's (Anderson's) and Hill's corps crossed the river on the same day on the way to Cold Harbor. *Hanover County: Route 1, 3 miles n. of Ashland.*

E-18 LAFAYETTE AND CORNWALLIS

Lafayette, commanding an American force, crossed the river west of this point, on May 29, 1781, while retreating before Cornwallis, who moved a few miles to the east. *Hanover County: Route 1, 3.6 miles n. of Ashland.*

E-19 LEE'S LEFT WING

On this stream, the Little River, and to the west, Lee's left wing rested while his army faced Grant along the North Anna, May 23–26, 1864. *Hanover County: Route 1, 5.2 miles n. of Ashland.*

E-20 LEE'S MOVEMENTS

A short distance east, at Taylorsville, Lee had his headquarters, May 24–26, 1864, as his army moved southeastward to intervene between Grant and Richmond. There Ewell's corps turned to Cold Harbor, May 27, 1864. *Hanover County: Route 1, 6.2 miles n. of Ashland.*

E-21* HANOVER JUNCTION

An important point because the junction of two railroads. The Virginia Central (C. & O.) was Lee's main line of supply in 1864 and was protected by the earthworks here. Lee camped here on May 22–23, 1864. *Hanover County: Route 1, 7.6 miles n. of Ashland.*

E-22* LAFAYETTE AND CORNWALLIS

Lafayette, commanding an American force, crossed this river, a few miles west, May 30, 1781. Cornwallis, the British commander, who had followed him from the James River, near here gave up the pursuit, June 1, and turned westward. Lafayette moved on to the Rapidan River, where he was joined by "Mad Anthony" Wayne. *Hanover County: Route 1, 3 miles s. of Carmel Church.*

E-23 LEE AND GRANT

Lee and Grant faced each other on the North Anna, May 23–26, 1864. Union forces crossed here and four miles to the west but found they could not dislodge Lee's center, which rested on the stream. Grant then turned east to Cold Harbor. *Caroline County: Route 1, 2.8 miles s. of Carmel Church.*

E-24 LONG CREEK ACTION

The earthworks in the angle between this stream and the North Anna River, held by a small Confederate force, were taken by Grant's troops moving southward on May 23, 1864. The Unionists then advanced to the river, on the south side of which was Lee's army. *Caroline County: Route 1, 2.4 miles s. of Carmel Church.*

E-25 GRANT'S OPERATIONS

Here, at Mount Carmel Church, on May 23, 1864, Hancock's (Second) Corps turned south to the North Anna River; Warren's (Fifth) Corps and Wright's (Sixth) Corps here turned west to Jericho Mills on the river. Grant had his headquarters in the church on May 24. On May 27, 1864, the four corps of Grant's army, returning from the North Anna, here turned east to Cold Harbor. *Caroline County: Route 1, at Carmel Church.*

E-26 DICKINSON'S MILL

Lee camped here, on May 21, 1864, on his way to the North Anna to oppose Grant moving southward. Ewell's and Longstreet's corps rested here that night. *Caroline County: Route 1, 2.2 miles s. of Ladysmith.*

E-27* BULL CHURCH

To the east, at Bull Church, a part of Warren's (Fifth) Corps camped on May 22, 1864, on the way to the North Anna River. *Caroline County: U.S. 1, at Ladysmith.*

E-28 NANCY WRIGHT'S

A little to the east, at Nancy Wright's, Warren's (Fifth) and Wright's (Sixth) Corps, coming from the east, on May 22, 1864, turned south. Wright camped here on May 22. *Caroline County: Route 1, 5.1 miles n. of Ladysmith.*

E-29* DOCTOR FLIPPO'S

Part of Warren's (Fifth) Corps, Army of the Potomac, camped at this place on May 22, 1864, on the way to the North Anna. *Caroline County: Route 1, 1.6 miles n. of Ladysmith.*

E-30 TURN IN SHERIDAN'S RAID

At this point in his Richmond raid, Sheridan, after a fight with Confederate cavalry commanded by General Williams C. Wickham, turned off the Telegraph Road to Beaver Dam, May 9, 1864. This change of route caused Sheridan to approach Richmond from the northwest instead of the north. *Spotsylvania County: Route 1, 1.8 miles s. of Thornburg.*

E-31 JERRELL'S MILL

Here, on May 9, 1864, Sheridan was attacked by Wickham's cavalry. Nearby, on May 22, 1864, Warren's (Fifth) Corps, moving to the North Anna, fought Rosser's cavalry. *Spotsylvania County: Route 1, 1.1 miles s. of Thornburg.*

E-32 MUD TAVERN

Mud Tavern was the old name of this place. Six miles east, at Guinea Station, Stonewall Jackson died, May 10, 1863. In the campaign of 1864, Ewell's and Longstreet's corps of Lee's army, coming from Spotsylvania Courthouse, here turned south, May 21, 1864. Lee fell back to the North Anna River as Grant swung around to the east. *Spotsylvania County: Route 1, at Thornburg.*

E-33* A RAIDS END

Here Gibbons and Hatch's Brigades, Army of the Potomac raiding south from Fredericksburg, were attacked by Stuart's Cavalry, on August 6, 1862, and retreated northward. *Spotsylvania County, U.S. 1, 2 miles n. of Thornburg*

E-34* WHERE BURNSIDE TURNED

Just to the east at Stanard's Mill, Burnside, on May 21, 1864, attempting to move south, found the river held by the Confederates in force and turned east to Guinea Station. *Spotsylvania County: Route 1, 1.3 miles n. of Thornburg.*

E-35* WHERE BURNSIDE CROSSED

Here, at Smith's Mill, Burnside's (Ninth) Corps, Army of the Potomac, crossed the Ny River, May 21, 1864, advancing southward. Repulsed at the Po River, it recrossed the Ny here and moved eastward. *Spotsylvania County: Route 1, 1.3 miles n. of Thornburg.*

E-36   UNION ARMY ROUTE

By this road the four corps of the Union army, coming from Spotsylvania, moved east to Guinea Station on May 21, 1864. *Spotsylvania County: Route 1, 3.8 miles n. of Thornburg.*

E-37*   MASSAPONAX CHURCH

Grant's army, moving east from Spotsylvania on May 21, 1864, reached this road here and followed it as far as the road to Guinea Station. *Spotsylvania County: Route 1, 4.5 miles n. of Thornburg.*

E-38   LEE'S HEADQUARTERS

Lee's headquarters in the winter of 1862–63 were a mile down this road. *Spotsylvania County: Route 1, 5.4 miles s. of Falmouth.*

E-39   START OF SHERIDAN'S RAID

Here Sheridan, moving from camp, came into the Telegraph Road on his raid to Richmond, May 9, 1864, while Lee and Grant were fighting at Spotsylvania. The 10,000 Union cavalry filled the road for several miles. Turning from the road ten miles south, Sheridan came into it again at Yellow Tavern near Richmond May 11, 1864. *Spotsylvania County: Route 1, 5.3 miles s. of Falmouth.*

E-40*   GRANT'S SUPPLY LINE

This road to Spotsylvania Courthouse was Grant's line of supply in May, 1864, in the Wilderness campaign. *Spotsylvania County: Route 1, 4 miles s. of Fredericksburg.*

E-41   HISTORIC AQUIA CREEK

Giles Brent built a house here in 1647. After the Indian War of 1676 this creek was for ten years the northern frontier of Virginia. The Army of the Potomac, coming from the James, landed here in August, 1862. For campaigns in 1862–63 this stream was the supply base of the Union army. *Stafford County: Route 1, 3.6 miles n. of Stafford.*

E-41*   LONGSTREET'S HEADQUARTERS

Here Longstreet had his headquarters in the winter of 1862–63. *Spotsylvania County: U.S. 1, 3.5 miles s. of Fredericksburg.*

E-42*   EARLY'S LINE OF BATTLE

Here Jubal A. Early formed line of battle across the road on the afternoon of May 3, 1863, after being driven from Fredericksburg by Sedgwick. *Spotsylvania County: Route 1, 3.5 miles s. of Fredericksburg.*

E-43*   LEE'S POSITION

On this hill, a little to the east, Lee watched the battle of Fredericksburg, December 13, 1862. *Spotsylvania County: Route 1, 1 mile s. of Fredericksburg.*

E-44*   BATTLES OF FREDERICKSBURG

The hill here is Marye's Heights, occupied by the Confederates in the battles of December 13, 1862, and May 3, 1863. In the first battle all attempts of the Union troops to take it failed. In the second battle (the Chancellorsville campaign) the Union troops carried the position, which was held by a small force. *Spotsylvania County: Route 1 at s. entrance of Fredericksburg.*

E-45*   FREDERICKSBURG

A settlement was made here at an early period. The town was established in 1727 and was named for Prince Frederick, father of George III. *Stafford County: Route 1, at n. entrance of Fredericksburg.*

E-46*   COLONIAL FORT

A fort was built at the falls here in 1676 to protect the settlers from the Indians, who were raiding the settlements. *Spotsylvania County: Route 1 at n. entrance of Fredericksburg.*

E-46-a   FREDERICKSBURG

Captain John Smith was here in 1608; Lederer, the explorer, in 1670. In May 1671 John Buckner and Thomas Royster patented the Lease Land Grant. The town was established in 1727 and lots were laid out. It was named for Frederick, Prince of Wales, father of George III. The court for Spotsylvania County was moved here in 1732 and the town was enlarged in 1759 and 1769. Fredericksburg was incorporated as a town in 1781, as a city in 1879, and declared a city of the first class in 1941. *Spotsylvania County: Alternate Route 1, 2 miles s. of Falmouth.*

E-46-b*   FREDERICKSBURG

Captain John Smith was here in 1608; Lederer, the explorer, in 1670. In May 1671 John Buckner and Thomas Royster patented the Lease Land Grant. The town was established in 1727 and lots were laid out. It was named for Frederick, Prince of Wales, father of George III. The court for Spotsylvania County was moved here in 1732 and the town was enlarged in 1759 and 1769. Fredericksburg was incorporated as a town in 1781, as a city in 1879, and declared a city of the first class in 1941. *Spotsylvania County: Route 1, 2 miles s. of Falmouth.*

E-47   HISTORIC FALMOUTH

Founded in 1727 as a trading center for the Northern Neck, Hunter's iron works here were an objective in the Virginia campaign of 1781. The Army of the Potomac camped here from November, 1862, to June, 1863, and moved hence to Chancellorsville and Gettysburg. *Stafford County: Route 1, .95 mile n. of Route 17.*

E-48   POTOMAC CREEK

Near the mouth of this creek, several miles east, was the Indian Village "Petomek," where Pocahontas was kidnapped by Captain Samuel Argall in 1613. There, travelers landed from steamers to take the stage to Fredericksburg, early railroad terminus. *Stafford County: Route 1, 3.8 miles n. of Falmouth.*

E-48* SMITH AND POCAHONTAS

At the mouth of this stream Captain John Smith in 1608 found an Indian "King's house" called "Petomek." The river takes its name from this. Here the Indian Princess, Pocahontas, was kidnapped by the English in June, 1612. *Stafford County: Route 1, 1.5 miles n. of Falmouth.*

E-48* POTOMAC CREEK

Near the mouth of this creek, several miles east, explorers in 1608 found an Indian village called "Petomek," from which the river took its name. There the Indian princess, Pocahontas, was kidnapped by Captain Argall in 1613. There travelers landed from steamers to take the stage to Fredericksburg, early railroad terminus. Charles Dickens landed there, going to Richmond, and returned the same way, March, 1842. *Stafford County: Route 1, 3 miles n. of Falmouth.*

E-49-a and E-49-b "FALL HILL"

On the heights one mile to the west, the home of the Thorntons from about 1736. Francis Thornton 2nd was a justice, a Burgess 1744–45, and Lieutenant Colonel of his Majesty's militia for Spotsylvania County. He and two of his brothers married three Gregory sisters, first cousins of George Washington. "Fall Hill" is still (1950) owned and occupied by direct Thornton descendants. *Spotsylvania County: Route 1, at Fredericksburg.*

E-49* ANCIENT IRON FURNACE

Here on Accokeek Run were iron mines and a furnace in which Augustine Washington, father of George Washington, began to smelt iron in 1727. *Stafford County: U.S. 1, two miles s. of Stafford Courthouse.*

E-50* INDIAN TRAIL

Here ran the original Indian trail. In 1664 a road was opened here and in 1666 it was extended to Aquia Creek. In 1750 this became a post road. In September, 1781, Washington passed over this road on the way to Yorktown, and over it the French army later marched north. *Stafford County: Route 1, .3 mile n. of Stafford.*

E-52 CHOPAWAMSIC

Settlement began here in 1651. Samuel Matthews, Governor of Virgina, 1659–60, patented land here. On December 27, 1862, Fitz Lee, raiding from Fredericksburg, struck the road here and moved northward, capturing wagons. *Prince William County: Route 1, 4.3 miles s. of Dumfries.*

E-53 CAMPAIGN OF 1781

Lafayette, coming to Virginia to take command, moved by this road, April 1781. Here passed Washington and Rochambeau going to Yorktown, September, 1781. *Prince William County: Route 1, at n. entrance of Dumfries.*

E-53* EARLY LAND PATENTS

Here on Quantico Creek, land was first patented by Richard Hawkins in 1653. *Prince William County: Route 1, s. of Dumfries.*

E-54*   ANCIENT ROAD TO VALLEY

Opened in 1731, this road by 1759 extended across the Blue Ridge Mountains, via Ashby's Gap. *Prince William County: Route 1, s. of Dumfries.*

E-55   HISTORY OF DUMFRIES

A tobacco warehouse was built here in 1730; the town was established in 1749 and became a noted port. In 1774 it elected one of the first Revolutionary committees of correspondence. Washington came to Dumfries frequently. On December 12, 1862, Wade Hampton here surprised a Union force, capturing some wagons; and, on December 27, 1862, J.E.B. Stuart had a skirmish with the Union troops holding the place. *Prince William County: Route 1, at Dumfries.*

E-56*   EARLY LAND PATENTS

Here on Marumsco Creek land was first patented by Thomas Burbage in 1653. *Prince William County: Route 1, 1.1 miles s. of Woodbridge.*

E-57*   EARLY LAND PATENTS

Land here on Powell's Run was first patented in 1757, at which time the stream was known as Yosococomico. *Prince William County: Route 1, 4 miles n. of Dumfries.*

E-58*   EARLY IRON FURNACE

Iron was mined on this stream before 1738 and John Tayloe had a furnace near by. A few miles to the east was "Leesylvania," home of Robert E. Lee's grandfather. *Prince William County: Route 1, 3.2 miles n. of Dumfries.*

E-59   THE OCCOQUAN

Near here in 1608 Captain John Smith found the "King's House" of the Doeg Indians. In 1729 "King" Carter built a landing here to ship copper ore. A town called Colchester was established here in 1753. Occoquan, to the west, was founded in 1804. On December 27, 1862, Wade Hampton raided Occoquan. *Prince William County: Route 1, at Woodbridge.*

E-60*   EVENTS ON POHICK CREEK

Here on Pohick Creek the second George Mason settled in 1690. Here the Iroquois Indians, by a treaty of 1722, agreed to deliver up runaway slaves. The fourth George Mason wished to build Pohick Church on the creek, but was overruled by George Washington. *Fairfax County: Route 1, 3.2 miles n. of Woodbridge.*

E-61   OCCOQUAN WORKHOUSE

In the nearby Occoquan Workhouse, from June to December, 1917, scores of women suffragists were imprisoned by the District of Columbia for picketing the White House demanding their right to vote. Their courage and dedication during harsh treatment aroused the nation to hasten the passage and ratification of the 19th Amendment in 1920. The struggle for woman's suffrage had taken 72 years. *Fairfax County: Route 123, at Lorton Penitentiary Youth Center.*

E-62   OLD TELEGRAPH LINE

One of the first telegraph lines in the world, a part of the Washington–New Orleans Telegraph Company, was built from Washington to Petersburg in 1847. From this the road took its name. *Fairfax County: Route 1, 4.1 miles n. of Woodbridge.*

E-63*   EARLY LAND PATENTS

Land was first patented on Accotink Creek in 1657. *Fairfax County: Route 1, 5.6 miles n. of Woodbridge.*

E-64*   FORT HUMPHREYS

Here stood "Belvoir" built by William Fairfax in 1741: In it Lawrence Washington was married in 1743. It was for many years the office of the Northern Neck proprietor. In the World War, 1918, camp for training engineers stood here. *Fairfax County: Route 1, .7 mile n. of Woodbridge.*

E-65   GUNSTON HALL

Gunston Hall, four miles to the east, is one of the most noted colonial places in Virginia. The land was patented in 1651 by Richard Turney, who was hanged for taking part in Bacon's Rebellion in 1676. In 1696 the second George Mason acquired it. The house was built in 1755–1758 by the fourth George Mason, Revolutionary leader and author of the Virginia Declaration of Rights and the first Constitution of Virginia. *Fairfax County: Route 1, 2.4 miles n. of Woodbridge.*

E-66*   WOODLAWN

The estate was inherited by Nellie Custis from George Washington. The house was built in 1805. A century later it became the home of Senator Oscar W. Underwood. *Fairfax County: Route 1, 7.4 miles s. of Alexandria.*

E-67*   HISTORY ON DOGUE RUN

Land on this stream, first patented in 1657, was later owned by William Dudley, one of Bacon's supporters in the rebellion of 1676. Rankin's Point near by was bombarded by British ships in 1814. *Fairfax County: Route 1, 7.1 miles s. of Alexandria.*

E-68*   MOUNT VERNON ESTATE

Two miles to the east. The original house was built in 1743 by Lawrence Washington. George Washington came into possession in 1752. From here he set out, in April, 1775, to take his seat in the Continental Congress. On December 24, 1783, he returned from the army and here he died on December 14, 1799. *Fairfax County: Route 1, 4.5 miles s. of Alexandria.*

E-69*   LITTLE HUNTING CREEK

Margaret Brent, secretary to Lord Baltimore, the first woman in America to demand a vote, patented land here in 1663. Augustine Washington lived here from 1734 to 1739, and here George Washington passed most of his infancy. *Fairfax County: Route 1, 4.5 miles s. of Alexandria.*

E-70* COLONIAL FORT

Here on Hunting Creek, Governor Berkeley in 1676, built a fort for defense against the Susquehannock Indians in the troubles that led to Bacon's Rebellion. *Fairfax County: Route 1, at Alexandria.*

E-71* HISTORIC ALEXANDRIA

Land was first patented here in 1657. In 1731 a warehouse was built on Hunting Creek about which grew up the village of Belhaven. The town of Alexandria was established in 1749 and became one of the main colonial trading centers. It was a part of the original District of Columbia but was returned to Virginia in 1847. *Alexandria: Route 1 at s. entrance to town.*

E-72 POHICK CHURCH

This building was begun in 1769 and completed by 1774, succeeding an earlier church two miles to the south. It was the lower church of Truro Parish, established in 1732, the parish of Mount Vernon and Gunston Hall. George William Fairfax, George Washington and George Mason, vestrymen, were members of the building committee under which the church was constructed. *Fairfax County: Route 1, 4.3 miles n. of Woodbridge.*

E-72* OLD ROAD TO WEST

Washington traveled by this road on his mission to Fort Duquesne in 1753. In 1754 he marched over it in command of the Virginia regiment. In 1755 a brigade of Braddock's army moved by it to the defeat near Pittsburg. *Fairfax County: Route 50 at n. entrance of Alexandria.*

E-73 WASHINGTON'S MILL

Just to the left is the restored mill operated by George Washington for years. (Restoration made by the State Commission on Conservation and Development—1932.) *Fairfax County: Route 1, 7.4 miles s. of Alexandria at Route 235.*

E-74 STUART'S RIDE AROUND McCLELLAN

Near here, on Winston's Farm, J.E.B. Stuart, advancing north, camped on June 12, 1862. Stuart was scouting to find the position of the right wing of McClellan's army besieging Richmond. At this point he turned east to Hanover Courthouse. Stuart made a complete circuit of the Union army. *Hanover County: Route 1, 1.9 miles n. of Ashland.*

E-75 MARLBOROUGH

In 1691, Marlborough, The Port Town in Stafford County, was laid off. Houses were built and the county court was held there for some years. The town did not develop. Nearby was the Indian Town where Pocahontas was sold in 1613 by the Indian Chief Japasaws to Captain Samuel Argall, 8 Miles East. *Stafford County: Route 1, 3.8 miles n. of Falmouth.*

E-79   PEYTON'S ORDINARY

In this vicinity stood Peyton's Ordinary. George Washington, going to Fredericksburg to visit his mother, dined here, March 6, 1769. On his way to attend the House of Burgesses, he spent the night here, October 31, 1769, and stayed here again on September 14, 1772. Rochambeau's army, marching north from Williamsburg in 1782, camped here. *Stafford County: Route 1, 1.8 miles n. of Stafford.*

E-80*   INDIAN MASSACRE

To the east, in Dogue Neck, Piscataway Indians attacked the house of Thomas Barton, killing eight persons, June 16, 1700. George Mason (2nd) described this as the "horriblest murder that ever was in Stafford." *Fairfax County: Route 1, 8.25 miles s. of Alexandria.*

E-81*   DEFENSES OF WASHINGTON

Just to the north lie Forts O'Rorke, Weed, Farnsworth, and Lyon. To the east is Fort Willard. These fortifications constituted the extreme southern defense line of the city of Washington, 1862–65. *Fairfax County: Route 1, .8 mile s. of Alexandria.*

E-90   AQUIA CHURCH

Here is Aquia Church, the church of Overwharton Parish, formed before 1680 by the division of Potomac Parish. It was built in 1757, on the site of an earlier church, in the rectorship of Reverend John Moncure, who was the parish minister from 1738 to 1764. The communion silver was given the parish in 1739 and was buried in three successive wars, 1776, 1812 and 1861. *Stafford County: Route 1, 2.7 miles n. of Stafford.*

E-91   LEE'S BOYHOOD HOME

Robert E. Lee left this home that he loved so well to enter West Point. After Appomattox he returned and climbed the wall to see "if the snowballs were in bloom." George Washington dined here when it was the home of William Fitzhugh, Lee's kinsman and his wife's grandfather. Lafayette visited here in 1824. *Alexandria: In front of 607 Oronoco Street.*

EH-8   ASBURY'S DEATHPLACE

A short distance southeast is the site of the George Arnold house where Bishop Francis Asbury died, March 31, 1816. Asbury, born in England in 1745, came to America in 1771 and labored here until his death. He was ordained one of the first two bishops of the Methodist Episcopal Church in America at the Baltimore Conference of December, 1784. *Spotsylvania County: Route 738, 5.5 miles s. of Spotsylvania Courthouse.*

EM-1 FREDERICKSVILLE FURNACE

Charles Chiswell established the iron-making community of Fredericksville near this point of Douglas Run, a tributary of the North Anna River. The furnace had been in blast for about five years when William Byrd in 1732 toured the site in the company of Chiswell and his iron-master, Robert Durham. An archaeological investigation of the furnace was financed by Virginia Electric and Power Company in 1970. *Spotsylvania County: Route 208, 100 yards s.w. of Furnace.*

EP-8 BIRTHPLACE OF MADISON

At this place, Port Conway, James Madison, Fourth President of the United States and Father of the Constitution, was born, March 16, 1751. His mother was staying at her paternal home, Belle Grove, 400 yards east, when her son was born. Madison's father, James Madison, Senior, lived in Orange County. The President had his home at Montpelier in that county. *King George County: Route 301, .4 mile n. of Port Royal.*

EP-20 JOHN WILKES BOOTH

This is the Garrett place where John Wilkes Booth, assassin of Lincoln, was cornered by Union soldiers and killed, April 26, 1865. The house stood a short distance from this spot. *Caroline County: Route 301, 9.1 miles n.e. of Bowling Green.*

EP-21 BIRTHPLACE OF GOVERNOR WISE

Here stood the birthplace of Henry Alexander Wise (1806–1876), Governor of Virginia (1856–1860) and General in The Confederate States Army. A talented orator and debator in an age of great orators, Wise was elected to six terms in Congress. He served as a delegate at the Virginia Conventions of 1850 and 1861, and as United States Minister to Brazil (1844–1847). *Accomack County: Route 13 business, town of Accomac.*

F-1 BATTLE OF BALL'S BLUFF

One mile east occurred the battle of Ball's Bluff, October 21, 1861. A Union force, which had crossed the river at this point, was driven back over it by the Confederates. *Loudoun County: Route 15, .9 mile n. of Leesburg.*

F-2 POTOMAC CROSSINGS

Here Lee turned east to the Potomac, crossing at White's Ford, September 6, 1862, in his invasion of Maryland. Jubal A. Early, returning from his Washington raid, crossed the river at White's Ford, July 14, 1864. *Loudoun County: Route 15, 6.9 miles n. of Leesburg.*

F-3 GREENWOOD

Home of Judge William Green. Judge Green entertained Lafayette here on August 22, 1825. *Culpeper County: Route 15, .8 mile s. of Culpeper.*

F-4   OAK HILL

The house to the northwest is Oak Hill, home of President James Monroe, who built it about 1818. Lafayette was entertained here in 1824. Monroe lived here most of the time from his retirement in 1825 to his death in 1831. *Loudoun County: Route 15, 3 miles n. of Aldie.*

F-5   WAYNE'S CROSSING

Three miles southeast, at Noland's Ferry, "Mad Anthony" Wayne, on his way to join Lafayette, crossed the Potomac River, May 31, 1781. He passed through Leesburg, June 3, and joined Lafayette near the Rapidan River, June 10. *Loudoun County: Route 15, 7.2 miles n. of Leesburg.*

F-6   SHARPSBURG (ANTIETAM)
      CAMPAIGN

Near here Stonewall Jackson bivouacked on the march into Maryland, September 4, 1862. *Loudoun County: Route 15, 2.7 miles n. of Leesburg.*

F-7   GOOSE CREEK CHAPEL

A short distance west is the site of the "Chapel above Goose Creek," built by the vestry of Truro Parish in 1736. Augustine Washington, father of George Washington, was a member of the vestry at the time. This was the first church on the soil of Loudoun County, erected as a chapel of ease for the benefit of early settlers. *Loudoun County: Route 15, 2 miles n. of Leesburg.*

F-8   COLONIAL HOME

Seven miles west is Roanoke Bridge, colonial homestead of Joseph Morton. The land was patented in 1746 and settled in 1755. Joseph Morton, one of the leading pioneers of this section, was a justice, a surveyor, and a founder of Briery Presbyterian Church. *Charlotte County: Route 15, 2.4 miles n. of Keysville.*

F-9   CAMPAIGN OF SECOND
      MANASSAS

Here Jackson, on his march around Pope to Bristoe Station, turned to the southeast, August 26, 1862. *Fauquier County: Route 55, at The Plains.*

F-10   WHERE PELHAM FELL

Four miles southeast, at Kelly's Ford, Major John Pelham, commanding Stuart's horse artillery, was mortally wounded, March 17, 1863. *Culpeper County: Route 15, at Elkwood.*

F-11   BATTLE OF BRANDY STATION

In this vicinity was fought one of the greatest Cavalry Battles of the Civil War. On June 9, 1863 Union forces under Pleasonton attacked Stuart, who was screening Lee's Northward movement toward Pennsylvania. After heavy fighting Pleasonton withdrew. *Culpeper County: Route 29, 1 mile n. of Brandy.*

F-11   BATTLE OF BRANDY STATION

This was the scene of many cavalry actions. A great cavalry battle took place here, on June 9, 1863, between Stuart, screening Lee's move to Gettysburg, and the cavalry of Hooker's army. *Culpeper County: Routes 15 and 29, .7 mile n.e. of Brandy.*

F-12*   BETTY WASHINGTON

Two miles south of this spot is the grave of Betty Lewis, sister of George Washington. She died March 31, 1797. *Culpeper County: Route 15, 3.1 miles n.e. of Culpeper.*

F-13   OPENING OF GETTYSBURG CAMPAIGN

On this plain Lee reviewed his cavalry, June 8, 1863. The next day the cavalry battle of Brandy Station was fought. On June 10, Ewell's Corps, from its camp near here, began the march to Pennsylvania. *Culpeper County: Route 15, .5 mile s.w. of Brandy.*

F-14   SIMON KENTON'S BIRTHPLACE

Near Hopewell Gap, five miles west, Simon Kenton was born, 1755. Leaving home in 1771, he became an associate of Daniel Boone and George Rogers Clark in Indian fighting. He won fame as a scout and as one of the founders of Kentucky. Kenton died in Ohio in 1836. *Prince William County: Route 15, 6.9 miles s. of Gilberts Corner.*

F-15*   MOTHER OF STONEWALL JACKSON

In this vicinity (and according to tradition two miles east at Peach Orchard) was born Julia Beckwith Neale, mother of Stonewall Jackson, February 29, 1798. She married Jonathan Jackson in 1818 and died, October 1831. *Loudoun County: Route 15, .9 mile s. of Gilberts Corner.*

F-15*   SIGNAL STATION

The lone peak to the northeast, Mount Pony, was used by Pope as a signal station, 1862. *Culpeper County: Route 15, 2 miles s. of Culpeper.*

F-16   LEE AND POPE

To the south is Clark's Mountain, behind which Lee's army was gathered, August 17, 1862. From a signal station on the mountain top Lee looked down on Pope's army, which he wished to attack. Pope, realizing his danger, retired northward. *Culpeper County: Route 15, 4.7 miles s. of Culpeper.*

F-17   KEMPER'S GRAVE

A mile south is the grave of James Lawson Kemper, who led his brigade of Virginia troops in Pickett's charge at Gettysburg, July 3, 1863, and fell desperately wounded. He became a major-general in 1864. Kemper was governor of Virginia, 1874–1878. *Orange County: Route 15, 2.7 miles n. of Orange.*

F-18   GOLDVEIN

Thomas Jefferson stated in NOTES ON THE STATE OF VIRGINIA (1782) that he found gold bearing rock weighing approximately four pounds near this site. Among the 19 gold mines that have been in operation since then in the area, the Franklin and the Liberty were the most productive with the Franklin producing 6259 ounces of gold as recently as 1936. *Fauquier County: Route 17, at Goldvein.*

F-19*   BATTLE OF CEDAR MOUNTAIN

Here Stonewall Jackson halted his advance late in the afternoon of August 9, 1862, having driven Banks back from Cedar Mountain. *Culpeper County: Route 15, 3 miles s. of Culpeper.*

F-20   BATTLE OF CEDAR MOUNTAIN

Near here Jackson formed line of battle and received the attack of Banks' Corps of Pope's army. From here he attacked in turn, driving the Union forces northwest. *Culpeper County: Route 15, 6.1 miles s. of Culpeper.*

F-21*   CROOKED RUN BAPTIST CHURCH

This church was organized in 1772. Among its first pastors was Thomas Ammon, who had once been imprisoned for preaching. In 1789, the first meeting of the Orange Association was held at this church. *Culpeper County: Route 15, 9.7 miles s. of Culpeper.*

F-22   JACKSON'S CROSSING

Here at Locust Dale, Stonewall Jackson's army crossed the river moving north to the battle of Cedar Mountain, August 9, 1862. The battle was fought a few hours later. *Madison County: Route 15, 7.6 miles n. of Orange.*

F-23   CHURCH OF THE BLIND PREACHER

Near here was the church of James Waddel, the blind Presbyterian preacher. Waddel, who had been a minister in the Northern Neck and elsewhere, came here about 1785 and died here in 1805. William Wirt, stopping in 1803 to hear a sermon, was impressed by Waddel's eloquence. He made it the subject of a classic essay. *Orange County: Route 15, .5 mile n. of Gordonsville.*

F-24   WOODBERRY FOREST SCHOOL

One mile east is Woodberry Forest School, a college preparatory school for boys founded in 1889 by Robert Stringfellow Walker, a captain in Mosby's Rangers. The school is named for the estate on which it stands, formerly owned by William Madison, brother of President James Madison. *Orange County: 1.5 miles n. of Orange.*

F-26   MONTPELIER AND MADISON'S TOMB

Five miles southwest is Montpelier, the home of James Madison, "Father of the American Constitution" and fourth President of the United States, 1809–1817. Near the house is the tomb of Madison, who died at Montpelier on June 28, 1836. *Orange County: Route 15, at Orange.*

F-32 CAMPAIGN OF SECOND MANASSAS

Near here Stonewall Jackson camped, August 13–15, 1862, just after the Cedar Mountain engagement. *Orange County: Route 15, 3.2 miles s. of Orange.*

F-40 CAMPAIGN OF 1781

Lafayette, moving west to protect stores in Albermarle from Tarleton, passed near here, June, 1781. *Louisa County: Route 15, 3.3 miles s. of Boswell's Tavern.*

F-50 POINT OF FORK

Four miles southeast is Point of Fork, near which an Indian village stood in 1610. In the Revolution a state arsenal was there. In June, 1781, Simcoe, sent by Cornwallis with a small force to destroy the stores there, succeeded in making Baron Steuben, the American commander, believe the whole British army to be near. Steuben retreated, leaving the stores to be destroyed. *Fluvanna County: Route 15, at Dixie.*

F-52 BREMO

To the west is Bremo, built by John Hartwell Cocke after plans made by Thomas Jefferson and completed about 1819. Two other houses once owned by Cocke, Lower Bremo and Recess, are in the vicinity. Cocke, one of the prominent men of his time and associated in the founding of the University of Virginia, was an early temperance advocate. *Fluvanna County: Route 15, 3.2 miles s. of Fork Union.*

F-53 CARTER G. WOODSON 1875–1950

Three miles east is the birthplace of the noted teacher, educator and historian, Dr. Carter G. Woodson. He was the founder of the association for the study of negro life and history, originated negro history week and authored more than a dozen important works dealing with his race in the United States. *Buckingham County: Route 15, 10 miles n. of Dillwyn.*

F-54 FEMALE COLLEGIATE INSTITUTE

Two miles east is the site of the first college for women in Virginia, the Female Collegiate Institute. Opened in 1837, it failed in 1843. Reopened in 1848, it survived until 1863. The school building has been destroyed but the "President's Cottage" still stands. *Buckingham County: Route 15, 5 miles n. of Dillwyn.*

F-55 GOLD MINES

This was the most notable gold-mining region in the country before the California gold rush in 1849. The Morrow Mine here, opened before 1835, was one of the earliest gold mines in which underground mining was employed. Profitably worked for a number of years, it was finally closed. Many other now unworked mines are near by. *Buckingham County: Route 15, at Dillwyn.*

F-56 OLD BUCKINGHAM CHURCH

The original, or southwest, wing was erected, circa 1758, as a church for the newly-formed Tillotson Parish. Abandoned soon after the Disestablishment (1784), the property was acquired by the Baptists during the next quarter century. It has since served continuously as the meeting house of Buckingham Baptist Church, which was itself constituted May 7, 1771. *Buckingham County: Route 15, .75 mile s.w. of Route 610.*

F-59 MARCH TO APPOMATTOX

Part of Lee's army passed here retreating westward, April 8, 1865. The Sixth (Wright's) Corps of Grant's army passed here, in pursuit, in the afternoon of the same day, moving on toward Appomattox. *Buckingham County: Route 15, 8.8 miles s. of Sprouses.*

F-60 EVE OF APPOMATTOX

Part of Lee's army passed here, April 8, 1865, retreating westward. The Second (Humphrey's) Corps of Grant's army passed, in pursuit, in the afternoon of the same day. Grant spent the night here, receiving early in the morning of April 9 a note from Lee in regard to surrender. He sent a reply and then went on to Appomattox. *Buckingham County: Route 15, 11.3 miles s. of Sprouses.*

F-61 NEW STORE VILLAGE

Four miles west is the site of New Store Village, in early times an important stop on the Stage Coach Road between Richmond and Lynchburg. Philip Watkins McKinney, Governor of Virginia 1890–1894, was born here in 1832. Peter Francisco, Revolutionary War hero, grew to maturity at nearby Hunting Towers, home of Judge Anthony Winston, an uncle of Patrick Henry. *Buckingham County: Route 15, 11.3 miles s. of Sprouses.*

F-65 OLD WORSHAM

A short distance south stands the colonial jail of Prince Edward County, built about 1755; the courthouse was near by. The British cavalryman, Tarleton, raided here in July, 1781. Here Patrick Henry made a great speech against the ratification of the United States Constitution, 1788. Washington was here on his southern tour, June 7, 1791. *Prince Edward County: Route 15, 5.6 miles s. of Farmville.*

F-66* SLATE HILL PLANTATION

A mile west is Slate Hill, home of Nathaniel Venable, who was a member of the Prince Edward Committee of Safety in the Revolution and a charter trustee of Hampden-Sydney College. Tarleton's British cavalry raided this place in 1781, seeking to capture Venable and army supplies stored here. *Prince Edward County: Route 15, 6.5 miles s. of Farmville.*

F-69   RANDOLPH-MACON MEDICAL SCHOOL

Just to the west was the medical school of John Peter Mettauer, which became a branch of Randolph-Macon College in 1847. It was discontinued, probably in 1861. Dr. Mettauer, one of the leading surgeons of the day, practiced until his death in 1875. *Prince Edward County: Route 15, 5 miles s. of Farmville.*

F-70   KINGSVILLE

Here, before the Revolution, stood King's Tavern. The British cavalryman, Tarleton, raiding, camped here in 1781. In the same year sick and wounded French soldiers were brought to this place from Yorktown; seventy of them are buried here. Nearby is the site of the colonial church of which Archibald Mc-Roberts was minister. *Prince Edward County: Route 15, 4.5 miles s. of Farmville.*

F-71   PROVIDENCE

Two miles east is the glebe house where the Rev. Archibald McRoberts lived during the Revolution. Tarleton, raiding through this section in July, 1781, set fire to the house, but a timely rain put out the flames. Accordingly, the place was named "Providence." *Prince Edward County: Route 15, 5.6 miles s. of Farmville.*

F-72   CAMPAIGN OF 1781

Tarleton, sent by Cornwallis to destroy supplies at Bedford, passed here going west, July, 1781. *Prince Edward County: Route 15, 5.6 miles s. of Farmville.*

F-75   OLD BRIERY CHURCH

Just to the north stands Briery Church, organized in 1755 following the missionary work of Presbyterian Minister Samuel Davies. The first church was built about 1760 and was replaced in 1824. The present Gothic Revival church was built about 1855 to designs of Robert Lewis Dabney. *Prince Edward County; Route 15, 2.4 miles n. of Keysville.*

F-77   EARLY EXPLORATION

Batts, Fallam and Thomas Wood, sent by Abraham Wood to explore western Virginia, passed near here, September, 1671. *Charlotte County: Route 15, .2 mile n. of Keysville.*

F-78   CAMPAIGN OF 1781

Tarleton, British cavalryman, returning from his raid to Bedford, passed near here, July, 1781. *Charlotte County: Route 15, at s. entrance of Keysville.*

F-80   ROANOKE PLANTATION

Nine miles west is Roanoke, home of John Randolph, a member of the House of Representatives for many years, and Senator. Randolph at first was Jefferson's lieutenant and later on an opponent and critic, but he never lost the love of his constituents. He died in Philadelphia, May 24, 1833, and was buried here; later his remains were removed to Richmond. *Charlotte County: Route 15, at Wyliesburg.*

F-82   STAUNTON BRIDGE ACTION

The railroad bridge over Staunton River, nine miles west, was held by a body of Confederate reserves and citizens from Halifax, Charlotte and Mecklenburg counties against Union cavalry raiding to destroy railroads, June 25, 1864. When the Unionists attempted to burn the bridge, they were repulsed. Meanwhile Confederate cavalry attacked from the rear. Thereupon the raiders retreated to Grant's army at Petersburg. *Charlotte County: Route 15, at Wyliesburg.*

F-95   PRESTWOULD PLANTATION

The second William Byrd obtained land here about 1730 and named the place "Blue Stone Castle." The estate extended ten miles along Roanoke River. Before the Revolution Sir Peyton Skipwith came into possession and built the present house, which he named "Prestwould." *Mecklenburg County: Route 15, 3 miles n. of Clarksville.*

F-98*   OCCANEECHEE ISLAND

Just to the west lies Occaneechee Island, former home of the Occaneechee Indians. It was visited by Abraham Wood in 1650. Bacon, the Rebel, following a band of savages ravaging the frontier, overtook them here and persuaded the Occaneechees to attack them. When the Occaneechees refused him food, Bacon turned on them, May 16, 1676. *Mecklenburg County: Route 15, near state line.*

FA-1   CAMPAIGN OF SECOND MANASSAS

Lee and Longstreet, moving eastward to join Jackson at Manassas, found this gap held by a Union force, August 28, 1862. They forced the gap, after some fighting, and moved on toward Manassas, August 29, 1862. *Prince William County: Route 55, 5 miles s.e. of The Plains.*

FB-2   JOHN MARSHALL'S HOME

The land was bought by Thomas Marshall, the Chief Justice's father, who built the old part of the house in 1773. John Marshall lived here until he entered the army in 1775. Years later he built the new house for his eldest son. *Fauquier County: Route 55, 4 miles w. of Marshall.*

FB-4   CAMPAIGN OF SECOND MANASSAS

Near here Stonewall Jackson, after a march of twenty-six miles on his way to Bristoe Station, halted for a few hours to rest his men, August 25–26, 1862. *Fauquier County: Route 55, at Marshall.*

FF-2   STATE FISH HATCHERY

One mile south. This fish cultural station was established in 1933 for hatching and rearing smallmouth bass and other species of sunfish for the stocking of the public waters of Virginia. *Warren County: Route 55, 5 miles w. of Riverton.*

FF-4*   GETTYSBURG CAMPAIGN

General R. E. Lee established his headquarters here, June 17, 1863. Ewell's advance had crossed the Potomac; Longstreet was near Snicker's Gap; Stuart in contact with the Union cavalry near Aldie; A. P. Hill moving to Chester Gap. The Army of Northern Virginia was about to invade the North. *Fauquier County: Route 55, at Markham.*

FF-5*   LEE'S ESCAPE

Near here Robert E. Lee and staff, moving to join Jackson for the battle of Second Manassas, narrowly escaped capture by the Ninth New York cavalry August 27, 1862. The staff, forming in line confronted the Unionists, who withdrew without charging. *Fauquier County: Route 55, 2 miles w. of Marshall.*

FF-8   McCLELLAN RELIEVED FROM COMMAND

At Rectortown, four miles north, General George B. McClellan received the order relieving him from command of the Army of the Potomac, November 7, 1862. As Burnside, his successor, was present, McClellan immediately turned over the command to him. *Fauquier County: Route 55, at Marshall.*

FL-8   ASH LAWN

Home of James Monroe, fifth President of the United States, from 1799 until Oak Hill was built. The house was designed by Thomas Jefferson; the rear part was constructed under his plans, 1794–1799. The place was in a neighborhood that included Monticello and the homes of other such noted men as William Short and Philip Mazzei. *Albemarle County: Route 695, 4 miles s. of Charlottesville.*

FR-3   RED HOUSE

This old tavern was built by Martin Hancock about 1813 on the site of his earlier cabin. It was a noted stopping place and trade center on the old south road to the West. *Charlotte County: Route 727, at Red House.*

FR-6   EDGEHILL

Three miles north is Edgehill, home of Clement Carrington. He ran away from Hampden-Sydney College to join the Revolutionary army, served in Lee's Legion, 1780–81, and was wounded at Eutaw Springs, September 8, 1781. *Charlotte County: Route 40, 2 miles e. of Charlotte.*

FR-7   GREENFIELD

Half a mile north is Greenfield, built in 1771 by Isaac Read. Read was a member of the House of Burgesses, 1769–1771, and of the Virginia conventions of 1774 and 1775. He served as an officer in the Revolutionary War, dying of wounds in 1777. *Charlotte County: Route 40, 2 miles e. of Charlotte.*

FR-8* COLONIAL HOME

Seven miles west is Roanoke Bridge, colonial homestead of Joseph Morton. The land was patented in 1746 and settled in 1755. Joseph Morton, one of the leading pioneers of this section, was a justice, a surveyor, and a founder of Briery Presbyterian Church. *Charlotte County: Route 40, 2 miles e. of Charlotte Courthouse.*

FR-10 HENRY AND RANDOLPH'S DEBATE

Here, in March, 1799, took place the noted debate between Patrick Henry and John Randolph of Roanoke on the question of States' Rights. Henry denied the right of a state to oppose oppressive Federal laws. Randolph affirmed that right. This was Henry's last speech and Randolph's first. Henry died three months later. *Charlotte County: Route 40, at Charlotte.*

FR-12 CAMPAIGN OF 1781

At Cole's Ferry on Staunton River, twelve miles southwest, Steuben halted his southward march, June 10, 1781. *Charlotte County: Route 40, at Charlotte.*

FR-14 CUB CREEK CHURCH

Six miles south is Cub Creek Presbyterian Church, the oldest church in this section. The neighborhood was known as the Caldwell Settlement for John Caldwell, grandfather of John C. Calhoun of South Carolina. About 1738 he brought here a colony of Scotch-Irish and obtained permission to establish a church. *Charlotte County: Route 40, 2 miles e. of Phenix.*

FR-15 ROUGH CREEK CHURCH

A chapel was built here in 1765–1769 by order of the vestry of Cornwall Parrish. Following the disestablishment and a brief period of irregular use, the property passed to the Republican Methodists, a denomination then active in the South. It was received under the care of Hanover Presbytery in 1822, and the present building was erected in 1838 on the original site. Rough Creek is the mother church of Madisonville, Oak View, and Phenix Presbyterian churches organized 1907–1914. *Charlotte County: Route 727, n. of Phenix.*

FR-16 HAT CREEK CHURCH

Four and a half miles north stands Hat Creek Presbyterian Church, founded by John Irvin and associates (first settlers) about 1742. William Irvin, son of John, and the noted blind preacher, James Waddel, were among its pastors. The first log building was replaced in 1788, and two other churches have been built on the original site. *Campbell County: Route 40, 2.1 miles e. of Brookneal.*

FR-25 PATRICK HENRY'S GRAVE

Five miles southeast of Red Hill, last home and resting place of Patrick Henry. He moved here in 1796 and died here, June 6, 1799. *Campbell County: Route 40, 2.5 miles e. of Brookneal.*

FR-26   ST. JOHN'S LUTHERAN CHURCH

German settlers formed a congregation here that was a center of Lutheranism in Virginia throughout the 19th century. The church built around 1800 was replaced by the present structure in 1854. The cemetery has distinctive stones dating from 1804 to the present. St. John's became a part of Holy Trinity, Wytheville, in 1924. *Wythe County: Route 21, at Wytheville.*

FR-27   BIRTHPLACE OF GENERAL PICK

Lt. Gen. Lewis Andrew Pick was born here on November 18, 1890. Educated at Rustburg and at VPI (where he was a member of the Corps of Cadets), General Pick served in two world wars and in the Korean conflict. Best known as the builder of the 1,030-mile long Ledo Road, used to supply American and Chinese troops in the China-Burma-India Theatre during World War II, Pick also served as chief of the Army Corps of Engineers before his death in 1956. *Campbell County: Route 40, in Brookneal.*

G-2   LEETON FOREST

Half a mile east is the site of Leeton Forest, latter-day home of Charles Lee, Attorney General in Washington's and Adams' cabinets, 1795–1801. The tract was patented by Thomas Lee, of Stratford, in 1718 and descended to his son, Richard Henry Lee, Revolutionary leader. The latter's daughter Anne married Charles Lee, who obtained title to the property in 1803, and who died here in June, 1815. *Fauquier County: Route 802, .5 mile s. of Warrenton.*

G-3   ST. JAMES UNITED CHURCH OF CHRIST

Formerly St. James Evangelical and Reformed Church, this is the oldest active congregation of the German Reformed tradition in Virginia. Lovettsville, a German settlement, was founded by settlers of the Reformed Faith in 1733. Early records indicate that Elder William Wenner, the first leader of the Lovettsville congregation, arrived in the area as early as 1720. *Loudoun County: Route 673, .1 mile e. of Route 287.*

G-9   CAMPAIGN OF SECOND MANASSAS

Here Lee and Jackson has their headquarters. Here, August 24, 1862, they formed the plan to attack Pope's line of supply and bring him to battle before McClellan could join him. *Culpeper County: Route 211, 7 miles n.w. of Warrenton.*

G-9   LITTLE FORK CHURCH

One-half mile east stands Little Fork Episcopal Church, begun 1753, destroyed by fire in 1773. Present structure completed in 1776. *Culpeper County: Route 229, 6 miles s. of Route 211.*

G-10   GENERAL EDWARD STEVENS

Here is buried General Edward Stevens, who served at Brandywine, Camden, Guilford Courthouse and Yorktown. He died on August 17, 1820. *Culpeper: Route 229, at n. entrance of Culpeper.*

G-11*   CAVALRY ENGAGEMENT

Near here J.E.B. Stuart, while fighting the Union cavalryman, Buford, was attacked in the rear by another cavalry force under Kilpatrick. Stuart, turning on Kilpatrick, cut his way out, September 22, 1863. Buford pursued him to the Rapidan River. *Madison County: Route 231, 5.5 miles s. of Madison.*

G-12   JOSEPH EARLY HOME

One mile west was the home of Joseph Early, Revolutionary soldier. Washington, in going West and returning, stopped at Early's overnight. His diary for October 2, 1784, shows that he spent the night before at "Widow Early's." *Madison County: Route 29, 3 miles s. of Madison.*

G-15   HENRY HOUSE

These are the grounds of the Henry House, where occurred the main action of the First Battle of Manassas, July 21, 1861, and the closing scene of the Second Battle of Manassas, August 30, 1862. *Prince William County: Route 234, 5.1 miles n.w. of Manassas.*

G-25*   GENERAL SUMTER'S BOYHOOD

Thomas Sumter, Revolutionary soldier in South Carolina for whom Fort Sumter was named, lived for a time in his youth at Sumter's Mill, five miles southeast. *Albemarle County: Route 29, 5 miles s. of Ruckersville.*

GA-32   POINT OF FORK

Here was an important supply depot and arsenal of the Virginia government in 1781, and here Baron von Steuben, commanding the American forces, trained recruits for Greene's army in the South. Threatened by Cornwallis's approach, Stueben moved stores across James River. On June 4, 1781, Colonel Simcoe, with his cavalry, made Steuben believe that the whole British army was at hand. Steuben retreated, leaving stores to be destroyed. *Fluvanna County: Route 6, .8 mile w. of Columbia.*

GA-33   FORK UNION ACADEMY

First classes of Fork Union Academy were held here October 15, 1898, in the residence of Susan Payne Cooper. Established as a coeducational English and classical school, it became Fork Union Military Academy for boys in 1903. Organized by ten guarantors who were members of Fork Church, the Academy was sustained mainly by private contributions from the Fork Union Community until 1913 when it became affiliated with the Baptist denomination. *Fluvanna County: Route 6 at Route 15.*

GA-34   RASSAWEK

Rassawek, a town of the Monacan Indians, stood near here at the time of the settlement in 1607. The Monacans, a Siouan tribe, were decimated by repeated attacks of the Iroquois from the north, and finally moved westward. *Fluvanna County: Route 6, .8 mile w. of Columbia.*

GA-35   BARCLAY HOUSE AND SCOTTSVILLE MUSEUM

Here stands the Barclay House, built about 1830, later the home of Dr. James Turner Barclay, inventor for the U.S. Mint and Missionary to Jerusalem. He founded the Adjacent Disciples Church in 1846 and served as its first preacher. It is now the Scottsville Museum. *Albemarle County: Route 6, at Scottsville.*

GA-36   HISTORIC SCOTTSVILLE

In 1745 Old Albemarle County was organized at Scott's landing, its first county seat, here on the Great Horseshoe Bend of the James River. In 1818 the town was incorporated as Scottsville. Beginning in 1840 it flourished as the chief port above Richmond for freight and passenger boats on the James River and Kanawha Canal. It played a vital role in the opening up of the west. The 1840s and '50s were its golden era. *Albemarle County: Route 20, Int. Route 6 in Scottsville.*

HD-1   COLONEL ABRAM PENN

200 yards south is "Poplar Grove," Penn's old home and burial place. At age 21, he "won his spurs," leading a company under General Lewis at Point Pleasant. During 1780–81 he organized the first Revolutionary troops from Henry and adjoining counties, and led his regiment to aid General Greene in the battles of Guilford Court House and Eutaw Springs. He helped organize Patrick County. *Patrick County: Route 58, 1.86 miles s.e. of Henry County line.*

I-1   VIRGINIA MILITARY INSTITUTE

A state military, engineering and arts college, founded in 1839. Graduates of it have taken a prominent part in every war since the Mexican War, 2,000 of them serving in the World War. The cadets fought as a corps at New Market in 1864. Among the members of the faculty were Stonewall Jackson and the noted scientists, Matthew F. Maury and John M. Brooke. *Rockbridge County: Route 11, at Lexington.*

I-2   SOUTHWEST VIRGINIA MUSEUM

Originated by Mrs. Janie Slemp Newman and developed by her brother, C. Bascom Slemp, as a neighborhood museum. It contains books by local authors, portraits of citizens, implements, machines, furniture, household utensils, furnishings and costumes. It presents a representative picture of the life of Southwestern Virginians of the past. The collection of museum pieces was bequeathed to Virginia by will of C. Bascom Slemp and accepted by the State in 1946. *Wise County: Alternate Route 58, at Big Stone Gap.*

I-2-a   VIRGINIA POLYTECHNIC INSTITUTE

Nine miles north is the Virginia Polytechnic Institute, a state college of agriculture, engineering and business, established in 1872, as a land-grant college, on the site of the Draper's Meadows massacre of 1755. Its founding marked the beginning of scientific agricultural and industrial instruction in Virginia. The college includes agricultural and engineering experiment stations. *Montgomery County: Route 11, .6 mile e. of Christiansburg.*

I-2-b VIRGINIA POLYTECHNIC INSTITUTE

Nine miles north is the Virginia Polytechnic Institute, a state college of agriculture, engineering and business, established in 1872, as a land-grant college, on the site of the Draper's Meadows massacre of 1755. Its founding marked the beginning of scientific agricultural and industrial instruction in Virginia. The college includes agricultural and engineering experiment stations. *Montgomery County: Route 11, at w. entrance of Christiansburg.*

I-2-c VIRGINIA POLYTECHNIC INSTITUTE

A state college of agriculture, engineering and business, established in 1872, as a land-grant college, on the site of the Draper's Meadows massacre of 1755. Its founding marked the beginning of scientific agricultural and industrial instruction in Virginia. The college includes agricultural and engineering experiment stations. *Montgomery County: Route 460, at Blacksburg.*

I-3 UNIVERSITY OF VIRGINIA

This institution was founded by Thomas Jefferson. The cornerstone of the first building was laid, on October 6, 1817, in the presence of three Presidents of the United States, Jefferson, Madison and Monroe, all members of the board of visitors. It became the state university in 1819 and was opened to instruction in 1825. The university was conducted by the faculty until 1904, when the first president was elected. *Albemarle County: Route 29, at Charlottesville.*

I-4 CATAWBA SANATORIUM

This institution, one mile northeast, stands on the site of the old Roanoke Red Sulphur Springs, which by 1859 was a noted summer resort. The sanatorium was established by the general assembly of Virginia in 1908 for the treatment of persons suffering with incipient tuberculosis. It opened its doors on July 30, 1909. The location was selected for its bracing and healthy climate. *Roanoke County: Route 311 at Catawba.*

I-5* STATE COLONY

One mile southeast is the state colony for epileptics and feebleminded, chartered by the General Assembly, February 20, 1906, opened to patients in May, 1911. In its grounds are earthworks erected in June, 1864, to defend Lynchburg against Sheridan's advance from the east. Sheridan, defeated by Hampton at Trevillians, did not reach here. *Amherst County: Route 29, 1 mile n. of Lynchburg.*

I-6 CENTRAL STATE HOSPITAL

Established in 1869 in temporary quarters at Howard's Grove near Richmond. In 1870 it came under control of the State. In 1885 it was moved to the present location, the site of "Mayfield Plantation," which was purchased and donated to the State by the City of Petersburg. The first hospital in America exclusively for the treatment of mental disease in the Negro. *Dinwiddie County: Route 1, .4 mile w. of Petersburg.*

I-7   EMORY AND HENRY COLLEGE

One mile north is Emory and Henry College, founded in 1836, the first institution of higher learning in Southwest Virginia. It was named for Bishop John Emory of the Methodist Church and Patrick Henry, the orator of the Revolution. Four bishops of the Methodist Church, three governors, and one United States Senator are among its alumni. *Washington County: Route 11, 8.3 miles e. of Abingdon.*

I-8   WASHINGTON AND LEE UNIVERSITY

Founded 1749, as Augusta Academy, near Greenville; reestablished at Timber Ridge, May, 1776, as Liberty Hall Academy; moved to Lexington and chartered as a college, 1782; endowed by George Washington, 1796, and named for him. Under presidency, 1865–1870, of Robert E. Lee (buried in the university chapel), whose name after death was incorporated in the official title. *Rockbridge County: Route 11, at Lexington.*

I-9*   HAMPDEN-SYDNEY COLLEGE

Formed in 1776 (six months before the Declaration of Independence) and named for John Hampden and Algernon Sydney, English patriots, it was brought into being by the love of liberty. Patrick Henry and James Madison were on the first board of trustees. President William Henry Harrison was a member of the class of 1791. The college is one of the leading educational institutions of the Presbyterian Church. *Prince Edward County: Route 133 at Hampden-Sydney.*

I-10-a   RANDOLPH-MACON COLLEGE

Three blocks west is Randolph-Macon College for men, the oldest Methodist college in America. It was chartered in 1830 and was named for John Randolph of Roanoke and Nathaniel Macon of North Carolina. Originally situated at Boydton in southside Virginia, it was moved to present location in 1868. *Hanover County: Route 1, at Ashland.*

I-10-b*   RANDOLPH-MACON COLLEGE

A liberal arts college for men, chartered February 3, 1830. Named for John Randolph and Nathaniel Macon. The oldest Methodist college in America. *Hanover County: Route 54, at Ashland.*

I-11-a   ROANOKE COLLEGE

Five miles west is the birthplace of Virginia Institute, founded in 1842 by David F. Bittle, assisted by Christopher C. Baughman. Chartered on January 30, 1845, as Virginia Collegiate Institute, the school was moved to Salem, Virginia, in 1847, and was chartered as Roanoke College, March 14, 1853. *Augusta County: Route 340, 2.1 miles n. of Greenville.*

I-11-b ROANOKE COLLEGE

At Salem is a liberal arts institution for men and women. Founded in Augusta County in 1842 as Virginia Institute, it was chartered in 1845 as Virginia Collegiate Institute; moved to Salem in 1847; chartered as Roanoke College in 1853, and was in operation throughout 1861–65. The students formed a company in the Confederate Army, Virginia Reserves, September 1, 1864. *Roanoke County: Route 11, .2 mile w. of Salem.*

I-13 BRIDGEWATER COLLEGE

Located two miles southwest in the town of Bridgewater, this liberal arts college is affiliated with the Church of the Brethren. It grew out of the Spring Creek Normal School and Collegiate Institute, founded in 1880, and became Bridgewater College nine years later. It has been coeducational from the beginning. *Rockingham County: Route 11, at Va. 257 (Mount Crawford).*

I-13-A BRIDGEWATER COLLEGE

Founded near this site in 1880, the college is now located 4.3 miles east in the town of Bridgewater. This liberal arts college is affiliated with the Church of the Brethren. It grew out of the Spring Creek Normal School and Collegiate Institute and became Bridgewater College nine years later. It has been co-educational from its founding. *Rockingham County: Routes 613 and 748 at Spring Creek.*

I-15* STATE TEACHERS COLLEGE AT FARMVILLE

The college opened here in October 1884 as a "State Female Normal School." In 1914 the name was changed to "State Normal School for Women at Farmville;" in 1924 to "State Teachers College at Farmville." In 1916 conferring the B. S. degree was authorized and later the B. A. degree. William H. Ruffner, first State Superintendent of Public Instruction, was the first president. The fourth, J. L. Jarman, served from 1902 to 1946, succeeded by Dabney S. Lancaster. *Prince Edward County: Route 15, at Farmville.*

I-15-a* LONGWOOD COLLEGE

The college, on High Street in Farmville, opened in 1884 as a "State Female Normal School." In 1914 the name was changed to "State Normal School for Women at Farmville"; in 1924 to "State Teachers College at Farmville;" in 1949 to "Longwood College." Conferring the B. S. degree was authorized in 1916, and later the B. A. degree. William H. Ruffner, first State Superintendent of Public Instruction, was the first president. The fourth, J. L. Jarman, served from 1902 to 1946. *Prince Edward County: Route 460, at Farmville.*

I-16 THE VIRGINIA SCHOOL FOR THE DEAF AND THE BLIND–FOUNDED 1839

A State residential school created by an act of the General Assembly of the Commonwealth of Virginia on March 31, 1838 for the purpose of educating the deaf and the blind children of the state. *Staunton: Route 11 (Bypass) just e. of the school.*

I-17   MARY BALDWIN COLLEGE

The oldest college for women related to the Presbyterian Church, U.S. Founded 1842 by Rufus W. Bailey as Augusta Female Seminary; renamed in 1895 to honor Mary Julia Baldwin, pioneer woman, educator and principal, 1863–1897. *Staunton: Route 340, at Mary Baldwin College.*

J-1*   A RAID OF MOSBY'S

Here Mosby attacked Sheridan's supply train, August 13, 1864, capturing 600 horses and mules and 200 prisoners. *Clarke County: Route 340, 1 mile n. of Berryville.*

J-1-a   BUCK MARSH BAPTIST CHURCH

Organized near this spot by Wm. and Daniel Fristoe in 1772. Constituted by Elders John Marks and John Garrand, the latter serving as its Pastor. James Ireland served as Pastor from 1778–1806 and is buried here. *Clark County: Route 340, n. of Berryville.*

J-2*   BUCK MARSH

Near here, in 1744, Joseph Hampton and his two sons, while pioneering, lived in a hollow sycamore tree for some months. *Clarke County: Route 340, 1.5 miles n. of Berryville.*

J-3*   THIRD BATTLE OF WINCHESTER

Here Early, facing east, received the attack of Sheridan's army, at noon on September 19, 1864. Early repulsed the attack and countercharged, breaking the Union line. Only Upton's prompt action in changing front saved the Unionists from disaster. At 3 P.M., Sheridan made a second attack, driving Early back to Winchester. *Frederick County: Route 522 at e. entrance of Winchester.*

J-4   THIRD BATTLE OF WINCHESTER

Near here Early, facing east, took his last position on September 19, 1864. About sundown he was attacked and driven from it, retreating south. Presidents Rutherford B. Hayes and William McKinley served in this engagement on the Union side. *Frederick County: Route 522 at national cemetery, Winchester.*

J-6*   JOHN S. BARBOUR'S BIRTHPLACE

Just to the south stood "Catalpa," birthplace of John Strode Barbour, December 29, 1820. Barbour was a member of the House of Representatives; chairman of the state Democratic committee 1883–90; United States Senator, March 4, 1889 until his death on May 14, 1892. *Culpeper County: Route 522, at w. entrance of Culpeper.*

J-7   THE McKAY HOME

A short distance west, at Cedarville, stands the old home of the pioneer Robert McKay. Built of walnut logs, it is one of the oldest houses in the Valley. In 1731, Joist Hite, Robert McKay and others received a grant of 100,000 acres. Hite settled on the Opequon and McKay at this place on Crooked Run. These men opened the Valley to succeeding settlers. *Warren County: Route 340, at Cedarville.*

J-8   CAPTURE OF FRONT ROYAL

Stonewall Jackson, moving against Banks, captured this town from a Union force under Colonel Kenly, May 23, 1862. *Warren County: Route 340, at Front Royal.*

J-9   MOSBY'S MEN

Near this spot several of Mosby's men were executed by order of General Custer, September 23, 1864. On the following November 6 Colonel Mosby, in retaliation, ordered the execution of an equal number of Custer's men near Berryville. *Warren County: Route 340, .5 mile n. of Front Royal.*

J-10   CULPEPER MINUTE MEN

On the hill to the south the famous Culpeper Minute Men were organized, 1775. John Marshall, later Chief Justice of the Supreme Court, was a lieutenant. *Culpeper: Route 522, at w. entrance of Culpeper.*

J-11*   GUARD'S HILL AFFAIR

General Fitz Lee's cavalry, supported by a brigade of Kershaw's infantry, detached from Anderson's Corps at Front Royal, near here attacked Merritt of Sheridan's cavalry, August 16, 1864. Merritt, on being reinforced, drove the Confederates back across the river. He then withdrew towards Charlestown. *Warren County: Route 340, .2 mile n. of Riverton.*

J-12   RECREATIONAL CENTER OF FRONT ROYAL

The lands in this part were presented to the people of this community by Mr. and Mrs. William E. Carson and the park facilities were developed under the supervision of the National Park Service of the Department of the Interior by enrollees of the Civilian Conservation Corps. *Warren County: Route 340, 1.1 miles n. of Riverton.*

J-13*   THIRD BATTLE OF WINCHESTER

On this hill, Sheridan, facing west, took his final position, September 19, 1864. Early held position a half mile to the west. At 4 P.M. Sheridan, massing his cavalry and infantry, advanced on Early, whose line was broken by the assault. *Frederick County: Route 50, at Winchester.*

J-14*   GETTYSBURG CAMPAIGN

Lee and Longstreet, on their way to Gettysburg, camped here, June 18–19, 1863. *Clarke County: Route 340, 1 mile n. of Berryville.*

J-15   SIGNAL STATIONS

The hilltop northeast of this spot is Cole's Hill. The mountain to the west is Mount Pony. Both were used by Pope as signal stations, 1862. *Culpeper County: Route 3, 3.6 miles e. of Culpeper.*

J-16   DEFENSES OF WINCHESTER

The fort on the hilltop to the north is one of a chain of defenses commanding the crossings of the Opequon. It was constructed by Milroy in 1863. *Frederick County: Route 522, 4 miles s. of Winchester.*

J-17   BROTHER AGAINST BROTHER

The first Maryland Regiment, U.S.A., was a part of the force holding this town when it was attacked by Stonewall Jackson, May 23, 1862. With Jackson was the First Maryland Regiment, C.S.A. The two regiments were arrayed against each other. *Warren County: Route 340, at Front Royal.*

J-25   GETTYSBURG CAMPAIGN

Ewell's Corps of Lee's army passed here going north, June 11–12, 1863; Hill's Corps, June 19. *Rappahannock County: Route 522, 5 miles s. of Front Royal.*

J-26   ALBERT GALLATIN WILLIS

A ministerial student, aged 20, of Mosby's command, he was hanged nearby October 14, 1864 by U.S. 2nd Cavalry (W.Va.) in reprisal for alleged murder of U.S. soldier by Mosby's men. Of two captured, one was to be hanged. Willis was offered chaplain's exemption, but refused to doom his companion, a married man. Professing his Christian readiness to die, he prayed for his executioners. *Rappahannock County: Route 522, 5.5 miles n. of Flint Hill.*

J-29*   POPE'S ARMY OF VIRGINIA

Here was organized, from the troops of Fremont, Banks and McDowell, the Union army of Virginia, June 26, 1862. *Rappahannock County: Route 522, at Sperryville.*

J-30*   ANDERSON AND CROOK

Near here R. H. Anderson, on his march to join Lee, then hard pressed at Petersburg, met Crook's Army of West Virginia. Anderson attacked, driving Crook back on Sheridan's main army, September 4, 1864. *Clarke County: Route 7, .7 mile w. of Berryville.*

J-33   OPENING OF THE WILDERNESS CAMPAIGN

Near here the Second Corps of Grant's army camped in the winter of 1863–64. To this point came Sheridan's cavalry, the Sixth Corps from Brandy Station, and the Fifth Corps from Culpeper. The Union army moved hence to Germanna and Ely's Fords on the Rapidan River, May 4, 1864, to open the Wilderness Campaign. *Culpeper County: Route 3, at Stevensburg.*

J-34*   GERMANNA

Here Governor Alexander Spotswood planted a colony of Germans in 1714. At that time this river was the frontier of Virginia. On August 29, 1716, Spotswood left this place with his Knights of the Golden Horseshoe on his exploring expedition across the mountains. The German colony moved hence to Fauquier County. Spotswood lived here for some years and was visited here by William Byrd in 1732. *Orange County: Route 3, 4.8 miles w. of Wilderness.*

J-35   GERMANNA FORD

One of the principal crossings of the Rapidan River from colonial times. Here a part of the Army of the Potomac crossed the river, April 30, 1863, preceding the battle of Chancellorsville. Here a part of Meade's army crossed on the way to Mine Run, November 26, 1863. Here the Fifth and Sixth corps of Grant's army crossed, May 4–5, 1864, to open the Wilderness campaign. *Orange County: Route 3, 4.8 miles w. of Wilderness.*

J-37   JACKSON'S AMPUTATION

Near here stood the hospital tent to which the wounded "Stonewall" Jackson was brought during the Battle of Chancellorsville. In that tent his left arm was amputated on May 3, 1863. He died seven days later at Guinea. *Spotslvania County: Route 3, e. of Route 20.*

J-38   ELY'S FORD

On this hill, May 3, 1863, Confederate General J.E.B. Stuart was notified that General Stonewall Jackson had been wounded at Chancellorsville and that he was to take command of Jackson's Corps. Moments before, Stuart had ordered his 1,000 men from North Carolina and Virginia to attack the 3,400 Pennsylvanians under General A. W. Averell at Ely's Ford. After ordering three volleys of musket fire at the Union troops below, Stuart cancelled the attack and left to assume his command at Chancellorsville. (Erected 1981 by the Spotsylvania Historical Association.) *Spotsylvania County: Route 610, .54 mile e. of Culpeper County line.*

J-39   WOUNDING OF JACKSON

Stonewall Jackson, coming from the west, surprised Howard's Corps of the Army of the Potomac, May 2, 1863. Howard retreated along this road toward Chancellorsville, pursued by the Confederates. Here, Jackson, in the early evening, moving in front of his line of battle to reconnoitre, fell, mortally wounded by his own men. *Spotsylvania County: Route 3, .9 mile w. of Chancellorsville.*

J-40   BATTLE OF CHANCELLORSVILLE

Hooker reached this point, April 30, 1863; next day he entrenched, with his left wing on the river and his right wing on this road several miles west. That wing was surprised by Jackson and driven back here, May 2. The Confederates stormed the position here, May 3. The Union army withdrew northward, May 5–6, 1863. *Spotsylvania County: Route 3, at Chancellorsville.*

J-42   SPOTSWOOD'S FURNACE

Four miles north on this side road is the site of an ancient iron furnace established about 1716 by Governor Alexander Spotswood, the first fully equipped iron furnace in the colonies. Iron was hauled along this road to the Rappahannock River for shipment. William Byrd visited the furnace in 1732 and described it. *Spotsylvania County: Route 3, 5.4 miles w. of Fredericksburg.*

J-60   CHATHAM

Here is Chatham, built about 1750 by William Fitzhugh. Here Robert E. Lee came to court his wife. In the battle of Fredericksburg, December 13, 1862, the house was occupied by General Sumner. It was General Hooker's headquarters for a time, 1863. *Stafford County: Route 3, .2 mile east of Fredericksburg.*

J-61   WASHINGTON'S BOYHOOD HOME

At this place, George Washington lived most of the time from 1739 to 1747. Here, according to tradition, he cut down the cherry tree. Washington's father died here in 1743; the farm was his share of the paternal estate. His mother lived here until 1771. *Stafford County: Route 3, 1.1 miles e. of Fredericksburg.*

J-62   LAMB'S CREEK CHURCH

This old church was probably built before 1750. The stepping stone at the door bears the date 1782. Near here Kilpatrick's Union cavalry, on a raid to destroy gunboats at Port Conway, fought a skirmish, September 1, 1863. *King George County: Route 3, 5.5 miles w. of King George.*

J-63   MARMION

Two miles north is Marmion, probably built by John Fitzhugh early in the eighteenth century and later named for Scott's poem. About 1785 it passed from Philip Fitzhugh to George Washington's favorite nephew, who died there. The place has come down in the Lewis family in direct line from him. The richly decorated interior is one of the best in Virginia. *King George County: Route 3, 2.3 miles w. of King George.*

J-64   BRISTOL IRON WORKS

On the river a short distance south is the site of the Bristol Iron Works, which were projected by John King and Company of Bristol, England, and established in 1721 by John Tayloe, John Lomax and associates. The works, which were on the Foxhall's Mill property owned in 1670 by Major Underwood, were in operation in 1729 and later. *Westmoreland County: Route 3, 2.6 miles w. of Oak Grove.*

J-65   ST. PAUL'S CHURCH

Eight miles northeast is St. Paul's Church, built about 1766. The building was in a ruinous condition in 1812 but was repaired by the State and used both as a church and as a schoolhouse. About 1828 it once more became exclusively a church. *King George County: Route 3, 1.5 miles w. of King George.*

J-66* HISTORIC PORT CONWAY

Six miles southeast is Port Conway on the Rappahannock. At the Conway place there, James Madison, fourth President of the United States, was born, 1751. There Kilpatrick's Union cavalry shelled two gunboats captured by the Confederates, September 1, 1863. There John Wilkes Booth, assassin of Lincoln, crossed the river, April 24, 1865. *King George County: Route 3, 2.7 miles e. of King George.*

J-67 HISTORY AT OAK GROVE

Here George Washington, while living at Wakefield with a brother, went to school, 1744–1746. Here Union cavalry came on a raid through the Northern Neck, May, 1863. Several miles north of this place, James Monroe, fifth President of the United States, was born, 1758. *Westmoreland County: Route 3, at Oak Grove.*

J-68 WESTMORELAND ASSOCIATION

At Leedstown, seven miles south, an association was formed to resist the enforcement of the Stamp Act, February 27, 1766. The resolutions, drafted by the Revolutionary leader Richard Henry Lee, were one of the first protests against the Stamp Act and influenced public opinion in all the Colonies. *Westmoreland County: Route 3, at Oak Grove.*

J-68* LEEDSTOWN

Six miles south on the Rappahannock River. An Indian village stood here in 1608; a settlement was made at the place in 1683. In February, 1766, a public meeting was held there at which resolutions were adopted denouncing the Stamp Act. *Westmoreland County: Route 3, s. of Colonial Beach.*

J-69* THE WASHINGTON HOME

John Washington settled at Wakefield in 1665. Augustine Washington, father of George Washington, was born here in 1694. George Washington was born here, February 22, 1732. In 1734 Washington's father moved away, but George Washington lived here again in 1744–46. Here at Wakefield are the tombs of the early Washingtons. *Westmoreland County: Route 3, 2.8 miles s.e. of Oak Grove.*

J-69-a POPES CREEK EPISCOPAL CHURCH

On this site, a part of "Longwood," stood Popes Creek Episcopal Church, built about 1744 on land given by the McCarty family. The Lees and Washingtons worshipped here. About 1826 it fell into disuse and was burned as being unsafe. *Westmoreland County: Route 3, 4.8 miles s.e. of Oak Grove.*

J-69-b   WASHINGTON'S BIRTHPLACE

Two miles north, on Pope's Creek, stood the house where George Washington was born, February 22, 1732. It was completed by his father, Augustine, about 1726. The present Memorial House is in the style of the original, which burned about 1779. *Westmoreland County: Route 3, 2.8 miles s.e. of Oak Grove.*

J-70*   LEE'S BIRTHPLACE

Two miles east is Stratford, built about 1727 by Thomas Lee. There January 20, 1732, was born Richard Henry Lee, who introduced the resolution in the Continental Congress for the Declaration of Independence. There Robert E. Lee was born, January 19, 1807. *Westmoreland County: Route 3, 4 miles n.w. of Montross.*

J-71   OLD WESTMORELAND COURTHOUSE

At a public meeting here, on June 22, 1774, resolutions of Richard Henry Lee offering aid to Boston, whose port had been closed by the British government, were adopted. Here, on May 23, 1775, the Westmoreland Committee of Safety passed resolutions denouncing the royal governor, Lord Dunmore, for seizing the colony's powder supply at Williamsburg. *Westmoreland County: Route 3, at Montross.*

J-72   NOMINI HALL

The house was built about 1730 and burned in 1850. It was not rebuilt. Only some poplar trees remain. A fine colonial mansion, it was the home of the celebrated "Councilor" Robert Carter. Philip Fithian, tutor at Nomini Hall, 1773–74, wrote his well-known "Journal" there. *Westmoreland County: Route 3, at Templeman's Cross Roads.*

J-73   MENOKIN

Near here is Menokin, home of Francis Lightfoot Lee, signer of the Declaration of Independence. Lee was a member of the Continental Congress from 1775 to 1779 and died at Menokin in 1797. *Richmond County: Route 690, 4.1 miles north of Warsaw.*

J-74*   CHANTILLY

One mile beyond Stratford is Chantilly, the home of Richard Henry Lee, a leader in the American Revolution and the proposer of the Declaration of Independence. Lee moved there about 1764 and died there in 1794. The house, which was named for a chateau in France, was destroyed many years ago. *Westmoreland County: Route 3, 4 miles n.w. of Montross.*

J-75 WESTMORELAND STATE PARK

This park was developed by the National Park Service, Interior Department, through the Civilian Conservation Corps, in conjunction with the Virginia Conservation Commission. It covers 1300 acres and was opened June 15, 1936. It was originally included in "Clifts Plantation," patented by Nathaniel Pope about 1650, and became a part of Stratford estate when purchased by Thomas Lee in 1716. *Westmoreland County: Route 3, 4.7 miles n.w. of Montross.*

J-76 STRATFORD AND CHANTILLY

Two miles east of Stratford, built about 1725 by Thomas Lee (1690–1750). President of the Virginia Council and father of Richard Henry Lee & Francis Lightfoot Lee, both signers of the Declaration of Independence. Here also was born Robert Edward Lee (1807–1870). Three miles east of Stratford stood Chantilly, the home of Richard Henry Lee in his later years. *Westmoreland County: Route 3, 4 miles n.w. of Montross.*

J-77 NORTH FARNHAM CHURCH

This is the church of North Farnham Parish, built about 1737. In 1814, a skirmish was fought here between raiders from Admiral Cockburn's British fleet and Virginia militia; bullet holes are still visible in the walls. The church was used as a stable by Union soldiers, 1863–65. It was restored in 1872, damaged by fire in 1887 and restored again in 1924. *Richmond County: Route 692, at Farnham.*

J-78 CYRUS GRIFFIN'S BIRTHPLACE

Four and a half miles southwest was born Cyrus Griffin, July 16, 1748. Educated in England, he served in the Virginia House of Delegates, 1777–8, 1786–7. He was a member of the Continental Congress, 1787–1788, in which last year he was president of the body. Griffin was president of the court of admiralty, commissioner to the Creeks, 1789, and a United States district judge. He died at Yorktown, December 14, 1810. *Richmond County: Route 2, 2.8 miles s.e. of Farnham.*

J-80 BIRTHPLACE OF WASHINGTON'S MOTHER

Seven-tenths mile west is Epping Forest. The land was patented by Colonel Joseph Ball, who died there in 1711. His daughter, Mary Ball, mother of George Washington, was born there in 1707/8. The house incorporates parts of the original structure. *Lancaster County: Route 3, 9.3 miles e. of Farnham.*

J-80* EPPING FOREST

In 1704 Colonel Joseph Ball obtained land here. Here, in 1707, was born Mary Ball, George Washington's mother. The old house burned some years ago, but the cook house and coach house remain. *Lancaster County: Route 3, 12 miles e. of Warsaw.*

J-81 BEWDLEY

About three miles southeast, on the north bank of the Rappahannock River. Bewdley was one of the most unusual houses in Virginia, with two rows of dormer windows. It was built by Major James Ball, cousin of Washington's mother, about 1750. The first steamboat on the river touched at its wharf. The house burned in 1917; only one chimney remains. *Lancaster County: Route 354, 2.13 miles e. of Route 3 intersection*

J-82 ST. MARY'S WHITE CHAPEL

Three miles southwest. A church was built there in 1669, and the tablets are of that date. The present church was built in 1741 and was later remodeled. St. Mary's White Chapel parish was united with Christ Church parish in 1752. The tombs of the Balls, ancestors and relatives of George Washington, are there. *Lancaster County: Route 3, at Lively.*

J-83 WHITE MARSH CHURCH

This church, founded in 1792, was the mother church of Methodism in the Northern Neck of Virginia. The first camp meeting in this section was held here. Bishops Enoch George and David S. Doggett were members of this church. Bishop Joshua Soule, author of the constitution of the General Conference of the American Methodist Church, preached at meetings here. *Lancaster County: Route 3, 3.6 miles n.w. of Kilmarnock.*

J-85 COROTOMAN

This place was three miles south. Little remains of the house. John Carter obtained patents for a large grant here before 1654, but the place is better known as the home of his son, Robert ("King") Carter. In April, 1814, the British, raiding in the Chesapeake region, pillaged the plantation. *Lancaster County: Route 646, .66 mile w. of Route 3 intersection.*

J-86 CHRIST CHURCH

Christ Church was built in 1732, on the site of an older church by Robert ("King") Carter, who reserved one quarter of it for seating his tenants and servants. It is one of the very few colonial churches in America that have [*sic*] never been altered, a typical early eighteenth-century structure. Robert Carter is buried here. *Lancaster County: Route 646, .66 mile w. of Route 3 intersection.*

J-87 WINDMILL POINT

Troops were stationed here in November, 1813. Here, April 23, 1814, the British made a landing and pillaged a vessel. They were driven off by militia stationed across the creek. *Lancaster County: Route 695, 6.50 miles e. of Route 3 intersection in Whitestone.*

J-88 DITCHLEY AND COBBS

Ditchley, five miles northeast, was patented in 1651 by Colonel Richard Lee. The first house dated from 1687; the present house was built by Kendall Lee in 1752. Cobbs Hall, near by, was acquired by Richard Lee, probably before 1651. A house was built there by Charles Lee in 1720; the present house is modern. *Lancaster County: Route 3, at Kilmarnock.*

J-89 FIRST AMERICAN WOMAN
MISSIONARY TO CHINA

Here was born, October 28, 1817, Henrietta Hall (daughter of Colonel Addison Hall), first American woman missionary to China. She married Rev. J. Lewis Shuck, and was sent with him to China by the Baptist Board of Foreign Missions, arriving there in September, 1836. She died at Hong Kong, November 27, 1844. *Lancaster County: Route 3, at Kilmarnock.*

JD-1 BELLE BOYD AND JACKSON

Near here Stonewall Jackson was met by the spy, Belle Boyd, and informed of the position of the Union troops at Front Royal, May 24, 1862. Jackson was advancing northward, attempting to get between Banks' army and Winchester. *Warren County: Route 340, 3 miles s.w. of Front Royal.*

JD-2 WILLIAM E. CARSON

William E. Carson, of Riverton, was the first chairman of the Virginia Conservation Commission, 1926–34. As such he was a pioneer and leading spirit in the establishment of the Shenandoah National Park and Skyline Drive; the Colonial National Historical Park; the state parks, and the state system of historical markers. *Warren County: Route 340, at Front Royal.*

JD-8 FIRST SETTLER (GREEN MEADOW)

To the west was the home of Adam Miller (1703–1783) one of the first Europeans to settle in the Valley. Property remained in the Miller (originally Mueller) family from the 1740s through 1936. *Rockingham County: Route 340, .5 mile n. of Elkton.*

JD-10 BATTLE OF PORT REPUBLIC

The cross road here roughly divides the Confederate and Union lines in the battle of June 9, 1862. Jackson attacked Shields, coming southward to join Fremont, but was repulsed. Reinforced by Ewell, Jackson attacked again and drove Shields from the field. At the same time he burned the bridge at Port Republic, preventing Fremont from coming to Shields' aid. *Rockingham County: Route 340, 3 miles n. of Grottoes.*

JD-14 JARMAN'S GAP

Five miles east is Jarman's Gap, formerly known as Woods' Gap. Through this pass Michael Woods, his three sons and three sons-in-law (Andrew, Peter, William Wallace), coming from Pennsylvania via Shenandoah Valley, crossed into Albemarle County in 1734—pioneers in settling this section. In 1780–81 British prisoners taken at Saratoga went through the gap en route to Winchester. In June 1862 part of Jackson's army, moving to join Lee at Richmond, crossed the mountain here. *Augusta County: Route 340, 1.2 miles n. of Waynesboro.*

JE-1 JACKSON'S MARCH TO FREDERICKSBURG

Stonewall Jackson, on his march from Winchester to Fredericksburg, preceding the battle of Fredericksburg, camped here, November 26, 1862. *Madison County: Route 231, at Madison.*

JE-2 KNIGHTS OF THE GOLDEN HORSESHOE

Near here Governor Alexander Spotswood and his troop of gentlemen, Knights of the Golden Horseshoe, on their way to explore the land beyond the mountains, camped on August 31, 1716. *Madison County: Route 15, 3.3 miles n. of Orange.*

JE-4 HEBRON CHURCH

One mile south stands Hebron Church, the oldest Lutheran church in the South, built about 1740. The first communion service bears the date, May 13, 1727; another the date, March 28, 1737. The organ was built in 1800. *Madison County: Route 231, 9.5 miles n. of Madison.*

JE-6 MAURY'S SCHOOL

Just north was a classical school conducted by the Rev. James Maury, Rector of Fredericksville Parish from 1754 to 1769. Thomas Jefferson was one of Maury's students. Matthew Fountaine Maury, the "Pathfinder of the Seas," was Maury's grandson. *Albemarle County: Route 231, 4.5 miles s.e. of Gordonsville.*

JE-15 A CAMP OF STONEWALL JACKSON'S

Just to the north, on the night of November 25, 1862, Stonewall Jackson, with his corps, camped. He was on his way to join Lee at Fredericksburg. *Madison County: Route 670, 1 mile n. of Criglersville.*

JE-35 LEE'S STOPPING PLACE

Here at Flannagan's (Trice's) Mill, Robert E. Lee spent the night of April 13–14, 1865, on his journey from Appomattox to Richmond. *Cumberland County: Route 690 at 612, 8.8 miles s. of Columbia.*

JE-36 CLIFTON

One mile north; home of Carter Henry Harrison, land patented, 1723. Harrison, as a member of the Cumberland Committee of Safety, wrote the instructions for independence (adopted April 22) presented by the county delegates to the Virginia convention of May, 1776. Apparently this was the first of such declarations publicly approved. The convention declared for independence. *CumberlandCounty: Route 690 at 605, 11 miles s. of Columbia.*

JF-15 WALNUT GROVE

Archibald Stuart—Revolutionary soldier, legislator, and judge was born here March 19, 1757, at the home of his grandfather and namesake, an early settler. The property was acquired by William A. Pratt in 1868 and G. Julian Pratt in 1900. *Augusta County: Route 340, .3 mile s. of Waynesboro city limits.*

JJ-2* LEE'S HEADQUARTERS

Half a mile west Robert E. Lee had his headquarters from December, 1863, to May, 1864, while his army held the line of the Rapidan River. Lee left this place to begin the Wilderness Campaign early in May, 1864. *Orange County: Route 20, 1.6 miles e. of Orange.*

JJ-4 BLOOMSBURY

A mile north is Bloomsbury, estate of the pioneer, James Taylor, ancestor of Presidents James Madison and Zachary Taylor. He was a member of Spotswood's expedition over the mountains in 1716. *Orange County: Route 20, 3.3 miles e. of Orange.*

JJ-6 CAMPAIGN OF SECOND MANASSAS

Two miles north, near Pisgah Church, Jackson, Ewell, and A. P. Hill camped, August 15–20, 1862, awaiting Longstreet. *Orange County: Route 20, 5.7 miles e. of Orange.*

JJ-10 MINE RUN CAMPAIGN

Meade, advancing south from the Rapidan River to attack Lee, found him in an entrenched position here on November 28, 1863. Heavy skirmishing went on until December 1. Then Meade, thinking Lee's lines too strong to assault, retired across the Rapidan in time to avoid a counterattack by the Confederates. *Orange County: Route 20, 6.6 miles e. of Unionville.*

JJ-12* STUART'S ESCAPE

Near here, early morning, August 18, 1862, General J.E.B. Stuart narrowly escaped capture. *Orange County: 4.1 miles e. of Unionville.*

JJ-15 ROBINSON'S TAVERN

Near here stood ancient Robinson's Tavern. Here Meade wished to concentrate his army in the Mine Run Campaign, November, 1863, but one corps, coming up late, disarranged his plans. Here Ewell, moving east from Orange in the Wilderness Campaign, camped on May 4, 1864. *Orange County: Route 20, at Locust Grove.*

JJ-20   BATTLE OF THE WILDERNESS

Ewell's Corps, the left wing of Lee's army, moving down this road from Orange, came into conflict near here with Warren's Corps of Grant's army, May 5, 1864. The fight moved to and fro until Ewell finally drove Warren back and entrenched here. Late the next afternoon, May 6, Ewell attacked the Unionists. Meanwhile, two miles south on the Orange Plank Road, the right wing of Lee's army was engaged with Grant's left wing. *Orange County: Route 20, 2.9 miles e. of Locust Grove.*

JJ-24   CAMPAIGN OF 1781

Lafayette, marching southward from Raccoon Ford, camped here, June 8–9, 1781. *Orange County: Route 20, 2.6 miles e. of Unionville (at Rhodesville).*

JP-6   BIRTHPLACE OF MONROE

In this vicinity stood the Monroe home where James Monroe, fifth President of the United States, was born, April 28, 1758. His father was Spence Monroe and his mother, Elizabeth Jones. He left home at the age of sixteen to enter William and Mary College and left college to enter the army. *Westmoreland County: Route 205, 1.8 miles s. of Colonial Beach.*

JT-2   NOMINY CHURCH

One of the two churches of Cople Parish. It was built in 1704 on land given by Youell Watkins, and was replaced in 1755 by a brick church on the same site. George Washington attended services here twice in 1768. The last colonial church was burned (1814) by the British Admiral Cockburn, who carried off the church silver. The present building was erected about 1852. The first Nominy Church of 1655 stood on the north side of the river opposite this place. *Westmoreland County: Route 202, 3.7 miles e. of Templemans Cross Roads.*

JT-3   THE GLEBE

Five miles north is the home of the rectors of Cople Parish, one of whom, Walter Jones, married Washington's parents, March 6, 1731. Here lived Thomas Smith, rector of the parish, 1764–1799, and chairman of the county Committee of Safety, 1775. He entertained Washington, May 25, 1771. The house is possibly the oldest in the Northern Neck. *Westmoreland County: Route 202, 4.4 miles e. of Templemans Cross Roads.*

JT-4   WASHINGTON'S MOTHER

At Sandy Point, seven and a half miles east, Mary Ball, Washington's mother, spent her youth in the home of her guardian, George Eskridge. There she was married to Augustine Washington, March, 1731. She is supposed to have named her eldest son for George Eskridge. *Westmoreland County: Route 202, 4.8 miles n.w. of Callao.*

JT-5   BUSHFIELD

A mile and a half east. This was the home of John Augustine Washington, younger brother of George Washington, who visited here. Here was born, in 1762, Bushrod Washington, who became a justice of the United States Supreme Court in 1798, and died in 1829. He inherited Mount Vernon. *Westmoreland County: Route 202, 4.4 miles e. of Templemans Cross Roads.*

JT-6   RICHARD HENRY LEE'S GRAVE

A mile and a half north, in the Lee burying ground, is the grave of Richard Henry Lee, who died, June 19, 1794. Lee was one of the first leaders of the American Revolution. On June 7, 1776, he introduced a resolution in the Continental Congress for a declaration of independence, and argued for it, June 7–10. The declaration was signed, July 4, 1776. *Westmoreland County: Route 202, 8.8 miles s.e. of Templemans Cross Roads.*

JT-7   YEOCOMICO CHURCH

Two miles east. Built in 1655 of oak timbers sheathed with clapboards. Rebuilt of brick in 1706. In this vicinity Mary Ball lived under the tutelage of Colonel George Eskridge, of Sandy Point, from 1721 until her marriage to Augustine Washington in 1730, and attended church here. In 1906 an association was formed to preserve the church. *Westmoreland County: Route 202, 8.1 miles n.w. of Callao.*

JT-8   KINSALE

Two miles east, on picturesque Yeocomico River, is Kinsale, the founding of which the Assembly ordered in 1705. The town was established in 1784. Near by at the old home of the Bailey family, "The Great House," is the tomb of Midshipman James B. Sigourney, who in command of the sloop "Asp" fell in an engagement with the British in Yeocomico River, June 14, 1813. *Westmoreland County: Route 202, 4.8 miles n.w. of Callao.*

JT-9*   COAN RIVER

This is a head stream of the Coan River, which flows into the Potomac. On this river Captain John Smith had an encounter with Indians in 1608. Marylanders made the first settlement in this region about 1640. In October, 1814, a force of British troops came up the Coan River and marched to Heathsville. *Northumberland County: Route 360, 2.2 miles w. of Heathsville.*

JT-12   NORTHUMBERLAND HOUSE AND MANTUA

Five miles northeast is the site of Northumberland House, built by the third Peter Presley, who was murdered in 1750. He was the last male descendant of the first William Presley, who settled there and who was a burgess as early as 1647. Mantua, near by, was built by James Smith, who died in 1832. It is a good house of the old Virginia type. *Northumberland County: Route 360, 1 mile e. of Heathsville.*

JT-15 LEEDSTOWN

Here at the then thriving port of Leedstown on February 27, 1766, ten years before the Declaration of Independence, the Leedstown Resolutions (or Westmoreland Association) were drawn. This association, a protest against the Stamp Act and a pledge of mutual aid in event of its execution, was signed by 115 men from Westmoreland and surrounding counties. *Westmoreland County: Route 637, at Leedstown.*

JT-16 SANDY POINT

Here at Sandy Point, Mary Ball, George Washington's Mother, spent her youth in the home of her Guardian, Colonel George Eskridge. Here she married Augustine Washington in March 1731. She is supposed to have named her eldest son, George, for Colonel Eskridge. *Westmoreland County: Route 604, at Sandy Point.*

JX-5 MORATTICO BAPTIST CHURCH

On the hill is Morattico church, organized in 1778, the mother Baptist Church of the Northern Neck. The present building was erected in 1856. Lewis Lunsford, first pastor, is buried here. *Northumberland County: Route 200, 2.8 miles n. of Kilmarnock.*

K-1 CUMBERLAND GAP

This pass was long the gateway to the West. On April 13, 1750, Dr. Thomas Walker reached the gap, which he named for the Duke of Cumberland, son of George II. A few years later Daniel Boone and numberless pioneers passed through it on the way to Kentucky. In August, 1863, Cumberland Gap was captured by a Union army under General Ambrose E. Burnside. *Lee County: Route 58, at Cumberland Gap.*

K-3 INDIAN MOUND

The knoll a short distance to the north is an Indian burial mound. The Cherokees were the principal tribe inhabiting this region. *Lee County: Route 58, 2 miles w. of Rose Hill.*

K-4 COLONIAL FORT

Near here Joseph Martin established a fort in 1768. It consisted of five or six cabins surrounded by a strong stockade. Indians soon forced the settlers to abandon this fort. *Lee County: Route 58, at Rose Hill.*

K-5 INDIAN MASSACRE

In this valley, in June, 1785, Indians led by the notorious half breed, Benge, massacred the family of Archibald Scott, killing the father and five children and taking the mother into captivity. She later escaped. *Lee County: Route 58, at Stickleyville.*

K-6   THOMPSON SETTLEMENT CHURCH

This Baptist church, a mile southeast, is the oldest church in Lee County. It was organized in 1800; the original site was on Powell's River, a short distance west. James Kinney was the first pastor. The church was removed to the present site in 1822. *Lee County: Route 758, 10.2 miles s.w. of Jonesville.*

K-7   HANGING ROCK

The cliffs to the north were a familiar landmark along the wilderness road which was blazed by Daniel Boone in March, 1775, and which was the principal route from Virginia to Kentucky. They are part of the Cumberland Mountains. *Lee County: Route 58, .25 mile w. of Ewing.*

K-8   DOCTOR STILL'S BIRTHPLACE

Andrew Taylor Still, physician and founder of osteopathy, was born two miles southwest, near the Natural Bridge of Lee County, August 6, 1828. Dr. Still served in the War between the States. He established the first American school of osteopathy in 1892 at Kirksville, Missouri. He died there, December 12, 1917. *Lee County: Route 58, at w. entrance of Jonesville.*

K-9   JONESVILLE METHODIST CAMP GROUND

This Camp Ground was established in 1810 as a place for religious services for the Methodists of Lee County on lands given by Elkanah Wynn. In June 1827, Rev. Abraham Still, Daniel Dickenson, George Morris, Evans Peery, Henry Thompson, Elkanah Wynn and James Woodward were appointed trustees and the present auditorium was built in 1827–28. The massive oak columns were hewn by Henry Woodward, David Orr, Robert Wynn and Rev. Joseph Haskew *Lee County: Route 58, 2 miles w. of Jonesville.*

K-10   JONESVILLE

This town was established in 1794 as the county seat of Lee County and was named for Frederick Jones. Here on January 3, 1864, General William E. Jones, assisted by Colonel A. L. Pridemore, defeated a Union force, capturing the battalion. Union troops burned the courthouse in 1864. The present courthouse was erected in 1933. The town was incorporated in 1834, and reincorporated in 1901. *Lee County: Route 58, at Jonesville.*

K-11   GATE CITY

The town was laid off in 1815 as the county seat of Scott County. The original name of Winfield, for General Winfield Scott, was changed to Estillville for Judge Benjamin Estill. In 1886, the name was changed to Gate City because of its situation in Moccasin Gap, through which the old Wilderness Road to the West passed. It was incorporated, 1892. *Scott County: Route 71, at Gate City.*

K-12   FARIS STATION

Near by stood the home and tavern of Elisha Faris, an early station on the Boone trail to Kentucky. Indians led by Chief Benge here massacred members of the Faris family in 1791. *Scott County: Route 71, at Gate City.*

K-13   FORT BLACKMORE

Ten miles north, on Clinch River near the mouth of Stony Creek, stood Fort Blackmore, the first settlement in Scott County, established about 1771. It was attacked by Indians several times but was never captured. *Scott County: Route 71, at Gate City.*

K-14   McCONNELL'S BIRTHPLACE

Four miles south was born John Preston McConnell, noted educator. He taught in Milligan College, the University of Virginia and Emory and Henry College. He was president of the Radford State Teachers' College, 1913–1937. Dr. McConnell was president of Southwestern Virginia, Incorporated, and was associated with many cultural agencies. He was active in every phase of educational work, writing several books and many articles. *Scott County: Route 58, 2 miles e. of Gate City.*

K-15   BIG MOCCASIN GAP

In March, 1775, Daniel Boone made a road through this gap to Boonesboro, Kentucky. It followed the original Indian path and was known as the Wilderness Road. For a long time it was the main route to Kentucky from the East. *Scott County: Route 58, 2.1 miles e. of Gate City.*

K-16   DONELSON'S INDIAN LINE

John Donelson's line, surveyed after the treaty of Lochaber with the Indians, 1770, crossed the road here. This line separated Indian territory from land open to settlement. Violations of the line by settlers contributed to Dunmore's War, 1774. *Scott County: Route 58, 2.1 miles e. of Gate City.*

K-17   HOUSTON'S FORT

The first settlement in what is now Scott County was established on this site by Thomas McCulloch in 1769. In 1771, the settlement was abandoned in fear of Indian attack. William Houston, assignee of Thomas McCulloch, constructed a fort here in 1774. During an attack on the fort by a large force of Cherokee Indians in 1776, Samuel Cowan, a messenger, was killed and scalped. *Scott County: Route 613, 6.8 miles s. of Route 71.*

K-19   SEVEN MILE FORD

The place takes its name from the highway ford on the Holston, seven miles west of Royal Oak. The land here belonged to General William Campbell, hero of King's Mountain, 1780. It descended to the wife of John M. Preston. The town originated as a railroad station. It was occupied in Stoneman's raid of December, 1864. *Smyth County: Route 11, 2.9 miles e. of Chilhowie.*

K-20 WILLIAM CAMPBELL'S GRAVE

A short distance north are the home site and grave of William Campbell, noted Indian fighter and commander of troops at the battle of King's Mountain, 1780. Later he was with Lafayette in eastern Virginia until his death, August 22, 1781, shortly before the siege of Yorktown. *Smyth County: Route 11, 2 miles e. of Chilhowie.*

K-21 FARTHEST WEST, 1750

Near here, in 1750, Dr. Thomas Walker, on his first journey southwest, assisted Samuel Stalnaker in building his cabin. At that time this was the farthest west settlement. *Smyth County: Route 11, at Chilhowie.*

K-22 CHILHOWIE

An Indian name meaning "Valley of Many Deer." Land was patented here by Colonel James Patton, 1746; Samuel Stalnaker, first settler, built a home here in 1750. In 1804 Robert Gannaway came here and in 1815 opened Chilhowie Springs. When the railroad came the town was called Greever's Switch, later changed to Chilhowie. It was incorporated, 1913. *Smyth County: Route 11, at Chilhowie.*

K-23 A COLONIAL SOLDIER'S HOME

Five miles north was the home of Walter Crockett, a captain in the Point Pleasant Indian expedition of 1774 and the suppressor of a Tory rising in 1779. He was county lieutenant and clerk of Wythe County. *Wythe County: Route 11, at e. entrance of Wytheville.*

K-24* EARLY CHURCH

Two hundred yards south is the site of the Old Upper Congregation Presbyterian Church, organized in 1776. *Smyth County: Route 11, .6 mile e. of Marion.*

K-25 NEW RIVER

This stream was reached by the explorers, Batts and Fallam, September, 1671. The expedition was sent out by Abraham Wood, who lived at Fort Henry (Petersburg). The river was known as Wood's River until renamed New River. *Pulaski County: Route 11, .5 mile n.w. of Radford.*

K-26 BATTLE OF MARION

Here, on December 17–18, 1864, General Stoneman, raiding to Saltville, fought an engagement with John C. Breckinridge, Confederate commander in southwest Virginia. *Smyth County: Route 11, at Marion e. corporate limits.*

K-27 SITE OF COLONIAL HOME

Royal Oak, home of Arthur Campbell, Indian fighter and Revolutionary leader, who settled here in 1769, stood three hundred yards south. The house was a neighborhood fort and in it, in 1832, the first court of Smyth County was held. *Smyth County: Route 11, at intersection with Route 16 in Marion.*

K-28 SALTVILLE HISTORY

William King built salt works there in 1795. In October, 1864, Union troops, raiding Saltville, were driven off; but in December, 1864, the works were destroyed by General Stoneman. *Washington County: Route 11, 4.1 miles w. of Chilhowie.*

K-29 FIRST SETTLEMENT

About five miles southwest is Dunkard Bottom, where Dr. Walker found [sic] a settlement in 1750. The fort there was built about 1756 and was the first fort in Virginia west of New River. The first store and first mill were also there. *Pulaski County: Route 11, 1.9 miles w. of Radford.*

K-30 EARLY SETTLERS

Stephen Holstein (Holston), coming here before 1748, gave his name to the river and valley. James Davis settled on this place, "Davis' Fancy," in 1748 and his home became a neighborhood fort. *Smyth County: Route 11, 8.5 miles e. of Marion.*

K-31 SITE OF MOUNT AIRY

A German settlement of colonial times had its center here. One of its leading men, Robert Doak, was a member of the House of Burgesses for Fincastle County, 1773–1775. *Wythe County: Route 11, 12.9 miles w. of Wytheville.*

K-32* DEATH OF BOONE'S SON

Near here, October 10, 1773, James Boone, son of Daniel Boone, and Henry Russell, members of Boone's party on the way to Kentucky, were surprised and killed by Indians. *Lee County: Route 58, 1 mile e. of Stickleyville.*

K-33 HUNGRY MOTHER STATE PARK

This park was developed by the National Park Service, Interior Department, through the Civilian Conservation Corps, in conjunction with the Virginia Conservation Commission. It covers 2150 acres and was opened, June 15, 1936. It takes its name from a legend of an Indian raid in which a woman was carried off with her infant. *Smyth County: Route 11, at intersection with Route 16 in Marion.*

K-34 MARION

The community center here was known as Royal Oak, home of Arthur Campbell, frontiersman. The place became the county seat when Smyth County was formed and was named for Francis Marion, Revolutionary hero. It was incorporated in 1832; the courthouse was built in 1834; the railroad came in 1856. A cavalry action was fought here, December 1864, in Stoneman's raid. *Smyth County: Route 11, at Marion.*

K-35   WYTHEVILLE

When Wythe County was formed, this place became the county seat under the name of Evansham. It was incorporated in 1839 as Wytheville. The old Wilderness Road to Cumberland Gap passed here. In July, 1863, Toland's raiders captured the town. In May, 1864, Averell passed here on a raid; the town was again occupied by Union troops in December, 1864, and April, 1865. *Wythe County: Route 11, at Wytheville.*

K-36   ANCHOR AND HOPE PLANTATION

One mile north is a plantation that was surveyed in March, 1748, and patented, in June, 1753, by Colonel John Buchanan and named by him "Anchor and Hope." There in 1792 an academy was established to teach oratory. The pioneer educator, Thomas E. Birch, was instructor and minister for the settlement. *Wythe County: Route 52, at Fort Chiswell.*

K-37   INGLESIDE

Home of Colonel R. E. Withers, Confederate officer, Lieutenant-Governor of Virginia, United States Senator and Consul at Hong Kong. *Wythe County: Route 11, at e. entrance of Wytheville.*

K-38*   BATTLE OF CLOYD'S MOUNTAIN

Five miles north, at Cloyd's Mountain, General George Crook, raiding south to destroy the Virginia and Tennessee railroad (N & W), met and repulsed General A. G. Jenkins in a fierce action, May 9, 1864. Jenkins was mortally wounded. *Pulaski County: Route 100, at Dublin.*

K-39   LEAD MINES

Nine miles south on New River. Discovered in 1756 by Colonel John Chiswell. These mines supplied lead for the patriots in the Revolutionary War. Tories attempted to seize them in 1780 but were suppressed. *Wythe County: Route 52, at Fort Chiswell.*

K-40   DRAPER'S VALLEY

To the south and west lies Draper's Valley, named for John Draper, who settled here in 1765. He moved hence from Draper's Meadows (Blacksburg), where his wife was captured by the Indians in the massacre of 1755. Six years later Draper ransomed her. He served as an officer in the Point Pleasant Indian expedition of 1774. *Pulaski County: Route 11, 1.9 miles s. of Pulaski.*

K-41   PULASKI

The town sprang up at the coming of the railroad and was first known as Martin's Tank. Governor John Floyd lived near by. The county seat was moved here from Newburn in 1894. The town, like the county, was named for Count Casimir Pulaski, killed in the siege of Savannah, 1779. It was incorporated in 1886. Zinc and iron were early industries. *Pulaski County: Route 11, at Pulaski.*

K-42*   BRISTOL, VIRGINIA

The Sapling Grove tract (Bristol) was surveyed for John Tayloe, 1749. It was owned by Isaac Baker and Evan Shelby, who built a post about 1770. The Virginia tract was bought by John Goodson, whose son founded the town of Goodson, incorporated in 1856. In 1863 and 1865 it was raided by Unionists and partly burned. In 1890 it was named Bristol when incorporated as a city. *Route 11, at Bristol.*

K-43*   HISTORIC BRISTOL

Evan Shelby, noted Indian fighter, settled here about 1765 on a tract called "Sapling Grove." His home was a neighborhood fort, the refuge of settlers in Indian attacks. Bristol grew around this place and became an early railroad center. *Route 11, at Bristol.*

K-45   PAGE'S MEETING HOUSE

One mile to the north stood this Methodist Chapel, an early one in the New River area. It was built on land given in 1795 by Alexander Page. Bishop Francis Asbury preached in the Chapel in 1802 and again in 1806. *Pulaski County: Route 11, 1.25 miles w. of Radford.*

K-46   SHERWOOD ANDERSON

A prolific author whose works influenced Faulkner, Hemingway, and other writers of the American School of Realism, Anderson lived in this area from 1925 until his death in 1941. He built his home "Ripshin" near Troutdale (22 mi. S.E.) and was for a time publisher of two Smyth County weekly newspapers. He is buried here in Round Hill Cemetery. *Smyth County: Route 11, at e. corporate limits of Marion.*

K-47*   KING'S MOUNTAIN MEN

From this vicinity went forth a force of Virginians, under the command of Colonel William Campbell, to fight against the British in the Carolinas, 1780. The Virginia troops played an important part in the victory of King's Mountain, South Carolina, won by the Americans over Patrick Ferguson, October 7, 1780. *Washington County: Route 11, at w. entrance of Abingdon.*

K-48   SITE OF BLACK'S FORT

The fort, built in 1776, stood a short distance to the south. Here the first court of Washington County was held, January 28, 1777. *Washington County: Route 11, at Abingdon.*

K-49 ABINGDON

First known as Wolf Hills, land was patented here by Dr. Thomas Walker in 1750. Black's Fort was built, 1776. The town of Abingdon was established in 1778 as the county seat of Washington County. A courthouse, built about 1800, was replaced in 1850. In 1862 the church bells were melted for cannon. In Stoneman's raid, December, 1864, the town was partly burned. A new courthouse was built, 1869. *Washington County: Route 11, at Abingdon.*

K-65 RADFORD

It originated as a railroad town in 1856 and was known as Central. In 1862–65 this section was in the range of Union raids; Confederates burned the bridge at Ingles Ferry to retard raiders. Incorporated in 1887 as a town, the place was incorporated as a city in 1892 and named Radford, for Dr. John B. Radford, prominent citizen. Radford State Teachers College was established here, 1913. *Montgomery County: Route 11, at Radford.*

K-66 STATE TEACHERS COLLEGE AT RADFORD

A state college for women established in 1910. Opened 1913. Empowered by legislature in 1916 to grant degrees in education and in the arts and sciences. Present name authorized in 1924. The John Preston McConnell Library, named for the first president of the college, contains a valuable collection on the history of Southwest Virginia. *Montgomery County: Route 11, at Radford.*

K-67 "FOTHERINGAY"

To the east is the home of Colonel George Hancock (1754–1820), Revolutionary soldier, Congressman, and father-in-law of explorer William Clark. In this vicinity George Washington and two companions escaped being ambushed by Shawnee Indians in October, 1756. *Montgomery County: Route 11, 4.5 miles w. of Roanoke County.*

K-70 INGLES FERRY ROAD

Ingles Ferry, several miles west, was the first rendezvous of Colonel William Byrd's expedition against the Cherokees, 1760. There Indians returning from their last foray in the New River region, 1763, were attacked by William Ingles and a party of settlers. *Montgomery County: Route 11, 1.4 miles e. of Radford.*

K-71 LEWIS-McHENRY DUEL

In this town occurred the duel between Thomas Lewis and John McHenry in May 1808. This was the first duel with rifles known to have taken place in Virginia. It resulted in the death of both men. Dr. John Floyd, later Governor of Virginia and member of Congress, was the attending surgeon. This affair contributed to the passage in January, 1810, of the Barbour Bill outlawing dueling in Virginia. *Montgomery County: Routes 11 and 460, at Christiansburg.*

K-72   CHRISTIANSBURG

Christiansburg, originally known as "Hans' Meadows," was established in 1792 and named for Colonel William Christian, noted Colonial and Revolutionary Indian fighter. It became an important place on the route to the West. On May 10, 1864, Averell raided the town on an expedition into southwest Virginia. On April 5, Stoneman raided it while destroying railroads. *Montgomery County: Route 11, .6 mile e. of Christiansburg.*

K-73   FORT VAUSE

The fort stood on this hill. It was attacked and burned by French and Indians in June, 1756. It was rebuilt by Captain Peter Hogg, and visited by George Washington in October, 1756. *Montgomery County: Route 11, .3 mile w. of Shawsville.*

K-74   COLONIAL MANSION SITE

The home of James Campbell, a prominent colonial pioneer, who settled here in 1742, stood on this site. On his land Fort Lewis was built in 1756. *Roanoke County: Route 11, 2.5 miles w. of Salem.*

K-75   GENERAL ANDREW LEWIS

Richfield, home of Andrew Lewis, famous colonial and Revolutionary soldier, is marked by the knoll and locust trees a half mile east of this spot. *Salem: Route 11, at intersection of College Avenue and Eighth Street.*

K-76   OLD LUTHERAN CHURCH

Tradition has it that the church near by was built where Moravian and Lutheran missionaries preached soon after the Revolution. Here, in 1796, Lutherans held services and, a little later, organized their first congregation in this section. In 1828, the Lutheran synod of North Carolina met here and consecrated the church. *Roanoke County: Route 11, .8 mile w. of Roanoke.*

K-77   GENERAL ANDREW LEWIS' GRAVE

This famous pioneer, patriot, statesman, and soldier, is buried here on part of his 625 acre estate. Member of House of Burgesses, 1772–1775; defeated Indians at battle of Point Pleasant, 1774; drove Lord Dunmore from Virginia, 1776. Died 1781. *Salem: Route 460, at Park Avenue and Main Street.*

K-88   OLD SALEM INNS

Salem, founded in 1803, was a notable stopping place on the route to the West. The inns located near this spot were the Bull's Eye, Ye Olde Time Tavern, the Globe, the Indian Queen, and the Mermaid. *Roanoke County: Route 11, .2 mile w. of Salem.*

K-95   ROANOKE

The first village here, at Pate's Mill and Tavern on Evans' Mill Creek, was called Big Lick for nearby salt marshes. In 1839 it was laid off as the town of Gainesborough. After the coming of the Virginia and Tennessee Railroad (later N & W) in 1852, another village sprang up about the old Stover House that was also named Big Lick. Gainesborough became known as Old Lick. *Roanoke: East Bullit and South Jefferson streets.*

K-95   ROANOKE

In June, 1864, General Hunter passed here retreating from Lynchburg. In 1874 Big Lick was incorporated. In 1881, with the junction of the new Shenandoah Valley Railroad with the N. & W., rapid growth began. In 1882 the name was changed to Roanoke; in 1884 it was incorporated as a city. In 1909 the Virginian Railroad operated its first train. In recent years Roanoke became the third city of Virginia. *Roanoke: East Bullit and South Jefferson streets.*

K-116   A COLONIAL FORD

Tosh's Ford and Evans' Mill, located on the river near this crossing, were the base of supplies for military expeditions of colonial days in all this region. *Roanoke: Franklin Road s.w. between Naval Reserve and Brandon avenues.*

K-119   INDIAN REMAINS

The large knoll three hundred yards to the east is an Indian mound. It is supposed to have been built by some tribe of the Siouan race which later was driven westward. *Bedford County: Route 460, 12 miles w. of Bedford.*

K-121   COLONIAL FORT

Near here stood a fort, or blockhouse, built for protection against Indian attacks. In this fort Mrs. William Ingles took refuge after her escape from captivity among the Indians in the spring of 1756. *Bedford County: Route 460, 11 miles w. of Bedford.*

K-130   HUNGER'S BIVOUAC

Near here General Hunter, on his retreat from Lynchburg, halted for the night of June 18, 1864. He resumed his retreat early in the morning of June 19. *Bedford County: Route 460, 3 miles w. of Bedford.*

K-132   HOME OF JOHN GOODE

Here is the home of John Goode, political leader, born 1829, died, 1909. Goode was a member of the secession convention of 1861; of the Confederate Congress and of the United States Congress; Solicitor General of the United States; president of the Virginia constitutional convention of 1901. *Bedford County: Route 460, at Bedford.*

K-134   BEDFORD

This place became the county seat of Bedford when it was moved from New London in 1782. First called Liberty (incorporated in 1839), the town changed its name to Bedford City in 1890 and to Bedford in 1912. A third courthouse, built in 1834, was replaced by the present building in 1930. The Union General Hunter, with his army, passed here in June, 1864, on his way to Lynchburg, and repassed on his retreat. *Bedford County: Route 460, at Bedford.*

K-136   PEAKS OF OTTER ROAD

This road was followed by General Hunter when he crossed the Blue Ridge at the Peaks of Otter and came to Bedford en route to Lynchburg, June 16, 1864. *Bedford County: Route 460, at Bedford.*

K-138   POPLAR FOREST

A mile and a half south is Poplar Forest, Thomas Jefferson's Bedford estate. He came here in June, 1781, after his term as governor expired, and while here was thrown from a horse and injured. During his recovery he wrote his "Notes on Virginia." *Bedford County: Route 460, 6.5 miles w. of Lynchburg.*

K-139   NEW LONDON

This place, on the old stage road, was the first county seat of Bedford; the first courthouse, built in 1755, was standing until 1856. In 1781, New London was raided by the British cavalryman, Tarleton, seeking military stores. It came into Campbell County in 1782. An arsenal here was afterward removed to Harper's Ferry. *Campbell County: Route 858, 4 miles w. of Lynchburg.*

K-139   NEW LONDON

At New London, Patrick Henry made one of his most famous speeches. John Hook, a Tory, brought suit for two steers impressed for the American army in 1781. Henry, the opposing counsel, so pictured the sufferings of the patriots in that critical year and their joy at Cornwallis's surrender, and so ridiculed Hook, that the case was laughed out of court. *Campbell County: Route 858, 4 miles w. of Lynchburg.*

K-140   ST. STEPHEN'S CHURCH

Half a mile north is St. Stephen's Church, built about 1825 under Rev. Nicholas Cobb, later Bishop of Alabama. In the old cemetery here many members of early families of the community are buried. *Bedford County: Route 460, 8 miles w. of Lynchburg.*

K-141   NEW LONDON ACADEMY

Chartered by the state in 1795, this is the oldest secondary school in Virginia in continuous operation under its own charter. Conducted for many years as a private school for boys, it began to receive public funds in 1884. It now operates as a public school. *Bedford County: Route 460, at New London Academy.*

K-142*   JOHN DANIEL'S HOME

Half a mile west is Westerly, once the home of Colonel Peyton Leftwick, War of 1812 soldier. Later it was the home of Judge William Daniel and of his son, John Warwick Daniel, Confederate soldier and for many years United States Senator from Virginia. *Lynchburg: 720 Court Street.*

K-146*   CHESTNUT HILL

Two miles north is Chestnut Hill, home of Charles Lynch, Sr., father of John Lynch, founder of Lynchburg, and of Charles Lynch, Revolutionary soldier. Charles Lynch, Sr., died in 1753 and is supposed to be buried at Chestnut Hill. *Lynchburg: Route 501, 4 miles e. of Lynchburg.*

K-148* MOUNT ATHOS

Two miles north are the ruins of Mount Athos, or Buffalo Lick Plantation. The house was built in 1796 by William J. Lewis, who commanded a corps of mountain riflemen at the siege of Yorktown in 1781. *Campbell County: Route 460, 6 miles e. of Lynchburg.*

K-150 OXFORD FURNACE

Across the stream stood Oxford Furnace, conducted in the Revolution by James Calloway to supply military materials. Iron mines were near by. The furnace was operated until 1875, the mill until 1900. *Campbell County: Route 460, 2.5 miles e. of Lynchburg.*

K-152 CONCORD STATION

The first railroad train passed this station in 1854. In 1864, the station building and the Confederate commissary here were burned by the Union General Hunter. This was the extreme eastern limit of Hunter's raid. *Campbell County: Route 460, at Concord.*

K-156 THE LAST FIGHT

Two miles north, at sunrise of April 9, 1865, Fitz Lee and Gordon, moving westward, attacked Sheridan's position. The attack was repulsed, but a part of the Confederate cavalry under Munford and Rosser broke through the Union line and escaped. This was the last action between the Army of Northern Virginia and the Army of the Potomac. *Appomattox County: Route 460 at Route 131 in Appomattox.*

K-157 SURRENDER AT APPOMATTOX

At the McLean house at Appomattox, two miles north, took place the meeting between Lee and Grant to arrange terms for the surrender of the Army of Northern Virginia. This was at 1:30 P.M. on Sunday, April 9, 1865. *Appomattox County: Route 460 at Route 131 in Appomattox.*

K-158* APPOMATTOX COURT HOUSE— NEW AND OLD

This building, erected in 1892 when the county seat was moved to this location, should not be mistaken for the original, built in 1846 and destroyed by fire in 1892. Three miles northeast is Old Appomattox Court House and the McLean House where Lee surrendered to Grant on April 9, 1865, thus ending the War Between the States. The village of Old Appomattox Court House is now preserved as a national shrine by the Federal Government. *Appomattox County: Route 131 at town of Appomattox.*

K-159 BATTLE OF APPOMATTOX STATION—1865

Near this building stood the station of the South Side Rail Road where, on April 8th, 1865, three trains unloading supplies for the Army of Northern Virginia were captured by units of Sheridan's Union Cavalry under General George Custer. Significant for its relationship to the surrender by General Robert E. Lee at Appomattox Court House, this action also marked the last strategic use of rail by Confederate forces. *Appomattox County: at corner of Main and Church streets in town of Appomattox.*

K-170   NOTTOWAY COURTHOUSE

Near here the Confederate cavalry-man, W. H. F. Lee, interposed between Wilson and Kautz raiding to Burkeville and fought a sharp action, June 23, 1864. Wilson then started on his return to Grant's army. Grant passed here with a part of his army in pursuit of Lee, April 5, 1865. Here he received word from Sheridan that the latter was at Jetersville across Lee's line of retreat. *Nottoway County: Route 460, .2 mile w. of Nottoway.*

K-172   BLACKSTONE

A tobacco center, originally known as "Black's and White's" for rival tavern-keepers. The Union General Wilson passed here on the raid of June, 1864. General Ord, with a corps of Grant's army, spent the night of April 5–6, 1865, here. The name of the town was changed to Blackstone about 1885; it was incorporated in 1888. Blackstone College for girls is here. *Nottoway County: Route 460, at Blackstone.*

K-204   ETTRICK

The site of an Appomattox Indian village burned in 1676 in Bacon's Rebellion, the present town of Ettrick stands on land that belonged to "Ettrick Banks" and "Matoax," the boyhood plantation of John Randolph of Roanoke. In 1810 Campbell's Bridge connected Ettrick with Petersburg, hastening the development of mills on the river. Virginia State University, formerly known as the Virginia Normal and Collegiate Institute, was established here in 1882. *Chesterfield County: Route 36, .2 mile w. of Petersburg.*

K-205   CITY POINT AND HOPEWELL

City Point is five miles northeast. There Governor Sir Thomas Dale made a settlement in 1613. In April, 1781, the British General Phillips landed there. Grant had his base of operations there in the siege of Petersburg, 1864–1865. Lincoln was there in April, 1865. In the World War the city of Hopewell grew up near by. *Prince George County: Route 36, .7 mile e. of Petersburg.*

K-206*   BAILEY'S CREEK

Named for Temperance Bailey, who owned land here in 1626. *Prince George County: Route 106, 5.5 miles e. of Petersburg.*

K-207   HISTORY AT PRINCE GEORGE COURTHOUSE

Lord Cornwallis, going toward the James in pursuit of Lafayette, passed here, May 24, 1781. A part of Grant's army passed here on the way to Petersburg, June, 1864. The place was occupied by Union troops in 1864–65. *Prince George County: Route 106, at Prince George.*

K-208   JORDAN'S POINT

Five miles north on James River. There, in 1619, Samuel Jordan established a place, Jordan's Journey. Near there, in April, 1676, the settlers in arms against the Indians chose Bacon as their leader. The Revolutionary leader, Richard Bland, had his home there, and near by the great agriculturist, Edmund Ruffin, lived. *Prince George County: Route 106, 2.9 miles e. of Prince George.*

K-209   MERCHANT'S HOPE CHURCH

Half a mile south. This church was built about 1657 and is, therefore, one of the oldest churches in Virginia. The first Prince George Courthouse was near it. The parish, that of Martin's Brandon, was one of the earliest established in Charles City County. *Prince George County: Route 10, 8.3 miles n.w. of Burrowsville.*

K-210   COGGIN'S POINT

Four miles north on James River. When Benedict Arnold fell back down the James after his raid to Richmond, Baron Steuben, at Coggin's Point, observed his fleet, January 10, 1781. From the bluff General D. H. Hill bombarded McClellan's camp on the north side of the river, July 31, 1862. *Prince George County: Route 10, 8.3 miles n.w. of Burrowsville.*

K-211   THE CATTLE RAID

Just to the north of the road here, at old Sycamore Church, Wade Hampton, coming from the south, attacked the Union cavalry guarding Grant's beef cattle, September 16, 1864. The Unionists were overpowered; Hampton, rounding up 2,500 beeves, succeeded in escaping with them across the Blackwater and into Lee's lines. *Prince George County: Route 106, 6.8 miles e. of Prince George.*

K-211*   UPPER CHIPPOKES CREEK

In 1610 an Indian chief, Chopoke [*sic*], lived near the mouth of this creek. In 1637 the first Benjamin Harrison obtained a land grant on the stream. *Surry County: Route 10, 13.5 miles w. of Surry.*

K-212   POWELL'S CREEK

The creek nearby was named for Nathaniel Powell, acting governor in 1619. Weyanoke Indian town was here. Nearby is the site of an old mill, known in the Revolution as Bland's, and later, Cocke's Mill. The British General Phillips passed here, May, 1781. Here Grant's army, after crossing the James, turned towards Petersburg, June, 1864. *Prince George County: Route 10, 5.3 miles n.w. of Burrowsville.*

K-213   MAYCOCK'S PLANTATION

Six miles north on James River. The place was patented about 1618 by Samuel Maycock, slain in the massacre of 1622. In 1774, David Meade became the owner. There Cornwallis crossed the river, May 24, 1781. Anthony Wayne crossed there, August 30, 1781. *Prince George County: Route 10, 5.3 miles n.w. of Burrowsville.*

K-214   FLOWERDEW HUNDRED

Four miles north. Governor Sir George Yeardley patented land there in 1619, and in 1621 built at Windmill Point the first windmill in English America. The place was named for Temperance Flowerdew, Yeardley's wife. Near there Grant's army crossed the James in June, 1864. *Prince George County: Route 10, 5.3 miles n.w. of Burrowsville.*

K-215 HOOD'S

Four miles north on James River. There, on January 3, 1781, Benedict Arnold, ascending the river, was fired on by cannon. On January 10, Arnold, returning, sent ashore there a force that was ambushed by George Rogers Clark. Fort Powhatan stood there in the War of 1812. *Prince George County: Route 10, at Burrowsville.*

K-216 WARD'S CREEK

Named for John Ward, who patented land here in 1619. The plantation was represented in the first General Assembly, 1619. *Prince George County: Route 10, at Burrowsville.*

K-218 BRANDON

This place, five miles northeast, has been owned by the Harrison family for two centuries. John Martin patented the land in 1617. Nathaniel Harrison bought it in 1720. The present house was built about 1770. The British General Phillips landed at Brandon, May 7, 1781. A mile farther is Upper Brandon. *Prince George County: Route 10, at Burrowsville.*

K-222 HISTORIC CABIN POINT

A village was here as early as 1689. Here Baron Steuben gathered militia in January, 1781, to resist Benedict Arnold's invasion, and here General Muhlenberg, watching Arnold at Portsmouth, had his headquarters. *Surry County: Route 10, 4 miles n.w. of Spring Grove.*

K-223 FLYING POINT

This is six miles north. William Rookings patented land there in 1636. His son, William Rookings, was one of the leaders in Bacon's Rebellion, 1676. *Surry County: Route 10, 4 miles n.w. of Spring Grove.*

K-224 PACE'S PAINES

This place, seven miles north, was settled by Richard Pace in 1620. On the night before the Indian massacre of March 22, 1622, an Indian, Chanco, revealed the plot to Pace, who reached Jamestown in time to save the settlers in that vicinity. *Surry County: Route 10, 3.5 miles w. of Surry.*

K-225* CLAREMONT

The Quiyoughcohannock Indian village nearby was first visited by English settlers in May, 1607. The first land patent at Claremont was 200 acres granted to George Harrison in 1621. Arthur Allen, who built the house now known as Bacon's Castle, first purchased land here in 1656. The estate was called "Cleremont" by William Allen by 1793, and Claremont Manor was probably built by him after 1754. Situated on land that had been part of the Allen estate, the town of Claremont was incorporated in 1886 *Surry County: Route 613, at Claremont.*

K-225* CLAREMONT

Four miles north. The village of the Quioughcohanock [*sic*] Indians nearby was first visited by English settlers in May, 1607. The estate was patented in 1649; the house was built some years later by Arthur Allen, rumored to be a prince. There is an underground passage to the river. A place of great romantic interest. Railroad iron from there was used to armor the Confederate battleship "Merrimac." *Surry County: Route 10, 4 miles n.w. of Spring Grove.*

K-226 WAKEFIELD AND PIPSICO

Five miles north is Wakefield, owned by the first Benjamin Harrison as early as 1635. Seven miles northeast is Pipsico, named for a noted Indian chief. In 1608 an Indian village was in that vicinity. *Surry County: Route 10, at Spring Grove.*

K-227 PLEASANT POINT

Four miles north is Pleasant Point on James River. William Edwards patented land there in 1657; the house is ancient. Edwards was clerk of the general court and a member of the House of Burgesses. *Surry County: Route 10, 1.3 miles s.e. of Surry.*

K-228* GLEBE HOUSE

Built before 1724, this was the glebe house of Southwark Parish. *Surry County: Route 10, 4.7 miles w. of Surry.*

K-229 SOUTHWARK CHURCH

Four miles northeast are the ruins of this church, built before 1673. *Surry County: Route 10, 3.5 miles w. of Surry.*

K-230 BELL FARM (COLONEL MICHAEL BLOW)

One mile south stood Bell Farm, home of Michael Blow. Colonel Blow was the first Chairman of the Committee of Safety of Sussex County, member of the House of Burgesses, member of the First Virginia Convention (1774), County Justice, and colonel in the Revolutionary Army. *Sussex County: Route 460, at Route 628.*

K-230* SETTLEMENT ON GRAY'S CREEK

First called Rolfe's Creek for Thomas Rolfe, son of Pocahontas, who was an early landowner here. Later it was named for Thomas Gray, who patented land here in 1639. *Surry County: Route 10, 2 miles n.w. of Surry.*

K-231 SWANN'S POINT

Ten miles northeast is Swann's Point on James River. In 1635 William Swann patented land there. The English commissioners investigating Bacon's Rebellion met at Swann's Point in 1677. William Swann's tomb, dated 1680, is there. *Surry County: Route 10, at Spring Grove.*

K-232* CYPRESS CHURCH

Eight miles southwest are the ruins of Cypress Church, built in 1753. *Surry County: Route 10, 1 mile s. of Surry.*

K-233 SMITH'S FORT PLANTATION

Two miles north is the Thomas Warren House, one of the oldest in Virginia. Erected during 1651–1652 some of the land had descended to Thomas Rolfe, son of Pocahontas, from her father, the Indian chief Powhatan. Earlier on this tract Captain John Smith and the colonists built a fort for the protection of Jamestown, just across the river. *Surry County: Route 10, at Surry.*

K-234* HISTORY ON CROUCH'S CREEK

Originally called Tappahannock Creek. In 1625 the poet, George Sandys, treasurer of the colony, had a settlement here and a building for raising silk worms. In 1638 Thomas Crouch patented land on this stream. *Surry County: Route 10, at Surry.*

K-235 BACON'S CASTLE

This house, just to the north, was built by Arthur Allen in 1655. In Bacon's Rebellion, 1676, the house was seized by a party of rebels and fortified. On December 29, 1676, it was captured by sailors from a ship in James River who were engaged in putting down the rebellion. *Surry County: Route 10, at Bacon's Castle.*

K-236 ORGANIZATION OF THE CHRISTIAN CHURCH

At "Old Lebanon Church" here, the Christian Church was established under the leadership of James O'Kelly, August, 1794. O'Kelly had withdrawn from the Methodist Church, 1792. *Surry County: Route 10, 1.5 miles w. of Surry.*

K-237 HOG ISLAND

On this point, in James River nine miles northeast, the settlers kept their hogs in 1608. When abandoning Jamestown in June, 1610, they stopped at the island for a night. The next morning, proceeding down the river, they met a messenger from Governor Lord Delaware, who had just arrived, and returned to Jamestown. *Surry County: Route 10, at Bacon's Castle.*

K-238 OLD TOWN

Half a mile north, stood the Warrascoyack Indian village. Captain John Smith obtained corn there for the starving colonists in 1608. The Warrascoyacks took part in the massacre of 1622 and their village was destroyed in 1623. In 1680, Old Town was established. *Isle of Wight County: Route 621, .1 mile e. of Route 10.*

K-239 LAWNE'S CREEK

Named for Christopher Lawne, who settled at the mouth of the creek in 1619. In 1634 the plantations hereabouts became the county of Warrascoyack. In 1637 the name was changed to Isle of Wight. *Isle of Wight County: Route 10, 8.1 miles n.w. of Smithfield.*

K-240* WRENN'S MILL SITE

Two miles south, on Pagan Creek, stood Wrenn's Mill as early as 1646. About 1685 George Hardy operated a mill there. On this site, which has seen several mill structures, a mill is still running. *Isle of Wight County: Route 10, 4.5 miles n.w. of Smithfield.*

K-240-b WRENN'S MILL

About one mile south, on Pagan Creek, stands a mill which was in operation by 1650. Once known as "Green's Mill," it was purchased by Charles Wrenn in 1821. A skirmish was fought there, April 14, 1864. *Isle of Wight County: Route 10, 4.5 miles w. of Smithfield.*

K-241* BENNETT'S PLANTATION

This place, two miles north, was settled by Edward Bennett in February, 1622. Houses were being built in March, 1622, when the Indians massacre occurred. More than fifty of the settlers perished; others, resisting, drove off the savages. *Isle of Wight County: Route 10, 2 miles n.w. of Smithfield.*

K-242* BASSE'S CHOICE

This place, three miles north, was settled by Nathaniel Basse in 1621. In the massacre of 1622, the Indians killed twenty settlers there. *Isle of Wight County: Route 10, 2 miles n.w. of Smithfield.*

K-243k SMITHFIELD

The town was established in 1752. The Masonic Hall was built in 1753. Benedict Arnold occupied the town, January 15, 1781. At Cherry Grove Landing near by, skirmishing took place on April 13–15, 1864, and the Confederates made a daring capture of a Union vessel on December 5, 1864. *Isle of Wight County: Route 10, at Smithfield.*

K-244 PAGAN POINT

Two miles north. There stood an Indian village named Mokete. "Pagan" refers to the heathenism of the Indians. *Isle of Wight County: Route 10, .4 mile w. of Smithfield.*

K-245 SAINT LUKE'S CHURCH

To the east is the venerable "Old Brick Church." By tradition it is dated 1632. It is the nation's only original Gothic house of worship surviving from colonial times and may also be the oldest church in the United States. *Isle of Wight County: Route 10, 4.25 miles s.e. of Smithfield.*

K-245* ST. LUKE'S CHURCH

The church, bricks of which bear the date of 1632, is one of the oldest churches in the United States. It was abandoned in 1830 and restored about 1890. Tarleton's British cavalry camped here in 1781. *Isle of Wight County: Route 10, .25 mile n.w. of Benn's Church.*

K-246 BENN'S CHURCH

This Methodist church was known in 1804 as Benn's Chapel. Bishop Asbury preached here in 1804. *Isle of Wight County: Route 10, 4.2 miles s.e. of Smithfield.*

K-247* MACCLESFIELD

Seven miles north. It was the home of Colonel Josiah Parker, Revolutionary officer. In 1781, British cavalry under Tarleton raided the place in the effort to capture Parker. A militia camp was at Macclesfield in the War of 1812. *Isle of Wight County: Route 10, 4.2 miles s.e. of Smithfield.*

K-248 CHUCKATUCK

A colonial church is here. In July, 1781, the British cavalryman Tarleton was at Chuckatuck. On May 3, 1863, a skirmish took place here between Union and Confederate forces as Longstreet withdrew from the siege of Suffolk. *Suffolk ("old" Nansemond County): Route 10, 9.2 miles n.w. of Suffolk proper.*

K-249 DUMPLING ISLAND

One mile east in Nansemond River. There, in 1608, the English settlers were attacked by Indians in canoes. The savages jumped overboard when the English fired their guns and later ransomed the canoes for corn. In 1609, the colonists sought to seize the Indians' corn on the island but were driven off. *Suffolk ("old" Nansemond County): Route 10, 6 miles n.w. of Suffolk proper.*

K-250 REID'S FERRY

The village of the Nansemond Indians stood near here, 1608, when the region was first explored by the English settlers. These savages took part in the massacre of 1622, and in the war that followed their town was destroyed by Sir George Yeardley. *Suffolk ("old" Nansemond County): Route 10, 5.5 miles n.w. of Suffolk proper.*

K-251* EARLY HISTORY OF SUFFOLK

A warehouse was established here in 1730 on land of the Widow Constance. The town was established in 1742. Robert Howe occupied it with Virginia and North Carolina troops in February, 1776. It was burned by a British raiding force under General Matthews, May 13, 1779. Lafayette visited it in February, 1825. Suffolk was destroyed by fire in 1837 but soon rose from its ashes. *Suffolk ("old" Nansemond County): Route 10, 1.5 miles n.w. of Suffolk proper.*

K-252 SIEGE OF SUFFOLK

The town was occupied by Union Troops from May, 1862, until the end of the Civil War. Confederate forces under Longstreet unsuccessfully besieged Suffolk, from April 11, to May 3, 1863, when they withdrew across the James on Lee's orders. *Suffolk: Route 460, .5 mile w. of old city limits.*

K-253* DISMAL SWAMP

The swamp, just to the south, was visited by William Byrd in 1728 while surveying the Virginia-North Carolina Line. In 1763, George Washington made explorations in it, and organized the Dismal Swamp Company to drain it. The company acquired 40,000 acres of land in the swamp. *Suffolk: ("old" Nansemond County): Route 58, 4.7 miles e. of Suffolk proper.*

K-254* REVOLUTIONARY CAMP

Here the Nansemond militia under Colonel Willis Riddick, opposing a British raid, camped on May 11, 1779. *Suffolk ("old" Nansemond County): Route 337, 6.2 miles n.e. of Suffolk proper.*

K-255   YEATES SCHOOL

Before 1731 John Yeates established two free schools in this neighborhood, one on each side of Bennett's Creek. By his will, September 18, 1731, he left his property for the use of these schools. They continued until 1861 and were sold in 1866 under an act of legislature. *Suffolk ("old" Nansemond County): Route 337, at Driver.*

K-255*   HISTORIC CLAREMONT

Claremont is four miles north. There stood the village of the Quioughcohanock Indians, visited by the first settlers in May, 1607. An English settlement was made there about 1632; the manor house is a colonial dwelling. Rails from a railroad there were used to armor the Confederate warship Merrimac. *Surry County: Route 10, at Spring Grove.*

K-256   SLEEPY HOLE FERRY

Three miles east, Benedict Arnold, returning from his Richmond raid, crossed the river there, January 16, 1781; Cornwallis, going to Portsmouth, crossed there in July, 1781. *Suffolk ("old" Nansemond County): Route 337, at Driver.*

K-257   BENNETT'S HOME

On this stream, Bennett's Creek, stood the home of Richard Bennett. He was one of the commissioners to "reduce" Virginia after the victory of Parliament in the civil war in England, 1651, and the first governor under the Cromwellian domination, 1652–55. *Suffolk ("old" Nansemond County): Route 337, at Driver.*

K-258   GLEBE CHURCH

Built in 1738. In 1775 the parish minister, Parson Agnew, was driven from the church for preaching loyalty to the king. The building was repaired in 1854. *Suffolk ("old" Nansemond County): Route 337 at Driver.*

K-259   SIEGE OF SUFFOLK

Across the road here ran the main line of Confederate works, built by Longstreet besieging Suffolk, April 1863. He abandoned the siege and rejoined Lee at Fredericksburg. *Suffolk ("old" Nansemond County): Route 10, 1.5 miles n.w. of Suffolk proper.*

K-261*   PIG POINT

Eight miles north, at the mouth of Nansemond River. A Confederate battery there had an engagement with the Union ship, Harriet Lane, June 5, 1861. *Suffolk ("old" Nansemond County): Route 460, 8 miles w. of Portsmouth.*

K-262   CRANEY ISLAND

This island in the Elizabeth River is about four miles northeast. British forces moving on Norfolk attacked American fortifications there June 22, 1813, but were repulsed. The Confederate Ironclad "Virginia" (MERRIMAC) was destroyed by her crew there May 11, 1862. *Chesapeake ("old" Norfolk County): Route 17, w. of Churchland bypass.*

K-262* CRANEY ISLAND

Seven miles northeast on Elizabeth River. The fortifications on the island were attacked, June 22, 1813, by the British, who were repulsed with loss. The Portsmouth artillery served with distinction. Here, May 11, 1862, the Confederates destroyed the iron-clad Merrimac. *Chesapeake ("old" Norfolk County): Route 337, 2.8 miles w. of Portsmouth.*

K-263* HODGES FERRY

Near here stood a colonial church, built about 1762. William Braidforth, a Scotchman who sided with the colonists in the Revolution, was chaplain here through the war period. *Chesapeake ("old" Norfolk County): Route 337, 2.3 miles w. of Portsmouth.*

K-264* DALE POINT

A short distance north, birthplace of Commodore Richard Dale, born 1756, Lieutenant on Bon Homme Richard in the fight with British ship Serapis, 1779. First Commandant Norfolk Navy Yard, 1794, commanded squadron against Barbary Pirates, 1801. *Chesapeake ("old" Norfolk County): Route 460, .25 mile w. of Portsmouth.*

K-265* FORT NELSON

In Portsmouth (Naval Hospital) stood Fort Nelson, built in the Revolution to protect the Norfolk area. In May, 1779, a British fleet under Sir George Collier, carrying troops under General Matthews, took the fort, which was abandoned by the garrison. The British destroyed ships, tobacco and supplies. The point was fortified again in 1861. *Chesapeake ("old" Norfolk County): Route 337, near w. city limits of Portsmouth.*

K-270* HARGROVE'S TAVERN

Nearby is the site of Hargrove's Tavern, known as the Halfway House, which was built before the Revolution. Here Captains King and Davis of the Virginia militia were surprised by the British, May, 1781, and Davis was killed. *Suffolk ("old" Nansemond County): .8 mile e. of Driver.*

K-272* KEMPSVILLE

Three miles east is Kempsville. There Lord Dunmore, royal governor, attacked a party of militia, November 16, 1775, and dispersed it. The place was Princess Anne County Courthouse from 1778 to 1822. Kempsville was established as a town in 1783. *Virginia Beach ("old" Princess Anne County): Route 165 at Kempsville.*

K-273* NEW TOWN

Two miles south, on the Eastern Branch, is the site of New Town, laid out in 1697 and established as a town in 1740. Princess Anne County Courthouse was there from 1753 to 1778. Norfolk people refugeed [sic] there after the burning of Norfolk, January 1, 1776. The British cavalryman Simcoe was stationed there in March, 1781. *Virginia Beach ("old" Princess Anne County): Route 58 3 miles e. of Norfolk.*

K-275* GREAT BRIDGE

Eight miles south is Great Bridge, which at the time of the Revolution was a causeway through a marsh. Lord Dunmore, the royal governor, had a British garrison here to protect this approach to Norfolk. On December 9, 1775, an action was fought there between the British and the Virginia troops, in which the former were defeated. This fight forced Dunmore to evacuate Norfolk. *Chesapeake ("old" Norfolk County): Route 17, 3 miles s. of Portsmouth.*

K-276* DONATION CHURCH AND WITCH DUCK

Two and three-tenths miles north is Donation Church, first built before 1694. Nearby is the site of Princess Anne County Courthouse, 1730–1753. One mile north of this place is "Witch Duck," where Grace Sherwood, accused of being a witch, was tested. She was put in water "above man's depth" to "try her how she swims therein." *Virginia Beach ("old" Princess Anne County): Route 58, 5 miles e. of Norfolk.*

K-277* FIRST EASTERN SHORE CHAPEL

About one mile northwest of this point near the head of Wolfsnare Creek stood the first Eastern Shore Chapel of Lynhaven Parish, built before 1689. Adjoining it was built in this year a secondary courthouse for Lower Norfolk County, which became the first courthouse of Princess Anne County upon its formation in 1691. Near the chapel also stood in 1693 the first recorded Presbyterian meeting-house in Virginia, founded by the Rev. Josias Mackie. *Norfolk: Route 58, 2.2 miles w. of Virginia Beach.*

K-278* EASTERN SHORE CHAPEL

One mile south is Eastern Shore Chapel. The land on which it stands, patented by William Cornick in 1657, was given to Lynnhaven Parish by his heirs. Two wooden buildings occupied the site; the present church was built in 1754. The communion service, which bears the date, 1759, was buried in a hen house, 1861–65, to save it from raiders. The chapel was abandoned in war time but was later reoccupied. *Virginia Beach ("old" Princess Anne County): Route 58, 2.2 miles w. of beach front.*

K-279 CHIPPOKES PLANTATION

This plantation, four miles to the northeast, was established in 1619 by Captain William Powell of Jamestown. Structures and artifacts on the property reflect plantation life from the early 17th century to the present. Donated to the Commonwealth by Mrs. Victor Stewart in 1967 for use as a state park, Chippokes is noted for its 350 years of continuous agricultural production and its modern recreational facilities. *Surry County: Route 10, 1.3 miles s.e. of Surry.*

K-300 LAWNES CREEK CHURCH

Approximately six miles to the north, near Hog Island Creek, is the site of Lawnes Creek Church. Authorized in 1629 as a "chapel of ease" for the settlers in the area by the Council and General Court of Colonial Virginia, the church was the site of a meeting in 1673 to protest unjust taxation and government without representation and to manifest a spirit of religious independence. *Surry County: Route 10, 7.2 miles s.e. of Surry.*

K-305 LEE'S RETREAT

Here the Confederates, under General Heth, made a gallant stand, April 2, 1865, but were finally overwhelmed. The loss of this point cut Lee's railway connection with Danville. On April 3, Grant and Meade camped here in pursuit of Lee. *Dinwiddie County: Route 460, .2 mile e. of Sutherland.*

K-306 EARLY PEANUT CROP

One mile northwest Dr. Matthew Harris grew the first commercial crop of peanuts in the United States, according to tradition, in or soon after 1842. *Sussex County: Route 460, 4 miles s.e. of Waverly.*

K-307 BATTLE OF FIVE FORKS

Four miles south is the battlefield of Five Forks. To that point Pickett retired from Dinwiddie Courthouse in the night of March 31, 1865. Sheridan, following, attacked him in the afternoon of April 1, 1865. The Confederates, outnumbered and surrounded, were overwhelmed. This defeat broke Lee's line of defense around Petersburg and forced him to retreat. *Dinwiddie County: Route 460, 4.9 miles w. of Sutherland.*

K-310 JAMES BOWSER PLANTATION

James Bowser, the only negro from Nansemond County to fight in the American Revolution, enlisted as a private in the Virginia Continental Line and was honorably discharged in 1782. Bowser returned to the county at the close of the Revolution and built his own business as a farmer and horse-breeder on land granted as bounty for his services to the Commonwealth. He married and reared a large family of free-born citizens. *Suffolk ("old" Nansemond County): 1 mile n. of Intersection of Routes 629 and 337.*

KA-8   DONELSON'S INDIAN LINE

John Donelson's line, surveyed after
the treaty of Lochaber with the Indians, 1770, crossed the road here. This
line separated Indian territory from
land open to settlement. Violations of
the line by settlers contributed to Dunmore's War, 1774. *Lee County:
Route 23, 5 miles s. of Big Stone Gap.*

KA-10   CARTER'S FORT

Three miles east, in Rye Cove, stood
Carter's Fort, built by Thomas Carter
in 1784. It was a station on the old
Wilderness Road from North Carolina
to Kentucky. *Scott County: Route
871, 1 mile e. of Sunbright.*

KA-11   BIG STONE GAP

Big Stone Gap, originally known as
Three Forks, received its charter February 23, 1888. A postoffice was established April 12, 1856. In the early
nineties it became the center of iron
and coal development. It was the
home and workshop of John Fox, Jr.,
novelist, and author of "Trail of the
Lonesome Pine." *Wise County: Alternate Route 58, at Big Stone Gap.*

KA-15   FIRST COURT OF SCOTT
COUNTY

The monument in the field to the east
marks the site of Benjamin T. Hollins'
home, in which was held the first
court of this county, February 14,
1815. *Scott County: Route 23, 2.1
miles e. of Gate City.*

KB-6   SALTVILLE

The land, patented by Charles Camp-
bell in 1753, passed to the wife of
General Francis Preston. General
William Russell began saltmaking
here in 1788; Thomas Madison di-
rected the work in 1790. William
King greatly enlarged the works. In
1861–64 the Confederate government
obtained salt here. In October, 1864,
Stoneman destroyed the salt works.
The town was incorporated in 1894.
Smyth County: Route 91, at Saltville.

KB-56   EGGLESTON'S SPRINGS

Near here Adam Harmon, probably in
1750, established what is believed to
be the first settlement in Giles County.
Here, in 1755, he found Mary Ingles
as she was making her way back to
Draper's Meadows after her escape
from the Indians. *Giles County:
Route 730, at Eggleston.*

KB-65   LINCOLN'S VIRGINIA
ANCESTORS

Thomas Lincoln, the father of the
president, was born just west of here
in 1778. He was a grandson of John
Lincoln who settled here about 1767,
and whose house stood to the east.
The Lincoln family graveyard is
nearby. *Rockingham County: Route
42, 2.5 miles n. of Edom.*

KB-75   FORT DICKINSON

The site was about one-half mile north of the river. This was one of a chain of frontier forts ordered erected by the Virginia Legislature early in 1756. The chain extended from Hampshire County (now West Virginia) to Patrick Co. on the North Carolina border. These forts were established under the supervision of Colonel George Washington, who made an inspection tour of the chain. This Fort was attacked by Indians at least once in 1756 and again the next year. *Bath County: Route 42, 3 miles s.e. of Milboro Springs.*

KC-1   BLAND

The community center was first known as Crab Orchard. The place became the county seat of Bland County when it was formed in 1861 under the name of Seddon, which was later changed to that of the county. At Rocky Gap a skirmish was fought in Crook's raid against the Virginia and Tennessee Railroad, May, 1864. *Bland County: Route 52, .35 mile s. of intersection with Route 98.*

KC-2*   A GREAT PREACHER

Some miles to the east was born William Elbert Munsey, July 13, 1833, and near here he preached his first sermon. Ordained to the Methodist ministry in 1855, Munsey was a noted preacher in several States. He died, October 23, 1877. *Bland County: Route 52, 2 miles s. of Rocky Gap.*

KC-3   ONE OF THE "BIG FOUR"

Here is the home of S. H. Newberry, who, with three others, composed the "Big Four" in the Virginia Senate. These four men united to defeat objectionable measures of the Readjuster movement. *Bland County: Route 52, 7 miles s. of Bland.*

KC-4   TOLAND'S RAID

Over this pass, Union cavalry under Colonel John T. Toland raided to Wytheville to destroy the Virginia and Tennessee Railway (N. & W.), July 1863. Mary Tynes, a girl of the neighborhood, rode ahead to warn the people. When the raiders reached Wytheville, they were repulsed by home guards and Toland was killed. *Wythe County: Route 52, at Bland-Wythe county line.*

KC-10   CATY SAGE

Two miles to the southwest was the home of James and Lovis Sage. From it their five-year-old daughter Caty was abducted in 1792. Fifty-six years later a brother found her in Eastern Kansas, living with Wyandot Indians. *Grayson County: Route 21, 4 miles s. of Wythe County line.*

KD-5   SEAT OF FINCASTLE COUNTY

Three miles southwest, on New River, was the seat of Fincastle County, which from 1772 to 1776 embraced Southwestern Virginia, including Kentucky. There are the ancient lead mines, visited and described by Thomas Jefferson. *Wythe County: Route 52, 5.5 miles s.e. of Fort Chiswell.*

KD-6   JACKSON'S FERRY AND OLD SHOT TOWER

Here on New River, Captain William Herbert, before the Revolution, established a ferry, later called Jackson's Ferry, that was in operation until 1930. The old tower across the river was built about 1820 for the manufacture of shot. *Wythe County: Route 52, 7.7 miles s.e. of Fort Chiswell.*

KD-8   AUSTIN'S BIRTHPLACE

Near Austinville, five miles west, was born Stephen F. Austin, "Father of Texas," November, 1793. He began his colonization work in 1821. *Wythe County: Route 52, at Poplar Camp.*

KD-12   HILLSVILLE

This place became the county seat when Carroll County was formed. The first court was held here, 1842; A. W. C. Nowlin was the first judge. The courthouse, built in 1872, was remodeled some years ago. The town was incorporated in 1900 and rechartered in 1940. *Carroll County: Route 52 at Hillsville.*

KE-5   BATTLE OF CLOYD'S MOUNTAIN

Just to the west took place the battle of Cloyd's Mountain, May 9, 1864. The Union General Crook, raiding to destroy the Virginia and Tennessee Railroad (N. & W.), met and repulsed General A. G. Jenkins, who was mortally wounded. *Pulaski County: Route 100, 5 miles n. of Dublin.*

KG-2   STUART'S BIRTHPLACE

A short distance west is the site of the home of Archibald Stuart, Jr., a statesman of a century ago. There was born, February 6, 1833, his son, James Ewell Brown Stuart, who became Major-General commanding the cavalry of the Army of Northern Virginia and whose fame is a part of the history of that army. Stuart closed his career by falling in the defense of Richmond, May 11, 1864. *Patrick County: Route 103, 4 miles s. of Friends Mission.*

KG-5   FLOYD

This place became the county seat when Floyd County was formed in 1831. First called Jacksonville for Andrew Jackson, its name was changed to that of the county. The courthouse was built on land given by the Phlegar family. The town was incorporated in 1892 and rechartered in 1936. Here was born Admiral Robley D. Evans, hero of the Spanish-American War. *Floyd County: Route 8, at Floyd.*

KG-8   COLONEL WILLIAM PRESTON

One mile west is "Smithfield," old home of Col. William Preston, who materially guided the destiny of the Virginia frontier from the French and Indian War through the Revolution. On this estate two Virginia governors were born: James P. Preston, 1816–19; John B. Floyd, 1849–52. The latter was the son of another Virginia governor, John Floyd, 1830–34, who while in office advocated before the legislature abolition of slavery in Virginia. *Montgomery County: Route 460, at Blacksburg.*

KG-10 DRAPER'S MEADOW MASSACRE

Here a settlement was made by the Ingles and Draper families in 1748. It was attacked in July, 1755, about the time of Braddock's Defeat, by Indians, who killed or captured every person found. Colonel James Patton was among the slain. Mrs. Draper and Mrs. William Ingles were carried into captivity. *Montgomery County: Route 460, at s. entrance of Blacksburg.*

KG-12 MONTGOMERY WHITE SULPHUR SPRINGS

Near here stood Montgomery White Sulphur Springs, popular resort area of 19th century America. During the Civil War the resort was converted into a military hospital staffed by Catholic nuns. Several hundred victims of smallpox including nurses and soldiers are buried nearby. The Southern Historical Society was reorganized here in August, 1873, when Jefferson Davis delivered the principal address. *Montgomery County: Interstate 81, ¾ mile n. of exit 38 at rest area, northbound lane.*

KG-15 MOUNTAIN EVANGELIST

The Reverend Robert Sayers Sheffey (1820–1902), although one of a kind as to style and personality, was a Methodist Circuit Rider in the classic frontier tradition. Celebrated for the intensity of his faith and prayer, as well as for his eccentricities, Sheffey's authority was recognized throughout this region. He is buried nearby, in Wesley Chapel Cemetery, beside his second wife, Elizabeth Stafford Sheffey. *Giles County: Route 100, at Route 730.*

KG-16 OLD-FASHIONED CAMP MEETING

Adjacent to and named for this stream, Wabash Campground was exemplary of a religious and social institution, indeed of a way of life, which flourished during the 19th century. Hundreds of families would camp for two weeks or more while attending the revival meetings first held here in 1834. The campground functioned until the early 1900's, when the large shed used during worship and many family shelters were destroyed by fire. *Giles County: Route 100, .6 mile n. of intersection with Route 659.*

KG-17 SNIDOW'S FERRY

In this vicinity Christian Snidow, pioneer, established a ferry over the river in 1786, and built a house in 1793. *Giles County: Route 460, 3 miles e. of Pearisburg.*

KG-19 DISCOVERY OF NEW RIVER

Abraham Wood, who lived at Fort Henry (Petersburg), possibly visited this stream in 1654. It was reached by Batts and Fallam, sent by Wood, on September 13, 1671. Long known as Wood's River, it came to be called New River. *Giles County: Route 460, 3 miles e. of Pearisburg.*

KG-20 FIRST COURT OF GILES COUNTY

About a mile north, in what is now Bluff City, was held the first court of Giles County, May 13, 1806. Near by stood the home of George Pearis, the first settler in this section. *Giles County: Route 460, 1 mile n. of Pearisburg.*

KG-21 PEARISBURG

The town was laid off in 1806 when Giles County was formed, and named for Captain George Pearis, early settler. Established in 1808, it was first incorporated in 1835, and reincorporated in 1914. Here, in May 1862, Union troops under Colonel Rutherford B. Hayes were defeated by Confederates under General Henry Heth. The present courthouse was erected in 1836. *Giles County: Route 460, at Pearisburg.*

KG-22 NARROWS

Named for the narrows in New River. The place was occupied by Confederate troops under French and Jackson in May, 1864. Combining with McCausland, they forced the Union General Crook to evacuate Blacksburg. Crook passed here on his way to West Virginia. The Norfolk and Western Railroad came in 1884; the Virginian in 1910. The town was incorporated in 1904. *Giles County: Route 460, at Narrows.*

KG-23 PITTSYLVANIA COURT HOUSE

This Greek Revival building was erected in 1853 as the third Court House of Pittsylvania County. The county, formed in 1767, and the Town of Chatham were named for William Pitt, First Earl of Chatham. The present Court House replaced a structure built in 1783 one block west where the old offices of the clerk still stands. The court was removed to this locality from Callands in 1777. *Pittsylvania County: Route 29 in front of court house.*

KH-1 GOVERNOR FLOYD'S GRAVE

A short distance across the State line is the grave of John Floyd, Governor of Virginia, 1830–34. Floyd while in Congress led in taking measures to secure Oregon for the United States. He died in 1837. *Alleghany County: Route 311, just s. of Sweet Chalybeate.*

KH-4 NEW CASTLE

This place became the county seat when Craig County was formed in 1851. The courthouse was built in 1851 and remodeled in 1935. General Averell passed through New Castle in his raid of December, 1863, and General Hunter in June, 1864. The town was incorporated in 1890. *Craig County: Route 311, at New Castle.*

KH-7 HANGING ROCK

On June 31, 1864 General Hunter, retreating from defeat at Lynchburg by General Early, met confederate forces led by General John McCausland. After losing some of his artillery here, Hunter continued his withdrawal northwest through New Castle to Lewisburg. *Roanoke County: Route 311, n. of Salem at Route 116.*

KM-5   QUAKER BAPTIST CHURCH

A Quaker meeting was established on Goose Creek in 1757, and a meeting house built. Fear of Indians caused most of the Quakers to move elsewhere though some of them returned. Unsuccessful attempts were made to reestablish the Goose Creek meeting. Before 1824 a church was established near here, known as Difficult Creek Baptist Church. The present Church (Quaker Baptist), built in 1898, stands near the site of the old building. *Bedford County: Route 24, 3.0 miles e. of intersection of Routes 122 and 24.*

KN-1   HOSPITAL OF ST. VINCENT DEPAUL

Founded in 1855, the Hospital of St. Vincent dePaul was Norfolk's first civilian hospital. Located two blocks south at the corner of Church and Wood streets, the hospital was opened in the home of Ann Plume Herron by eight Daughters of Charity during a yellow fever epidemic. It was incorporated March 3, 1856, and later named dePaul Hospital when moved to the present site at Kingsley Lane and Granby Street. *Norfolk: Kingsley Lane and Granby Street.*

KO-1   ST. JOHN'S CHURCH

Founded about 1643 and formerly known as Chuckatuck Church. The present building, the third on or near the site, was built in 1755 and is the second oldest church building in Nansemond County. Renamed St. John's Church in 1828. *Suffolk ("old" Nansemond County): Route 125, 1 mile e. of Chuckatuck.*

KP-4   BOOKER WASHINGTON'S BIRTHPLACE

Nearby was born Booker Taliaferro Washington, probably in 1858, the son of a slave woman. He graduated at Hampton Institute, 1875, and became an instructor there. In 1881, he was appointed principal of the later famous Tuskegee Institute, Alabama. Recognized as an orator and the leader of the Negroes in America, he used his influence to promote harmony between the races and to advance the colored people educationally and economically. He died, November 14, 1915. *Franklin County: Route 122, just w. of Hales Ford Church.*

KV-1   FIRST FLIGHT SHIP TO SHORE

On 14 November, 1910, Eugene Ely in a Curtiss built "Hudson Flyer," utilizing a specially constructed platform with an uptilt at the end, took off from the cruiser *Birmingham* anchored off Fort Monroe and landed at Willoughby Spit, 2½ miles distant, thus completing the first flight from ship to shore and the first flight to utilize the "Ski Jump" deck. This was the birth of Naval aviation. *Norfolk: Fourth View Street and Interstate 64, at visitors center.*

KV-4   SEASHORE STATE PARK

This park was developed by the National Park Service, Interior Department, through the Civilian Conservation Corps, in conjunction with the Virginia Conservation Commission. It covers 3400 acres and was opened, June 15, 1936. Two miles west is Lynnhaven Bay, in or near which there were naval actions in 1672 and 1700, and naval movements in 1781 and 1813. *Virginia Beach ("old" Princess Anne County): Route 60, 1 mile e. of Route 615.*

KV-5   LANDING OF WOOL AND SURRENDER OF NORFOLK

Near here Major-General John E. Wool, on May 10, 1862, landed with 6,000 Union troops. President Lincoln, Salmon P. Chase, Secretary of the Treasury, and Edwin M. Stanton, Secretary of War, watched the movement from a ship in Hampton Roads. As the Confederate troops had withdrawn, Wool marched to Norfolk, which was surrendered to him by Major W. W. Lamb that afternoon. *Norfolk: West Ocean View Avenue near Mason Creek Road.*

KV-6   SARAH CONSTANT SHRINE

This shrine commemorates the name of Captain Christopher Newport's flagship, the "Sarah Constant." The "Sarah Constant," with the two other ships, the "Godspeed," Captain Bartholomew Gosnold, and the "Discovery," Captain John Ratcliffe, first came to anchor in Virginia waters near here, April 26, 1607. *Norfolk: West Ocean View Avenue near Fourth View Street.*

KV-7   OPERATION TORCH, 1942

The first major amphibious action of World War II was planned near here in the Nansemond Hotel, Hdq. of Amphibious Force U.S. Atlantic Fleet. An Army-Navy staff under Adm. H. K. Hewitt met with General G. S. Patton to plan the movement of Task Force "A" from Hampton Roads to North Africa. *Norfolk: 350 ft. e. of Route 60 and Tidewater Drive.*

KV-15   FIRST LANDING

Near here the first permanent English settlers in North America first landed on American soil, April 26, 1607. From here they went on to make the settlement at Jamestown. The brick lighthouse was built in 1791. *Virginia Beach ("old" Princess Anne County): Route 60, .85 mile w. of Route 305, at Cape Henry.*

KW-16*   OLDEST BRICK HOUSE IN VIRGINIA

One mile east stands the house of Adam Thoroughgood, built in 1636, the oldest brick residence in Virginia. Nearby is the site of the first church of Lynnhaven Parish, erected before 1640. *Virginia Beach ("old" Princess Anne County): Route 500, 7 miles e. of Norfolk.*

KY-4* BATTLE OF GREAT BRIDGE

A short distance east was a stockade fort built by the British to command a causeway and bridges over the swamp. Lord Dunmore, the royal governor, held this fort with a force of British regulars, tories and Negroes. On December 9, 1775, the regulars, led by Captain Fordyce, tried to cross the causeway to attack the Americans. Most of the British were killed or wounded, and Dunmore withdrew to his fleet. *Chesapeake ("old" Norfolk County): Route 170, at Great Bridge.*

KY-5 BATTLE OF GREAT BRIDGE

In this vicinity, in 1775, was the southern end of a causeway, with bridges, by which the swamp and stream were crossed. Here William Woodford's Virginia riflemen defended the passage. When Lord Dunmore's British regulars attempted to cross the swamp, on December 9, 1775, they were cut to pieces by the fire of the riflemen. This defeat forced Dunmore to evacuate Norfolk. *Chesapeake ("old" Norfolk County): Route 168 at Great Bridge.*

L-3 DOUTHAT STATE PARK

This park was developed by the National Park Service, Interior Department, through the Civilian Conservation Corps, in conjunction with the Virginia Conservation Commission. It covers nearly 4,500 acres and was opened, June 15, 1936. It lies in a region once extensively devoted to iron smelting. *Alleghany County: Route 60, 1.5 miles e. of Clifton Forge.*

L-5 LUCY SELINA FURNACE

This furnace was built in 1827 by Ironmasters John Jordan and John Irvine and was named for their wives. During the Civil War, iron produced here was used in the manufacture of Confederate Munitions. *Alleghany County: Route 60, at Longdale.*

L-8 NEW MONMOUTH CHURCH AND MORRISON'S BIRTHPLACE

This is the site of the first church, built 1746. Just northeast was the birthplace of William McCutchan Morrison, born, 1867, died, 1918. A missionary to the Belgian Congo, he translated the Bible into native languages and exposed conditions there. Buried at Luebo, Congo. *Rockbridge County: Route 60, 2 miles w. of Lexington.*

L-10 FIRST INDIAN FIGHT

The first clash between settlers and Indians in Rockbridge County occurred near here, December 18, 1742. Captain John McDonald led the settlers; the Indians were the Iroquois. *Rockbridge County: Route 130, at Glasgow.*

L-11 MOOMAW'S LANDING

Here was Moomaw's Landing on the North River Canal. In May 1863 the Packet Marshall passed here bearing the body of Gen. Thomas J. (Stonewall) Jackson to Lexington. Mrs. Robert E. Lee used the canal in 1865 to join her husband at Washington College (now Washington & Lee University) in Lexington. *Rockbridge County: Route 60, w. end of Buena Vista.*

L-12   SHADY GROVE

Two miles east is Shady Grove, built by Patrick Henry for his son, Spotswood Henry. *Campbell County: Route 501, at Gladys.*

L-20   QUAKER MEETING HOUSE

The first Quaker meeting house here was built in 1757; it was remodeled in 1765. Sarah Lynch, mother of Charles and John Lynch, founder of Lynchburg, gave the land for the church. This church is now the Quaker Memorial Presbyterian Church. *Lynchburg: Fort Avenue at Quaker Parkway.*

L-22   SANDUSKY

In the grove to the northwest is Sandusky, built by Charles Johnston in 1797 and named for the city in Ohio, then a trading post, where Johnston stayed after escaping from the Indians. Here the Union General Hunter had his headquarters, June 17–18, 1864. Presidents Rutherford B. Hayes and William McKinley, then officers under Hunter, roomed together in this house. *Lynchburg: Fort Avenue at Quaker Parkway.*

L-30*   ORIGIN OF LYNCH LAW

A hundred yards west stands a walnut tree under which Colonel Charles Lynch, William Preston, Robert Adams, Jr., James Callaway and others held an informal court for the trial of tories and criminals, 1780. Punishment usually consisted of whipping. From this rude justice the term "Lynch Law" was evolved. *Campbell County: Route 29, 1 mile n. of Alta Vista.*

L-32   CLEMENT HILL

The house on the hill three hundred yards to the west was the home of Captain Benjamin Clement, who was one of the first makers of gunpowder in Virginia, 1775. The land grant was made in 1741. *Pittsylvania County: Route 29, 1 mile s. of Alta Vista.*

L-50*   PEYTONSBURG

This place, fifteen miles east, was a village in 1752, when Halifax County was formed. It was established as a town in 1759, and fell within Pittsylvania when that county was formed in 1767. Canteens were made there for Greene's army in 1780–81. Washington stopped there on his Southern tour, June 4, 1791. *Pittslyvania County: Route 29, at Chatham.*

L-52   MARKHAM

Some miles northeast is the site of Markham, where was born Rachel Donelson, wife of President Andrew Jackson, 1767. Her father, John Donelson, leaving Virginia, became one of the first settlers of Tennessee. Fort Donelson was named for him. *Pittsylvania County: Route 29, at Chatham.*

L-61   BEAVERS TAVERN

The house to the east was Beavers Tavern, 1800–1840. This was the muster ground of the county militia and a popular stage station. John C. Calhoun was a frequent visitor here. *Pittsylvania County: Route 29, 5 miles n. of Danville.*

LT-1 CALLANDS

Pittsylvania was cut off from Halifax in 1767 and the courthouse built here. In 1769 a town named Chatham was established here on land of James Roberts. A few years later Samuel Calland opened a store and the town took his name. In 1777 Henry County was cut off from Pittsylvania, and the county seat moved to Competition, more centrally located. The name Competition became Chatham in 1874. *Pittsylvania County: Route 57, at Callands.*

M-1 ROBERT RUSSA MOTON HIGH SCHOOL

On this site 4–23–51, the students staged a strike protesting inadequate school facilities. Led by Rev. L. Francis Griffin, these students' actions became a part of the 1954 U.S. Supreme Court's Brown v. Board of Education decision, which ruled racial segregation in public schools unconstitutional. To avoid desegregation, the Prince Edward County public schools were closed 6–4–59 and remained closed until 9–2–64. *Prince Edward County: Route 15 and Ely Street in Farmville.*

M-9 PAUL CARRINGTON

Member of House of Burgesses 1765–1775, of Virginia conventions, 1774–1788, including Constitutional Conventions, of first Supreme Court of Appeals of Virginia. A founder of Hampden-Sydney College. Lived and is buried at Mulberry Hill nearby. *Charlotte County: Route 360, at Route 607 in Wylliesburg.*

M-10 GOODE'S BRIDGE

Here Anthony Wayne took station in July, 1781, to prevent the British from moving southward. Here, April 3, 1865, Longstreet's, Hill's and Gordon's corps of Lee's army, retreating from Petersburg toward Danville, crossed the river. *Chesterfield County: Route 360, 7.8 miles e. of Amelia.*

M-11 LEE'S RETREAT

Lee's army reached Amelia, April 4–5, 1865, moving southward. Here it was delayed by having to forage for food. In the afternoon of April 5, Lee advanced toward Jetersville. *Amelia County: Route 360, at Amelia.*

M-12 LEE'S RETREAT

Near here Lee, moving south toward Danville in the afternoon of April 5, 1865, found the road blocked by Sheridan. He then turned westward by way of Amelia Springs, hoping to reach the Southside (Norfolk and Western) Railroad. *Amelia County: Route 360, 4.8 miles s.w. of Amelia.*

M-13 LEE'S RETREAT

Near here, April 6, 1865, Meade, who was advancing northward on Amelia Courthouse, learned that Lee had turned westward. Meade sent the Second Corps on the Deatonsville Road, the Fifth Corps on the Paineville Road, and the Sixth Corps on a parallel route. *Amelia County: Route 360, 5.3 miles s.w. of Amelia.*

M-14 LEE'S RETREAT

Sheridan reached here on April 4, 1865, with cavalry and the Fifth Corps, and entrenched. He was thus squarely across Lee's line of retreat to Danville. On April 5, Grant and Meade arrived from the east with the Second Corps and the Sixth Corps. *Amelia County: Route 360, .7 mile s.w. of Jetersville.*

M-15 LEE'S RETREAT

From here Union cavalry moved north on April 5, 1865, to ascertain Lee's whereabouts. On the morning of April 6, the Second, Fifth and Sixth corps of Grant's army advanced from Jetersville toward Amelia Courthouse to attack Lee. *Amelia County: Route 360, at Jetersville.*

M-16 LEE'S RETREAT

The Union General Ord reached this place in the night of April 5, 1865, to head off Lee. On April 6, Ord sent a cavalry force from here to burn the bridges near Farmville and then moved westward with the Twenty-fourth Corps *Nottoway County: Route 360, at Burkeville.*

M-17 HISTORIC BURKEVILLE

Tarleton's British cavalry, raiding west, stopped here in July, 1781. When railroads were built, the place was known as Burke's Junction. The Union cavalryman Kautz destroyed the railways here in June, 1864. Jefferson Davis passed through Burkeville, going south, April 3, 1865. Grant's headquarters were here, April 6, 1865. *Nottoway County: Route 360, at Burkeville.*

M-18 FRANCISCO'S FIGHT

A few miles east Peter Francisco, a soldier in the Virginia service, defeated, singlehanded, nine of Tarleton's British dragoons, July 1781. Francisco weighed two hundred and sixty pounds and was considered the strongest man in Virginia. After the Revolution he became doorkeeper of the House of Delegates. He died in 1836. *Nottoway County: Route 360, 6 miles n.e. of Burkeville.*

M-19 LEE'S RETREAT

Three miles north is Amelia Springs, once a noted summer resort. There Lee, checked by Sheridan at Jetersville and forced to detour, spent the night of April 5–6, 1865. *Amelia County: Route 360, at Jetersville.*

M-20 T. O. SANDY (FIRST COUNTY AGENT)

First Farm Demonstration Agent in Virginia lived one mile south. Appointed State Agent in 1907. Under his able leadership programs in Farm and Home Demonstration work, Boys Corn Clubs and Girls Canning Clubs were developed. In 1914 the Agency was transferred to the Virginia Polytechnic Institute and became the Extension Service now embracing mens and womens work and 4–H clubs. *Nottoway County: Route 460, 2.1 miles e. Burkeville.*

M-24* LEE'S RETREAT

Two miles north are the battlefields of Sailor's Creek, April 6, 1865. There Grant captured more men than were captured in any other one day's field engagement of the war. *Prince Edward County: Route 307, 3 miles e. of Rice.*

M-25 BATTLE OF SAILOR'S CREEK

Six miles north took place the battle of Sailor's Creek, April 6, 1865. Lee's army, retreating westward from Amelia Courthouse to Farmville by way of Deatonsville, was attacked by Sheridan, who surrounded Ewell's Corps. After a fierce action the Confederates were overpowered. Ewell, eleven other generals, and several thousand men were captured. This was the last major engagement between Lee's and Grant's armies. *Prince Edward County: Route 460, at Rice.*

M-26 BATTLE OF SAILOR'S (SAYLER'S) CREEK

This is the Hillsman House, used by the Unionists as a hospital in the engagement of April 6, 1865. From the west side of the creek the Confederates charged and broke through the Union infantry, but were stopped by the batteries along the hillside here. A mass surrender followed, including a corps commander, Gen. R. S. Ewell, several other generals, many colonels, about 7000 rank and file, and several hundred wagons. It was the largest unstipulated surrender of the war. *Amelia County: Route 617, 5 miles n.e. of Rice.*

M-26 BATTLE OF SAILOR'S (SAYLER'S) CREEK

At the same time another engagement took place two miles north, on the main Sailor's (Sayler's) Creek, where Gen. John B. Gordon repulsed pursuing Union troops. He lost most of his wagons but saved the majority of his men. At this time Gen. Robert E. Lee was retreating from Petersburg toward Danville, closely followed by Gen. Grant. Lee lost half of his troops in these two memorable rearguard actions, which foreshadowed the surrender at Appomattox three days later. *Amelia County: Route 617, 5 miles n.e. of Rice.*

M-30* ACTION OF HIGH BRIDGE

Three miles north took place the engagement of High Bridge, April 7, 1865. Lee's rear guard at the bridge head on the west bank of the Appomattox was driven off by the Second Corps of Grant's army after setting fire to the bridge. *Prince Edward County: Route 460, at Rice.*

M-33* LONGWOOD ESTATE

Birthplace, and until 1811, residence of Peter Johnston, Lieutenant in Lee's Legion in the Revolution; and birthplace of his son, Joseph E. Johnston, Brigadier General U.S.A., and General C.S.A. *Prince Edward County: Route 460, at Farmville.*

M-60 LYNCHBURG DEFENSES

The earthwork on the hilltop two hundred yards to the east was thrown up as a part of the system of defenses for Lynchburg, 1861–65. The city was an important supply base and railroad center. *Bedford County: Route 501, e. entrance of Lynchburg.*

M-66 ELDON

Three miles north is Eldon, birthplace and home of Henry D. "Hal" Flood (1865–1921). A member of the United States House of Representatives (1901–1921), and Chairman of the Committee on Foreign Affairs (1913–1919), he drafted the Resolution declaring war on Germany and Austria, April 6, 1917. *Appomattox County: Route 460 at 131, in Appomattox.*

M-66* ELDON

Three miles north is Eldon, birthplace and home of Hal D. Flood, for many years a member of the United States House of Representatives. He was chairman of the Committee on Foreign Affairs, January, 1913–March, 1919, and the author of the resolution declaring war on Germany and Austria, April, 1917. He died in Washington, December 8, 1921. *Appomattox County: Route 24, 1.1 miles n. of Appomattox.*

M-66 INVENTOR OF THE BANJO

Nearby is buried Joel Walker Sweeney (circa 1810–1860), musician and developer of the five-string banjo. In 1831 Sweeney launched himself and his two brothers, Sam and Dick, on a series of minstrel tours that continued until his death twenty-nine years later. *Appomattox County: Route 24, 3.2 miles e. of Appomattox.*

M-67 CLAY SMOKING PIPES

For many years, residents of the vicinity made clay smoking pipes. Products of this industry were distributed to all parts of America during the nineteenth century. More recently, smoking pipes were factory produced in Pamplin City. *Appomattox County: Route 460, at Pamplin.*

MG-1 APPOMATTOX COURT HOUSE CONFEDERATE CEMETERY

Here were buried eighteen Confederate soldiers who died April 8 and 9, 1865 in the closing days of the War Between the States. The remains of one unknown Union soldier found some years after the war are interred beside the Confederate dead. About 500 yards east of this cemetery is the McLean House where Lee and Grant signed the surrender terms. *Appomattox County: Route 24, .2 mile e. of Appomattox.*

MG-2* THE LAST POSITIONS

Lee, retreating from Petersburg, reached the hills to the northeast, only to find Grant in position here across his line of retreat, April 8, 1865. The Confederates made an attack early in the morning of April 9. John B. Gordon broke through the opposing cavalry but was stopped by the infantry. Some hours later Lee rode along this road to meet Grant for surrender. *Appomattox County: Route 24, 2 miles n. of Appomattox.*

MG-3   WILDWAY

Three miles north is Wildway, home of Thomas S. Bocock, member of the United States Congress and only speaker of the Confederate House of Representatives. He was born, May 18, 1815, and died, August 25, 1891. *Appomattox County: Route 24, at Vera.*

MJ-1   BIZARRE

Near here is the site of Bizarre, owned in 1742 by Richard Randolph of Curles. In 1781, his grandson, John Randolph of Roanoke, took refuge at Bizarre with his mother on account of Arnold's invasion. John Randolph lived here until 1810, when he moved to Roanoke in Charlotte County. *Cumberland County: Route 45, at n. entrance of Farmville.*

N-4   FREDERICKSBURG CAMPAIGN

Here passed part of the Army of the Potomac, under General Burnside, on the way from Warrenton to Fredericksburg, November, 1862. The battle of Fredericksburg was fought, December 13, 1862. *Stafford County: Route 17, 4.1 miles n.w. of Falmouth.*

N-5   CAVALRY AFFAIRS

Near here Wade Hampton with a small cavalry force surprised and captured 5 officers and 87 men of the Third Pennsylvania Cavalry, November 28, 1862. At that time Burnside was moving toward Fredericksburg. On February 25, 1863, Fitz Lee, on a reconnaissance, attacked Union cavalry here, driving it back on Falmouth where the Union army was encamped. *Stafford County: Route 17, 8 miles n.w. of Falmouth.*

N-6*   THE MUD MARCH

Here passed a part of the Army of the Potomac moving westward toward the fords of the Rappahannock, January 20–21, 1863. Burnside, commanding, sought to get in the rear of Lee, who was at Fredericksburg. A storm, making the roads deep in mud, forced the abandonment of the movement. *Stafford County: Route 17, 4.1 miles n.w. of Falmouth.*

N-8   LEDERER EXPEDITION

The explorer, John Lederer, and his companions started near here in August, 1670 on their way to the Blue Ridge Mountains. Lederer was one of the first to explore the Piedmont north of the James River. *Caroline County: Route 17, 12.5 miles s.e. of Fredericksburg.*

N-9   EARLY SETTLEMENT

Two miles east near the river, Richard Coleman planted a frontier settlement and trading post in 1652. By 1660 a church was built to which every man was required to come armed for protection against the Indians. *Essex County: Route 17, 7 miles northwest of Caret.*

N-10   COLONIAL POST OFFICE

Here was Newpost, headquarters of Alexander Spotswood (Governor of Virginia, 1710–22), deputy postmaster general for the colonies, 1730–39. Spotswood also had an iron furnace here. *Spotsylvania County: Route 17, .4 mile n.w. of New Post.*

N-11   JACKSON'S HEADQUARTERS

In an outhouse, here at Moss Neck, Stonewall Jackson had his headquarters, December, 1862–March, 1863. He was engaged in guarding the line of the Rappahannock with his corps of Lee's army. *Caroline County: Route 17, 5.7 miles s.e. of New Post.*

N-12   WINDSOR

This is the ancient Woodford estate. Governor Spotswood and the Knights of the Golden Horseshoe stopped here on their way to the mountains, August, 1716. Here General William Woodford was born, October 6, 1734. He defeated Governor Lord Dunmore at the Great Bridge, December, 1775, and took an important part in the Revolutionary War. *Caroline County: Route 17, 6.9 miles s.e. of New Post.*

N-13   SKINKER'S NECK

Two miles north on the Rappahannock River. There Jubal A. Early, in December, 1862, confronted Burnside's army on the other side of the river. His alertness prevented a crossing and battle at this point. *Caroline County: Route 17, 6.9 miles s.e. of New Post*

N-14   HAZELWOOD

Here was the home of John Taylor of Caroline, Jefferson's chief political lieutenant and a leading advocate of States Rights. He died here in 1824. *Caroline County: Route 17, 12.7 miles s.e. of New Post*

N-15   RAPPAHANNOCK ACADEMY

On this site colonial Mount Church, built about 1750. In 1808 the parish glebe was sold and the proceeds were used to establish a school; the church building was turned into Rappahannock Academy, one of the most noted schools in Virginia. *Caroline County: Route 17, 10 miles s.e. of New Post.*

N-16   WHERE BOOTH DIED

On this road two miles south is the Garrett place. There John Wilkes Booth, Lincoln's assassin, was found by Union cavalry and killed while resisting arrest, April 26, 1865. *Caroline County: Route 301, at Port Royal Cross Roads.*

N-17   OLD PORT ROYAL

The town was established in 1744 and was one of the principal shipping points on the Rappahannock River in colonial times. In December, 1862, Burnside, commanding the Army of the Potomac, considered crossing the river here but finally moved up to Fredericksburg. Union gunboats, attempting to pass up the river at that time, were driven back by D. H. Hill. *Caroline County: Route 301, at Port Royal Cross Roads.*

N-18   OLD RAPPAHANNOCK COURTHOUSE

About half a mile northeast stood the old courthouse and clerk's office of Rappahannock County, 1665–1693. To this courthouse Thomas Goodrich and Benjamin Goodrich, ordered to appear with halters around their necks, came to express their penitence for taking part in Bacon's Rebellion in 1676. *Essex County: Route 17, at Caret.*

N-19   PORTOBAGO INDIAN TOWNS

On the river two and a half miles north and two miles northeast were the two principal towns of the Portobago Indians. In 1669 these Indians had sixty bowmen and hunters. *Essex County: Route 17, 11.8 miles northwest of Caret.*

N-20   FONTHILL

A mile and a half west is Fonthill, home of R.M.T. Hunter, United States Senator, Confederate Secretary of State, and Confederate Senator. The place was raided by Union troops in 1863. In 1865, Hunter was arrested here and taken to prison in Fort Pulaski. *Essex County: Route 17, 3 miles n.w. of Caret.*

N-21   HISTORIC TAPPAHANNOCK

The town was founded in 1680 under the name of Hobbs His Hole. In 1682, a port was established here and called New Plymouth. In 1808, the name was changed to Tappahannock. The British Admiral Cockburn shelled the town, December 1, 1814. An old customs house and a debtors' jail are here. *Essex County: Route 360, at Tappahannock.*

N-22   RITCHIE'S BIRTHPLACE

Here was born Thomas Ritchie, November 5, 1778. In 1804, he established the Richmond Enquirer, which ran until 1877, the most noted of Virginia newspapers. Ritchie was a political leader in Virginia and an editor of national fame. In 1845, he became editor of the Washington Union. He retired in 1851 and died, July 3, 1854. *Essex County: Route 17, at Tappahannock.*

N-23   VAUTER'S CHURCH

This was the upper church of St. Anne's Parish, formed in 1693. The northern half of the structure was built about 1719, the southern wing in 1731. The church still has a communion service set presented by Queen Anne. *Essex County: Route 17, 10.7 miles n.w. of Caret.*

N-24   FORT LOWRY—CAMP BYRON

Located two miles N.E. on Rappahannock River at Lowry's Point was a Confederate eight gun "water battery" constructed in 1861. Here at Dunnsville was located Camp Byron, home of Company F (Essex Light Dragoons), Ninth Cavalry, C.S.A.; the company moved to Fort Lowry in October 1861 to assist in the fort's defense and to conduct scouting missions. *Essex County: U.S. 17, at Route 611.*

N-25   ANCIENT INDIAN TOWN

Two hundred yards northeast on the river stood an early Indian town, seemingly the one known as "Appamatuck" to Captain John Smith in 1607. *Essex County: Route 17, 1.75 miles w. of Tappahannock.*

N-26   MANN MEETING HOUSE

Just to the east stood Mann Meeting House, the first Methodist Episcopal Church in this region. It was built before 1794 and abandoned about 1880. The site is now occupied by the Macedonia Colored Baptist Church. *Essex County: Route 17, 12.4 miles s.e. of Tappahannock.*

N-27   GOULDBOROUGH PLANTATION (LATER GOLDBERRY)

Just east of here was the seat of the Waring family, members of which served the colony and our fledgling nation in elected and appointed offices and as officers in the county militia and the Continental Line. Thomas Waring II (ca. 1690–1754), Burgess 1736–1754, built a mansion here in 1733. His son Francis (1717–1771) Burgess 1758–1769, was an organizer of the Sons of Liberty and a signer of the Leedstown Resolves. The house, having survived three wars, burned in the late 19th century. *Essex County: Route 17, 2.27 miles s. of Caret.*

N-28   DEPARTURE OF THE INDIANS

In the forest west of this point the Rappahannock Indians built a wooden fort as a defense against hostile Northern Indians. From the shore just to the northeast the Rappahannocks were transported thirty-five miles up the river, February 4, 1684. *Essex County: Route 17, 2.8 miles n.w. of Tappahannock.*

N-29   FORT LOWRY

Here in 1861 Confederates constructed an eight gun "water battery" principally for the defense of Fredericksburg. The guns were manned by the 55th Infantry Regiment located 500 yards N.W. The cannons were moved and the fort abandoned March 1862 after Northern Neck troop withdrawal left unit defenseless. On April 14, 1862, six Union gun boats bombarded and burned the installation. Thereafter, the fort functioned in limited capacity until the war ended. *Essex County: Route 646 at fort site.*

N-40   GLEBE LANDING CHURCH

This church was constituted in 1772 by the noted Baptist preacher, John Waller. The first building stood on the old glebe overlooking the Rappahannock River; hence the name Glebe Landing. The present building was erected in 1839. *Middlesex County: Route 17, 12.1 miles n.w. of Saluda.*

N-45   HEWICK

Three miles east is Hewick, built about 1678 by Christopher Robinson, clerk of Middlesex County. It was the birthplace of John Robinson, Speaker of the House of Burgesses and Treasurer of Virginia, 1738–1766, the leading man of the colony.

N-48   CHRIST CHURCH

Half a mile east is Christ Church, Middlesex. The first building was erected about 1666; the present one in 1712. About 1840 the church was restored. The colonial governor, Sir Henry Chicheley, is buried there. *Middlesex County: Route 33, 2.4 miles s. of Urbanna.*

N-49 TOMB OF PULLER

In Christ Churchyard immediateley to north lies buried Lt. Gen. Lewis Burwell Puller, USMC. He led Marines in 19 campaigns from Haiti and Nicaragua through the Korean War receiving 53 decorations and the admiration and affection of those he led. He was a Marine's Marine and is a tradition of Virginia and our nation's history. *Middlesex County: Route 33, 3 miles e. of Saluda.*

N-50 LOWER METHODIST CHURCH

Built 1717, this was the second lower chapel of Christ Church Parish, Middlesex County. It occupies the site of the first lower chapel of this parish, built before 1661 as the church of Piankatank Parish. Bartholomew Yates was the first minister of the present church. After 1792 the church was unused, except by the Methodists or Baptists. In 1857 Robert Healy bought the church from the parish and gave it to the Methodists, who have worshipped here ever since. *Middlesex County: Route 33, 9.3 miles s.e. of Saluda.*

N-58* THE SERVANTS' PLOT

On this Poropotank Creek, in 1663, the indentured servants of Gloucester County, weary of their hard lot, plotted an insurrection. The plot was matured, but it was betrayed by one Birkenhead, a servant at Purton, who thereby probably prevented a massacre. He was freed and given a present of tobacco. Mary Johnston's novel, "Prisoners of Hope," uses this incident. *King and Queen County: Route 14, 1.1 miles w. of Adner.*

N-61 POPLAR SPRING CHURCH

This is the site of Poplar Spring Church of Petsworth Parish. In 1694, old Petsworth Church was abandoned in favor of this church. It was considered the finest church of colonial Virginia. In 1676, the followers of Bacon, the Rebel, interred here a casket supposed to contain his remains, but in reality filled with stones. The body was buried secretly. *Gloucester County: Route 17, 5 miles n.w. of Gloucester.*

N-66* MARLFIELD

A mile and a half west is Marlfield, home of John Buckner, clerk of Gloucester County, who brought the first printing press into Virginia. Buckner printed the laws of 1680 without license, for which he was reproved in 1682 by Governor Lord Culpeper and his printing was prohibited. *Gloucester County: Route 17, 4.5 miles n.w. of Gloucester.*

N-77 STINGRAY POINT

Eight miles east, where the Rappahannock River joins Chesapeake Bay. Near there, in June, 1608, Captain John Smith, the explorer, was hurt by a stingray while fishing in the river. The point took its name from this incident. *Middlessex County: 8.6 miles west of Deltaville.*

N-85 BATTLE OF CRICKET HILL

On the shore here General Andrew Lewis, commanding the Virginia forces, erected a battery facing a stockaded camp on Gwynn's Island established by Governor Lord Dunmore, July, 1776. The fire from this point, Cricket Hill, damaged the camp and the British ships and forced the evacuation of the island. A little later Dunmore put out to sea. *Mathews County: Route 223, 4 miles n. of Mathews.*

N-86 FITCHETT'S WHARF

Fitchett's Wharf was a center of commercial activity for this area of Mathews County from 1845 until the early 20th century. It also served as a major port of call for vessels plying the Chesapeake Bay until 1932. An important shipyard, owned and operated by Lewis Hudgins, stood here until it was burned by Union forces in 1864. Several well-known brig and schooner class commercial ships were built here, including the *Victory* and the *Conquest.* The shipbuilder's house still stands nearby, and the wharf store has been restored as a residence. *Mathews County: Route 642, at Moon Post Office.*

ND-4 PATRICK HENRY'S BIRTHPLACE

Seven miles east, at Studley, May 29, 1736, was born Patrick Henry, the orator of the Revolution. *Hanover County: Route 2, 8.9 miles s. of Hanover.*

ND-5 EDMUND PENDLETON'S HOME

Six miles southeast is the site of Edmundsbury, home of Edmund Pendleton. Pendleton, born September 9, 1721, was in the House of Burgesses; a delegate to the Continental Congress; chairman of the Virginia Committee of Safety, 1775–6; president of the May 1776 convention and the convention that ratified the United States constitution, 1788; president of the Virginia supreme court. He died, October 26, 1803, and was buried there but was later removed to Williamsburg. *Caroline County: Route 2, 2.5 miles s. of Bowling Green.*

ND-6 CLAY'S BIRTHPLACE

Three miles northwest is Clay Spring, where Henry Clay was born, April 12, 1777. He passed most of his early life in Richmond, removing to Kentucky in 1797. His career as a public man and as a peacemaker between North and South is an important part of American history. *Hanover County: Route 2, 4.5 miles s. of Hanover.*

ND-7 CAMPAIGN OF 1781

Lafayette, marching from Head of Elk, Maryland, to Richmond, camped here the night of April 27, 1781. *Caroline County: Route 2, at Bowling Green.*

ND-9 CORNWALLIS'S ROUTE

Lord Cornwallis, marching northward in pursuit of Lafayette's American force, camped near here, May 30, 1781. He entered this road from the east on his way from Hanover Town to the North Anna at Chesterfield Ford (Telegraph Bridge). *Hanover County: Route 2, 1.3 miles s. of Hanover.*

NN-3 JOHN CLAYTON, BOTANIST

One and a half miles north is the site of his home "Windsor" where he developed an excellent botanical garden. He was the first president, Virginia Society for the promotion of Useful Knowledge, and clerk of Gloucester County from 1722 until his death in 1773. His herbarium specimens, some still preserved in the British Museum, were the basis of "Flora Virginia," compiled by Gronovius with the collaboration and Linnaeus and originally published at Leyden in 1739. *Mathews County: Route 14 e. of Gloucester County line.*

NP-1 CHARLES CHURCH

About one mile east, on north (left-hand) side of road (see stone marker and old foundations) stood the last colonial church of Charles Parish, built about 1708 and burned a century later, on the site of two earlier churches of the parish, built about 1636 and 1682. This parish was first known as New Poquoson Parish in 1635 and was renamed Charles Parish in 1692. *York County: Routes 134 and 17 at Tabb.*

NW-1 GLOUCESTER COURTHOUSE

The courthouse was built in 1766. The debtor's prison is also old. A skirmish occured near here between Confederate and Union cavalry, January 29, 1864. *Gloucester County: Route 17, at Gloucester.*

NW-2 WARE CHURCH

A mile east is Ware Church, built about 1693. Near by is Church Hill, another relic of colonial days. Not far distant is White Hall, a colonial mansion built by the Willis family. *Gloucester County: Route 17, at e. entrance of Gloucester.*

NW-3 TO GWYNN'S ISLAND

Two miles east is Toddsbury, home of the Todd family, built in 1722. Farther east, in Mathews County are the old homes, Green Plains, Auburn, and Midlothian. Some miles beyond them is Gwynn's Island, where General Andrew Lewis drove the last royal governor, Lord Dumore, from Virginia soil, July, 1776. *Gloucester County: Route 17, at e. entrance of Gloucester.*

NW-4 WARNER HALL

Three miles east is Warner Hall. The estate was patented about 1650 by Augustine Warner, who built the first house in 1674. Bacon, the Rebel, was here for a time in 1676. The later house, built about 1740 and burned in 1849, has been beautifully restored. *Gloucester County: Route 17, 4.2 miles s. of Gloucester.*

NW-5 ABINGDON CHURCH

This is the third church of Abingdon Parish and was erected in 1755 on the site of an earlier one. The parish, established between 1650 and 1655, had its first church near the river. *Gloucester County: Route 17, 6.2 miles s. of Gloucester.*

NW-6 WHITE MARSH AND REED'S BIRTHPLACE

Near here is White Marsh, a fine old house with terraced garden. Five miles west is the birthplace of Dr. Walter Reed, of the United States army, who first proved that yellow fever is conveyed by mosquitoes. *Gloucester County: Route 17, 5.3 miles s. of Gloucester.*

NW-7 TARLETON'S LAST FIGHT

Here, at the Hook, Tarleton, commanding the cavalry of Cornwallis's army, fought an action with Choisy's French force and Virginia militia, October 3, 1781. The Duke de Lauzun's cavalry charged Tarleton, who retired to Gloucester Point. There he was blockaded by the French and by Virginia militia. *Gloucester County: Route 1216, 2.1 miles n. of Gloucester Point.*

NW-8 ROSEWELL AND WEROWOCOMOCO

Several miles west is Rosewell, built about 1750, home of the Page family, and the largest of colonial Virginia houses. On York River, probably at Purtan Bay some miles west of Rosewell, was Werowocomoco, chief town of the Indian ruler Powhatan in 1607. *Gloucester County: Route 17, 5.3 miles s. of Gloucester.*

NW-9 GLOUCESTER POINT

Known first as Tyndall's Point. The colonists built a fort here in 1667. In 1676 Bacon led his rebels across the river here. Tarleton and Dundas occupied the place in October, 1781, in the siege of Yorktown. Cornwallis planned to break through the blockade here, but a storm kept him from crossing the river. The point was fortified by the Confederates in 1861 and occupied by Union troops in 1862. *Gloucester County: Route 17, at Gloucester Point.*

NW-10 EARLY LAND PATENT

Argoll Yeardley patented 4,000 acres of land, known as Tyndall's Neck, here on the north side of Charles (now York) River, October 12, 1640. This was one of the first land patents north of the York River. *Gloucester County: Route 17, at Gloucester Point.*

NY-15* DISMAL SWAMP CANAL

This canal, which connects Chesapeake Bay and Albermarle Sound, was charted by Virginia in 1787 and by North Carolina in 1790. It was opened to local traffic in 1806. The canal is now part of the inland waterway. *Chesapeake: Route 17, 1 mile s. of Route 104.*

O-5 OUTER FORTIFICATIONS

On the hilltops here ran the outer line of Richmond fortifications, 1862–1865. *Henrico County: Route 360, 1.4 miles s.w. of Mechanicsville.*

O-6 SEVEN DAYS' BATTLES

Longstreet's and D. H. Hill's divisions of Lee's army crossed the river here, in the afternoon of June 26, 1862, to attack the Union force at Mechanicsville. It was the opening of the Seven Days' Battles. *Hanover County: Route 360 at Hanover/Henrico county line.*

O-7* SEVEN DAYS' BATTLES

By this road the Confederates moved to attack McClellan's fortified position at Ellerson's Mill on Beaver Dam Creek, June 26, 1862. Beyond is the field of Gaines's Mill, fought on June 27, 1862. *Hanover County: Route 156, .5 mile s. of Mechanicsville.*

O-8* SHERIDAN'S RAID

Sheridan, moving around Richmond, reached this point on May 12, 1864, after a fight, and passed on to the James River near Shirley. *Hanover County: Route 360, e. entrance of Mechanicsville.*

O-9 SEVEN DAYS' BATTLES

Here the Confederates attacked the force holding McClellan's fortified position on the east bank of Beaver Dam Creek, June 26, 1862. *Hanover County: Route 360, .2 mile n.e. of Mechanicsville.*

O-11 BATTLE OF COLD HARBOR

The left of Lee's line at Cold Harbor, June 3, 1864, crossed the road here. The main battle took place to the east, where Grant attacked Lee's trenches without success. *Hanover County: Route 360, 3.6 miles n.e. of Mechanicsville.*

O-12* BETHESDA CHURCH

This is the site of Old Bethesda Church. Here, on May 30, 1864, a part of Warren's (Fifth) Corps of Grant's army, advancing southward, was attacked by Early. On June 2, 1864, Early here attacked Burnside's (Ninth) Corps. *Hanover County: Route 360, 4.6 miles n.e. of Mechanicsville.*

O-13* CORNWALLIS'S ROUTE

Lord Cornwallis, in the pursuit of Lafayette that led him to the North Anna River, passed near here, May 30, 1781. *Hanover County: Route 360, 10.6 miles n.e. of Mechanicsville.*

O-14* GRANT'S CROSSING

Some miles west of this spot the four corps of Grant's army crossed the river, May 28–29, 1864, moving toward Richmond. This move was followed by the battle of Cold Harbor. *Hanover County: Route 360, 11.8 miles n.e. of Mechanicsville.*

O-15 HENRY'S CALL TO ARMS

One mile east on the river was Newcastle. There, on May 2, 1775, Patrick Henry put himself at the head of the Hanover volunteers and marched against the royal governor, Lord Dunmore, who had seized the colony's powder. *Hanover County: Route 360, 11.8 miles n.e. of Mechanicsville.*

O-16 RUMFORD ACADEMY

Two miles east was Rumford Academy, established in 1804. It was one of the most noted Virginia schools of its time. *King William County: Route 360, at Central Garage.*

O-17* OLD PLACES

About twelve miles to the east are
Mount Pleasant, built about 1734; and
Sweet Hall, built about 1720, one of
the quaintest old houses in Virginia.
A little beyond is Romancoke, once
the home of Lee's son, R. E. Lee, Jr.,
and visited by General Lee. *King
and Queen County: Route 631, 2
miles n. of Manquin.*

O-18 CAVALRY RAIDS

Kilpatrick, coming from the east,
burned Confederate stores here, May
5, 1863. Dahlgren, coming from
Richmond, crossed the Mattapony
here March 2, 1864. Sheridan, returning from his Richmond raid, was
here, May 22–23, 1864, and on his
Trevillian raid passed here, June 7,
1864. *King William County: Route
360, at Aylett.*

O-20 CLARK HOME

About twelve miles east is the site
of the original home of the family of
George Rogers Clark, conqueror of
the Northwest. The family moved
from here to Albemarle County.
*King and Queen County: Route 360,
at Saint Stephens Church.*

O-21* WHERE DAHLGREN DIED

Colonel Ulric Dalgren, returning
from his raid to Richmond, was killed
by Confederate soldiers and home
guards about twelve miles to the
southeast, March 2, 1864. *King and
Queen County: Route 360, at Saint
Stephens Church.*

O-22 MATTAPONY INDIAN TOWN

Three miles north, on Piscataway
Swamp, the Mattapony Indians
settled after the massacre of 1644.
Here they lived in peace until 1668,
when they moved west to the Mattapony River. *Essex County: Route
360, at Millers Tavern.*

O-23 BACON'S NORTHERN FORCE

At Piscataway, near here, the northern
followers of Bacon the Rebel assembled in 1676. On July 10, 1676,
an action was fought with Governor
Berkeley's supporters, some of whom
were killed and wounded. Several
houses were burned. Passing here, the
rebels marched south to the Pamunkey
River, where they joined their leader,
Bacon. *Essex County: Route 360, at
Millers Tavern.*

O-24 EDMUND RUFFIN'S GRAVE

Here at Marlbourne (named for marl)
is the grave of Edmund Ruffin, one of
the greatest of American agricultur-
ists. Ruffin moved here in 1843 and
here carried on many of the experiments that made him famous. An ar-
dent secessionist, he fired the first gun
at Fort Sumter, April, 1861, and
served in the Confederate army until
incapacitated by age. He died in June,
1865. *Hanover County: Route 360,
8.9 miles n.e. of Mechanicsville.*

O-25   DUNLORA ACADEMY

Two and a half miles north, on Dunlora plantation then owned by Mrs. Ann Hickman, the Virginia Baptist Education Society established, in 1830, a school for ministers. This school, under the principalship of Rev. Edward Baptist, M.A., was known locally as Dunlora Academy. Edward Baptist resigned in 1832, and the school was removed to Henrico County and then to Richmond. From it developed Richmond College and later, the University of Richmond. *Powhatan County: Route 60, 5.7 miles w. of Powhatan.*

O-25*   MONTVILLE ESTATE

This typical plantation house was built by a member of the Aylett family in 1803 on the site of an older house. *King William County: Route U.S. 360, 1 mile s.w. of Aylett.*

O-27*   BETHLEHEM BAPTIST CHURCH

Formerly Spring Creek Church. Organized, July 25, 1790. Benjamin Watkins, founder and first pastor, 1790–1831. Located four miles northwest, 1790–1855. Then four miles southwest, 1855–1897. Moved to this location, 1897. Home church of Nannie Bland David, Missionary to Africa, 1880–1885. Her dying words: "Never give up Africa." *Chesterfield County: Route 60, 5.4 miles w. of Richmond.*

O-28   HUGUENOT SETTLEMENT

In this vicinity Huguenots, refugees from the tyranny of Louis XIV, settled in 1700 under the leadership of the Marquis de la Muce. The region had been deserted by its former occupants, the Monacan Indians, and the Huguenot settlement centered at the site of their village, called "Manakin Town." Later parties of Huguenots settled on both sides of James River and elsewhere. *Chesterfield County: Route 60, 1.7 miles e. of Midlothian.*

O-29   SALISBURY

Two miles north stood Salisbury, built in the eighteenth century as a hunting lodge. There Patrick Henry lived during his fourth and fifth terms as Governor of Virginia, 1784–1786. The Confederate General Edward Johnson lived there in his later years and died there. *Chesterfield County: Route 60, at Midlothian.*

O-30   DERWENT

Ten miles north is "Derwent" where Robert E. Lee lived in the summer of 1865 as the guest of Mrs. E. R. Cocke. Lee arrived at "Derwent" early in July. While there he was offered the presidency of Washington College, Lexington, which he accepted on August 24, 1865. On September 15, he left "Derwent" for Lexington. *Powhatan County: Route 13, 2 miles e. of Tobaccoville.*

O-31   GILES'S HOME

Five miles southwest is the Wigwam, the home of William B. Giles, Jefferson's chief lieutenant; United States Senator, 1804–1815, and Governor of Virginia, 1827–1830, an orator and famous political leader. Giles died there, December 4, 1830. *Powhatan County: Route 60, 1.7 miles w. of Powhatan.*

O-32   POWHATAN COURTHOUSE

The first courthouse was built about 1777. The village that grew up around it was long known as Scottsville for General Charles Scott, Revolutionary soldier, who lived in this county. A skirmish occurred here, January 25, 1865. Nearby is a tavern of the Revolutionary period. *Powhatan County: Route 13, at Powhatan.*

O-34   BLACK HEATH

Half a mile north is Black Heath, originally owned by John Heth, Revolutionary soldier. Here Major-General Henry Heth of the Confederate army was born, 1825. The best coal in Virginia was long found in the Black Heath mine. *Chesterfield County: Route 60, 1.7 miles e. of Midlothian.*

O-35*   MIDLOTHIAN COAL MINES

A mile south are the Midlothian Coal Mines, probably the oldest coal mines in America. Coal was first mined here before 1730 and a railway was built from the mines to James River before 1830. Operations went on continuously until 1865, and the coal used in cannon casting at the Tredegar Iron Works, Richmond, was obtained here. *Chesterfield County: Route 60, at Midlothian.*

O-39   GEOGRAPHICAL CENTER OF VIRGINIA

About two miles south and one-half mile west is the geographical center of the state. Latitude: 37 degrees 30.6′ north, Longitude: 78 degrees 37.5′ west. *Buckingham County: Routes 60 and 24 at Mount Rush.*

O-40*   BELLONA ARSENAL

Five miles north are the ruins of Bellona Arsenal, established by the United States government in 1816. It was used as an arsenal and barracks until 1835. A foundry was also here and cannon were cast. In 1853 the arsenal was sold; in 1861 it was taken over by the Virginia government and served the Confederate cause. *Chesterfield County: Route 60, 5.7 miles w. of Richmond.*

O-41*   PISCATAWAY CHURCH

Five miles north is Mt. Zion Church, successor of Piscataway Church, organized in 1774, the mother Baptist church of the vicinity. In 1813 the congregation occupied a colonial Episcopal church, which was not far from the present Mt. Zion Church. *King and Queen County: Route 360, 1.6 miles s.w. of Millers Tavern.*

O-42   AFTER APPOMATTOX

Just to the south a monument marks the spot where the tent of Robert E. Lee stood the night of April 12–13, 1865. *Buckingham County: Route 60, 1.1 miles e. of Buckingham.*

O-44   CAMPAIGN OF 1781

Steuben, both on his retreat from Simcoe and on his return north to join Lafayette, passed near here, June, 1781. *Cumberland County: Route 60, 1.8 miles w. of Cumberland.*

O-45   SABINE HALL

A mile and a half southeast is Sabine Hall, built in 1730 for Landon Carter, son of Robert ("King") Carter, and one of the noted colonial homes. In 1861, the estate passed to Elizabeth Carter, wife of Dr. Armistead N. Welford. *Richmond County: Route 360, .3 mile west of Warsaw.*

O-46   WARSAW

When Richmond County was formed in 1692, this place became the county seat and was known as Richmond (County) Courthouse. The present courthouse building was erected in 1748–49. The village was renamed Warsaw about 1846 in sympathy with the Polish struggle for liberty. It was the home of Congressman William A. Jones, advocate of Philippine independence. *Richmond County: Route 360, at Warsaw.*

O-49   ST. STEPHEN'S PARISH

Formed in 1653 as Chickacone Parish and renamed Fairfield in 1664. The upper part was known locally as Bowtracy Parish. When St. Stephen's Parish was formed in 1698, Fairfield became its lower part and Bowtracy its upper part. *Northumberland County: Route 360, at Heathsville.*

OB-2   BRUINGTON CHURCH

This is Bruington Church, organized in 1790. Here Robert Semple, one of the most noted Baptist ministers in Virginia, long served and here he is buried. *King and Queen County: Route 14, 6.2 miles n.w. of Stevensville.*

OB-3   MATTAPONY CHURCH

This is the ancient colonial Mattapony Church, used by the Baptists since 1824. Here are tombs of members of the family of Carter Braxton, signer of the Declaration of Independence. *King and Queen County: Route 14, 4.1 miles n.w. of King and Queen Courthouse.*

OB-5   HILLSBORO

This house, four miles south, was built by Colonal Humphrey Hill about 1722. It is of quaint architecture having brick ends and frame front and rear. The place was raided by the British during the Revolution. *King and Queen County: Route 14, 4.7 miles n.w. of Stevensville.*

OB-6   WHERE DAHLGREN DIED

Colonel Ulric Dahlgren, Federal officer, met death in the early morning, March 2, 1864, three hundred yards to the north. After the raid on Richmond, his force bivouaced here and, in breaking camp he fell to the fire of Confederate detachments and Home Defense forces who had gathered during the night. *King and Queen County: Route 631, 2.5 miles n.w. of King and Queen Courthouse.*

OB-9 NEWTOWN

Newtown began as a pre-Revolutionary tavern crossroads on the intercolonial King's Highway. The settlement prospered in the antebellum period, becoming King and Queen's largest post village and supporting several fine academies and schools. In June 1863 Newtown witnessed the last tactical action of General George Pickett's Division before its long march to Gettysburg.

Erected 1981 *King and Queen County: Va. Routes 625 and 721.*

OB-10 NEWINGTON

A mile south on the Mattapony River is the site of Newington, birthplace of Carter Braxton (born September 10, 1736), signer of the Declaration of Independence. In earlier times, Colonel Jacob Lumpkin, supporter of Governor Berkeley in Bacon's Rebellion, 1676, lived there. *King and Queen County: Route 14, 1 mile n.w. of King and Queen Courthouse.*

OB-16 LANEVILLE

A mile and a half southwest stood Laneville, built by Richard Corbin, receiver general (treasurer), about 1760 on the site of an earlier house. There Patrick Henry sent, May, 1775, to obtain money in payment for the colony's powder seized by Lord Dunmore. Laneville was one of the largest and finest houses in Virginia. *King and Queen County: Route 14, 10 miles s.e. of King and Queen Courthouse.*

OB-18 COLONIAL CHURCH

This church, the new church of Stratton Major Parish, was built in 1767. Rev. William Robinson, the Bishop of London's commissary, came to the parish in 1744 and was the first minister of the new church. It fell into disuse after the Revolution but later became a Methodist church. *King and Queen County: Route 14, 8.5 miles s.e. of King and Queen Courthouse.*

OB-50 POROPOTANK CREEK

Land was patented on this creek as early as 1640. In 1653, John Lewis settled here. John Lewis, Jr., was living here in 1676 when Bacon's troops were encamped near by. He suffered from the depredations of the rebels. *King and Queen County: Route 14, 1.1 miles w. of Adner.*

OC-14 PAMUNKEY RESERVATION

Eight miles south is the reservation where live descendants of the ancient tribe of Pamunkey Indians. It has always been Indian property, all that remains of the domain of Powhatan, who at the time of the first settlement (1607) ruled over the tribes of eastern Virginia and Maryland. *King William County: Route 30, .6 mile s.e. of King William.*

OC-15 MATTAPONY RESERVATION

Two miles east is the Mattapony Indian Reservation. The Mattaponies were one of the tribes ruled by the great Chief, Powhatan. The reservation is governed by the chief and the council, which make the tribal laws. *King William County: Route 30, 4.9 miles s.e. of King William.*

OC-18 ST. JOHN'S CHURCH

This was the parish church of St. John's Parish, formed in 1680. It was built in 1734. Earlier churches stood at West Point and about one mile north of this site. Carter Braxton, Revolutionary Statesman, was a vestryman. Preserved by joint effort. *King William County: Route 30, 8.9 miles n.w. of West Point.*

OC-22* CAMPAIGN OF 1781

About one mile south Lafayette placed in camp his Light Infantry consisting of Muhlenberg's and Febiger's commands, August 13, 1781. The troops had just been brought across the Pamunkey at Ruffins's Ferry, from New Castle, to observe Cornwallis, then entrenching at Yorktown. Within six weeks the Yorktown Campaign, in which these troops took part, opened. *King William County: Route 30, 6.6 miles n.w. of West Point.*

OC-25 CAMPAIGN OF 1781

About a mile to the east, August 13, 1781, Lafayette, then commanding American forces in Virginia, placed in camp his militia, consisting of Campbell's, Stevens' and Lawson's brigades. Wayne was at Westover; Muhlenberg and Febiger were in camp on the Pamunkey four miles northwest. The campaign of Yorktown was about to open; these troops were later engaged there. *King William County: Route 30, 3.4 miles n.w. of West Point.*

OC-26 CHERIOCOKE (HOME OF SIGNER)

Carter Braxton, Signer of the Declaration of Independence, lived at West Point 1777–1786 after fire destroyed his plantation Chericoke, upriver on the Pamunkey. The Town House no longer stands. From West Point Braxton channeled war goods to Patriot Troops. *King William County: Route 33 at West Point.*

OC-35 ROSEGILL

A short distance east is Rosegill. The house was built about 1650 by the first Ralph Wormeley; it became the summer home of the colonial governors, Sir Henry Chicheley and Lord Howard of Effingham. In 1776, the owner, the fifth Ralph Wormeley, was put under restraint as a Tory. In 1781, Rosegill was plundered by British privateersmen. *Middlesex County: Route 227, .7 mile s. of Urbanna.*

OC-40* URBANNA CREEK

This creek, mentioned in an act of 1680 as "Wormeley's Creek," was earlier known as "Nimcock Creek." After Urbanna was named in 1705 for Queen Anne, the stream took the same time. British privateersmen entered the creek, June 5, 1781, and pillaged Urbanna and Rosegill. *Middlesex County: Route 227, at Urbanna.*

OH-10* LEE'S LAST CAMP

Here Robert E. Lee, returning from Appomattox, pitched his tent for the last time, April 14, 1865. He stopped here to visit his brother, Charles Carter Lee, who lived at nearby "Windsor." Fearing to incommode his brother, Lee camped by the roadside and the next day ended his journey at Richmond. *Powhatan County: Route 711, 9.5 miles n. of Powhatan.*

OL-10 LEE'S RETREAT

Near here Custer, commanding advance guard of the Army of the Potomac, struck and drove back Fitz Lee, left flank guard of Army of Northern Virginia, April 3, 1865. *Amelia County: Route 38, 7 miles e. of Mannboro.*

ON-5 CAMPAIGN OF 1781

At Carter's Ferry, near here, Steuben, marching northward to join Lafayette, crossed the James, June 16, 1781. *Cumberland County: Route 45, at Cartersville.*

ON-7 CAMPAIGN OF 1781

Two miles north, near the mouth of Willis River, Steuben camped, June 5–6, 1781, when driven from Point of Fork by Simcoe. *Cumberland County: Route 45, 1.8 miles s. of Cartersville.*

OQ-4* THOMAS MASSIE

One mile from here is "Level Green," the home of Major Thomas Massie (1747–1834). Commander of the Sixth Virginia Regiment of Infantry, later Aid to Governor Thomas Nelson at the siege of Yorktown, and one of first magistrates of Nelson County when it was formed in 1807. *Nelson County: Routes 56 and 666 at Massie's Mill.*

OQ-5 WILLIAM CABELL

Three miles southwest is Union Hill, home of William Cabell. He was born, March 30, 1730. Cabell was a burgess, signer of the Articles of Association, member of the Revolutionary conventions and of the ratifying convention of 1788. He died, March 23, 1798. *Nelson County: Route 56, at Wingina.*

PA-2 SEVENS DAYS' BATTLES— MECHANICSVILLE

Mechanicsville was held by Union outposts when, in the early afternoon of June 26, 1862, A. P. Hill reached it coming from the north. The Unionists were quickly driven back to their position on Beaver Dam Creek. Then D. H. Hill, followed by Longstreet, crossed the Chickahominy on this road and joined A. P. Hill. *Hanover County: Route 360, at Mechanicsville.*

PA-4 SEVEN DAYS' BATTLES—
MECHANICSVILLE

Down this slope in the late afternoon of June 26, 1862, A. P. Hill moved to attack the Unionists holding the east side of Beaver Dam Creek. Pender's brigade was on the left, Ripley's on the right. Exposed to a terrible fire from entrenched troops, Pender and Ripley were driven back, though some men reached the stream. *Hanover County: Route 156, .8 mile s. of Mechanicsville.*

PA-6 SEVEN DAYS' BATTLES—
MECHANICSVILLE

This ridge was occupied by Porter's Corps (facing west), which formed the right wing of McClellan's army, June 26, 1862. The strong position was strengthened by earthworks and by an abatis along the creek. When A. P. Hill attacked late in the afternoon, the Confederates were driven back with severe loss. *Hanover County: Route 156, 1.2 miles s. of Mechanicsville.*

PA-8 SEVEN DAYS' BATTLES—
PORTER'S WITHDRAWAL

Along this road Fitz-John Porter withdrew from Beaver Dam Creek in the early morning of June 27, 1862. McClellan, having learned that Stonewall Jackson was approaching Porter's rear, late at night ordered the withdrawal to another position. This was on Boatswain Creek, not far from New Cold Harbor. *Hanover County: Route 156, 1.7 miles s. of Mechanicsville.*

PA-9* SEVEN DAYS' BATTLES—
GAINES'S MILL

Stonewall Jackson, coming from the Shenandoah Valley to join Lee, crossed the road here in the morning of June 27, 1862. He met Lee at Walnut Grove Church not far to the south. That afternoon Jackson joined in the attack that carried the position held by Porter of McClellan's army on Boatswain Creek. *Hanover County: Route 360, 1.8 miles n.e. of Mechanicsville.*

PA-10 SEVEN DAYS' BATTLES—
GAINES'S MILL

Here Lee and Stonewall Jackson conferred in the morning of June 27, 1862. Jackson's troops halted here until A. P. Hill arrived from Beaver Dam Creek. Hill then moved southward by Gaines's Mill and Longstreet along a road near the river; Jackson turned to the east. All three columns approached the Union position on Boatswain Creek. *Hanover County: Route 156, 2.7 miles s. of Mechanicsville.*

PA-12* SEVEN DAYS' BATTLES—NEW BRIDGE

The road to the south is the New Bridge road leading to Old Tavern (Highland Springs). In the 1862 campaign bridge and road played an important part in the movements of both armies. The Unionists moved from New Bridge to Mechanicsville on May 24, 1862. Longstreet and A. P. Hill crossed the bridge on June 29 going to the battle of Glendale. *Hanover County: Route 156, 4.3 miles s. of Mechanicsville.*

PA-16 SEVEN DAYS' BATTLES—
GAINES'S MILL

This is the site of Gaines's Mill, which gave its name to the battle of June 27, 1862. Here A. P. Hill's advance guard, following Porter, came in contact with the Union rear guard. After a short action the Unionists withdrew to a position on Boatswain Creek, closely pursued by the Confederates. *Hanover County: Route 156, 5 miles s. of Mechanicsville.*

PA-20* SEVEN DAYS' BATTLES—
GAINES'S MILL

Half a mile south is Boatswain Creek. The battle that was begun at Gaines's Mill by A. P. Hill, following Porter's rear guard, culminated at the Union position on Boatswain Creek. There A. P. Hill and Longstreet, moving eastward, and Jackson coming from the north converged to attack Unionists. *Hanover County: Route 156, 5.7 miles s. of Mechanicsville.*

PA-23* SEVEN DAYS' BATTLES—
GAINES'S MILL

A. P. Hill, in the afternoon of June 27, 1862, moved down this slope, crossed the creek and repeatedly charged the hill to the east, only to be driven back. Lee sent in Longstreet on Hill's right; but the position was not taken until Jackson, on the north, joined in the attack. *Hanover County: Route 156, 6.3 miles s. of Mechanicsville.*

PA-25 SEVEN DAYS' BATTLES—
GAINES'S MILL

Along the slopes of Boatswain Creek, facing north and west, extended Porter's position in the afternoon of June 27, 1862. The line was held by Sykes's division facing north, and Morell's facing west. Later McCall was thrown in to assist Morell. At dark Lee broke the Union line, and Porter retreated across the Chickahominy. *Hanover County: Route 718, 6.5 miles s. of Mechanicsville.*

PA-60 SEVEN DAYS' BATTLES—
GAINES'S MILL

Stonewall Jackson reached this point in the afternoon of June 27, 1862, after a circuit of Gaines's Mill. When he learned that A. P. Hill and Longstreet to the west were hard pressed, he moved south to join in the attack. *Hanover County: Route 156, 7.8 miles s. of Mechanicsville.*

PA-70 SEVEN DAYS' BATTLES—
GAINES'S MILL

The hill to the south, part of the Union line, was assailed by Stonewall Jackson (with D. H. Hill) in the late afternoon of June 27, 1862, after A. P. Hill's and Longstreet's first assaults on the west had failed. Jackson's men carried the Union position at the bayonet's point, while A. P. Hill and Longstreet were also successful. *Hanover County: Route 156, 8.2 miles s. of Mechanicsville.*

PA-80   SEVEN DAYS' BATTLES—
GAINES'S MILL

On this hill, facing north, Sykes's division was posted in the afternoon of June 27, 1862, holding the eastern end of the Union line. Here Jackson attacked, while to the west A. P. Hill and Longstreet renewed their assaults. When the Union line was broken on their left, Sykes's regulars fell back to the river still fighting. *Hanover County: Route 156, 8.5 miles s. of Mechanicsville.*

PA-105   SEVEN DAYS' BATTLES—GRAPE VINE BRIDGE

Here Sumner crossed the river to reinforce the part of McClellan's army fighting at Fair Oaks, May 31, 1862. Here a part of Porter's force crossed in the night of June 27, 1862, after the battle of Gaines's Mill. Here Stonewall Jackson, rebuilding the bridges destroyed by the retreating Unionists, crossed in pursuit, June 29. *Hanover County: Route 156, 11.1 miles s. of Mechanicsville.*

PA-125   SEVEN DAYS' BATTLES—
GOLDING'S FARM

Half a mile northwest occurred the action of Golding's Farm at dusk on June 27, 1862, as the battle of Gaines's Mill, on the other side of the river, was ending. The Confederates, sallying from their defenses, attacked Hancock's brigade holding the right of the Union line south of the river. A severe fight followed that was ended by darkness. *Henrico County: Route 156, 12.8 miles s. of Mechanicsville.*

PA-140   SEVEN DAYS' BATTLES—
ALLEN'S FARM

Half a mile north took place the action of Allen's Farm, or Peach Orchard, in the morning of June 29, 1862. There Sumner's Corps, forming the Union rear, was attacked by Magruder at 9 A.M. Fighting lasted until 11 A.M. when the Unionists fell back to Savage's Station on the York River Railroad. *Henrico County: Route 156, at Seven Pines.*

PA-142   SEVEN DAYS' BATTLE—
SAVAGE'S STATION

Here Magruder's line of battle, facing east, formed in the late afternoon of June 29, 1862. Barksdale's, Semmes's and Kershaw's brigades, extending from south of this road to the railroad, made a desperate effort to prevent the Union withdrawal. After a fierce struggle the Confederates fell back. In this battle they made the first known use of railway artillery. *Henrico County: Route 60, 3.6 miles e. of Seven Pines.*

PA-144   SEVEN DAYS' BATTLES—
SAVAGE'S STATION

Here, facing west, stretched the Union line in the afternoon of June 29, 1862. Brook's brigade was south of the road with Gorman's and Burns's brigades to the north. In a furious conflict Burns's line was broken but was restored by Sumner in person. Darkness ended the conflict. The Unionists withdrew   southward. *Henrico County: Route 60, 3.6 miles e. of Seven Pines.*

PA-148   SEVEN DAYS' BATTLES—WHITE OAK SWAMP

In the hill just to the west Stonewall Jackson placed his artillery about midday on June 30, 1862. An artillery duel then began with Franklin, guarding the south side of White Oak Swamp, that lasted until dark. *Henrico County: Route 156, 6.7 miles s.e. of Seven Pines.*

PA-152   SEVEN DAYS' BATTLES—WHITE OAK SWAMP

Here the greater part of McClellan's army and wagon trains crossed the swamp, June 28–30, 1862. Jackson, pursuing, arrived about noon on June 30, to find the bridge destroyed and the Unionists holding the south side. Failing to force a passage that day, Jackson rebuilt the bridge and crossed early on July 1. *Henrico County: Route 156, 7.1. miles s. of Seven Pines.*

PA-159*   SEVEN DAYS' BATTLES—GLENDALE (FRAYSER'S FARM)

Across the road here, June 30, 1862, extended the Union line of battle, facing west. Slocum's and Kearny's divisions were north of the road, McCall's and Hooker's south of it. The battle opened with an attack on Seymour's brigade of McCall's division and raged furiously until after nightfall. In the night the Unionists withdrew to Malvern Hill. *Henrico County: Route 156, on Darbytown Road, 10.2 miles s. of Seven Pines.*

PA-163   SEVEN DAYS' BATTLES—GLENDALE (FRAYSER'S FARM)

Here stood the center of Longstreet's line of battle in the afternoon of June 30, 1862. The Confederates, coming from the west, attacked the Union line just beyond. The battle lasted all afternoon, with varying fortunes and much hand-to-hand fighting. Near nightfall Longstreet sent in A. P. Hill to relieve his exhausted men. *Henrico County: Route 156, on Darbytown Road, 10.5 miles s. of Seven Pines.*

PA-175   SEVEN DAYS' BATTLES—GLENDALE (FRAYSER'S FARM)

The possession of this, the Quaker road, on June 30, 1862, saved McClellan's army from destruction. The Confederates, coming from the west, sought to seize the road and block the Union withdrawal to James River. While Longstreet was fighting a rearguard battle at Glendale, the Union wagon trains and artillery passed along this road and another road two miles east. *Henrico County: Route 156, 10 miles s. of Seven Pines.*

PA-180   SEVEN DAYS' BATTLES—MALVERN HILL

Here Lee met Longstreet and Jackson in the morning of July 1, 1862. D. H. Hill reported the strength of the Union position on Malvern Hill; but Lee, having cause to believe the Unionists were weakening, prepared to attack. Jackson and D. H. Hill moved on this road southward to Malvern Hill. *Henrico County: Route 156, 10.6 miles s. of Seven Pines.*

PA-190 SEVEN DAYS' BATTLES—
GLENDALE (FRAYSER'S FARM)

This was the extreme left of the Union line at Glendale, and was held by Hooker's division. When McCall (just to the north) was broken, Hooker, supported by Burns's brigade, drove the Confederates back. In the night the Union army moved southward. *Henrico County: Route 156, 11.1 miles s. of Seven Pines.*

PA-195 SEVEN DAYS' BATTLE—
MALVERN HILL

Across the road here stretched the Confederate line of battle, facing south, in the afternoon of July 1, 1862. Jackson commanded here, Magruder to the west. Longstreet and A. P. Hill were in reserve. The battle lasted intermittently from morning to night, reaching its crisis late in the afternoon. The disjointed Confederate attacks were repulsed with heavy loss. *Henrico County: Route 156, 12.3 miles s. of Seven Pines.*

PA-220 SEVEN DAYS' BATTLES—
MALVERN HILL

Here from east to west, Berdan's sharpshooters of Morell's division were strung out in the afternoon of July 1, 1862. Their rapid and accurate fire harassed the Confederates as they emerged from the woods and charged up the hill. *Henrico County: Route 156, 12.5 miles s. of Seven Pines.*

PA-230 SEVEN DAYS' BATTLES—
MALVERN HILL

Across the hill here from east to west the Union artillery was in position in the afternoon of July 1, 1862. The Union batteries overpowered the few cannon the Confederates were able to bring up. When the Southern infantry charged from the woods, they were met by a terrible artillery fire but continued to advance until they came under the fire of the Union infantry. *Henrico County: Route 156, 12.6 miles s. of Seven Pines.*

PA-235 SEVEN DAYS' BATTLES—
MALVERN HILL

Across the road here stretched the Union line of battle in the afternoon of July 1, 1862. Couch's, Kearney's and Hooker's divisions were to the east of the road, Morell to the west, with Sykes in reserve. The Confederates made several attacks and, for a time, the battle trembled in the balance; but the assailants were finally repulsed. In the night the Union army withdrew to James River. *Henrico County: Route 156, 12.7 miles s. of Seven Pines.*

PA-240* SEVEN DAYS' BATTLES—
MALVERN HILL

The troops of T.H.H. Holmes reached this point on June 30, 1862. It was Holmes' part in Lee's plan to take Malvern Hill; but the fire of the Union artillery there and the Gunboats in the river held him here, inactive. He remained here the next day, July 1, while the battle of Malvern Hill was being fought. *Henrico County: Route 156, 13.8 miles s. of Seven Pines.*

PA-250   BENJAMIN HARRISON BRIDGE

Benjamin Harrison (1726–1791), a signer of the Declaration of Independence, was born at Berkeley (2 miles east). He served in the Virginia General Assembly, The Continental Congress, as Governor, and in the Virginia Convention which ratified the U.S. Constitution. *Charles City County: Route 156, at bridge.*

PB-4   STATE FISH HATCHERY

Half a mile north. This fish cultural station was established in 1937 for hatching and rearing largemouth bass and other species of sunfish for the stocking of the public waters of Virginia. *King and Queen County: Route 14, 1 mile n.w. of Stevensville.*

PH-6   ACTION OF NANCE'S SHOP

In this vicinity the Union cavalryman, Gregg, guarding army trains moving to Petersburg, was attacked by Wade Hampton, June 24, 1864. Gregg was driven back toward Charles City Courthouse, but the wagon trains crossed the James safely. This action closed the cavalry campaign that began at Trevillians, June 11–12, 1864. *Charles City County: Route 603, 13.4 miles s.e. of Seven Pines.*

Q-1-1   TARLETON'S OAK

Tradition says that under this oak the British cavalryman, Banastre Tarleton, pitched his tent on his raid to Charlottesville, June 4, 1781. He attempted to capture Governor Jefferson and the legislature, but Captain Jack Jouett, by taking a shorter route, arrived in time to warn the patriots of their danger. *Charlottesville: Intersection High Street and Lexington Avenue.*

Q-1-a-b-d   CHARLOTTESVILLE

The site was patented by William Taylor in 1737. The town was established by a law in 1762, and was named for Queen Charlotte, wife of George III. Burgoyne's army, captured at Saratoga in 1777, was long quartered near here. The legislature was in session here, in June, 1781, but retired westward to escape Tarleton's raid on the town. Jefferson, who lived at Monticello, founded the University of Virginia in 1819. *Charlottesville: a. High Street near Hazel Street intersection. b. Monticello Road at Henderson and Ervin factory. d. Route 29 near Piedmont Avenue intersection.*

Q-2-a-b   WAYNESBORO

Here, on one of the first roads west of the Blue Ridge, a hamlet stood in colonial times. The Walker exploring expedition started from this vicinity in 1748. Here, in June, 1781, the Augusta militia assembled to join Lafayette in the East. A town was founded in 1797. It was established by law in 1801 and named for General Anthony Wayne. *Waynesboro: a. Route 250 at e. entrance of Waynesboro. b. Route 250 at w. entrance of Waynesboro.*

Q-3-a-b-c-d* BERRYVILLE

The town was laid out in 1798 on land of Benjamin Berry and was first known as Battletown. Here at "Audley" lived Nellie Custis, Washington's adopted daughter. Here at "Soldier's Rest" lived General Daniel Morgan, who built "Saratoga." Here Lee's army camped on the way to Gettysburg. Near here many engagements occurred, 1862–64. *Clarke County: a and c. Route 7, at e. and w. entrance of Berryville. b. Route 340, at n. entrance of Berryville. d. Route 12, at s. entrance of Berryville.*

Q-4-a GENERAL DANIEL MORGAN

Morgan used this road in traveling from his home, "Saratoga," to Winchester. He was a frontiersman, Indian fighter and the commander of Morgan's famous riflemen in the Revolution. He won glory at Quebec and Saratoga, and defeated Tarleton at the Cowpens. He died in 1802 and is buried in Winchester. *Winchester: Route 50, at e. limits of Winchester.*

Q-4-a WINCHESTER (back of marker)

At first called Fredericktown, it was founded in 1744, near a Shawnee Indian village, by Colonel James Wood, a native of the English city of Winchester. The town was situated in Lord Fairfax's proprietary of the Northern Neck. It was chartered in 1752. *Winchester: Route 50, at e. limits of Winchester.*

Q-4-b* JOIST HITE AND BRADDOCK

By this road, then an Indian trail, Joist Hite and his followers came to make the first permanent settlement in this section, 1732. In 1755, General Edward Braddock of the British army, accompanied by George Washington, passed here on his way to defeat and death at Fort Duquesne. *Winchester: Route 7, at e. limits.*

Q-4-b* WINCHESTER (back of marker)

At first called Fredericktown, it was founded in 1744, near a Shawnee Indian village, by Colonel James Wood, a native of the English city of Winchester. The town was situated in Lord Fairfax's proprietary of the Northern Neck. It was chartered in 1752. *Winchester: Route 7, at e. limits.*

Q-4-c GEORGE WASHINGTON

George Washington began his career here in 1748 as surveyor to Lord Fairfax. Here he had his headquarters as commander on the Virginia frontier against the French and Indians, 1755–1758. Here he built Fort Loudoun, and he was a member of the House of Burgesses for this county, 1758–1761. *Winchester: Route 11, at n. limits.*

Q-4-c* WINCHESTER (back of marker)

At first called Fredericktown, it was founded in 1744, near a Shawnee Indian village, by Colonel James Wood, a native of the English city of Winchester. The town was situated in Lord Fairfax's proprietary of the Northern Neck. It was chartered in 1752. *Winchester: Route 11, at n. limits.*

Q-4-d* LORD FAIRFAX

By this road Thomas Lord Fairfax, proprietor of the Northern Neck of Virginia, was accustomed to pass from his home, "Greenway Court" to preside over the sessions of the justices' court at Winchester, 1749–1769. His tomb is in the crypt of Christ Church, Winchester. *Frederick County: Route 522 at n. limits of Winchester.*

Q-4-d* WINCHESTER (back of marker)

At first called Fredericktown, it was founded in 1744, near a Shawnee Indian village, by Colonel James Wood, a native of the English city of Winchester. The town was situated in Lord Fairfax's proprietary of the Northern Neck. It was chartered in 1752. *Frederick County: Route 522 at n. limits of Winchester.*

Q-4-e COLONEL JAMES WOOD

James Wood, founder of Winchester, named for his native city in England, was the first clerk of Frederick County Court, which was organized in 1743 at the house on his estate, "Glen Burnie," His son, General James Wood, was Governor of Virginia, 1796–1799. *Frederick County: Route 50, just w. of Route 11.*

Q-4-e WINCHESTER (back of marker)

At first called Fredericktown, it was founded in 1744, near a Shawnee Indian village, by Colonel James Wood, a native of the English city of Winchester. The town was situated in Lord Fairfax's proprietary of the Northern Neck. It was chartered in 1752. *Frederick County: Route 50, just w. of Route 11.*

Q-4-F JACKSON'S HEADQUARTERS

This house was used by Major General Thomas J. Jackson, then commanding the valley district, department of Northern Virginia, as his official headquarters from November 1861, to March, 1862 when he left Winchester to begin his famous valley campaign. *Winchester: 415 North Braddock Street.*

Q-5 FORT DINWIDDIE

Known as Byrd's Fort and Warwick's Fort. Probably built in 1755, it was visited in that year by George Washington. *Bath County: Route 39, 5 miles w. of Warm Springs.*

Q-5-a LAST CONFEDERATE CAPITOL

This, the former home of Major W. T. Sutherlin, is regarded as the last capitol of the Confederacy, April 3–10, 1865. Here President Davis stayed and here was held the last full cabinet meeting, Breckinridge alone being absent. The establishment of the Confederate government in Danville ended when the news of Lee's surrender arrived on April 10. *Danville: at Sutherlin Avenue and Main Street.*

Q-5-b WRECK OF THE OLD 97

Here, on September 27, 1903, occurred the railroad wreck that inspired the popular ballad, "The Wreck of the Old 97." The southbound mail express train on the Southern Railroad left the tracks on a trestle and plunged into the ravine below. Nine persons were killed and seven injured, one of the worst train wrecks in Virginia history. *Danville: between Pickett and Farrar streets.*

Q-5-C LADY ASTOR

Here stood the residence in which Nancy Langhorne, Viscountess Astor, 1879–1964, was born. Lady Astor, noted for her wit, advocacy of Women's Rights, strong views on temperance, and articulate affection for her native state, was the first woman to sit, 1919–1945, in the British House of Commons. *Danville: corner of Main and Broad streets.*

Q-5-C THE GIBSON GIRL

Here stood the residence in which Irene Langhorne Gibson, 1873–1956 was born. Her beauty, charm, and vivacity captivated the artist Charles Dana Gibson who, following their marriage in 1895, cast his celebrated, style-setting "Gibson Girl" illustrations in her image. *Danville: Main and Broad streets.*

Q-5-C LOYAL BAPTIST CHURCH

In 1870 the Loyal Street Baptist Church, organized between 1865–66 by a group of former slaves on "Old Hospital-Dance Hill," was built. Worship continued here until 1924 when the church moved to Holbrook Street. The name was then changed to Loyal Baptist Church. *Danville: 400 Block of Loyal Street.*

Q-5-D DANVILLE SYSTEM

On this site stood Neal's Warehouse where the "Danville System" of selling tobacco began in 1858. Previously tobacco had been sold by sample from hogsheads, but under the new system it was sold at auction in open, loose piles so buyers could examine the whole lot. It is in general use today. *Danville: 126 N. Union Street.*

Q-5-E STRATFORD COLLEGE

Stratford College (1930–1974) and its constituent preparatory school, Stratford Hall (1930–1954), maintained the tradition of liberal arts education for women begun in 1854 at the Danville Female College. Main hall was built in 1883 to house the Danville College for Young Ladies (1883–1897) and is a landmark also of its successors Randolph-Macon Institute (1897–1930) and Stratford. *Danville: 1125 W. Main Street.*

Q-5-f CALVARY UNITED METHODIST CHURCH

An outgrowth of the mother church on Lynn Street in Danville, the North Danville Methodist Episcopal Church, South, was founded by 47 devoted members at the corner of Church and Keen streets on November 14, 1879. This was the first organized religious group in North Danville. On November 14, 1887, a new sanctuary on this site was dedicated and known as Calvary Methodist Episcopal Church, South. In 1968 the name was changed to Calvary United Methodist Church. *Danville: 924 N. Main Street.*

Q-6-1 FORT EARLY

The redoubt is part of the outer Lynchburg defenses, June, 1864. General Early arrived with the Second Corps of Lee's army in the afternoon of June 17. The redoubt (erected by Early) was occupied by part of Ramseur's and Gordon's divisions. The Union General Hunter attacked in the afternoon of June 18. Repulsed, he began to retreat in the night of June 18–19, followed by Early. *Lynchburg: Fort Avenue, near Early Monument.*

Q-6-2 FORT McCAUSLAND

The fort on the hill here was constructed by General J. A. Early to protect the approach to Lynchburg from the west. Union cavalry skirmished with the Confederates along the road immediately west of the fort. The Unionists, driven back by General McCausland, were unable to enter the city from this direction. *Lynchburg: Langhorne Road, about 1200 feet w. of Clifton Street.*

Q-6-3 INNER DEFENSES, 1864

Here ran the inner line of Lynchburg defenses thrown up by General D. H. Hill in June, 1864. General John C. Breckinridge, confronting General Hunter in the Shenandoah Valley, made a forced march to forestall Hunter. Hill constructed a shallow line of trenches, occupied by Breckinridge, and hospital convalescents and home guards. It became a reserve line when General Early arrived. *Lynchburg: on Twelfth Street, between Fillmore and Floyd streets.*

Q-6-4 INNER DEFENSES

A line of shallow entrenchments extended across Bedford Avenue near this spot, making connection with other trenches crossing the present Southern Railroad. These works protected Lynchburg from entrance by the Lexington Turnpike (now the Hollins Mill road). They were occupied by General Breckinridge's troops. *Lynchburg: corner of Bedford Avenue and Holly Street.*

Q-6-5 DEFENSE WORKS

On the crest of the hill just to the south was a redoubt forming part of the defenses thrown up by General D. H. Hill, June, 1864. These works were held by General Imboden's cavalry. A military road was constructed to conduct this point with Fort McCausland. Signs of this road may still be seen in old Rivermont Park. *Lynchburg: corner of Rivermont Avenue and Langhorne Road.*

Q-6-6 MUSTERED AND DISBANDED, 1861–1865

At this point the Second Virginia Cavalry was mustered into service, May 10, 1861. At the same place the remnant of this regiment was disbanded, April 10, 1865, completing a service of four years lacking one month. The regiment participated in many campaigns and engagements. *Lynchburg: between Rivermont Avenue and Monsview Drive.*

Q-6-7 INNER DEFENSES, 1864

A line of shallow entrenchments extended from near this point along the crest of the hill to the east. These works were occupied by the cadets of the Virginia Military Institute, who had marched here with General Breckinridge after the Institute at Lexington was burned by General Hunter. *Lynchburg: corner of Ninth and Polk streets.*

Q-6-8 INNER DEFENSES

Here, facing west, ran the inner defenses of the city, located by General D. H. Hill. They were constructed by convalescents and home guards. General Early, after an inspection of the system, moved most of the men to the outer works well to the westward. *Lynchburg: between Ninth and Polk streets.*

Q-6-9* INNER DEFENSES

Near here ran the line of inner defenses located by General D. H. Hill, June, 1864. He had been sent from Petersburg by General Beauregard to assist General Breckinridge, then in command. On General Early's arrival troops were moved to the outer works. *Lynchburg: between Wise and Floyd streets.*

Q-6-10 MILLER-CLAYTOR HOUSE

This building formerly stood at Eighth and Church streets. It now stands one block north. It was built by John Miller about 1791. Thoma Wiatt bought the house, long known as the "Mansion House." Samuel Claytor purchased it in 1825. For many years doctors' officers were here. For ninety years the house was owned by the Page family. The Lynchburg Historical Society moved and restored it. *Lynchburg: Rivermont Avenue and Treasure Island Road.*

Q-6-11 LYNCHBURG

In 1757 John Lynch opened a ferry here; in 1765 a church was built. In 1786 Lynchburg was established by act of assembly; in 1791 the first tobacco warehouse was built. Lynchburg was incorporated as a town in 1805. In 1840 the James River and Kanawha Canal, from Richmond to Lynchburg, was opened; the section of Buchanan, in 1851. Lynchburg became a city in 1852. *Lynchburg: Ninth and Church streets.*

Q-6-11 LYNCHBURG (back of marker)

Trains began running on the first railroad, the Virginia and Tennessee, in 1852. Lynchburg was a main military supply center, 1862–65. Here the Confederates under General Early defeated the Union General Hunter, June 18, 1864. In 1893 Randolph-Macon Woman's College opened; in 1903, Lynchburg College. In 1920 the council manager form of government was adopted. *Lynchburg: Ninth and Church streets.*

Q-6-12 CARTER GLASS

Born January 4, 1858, in a house which stood on this site. Newspaper publisher; member of the State Senate and Delegate to the State Constitutional Convention of 1901–1902; member of the United States House of Representatives, 1902–1918, and principal author of the Federal Reserve Act; Secretary of the Treasury, 1918–1920; member of the United States Senate from 1920 until his death in 1946. *Lynchburg: 829 Church Street.*

Q-6-13 LYNCHBURG COLLEGE

Situated on the hill to the southeast, this institution was established in 1903 by Dr. Josephus Hopwood and eight associates to promote Christian Higher Education. It was originally chartered as Virginia Christian College. The name was changed to Lynchburg College in 1919. This College is an educational institution of the churches of the Disciples of Christ. *Lynchburg: Lakeside Drive (Route 221), w. of Old Forest Road*

Q-6-14 RANDOLPH-MACON WOMAN'S COLLEGE

Founded by Dr. William Waugh Smith in 1891 and opened in 1893 as a member of the Randolph-Macon System of Educational Institutions, this Liberal Arts College has been recognized from its opening year for its high standards of scholarship. The scenic campus of 100 acres extends to the James River. *Lynchburg: Corner of Rivermont Avenue and Princeton Circle.*

Q-6-15 VIRGINIA SEMINARY AND COLLEGE

This college, one block to the southwest, was organized by the Virginia Baptist State Convention, May 1886, as a Negro College of "Self-Help" and "Spiritual Independence." The Charter was granted by an act of the Legislature, February 1888. It was opened January 1890 with 33 students. The College is the outgrowth of Gregory Willis Hayes' "Do-For-Thy-Self" philosophy. *Lynchburg: Campbell Avenue and DeWitt Street.*

Q-6-16* ALLEN WEIR FREEMAN, M.D. 1881–1954

Born at 416 Main Street, he was a pioneer in public health administration and education. He served as First Assistant Commissioner of Health, Virginia; Epidemiologist, United States Public Health Service; Health Commissioner, Ohio; Professor and Dean, School of Hygiene and Public Health, Johns Hopkins University; and Consultant to Foreign Governments in Developing Health Programs. *Lynchburg: in front of 416 Main Street.*

Q-6-17 DOUGLAS SOUTHALL FREEMAN, Ph.D. (1886–1953)

Born at 416 Main Street, he moved to Richmond at an early age and became a distinguished editor and historian. Editor of the Richmond News Leader, 1915–1959; Rector and President of The Board of Trustees, University of Richmond, 1934–1949; Professor of Journalism, Columbia University, 1935–1941; and Author of Pulitzer Prize biographies of both Robert E. Lee and George Washington, as well as other standard historical works. *Lynchburg: s. end of Rivermont Bridge.*

Q-6–18   SAMUEL D. ROCKENBACH (1869–1952) BRIGADIER GENERAL, U.S. ARMY CAVALRY

Nearby at 805 Madison St. is the birthplace of General Rockenbach, "Father of the U.S. Army Tank Corps." He began his education in Lynchburg schools and was a honor graduate of Virginia Military Institute in 1889. As first chief of the Army's tank corps in 1917, he pioneered training schools and field organization for tank warfare in World War I. *Lynchburg: Corner of Eighth and Court streets.*

Q-6-20   THE ANNE SPENCER HOUSE

This was the home of Edward Alexander and Anne Bannister Spencer from 1903 until her death on July 25, 1975. Born on February 6, 1882, in Henry County, Virginia, Anne Spencer was to receive national and international recognition as a poet. Published extensively between 1920 and 1935, she belonged to the Harlem Renaissance school of writers. *Lynchburg: 1313 Pierce Street.*

Q-7-a   TANGIER ISLAND

The island was visited in 1608 by Captain John Smith, who gave it the name. A part was patented by Ambrose White in 1670. It was settled in 1686 by John Crockett and his sons' families. In 1814, it was the headquarters of a British fleet ravaging Chesapeake Bay. From here the fleet sailed to attack Fort McHenry near Baltimore. The Rev. Joshua Thomas, in a prayer, predicted the failure of the expedition. It was in this attack that the Star-Spangled Banner was written. *Accomack County: on Tangier Island.*

Q-7-e   750 MAIN STREET—DANVILLE

On this site stood the residence of James E. Schoolfield. In the parlor of his house were held the meetings to organize both Dan River, Inc. on July 20, 1882 and the Young Women's Christian Association of Danville on December 19, 1904. *Danville: 750 Main Street.*

Q-8-a   TRINITY CHURCH

Built in 1762 as the parish church of Portsmouth parish, established in 1761. Later named Trinity; enlarged in 1829; remodeled in 1893. Colonel William Crawford, founder of Portsmouth in 1752, was a member of the first vestry. Buried here is Commodore James Barron, commander of the U.S. frigate Chesapeake when attacked by H.M.S. Leopard in 1807; the result was his celebrated duel with Stephen Decatur in 1820. The graves of many Revolutionary patriots are here. *Portsmouth: corner of High and Court streets.*

Q-8-b   MONUMENTAL METHODIST CHURCH

This church, founded 1772, is one of the oldest Methodist churches in Virginia. The first building was erected, 1775, at South and Effingham streets. The church was moved to Glasgow Street near Court in 1792. It established the first Sunday School in Portsmouth in 1818. Monumental was moved to this site, Dinwiddie Street, in 1831. *Portsmouth: Dinwiddie Street near High Street.*

Q-8-c   WATTS HOUSE

Built by Colonel Dempsey Watts in 1799 and inherited by his son, Captain Samuel Watts, who lived here until his death in 1878. Here Chief Black Hawk, of the Black Hawk Indian War, was entertained in 1820, and Henry Clay in 1844. *Portsmouth: at 517 North Street.*

Q-8-d   BALL HOUSE

Built about 1784 by John Nivison at the corner of Crawford and Glasgow streets and moved to this site in 1869. It served as a barracks in the War of 1812. Lafayette was entertained here in 1824 and President Andrew Jackson in 1833. The Ball family acquired the property in 1870. *Portsmouth: at 213 Middle Street.*

Q-8-e   BENEDICT ARNOLD AT PORTSMOUTH

Arnold, after going over to the British, was sent to Virginia to make war on the state. He reached Hampton Roads in December, 1780, raided to Richmond and came to Portsmouth, January 19, 1781. Establishing his headquarters in Patrick Robinson's house, and using the old sugar house on Crawford Street as a prison and barracks, Arnold remained here until spring. Then again he went up the James to open the fateful campaign of 1781 that won the war for America. *Portsmouth: Bayview and Maryland avenues.*

Q-8-f   CORNWALLIS AT PORTSMOUTH

Lord Cornwallis, commanding the British troops in the South, reached Portsmouth, July, 1781. He prepared to send a portion of his force to New York. Before the movement was made, orders came for him to take up a position at Old Point. Cornwallis selected Yorktown, however, and Portsmouth was abandoned. *Portsmouth: Crawford Parkway e. of Court Street.*

Q-8-g*   COLLIER'S RAID

A British fleet under Sir George Collier sailed up Elizabeth River and captured Fort Nelson, May, 1779. British troops commanded by General Matthews took possession of Portsmouth and destroyed quanities of tobacco and naval stores. Suffolk was burned. The troops then returned by sea to New York. *Portsmouth: Bayview and Maryland avenues.*

Q-8-h   PORTSMOUTH NAVAL HOSPITAL

This was begun in 1827 and opened in 1830. The hospital was taxed to its capacity in the great yellow fever epidemic of 1855 which decimated Portsmouth and Norfolk. This hospital has cared for the sick and wounded of the Navy in all wars of the United States since its establishment. It is the oldest hospital of the Navy. *Portsmouth: On hospital grounds.*

Q-8-k ELIZABETH RIVER

The Elizabeth River, explored by Captain John Smith in 1608, was named for Princess Elizabeth. Shipbuilding activity began in 1620 when John Wood, a shipbuilder, requested a land grant. Many historic ships were built at the naval shipyard here, including the USS Delaware, first ship dry-docked in America, and CCS Virginia, (Ex-Merrimac), first ironclad to engage in battle. *Portsmouth: Crawford Parkway at Court Street.*

Q-8-L CITY OF PORTSMOUTH

The site of this city was patented in 1659 by Captain William Carver. Established as a town in 1752 and named by its founder, Lt. Col. William Crawford. Chartered as a city in 1858, it has the country's oldest naval shipyard, established in 1767, the nation's oldest naval hospital, commenced in 1827, and is the birthplace of the world's largest naval installation. *Portsmouth: Route 17 at Churchland Bridge.*

Q-8-m CRAWFORD HOUSE

Erected 1835 by J. W. Collins, Portsmouth's first five-story building and for many years a leading hotel. Presidents Van Buren, Tyler, and Fillmore were entertained here. *Portsmouth: corner of Crawford and Queen streets.*

Q-8-n NORFOLK COUNTY COURT HOUSE, 1845–1962

Begun 1845, occupied 20 July 1846. The architect, William R. Singleton, a Portsmouth native, also designed the old Norfolk City Court House. This building stands on one of the four corners dedicated for public use in 1752 by Lt. Col. William Crawford, founder of Portsmouth. The site was formerly occupied by the clerk's office when an earlier court house, occupied in 1803, stood on the northeast corner, opposite. *Portsmouth: High and Court streets.*

Q-8-o ARNOLD'S BRITISH DEFENSE, 1781

This marks a line of British redoubts erected in March 1781 by order of Brigadier General Benedict Arnold who, under Major William Phillips, commanded British troops occupying Portsmouth. The line of fortifications extended in an arc along Washington Street from the northern waterfront to Gosport Creek and defended Portsmouth from American attack from the west. *Portsmouth: corner of Washington Street at King Street.*

Q-8-p ARNOLD'S BRITISH DEFENSES, 1781

This marks the Northern limit of a line of British redoubts erected in March 1781 by order of Brigadier General Benedict Arnold who, under Major General William Phillips, commanded British troops occupying Portsmouth. This line of fortifications extended in an arc south along Dinwiddie and Washington Streets to Gosport Creek and defended Portsmouth from American attack from the West. *Portsmouth: Crawford Parkway at Court Street.*

Q-8-q* ARNOLD'S BRITISH DEFENSES, 1781

A brick windmill near here was close to the southern limit of a line of British redoubts erected in March 1781 by order of Brigadier General Benedict Arnold who, under Major General William Phillips commanded British troops occupying Portsmouth. This line of fortifications extended north in an arc along Washington Street to the waterfront near Court Street. *Portsmouth: Corner of Washington and Brighton streets.*

Q-9 WARRENTON

Chosen as county seat in 1759, and first called Fauquier Court House, Warrenton was laid out as a town in 1790. John Marshall began law practice here. In the War Between the States it was the center of operations north of the Rappahannock and many wounded were hospitalized here. Union General Pope headquartered here in the Second Manassas Campaign. Seizing the local press, the Unionists edited the newspaper as "The New York Ninth." Mosby, the ranger, made forays in this vicinity. *Fauquier County: Route 802, at Warrenton.*

Q-10-a CAPPAHOSIC

Seven and one-half miles southwest is Cappahosic, where a ferry was established early in the eighteenth century. On the old charts, this Indian district lay between Werowocomoco and Timberneck Creek. Powhatan is said to have offered it to Capt. John Smith for "two great guns and a grindstone." John Stubbs patented the Cappahosic tract in 1652 and 1702 and a few years later built "Cappahosic House," which has clipped gables and inside chimneys with eight unique corner fireplaces. *Gloucester County: Route 17, at Gloucester.*

Q-11-a* STONEWALL JACKSON'S HOME

This house was purchased late in 1858 by Thomas Jonathan Jackson, then of the V.M.I. faculty. He and his wife lived here, in the only home he ever owned, from early 1859 to April, 1861, when he entered the service of the Confederacy. *Lexington: Washington and Main streets.*

Q-12-a CLERK'S OFFICE

Site of first county seat of Pittsylvania County. The building that served as the debtor's prison, 1767–1771, and later as the clerk's office, 1771–1777, remains. Nearby stands the debtor's gaol, built in 1773. It later served as Samuel Calland's store and in 1803 became the post office for Callands. *Pittsylvania County: Route 969, at Callands.*

QA-1 FOLLY CASTLE

This house was the town home of Peter Jones, who built it in 1763. It was called "Folly Castle" because it was a large house for a childless man, but Jones later had offspring. Major Erasmus Gill, Revolutionary soldier, also lived here. *Petersburg: West Washington Street.*

QA-2 TRADING STATION AND TAVERN

One block north and one block west is the traditional site of the station where Peter Jones, for whom Petersburg probably was named, traded with the Indians. It was established before 1675. There also is the colonial Durell's, or Golden Ball, Tavern, where British officers were quartered in the occupation of 1781. *Petersburg: corner of Sycamore and Bollingbrook streets.*

QA-3* WORLD WAR MEMORIALS

West on Wythe Street from this corner the trees were planted as memorials to the Petersburg men who died in the World War. Each tree bears the name of a soldier. The street was first known as Week's Cut, from ancient Week's Tavern. *Petersburg: corner of Wythe Street and Crater Road.*

QA-4 WORLD WAR MEMORIALS

Two blocks east on Wythe Street begin the trees planted as memorials to Petersburg men who died in the World War. Each tree bears the name of a soldier. Wythe Street was first known as Weeks's Cut and on it, diagonally opposite this spot, stood ancient Weeks's Tavern. *Petersburg: corner of Sycamore and Wythe streets.*

QA-5 POPLAR LAWN

Poplar Lawn is now known as Central Park. Here the Petersburg volunteers camped in October, 1812, before leaving for the Canadian border. Here Lafayette was greeted with music and speeches in 1824. The place was bought by the city in 1844. Volunteer companies enlisted here, April 19, 1861. In the siege of 1864–65 a hospital stood here. *Petersburg: corner of Filmore and South Sycamore streets.*

QA-6 FORT HENRY

Four blocks north is the traditional site of Fort Henry, established under the act of 1645. In 1646 the fort was leased by Abraham Wood. From it, in 1650, Abraham Wood and Edmund Bland set out on an exploring expedition; and, in 1671 Batts and Fallam, on the first expedition known to have crossed the Appalachian Mountains. The fort was garrisoned again in 1675, with Peter Jones as commander. *Petersburg: corner of West Washington and North South streets.*

QA-7 GENERAL LEE'S HEADQUARTERS

Three blocks north and a half block west is the Beasley house where General Robert E. Lee had his headquarters in 1864 during the siege of Petersburg. He moved thence to Edge Hill to be in closer touch with his right wing. *Petersburg: corner of West Washington and Lafayette streets.*

QA-8 NIBLO'S TAVERN

On the northeast corner stood a famous colonial tavern. Lafayette was entertained there in 1824. It was replaced in 1828 by Niblo's Hotel, built by William Niblo. Later it was known as the Bollingbrook Hotel. It was a favorite resort of generals in the siege of 1864–65. *Petersburg: corner of Bollingbrook and Second streets.*

QA-9* BATTERSEA

Four blocks north is Battersea, home of John Banister, Revolutionary soldier, who was elected the first mayor of Petersburg in 1784. In 1781 British officers were quartered there. In the same year the noted French traveler Chastellux visited it, and later the Italian Court Castiglioni. *Petersburg: West Washington Street and Battersea Lane.*

QA-10 ST. PAUL'S CHURCH

St. Paul's Church was built in 1856. Here Robert E. Lee and his staff worshipped during the siege of Petersburg, 1864–65. Lee attended the wedding of his son, W.H.F. Lee, in this church in 1867. *Petersburg: West Washington Street.*

QA-11 BLANDFORD CHURCH AND CEMETERY

The Brick Church on Well's Hill, now known as Old Blandford Church, was built between 1734 and 1737. The British General Phillips was buried in the churchyard in 1781. In the cemetery is a monument to Captain McRae and the Petersburg volunteers, who at Fort Meigs in 1813 won for Petersburg the name of the "Cockade City of the Union." Soldiers of six wars rest here, among them 30,000 Confederates. *Petersburg: Crater Road near Cameron Street.*

QA-12 BATTLE OF PETERSBURG

Here was fought the Battle of Petersburg, April 25, 1781. The Southside militia, 1,000 strong and commanded by Baron Steuben and General Muhlenberg, made a brave resistance to 2,500 British regulars under Phillips and Arnold. *Petersburg: Crater Road at Cameron Street.*

QA-13 EAST HILL

On the hilltop to the south is the site of East Hill, also known as Bollingbrook. There the British General Phillips, Benedict Arnold and Lord Cornwallis stayed in April and May, 1781. The house was bombarded by Lafayette, May 10, 1781. There Phillips died, May 13, 1781. *Petersburg: East Bank at Fourth streets.*

QA-14 TWO NOTED HOMES

Half a block south is the home of Major General William Mahone, famed for his gallant conduct at the Battle of the Crater, July 30, 1864. Two blocks south is the Wallace home, where Abraham Lincoln conferred with General Grant, April 3, 1865, preceding Grant's march to Appomattox. *Petersburg: Corner of West Washington and South Market streets.*

QA-15 FORMATION OF THE SOUTHERN METHODIST CHURCH

One block west stood the Union Street Methodist Church, completed in 1820. There was held the first general conference of the Methodist Episcopal Church South, May 1–23, 1846. At this meeting the Southern Methodist Church, which had separated from the Northern Church, effected its organization. *Petersburg: North Sycamore Street near Washington Street.*

QA-16 GRAHAM ROAD

On June 9, 1864, Kautz's Union cavalry, 1300 men, after overwhelming Archer's militia, one mile south, moved westward on this road to attack the city. Upon the hillside, one mile west, they were repulsed by the battery of Captain Edward Graham, and later driven to retreat by General James Dearing's cavalry. This attack, in conjunction with an infantry force that did not come up, was the first attempt to capture Petersburg. *Petersburg: corner of Crater and Graham roads.*

QA-17 GRAHAM ROAD

Upon this site, on June 9, 1864, Captain Edward Graham, commanding two guns of the Petersburg artillery, repulsed the attack of Kautz's cavalry, 1300 men, and by this gallant defense the city was saved. Later the Union forces were driven to retreat by the supporting cavalry of General James Dearing. *Petersburg: corner of Graham Road and Clinton Street.*

QB-1 FIRST SUFFOLK CHURCH

Here stood the Colonial Suffolk Church, a large, cross-shaped brick building erected in 1753 as the second parish church of Upper Parish, Nansemond County, and the first house of worship in the town of Suffolk. It survived the burning of Suffolk by the British in 1779 but fell to ruin and was torn down by 1802. *Suffolk: Western Avenue. 200 feet w. of Church Street.*

QC-1 TRINITY CHURCH

Known originally as Augusta Parish Church, it was founded in 1746 as the County Parish. The Virginia General Assembly met here in June 1781 to avoid capture by British Raiders. The present church was erected in 1855 and was used by the Virginia Theological Seminary during the War Between the States. The first Bishop of Virginia, James Madison, was a member of the church. *Staunton: 214 W. Beverley Street.*

R-4* LYNCHBURG DEFENSES

Half a mile southeast, on Madison Heights, are two large earthworks forming part of the Confederate defense system, 1861–65. *Amherst County: Route 29, 1 mile n. of Lynchburg.*

R-15* PATRICK HENRY'S GRAVE

Five miles east is Red Hill, last home and grave of Patrick Henry, orator of the Revolution. He moved there in 1796 and died there, June 6, 1799. Henry is especially famous for his "Liberty or Death" speech made in 1775 at the beginning of the Revolution. *Campbell County: Route 501 at Brookneal.*

R-20 SWEET BRIAR COLLEGE
CHARTERED 1901

This Liberal Arts College for women, opened in 1906, granted its first Bachelor of Arts Degrees in 1910. Established under the will of Indiana Fletcher Williams as a memorial to her only daughter, Daisy, the College is located on a 2800-acre tract of land acquired by Elijah Fletcher before 1830. The eighteenth-century homestead, remodeled and named "Sweet Briar House" by the Fletchers, is set in a boxwood garden. *Amherst County: Route 29, 2 miles s. of Amherst.*

R-50* BOYHOOD HOME OF COLONEL MOSBY

Five miles south near the "Thoroughfare Gap" was the early boyhood home of Colonel John Singleton Mosby (1833–1916), famous Confederate Ranger. He attended the school near Murrell's Shop, east of Elmington. *Nelson County: Route 6, 3 miles n. of Woods Mill.*

R-51 HURRICANE CAMILLE

On August 20, 1969, torrential rains, following remnants of Hurricane Camille, devastated this area. A rainfall in excess of 25 inches largely within a 5-hour period, swept away or buried many miles of roads, over 100 bridges, and over 900 buildings. 114 people died and 37 remain missing. The damage totalled more than $100,000,000 and Virginia was declared a disaster area. *Nelson County: Route 29 at Woods Mill Wayside.*

R-56 LOVINGSTON

This place became the county seat of Nelson when it was formed from Amherst in 1807. It was named for James Loving, Jr., who gave the land for the courthouse, built in 1808–09. The town was incorporated in 1807 and again in 1871, and deincorporated in 1938. *Nelson County: Route 250, at Lovingston.*

R-58. BIRTHPLACE OF RIVES

Two miles east, at Oak Ridge, was born William Cabell Rives, May 4, 1792. He was minister to France, 1829–32 and 1849–53; United States Senator, 1832–45; member of the Peace convention of 1861 and of the Confederate Congress. He died, April 25, 1868. Later, Oak Ridge was owned by Thomas Fortune Ryan. *Nelson County: Route 29, 4 miles s. of Lovingston.*

R-60 GRAVE OF PATRICK HENRY'S MOTHER

In the grove of trees some hundreds of yards to the west is the grave of Sarah Winston (Henry), mother of Patrick Henry, who died in November, 1784. *Amherst County: Route 151, just s. of Clifford.*

R-61 ACTION AT TYE RIVER

About 800 yards east, on June 11, 1864, the Botetourt Battery, C.S.A., prevented Federal Raiders from burning the Orange and Alexandria Railroad Bridge, thus enabling General Jubal Early to reach Lynchburg in time to save it from capture by General Hunter. *Amherst County: Route 29, s. of Tye River Bridge.*

R-62 OLD RUSTBURG

The place was named for Jeremiah Rust, who patented land here in 1780. The first courthouse of Campbell County was built here, in 1783; the present building was erected about 1848. The old "Fountain Hotel" was built in 1795 and has been conducted by the Finch family ever since. *Campbell County: Route 501, at Rustburg.*

R-63 FALLING SPRING PRESBYTERIAN CHURCH

The oldest congregation in the Fincastle Presbytery, the Falling Spring Presbyterian Church, was organized before 1748. The Hanover Presbytery met here in October, 1780. The present Gothic Revival Church was constructed of slave-made brick during the Civil War. At the time of its dedication in April, 1864, General Thomas L. Rosser's Cavalry Brigade was camped here. The first burial in the present cemetery was that of John Grigsby of Fruit Hill (1720–1794). Erected by the National Grigsby Family Society, 1981. *Rockbridge County: Route 11, 7 miles s. of Lexington.*

R-77* HISTORY AT HALIFAX

A part of Greene's army was here in February, 1781, just after Cornwallis's pursuit. Here Washington stopped, June 4, 1791, in his tour of the Southern States. Here John Randolph of Roanoke in 1827 made one of his great speeches. Here General Custer camped in April, 1865. *Halifax County: Route 360, at Halifax.*

R-79 GREEN'S FOLLY

Built about 1789 by Captain Berryman Green, a quartermaster in Washington's army at Valley Forge and later a deputy clerk of Halifax County. *Halifax County: Route 501, 2 miles s. of Halifax.*

R-80   MINISTER WHO MARRIED LINCOLN

Here lived Rev. Charles A. Dresser, rector of Antrim Parish and builder of St. Mark's Church, 1828. Dresser left this parish in 1835 for Peoria, Illinois, whence he moved to Springfield. There he married Abraham Lincoln to Mary Todd, November 4, 1842. *Halifax County: Route 501, 2 miles s. of Halifax.*

RA-4   ROCKFISH CHURCH

This Presbyterian church was established in 1746; James McCann conveyed the land for the church and school. Samuel Black became the first pastor in 1747. The first building was erected in 1771 by Thomas Mason. The church was reorganized in 1849. The present church was built in 1853. *Nelson County: Route 151, 10.6 miles s. of Afton.*

RA-6   WILLIAM H. CRAWFORD

William Harris Crawford was born in this vicinity, February 24, 1772. Early in life he was taken to Georgia and became a leading politician of the era. He was United States Senator; Minister to France; Secretary of War and of the Treasury; candidate, 1824, for the Presidency, which was decided by the House of Representatives. *Nelson County: Route 151, 12.7 miles s. of Afton.*

RG-5*   JOHN WEATHERFORD'S GRAVE

One half mile west is the grave of Elder John Weatherford (1740–1833) Baptist preacher for 70 years and early advocate of religious liberty. Jailed five months in Chesterfield in 1773 for unlicensed preaching, his release was secured by Patrick Henry. *Pittsylvania County: Route 29, 9 miles s.e. of Chatham.*

S-1*   STEUBEN AND LAFAYETTE

Steuben's militia here, on January 6, 1781, kept the British in Richmond from crossing the James. On April 30, 1781, the British (then south of the river) were kept from crossing to Richmond by Lafayette. *Richmond: Route 1 at s. entrance to city.*

S-2*   ARNOLD AT WARWICK

Warwick was on the James just to the east. Benedict Arnold burned it, with some ships, on April 30, 1781. *Chesterfield County: Route 1, 1.5 miles s. of Richmond.*

S-3   AMPTHILL ESTATE

Built before 1732 by Henry Cary, this was the home of Colonel Archibald Cary, a Revolutionary leader of Virginia. The house was moved, 1929–30, to its present location off Cary Street Road in Richmond's West End. *Chesterfield County: Route 1, .7 mile s. of Richmond.*

S-4   FIRST IRON FURNACE

On the creek nearby stood the first iron furnace in English America, built in 1619. It was destroyed by the Indians in the massacre of 1622. *Chesterfield County: Route 1, 1.5 miles s. of Richmond.*

S-5   DREWRY'S BLUFF

This bluff on the James River, a mile east, was fortified by Captain A. H. Drewry in 1862. A Union fleet, attempting to pass it, was driven back, May 15, 1862; and thereafter it served as a bar to attacks on Richmond by water. On June 16, 1864, Longstreet's Corps of Lee's army crossed the river there going to the defense of Petersburg. *Chesterfield County: Route 1, 2.5 miles s. of Richmond on northbound lane.*

S-6*   MAIN CONFEDERATE LINE

The main line of Confederate earthworks, 1864–65, ran from the creek here to Drewry's Bluff on James River. *Chesterfield County: Route 1, 8 miles s. of Richmond.*

S-7*   CHESTERFIELD COURTHOUSE

It was several miles to the west. Here Steuben had his militia camp in 1780–81. The barracks were burned by the British General Phillips on April 27, 1781. *Chesterfield County: Route 1, 3.9 miles s. of Richmond.*

S-8   BATTLE OF DREWRY'S BLUFF

From this point the Confederates, on May 16, 1864, moved to attack the Union Army of the James under Butler advancing northward on Richmond. *Chesterfield County: Route 1, 3.9 miles s. of Richmond.*

S-9*   BATTLE OF DREWRY'S BLUFF

Here ran the line of battle of the Union army on the morning of May 16, 1864. The earthworks, taken by the Unionists on May 14, were given up by them on May 16. *Chesterfield County: Route 1, 4.5 miles s. of Richmond.*

S-10   HALF-WAY HOUSE

Headquarters of the Union Army of the James, this old inn was a central point in the battle of Drewry's Bluff, May 16, 1864. *Chesterfield County: Route 1, 5.4 miles s. of Richmond.*

S-11*   PROCTOR'S CREEK FIGHT

To the west of the road here the Army of the James, on May 13–14, 1864, attacked the outer line of the Drewry's Bluff defenses. The Confederates withdrew to their second line on Kingsland Creek. *Chesterfield County: Route 301 at Proctor's Creek.*

S-12   INTO THE BOTTLE

The Union Army of the James, retiring across Proctor's Creek in this vicinity after the battle of Drewry's Bluff, May 16, 1864, turned east into the Peninsula between the James and Appomattox Rivers, where it was "Bottled" by Confederate forces. *Chesterfield County: Route 1, 6.5 miles s. of Richmond.*

S-12* INTO THE "BOTTLE"

The Union army, retiring across Proctor's Creek after the battle of May 16, 1864, in this vicinity turned east into the "bottle" between the James and Appomattox Rivers. *Chesterfield County: Route 1, 6 miles s. of Richmond.*

S-13 DUTCH GAP

This great bend in the James River lies due east. The town of Henrico was established here in 1611. In August, 1864, B. F. Butler cut a canal through the neck, shortening the river five miles. *Chesterfield County: Route 1, 6.7 miles s. of Richmond.*

S-14* OSBORNE'S WHARF

This old wharf lay to the east. Here Benedict Arnold burned state warships on April 27, 1781, and was here joined by Phillips. Lafayette, crossing the James, camped here, May 8–10, 1781, on his way to Petersburg. *Chesterfield County: Route 1, 6.7 miles s. of Richmond.*

S-15 DREWRY'S BLUFF

A mile east is Drewry's Bluff, James River fortification of Richmond, 1862–65. Earthworks remain. *Chesterfield County: Route 1, 2.5 miles s. of Richmond on southbound lane.*

S-16 POCAHONTAS STATE PARK

This park of 7604 acres was originally known as the Swift Creek Recreational Area. Its purchase in 1934 and subsequent development by the federal government were with the understanding that eventually the State would accept and maintain the property, incorporating it into its Park System. On June 6, 1946 the Virginia Conservation Commission dedicated the park, naming it for the Indian princess Pocahontas. *Chesterfield County: Route 655, 4.1 miles w. of Chesterfield.*

S-16* REDWATER CREEK

Here, on May 12, 1864, the Union Army, advancing northward, formed line of battle across the road and drove the Confederates back on Proctor's Creek. *Chesterfield County: Route 1, 4.5 miles n. of Petersburg.*

S-17 CHESTER STATION FIGHT

At this station, two miles west, the Union army of the James, turning toward Richmond, fought an action on May 10, 1864, and tore up the railroad. *Chesterfield County: Route 1, 7.8 miles s. of Richmond.*

S-18* THE "BOTTLE"

This is the peninsula between the James and Appomattox Rivers in which the Army of the James was "bottled" by Beauregard in 1864–65. The line of Union earthworks was enclosed by a line of Confederate works. *Chesterfield County: Route 1, 6.2 miles n. of Petersburg.*

S-19*   FEELING OUT FIGHT

The Confederates, feeling out the Union lines, attacked them just to the east on June 2, 1864, but soon withdrew. *Chesterfield County: Route 1, 6.9 miles n. of Petersburg.*

S-20*   A RAILROAD RAID

The Union Army of the James drove off the defenders and destroyed the railroad here for several miles, May 6–12, 1864. *Chesterfield County: Route 1, 4.25 miles n. of Petersburg.*

S-21   BERMUDA HUNDRED

This place, some miles to the east, is on the James at the mouth of the Appomattox. A town was established there in 1613. Phillips and Arnold sailed from there in May, 1781. In May, 1864, it became the base of operations of the Army of the James. *Chesterfield County: Route 1, 7.8 miles s. of Richmond.*

S-22*   PORT WALTHALL JUNCTION

This is on the railroad just to the east. Here the Union army, coming from the James River on May 7, 1864, began to tear up the railroad. *Chesterfield County: Route 1, 5.4 miles n. of Petersburg.*

S-23*   LEE'S HEADQUARTERS

At the Clay house to the east Lee, going to the defense of Petersburg, had his headquarters on June 17, 1864. *Chesterfield County: Route 1, 7.5 miles n. of Petersburg.*

S-24*   ADVANCE ON PETERSBURG

Here the Union Army of the James, on May 9, 1864, turned southward toward Petersburg. *Chesterfield County: Route 1, 4.1 miles n. of Petersburg.*

S-25   UNION ARMY CHECKED

Here the Army of the James, moving on Petersburg, May 9, 1864, was checked by the Confederate defenses on the creek and turned northward. *Chesterfield County: Route 1, 3.4 miles n. of Petersburg.*

S-26   LAFAYETTE AT PETERSBURG

From this hill Lafayette, on May 10, 1781, shelled the British in Petersburg. *Chesterfield County: Route 1, at Colonial Heights.*

S-27   LEE'S HEADQUARTERS

Lee's headquarters from the latter part of June, 1864, to September, 1864, were here. *Chesterfield County: Route 1, at Colonial Heights.*

S-28   JOHN BAPTIST PIERCE (1875–1942)

A Cooperative Extension Service pioneer, innovator, and educator, John Baptist Pierce was appointed in 1906 by Seaman Knapp and H. B. Frissell of Hampton Institute as the first Negro farm demonstration agent for Virginia. Pierce served for 35 years as district agent for Virginia and North Carolina and as the United States Department of Agriculture field agent for the upper southern states. Pierce's "Live-at-Home and Community Improvement Program" was a unique innovation which helped many rural Virginians raise their standards of living. *Hampton: Route 60 between Interstate 64 and Emancipation Drive.*

S-40   SAPONEY CHURCH

Five miles southeast stands Saponey Church, built in 1728. This church, the oldest in Dinwiddie County, is still in use. *Dinwiddie County: Route 1, at Dewitt.*

S-41*   DINWIDDIE TAVERN

This is the site of old Dinwiddie Tavern, famous stopping-place in the latter part of the eighteenth century. It was burned in 1865. *Dinwiddie County: Route 1, at Dinwiddie.*

S-42*   QUAKER SETTLEMENT

Two miles east was a Quaker settlement, founded about 1794. Some of the houses still stand. *Dinwiddie County: Route 1, 6 miles s.w. of Petersburg.*

S-43   COTTAGE FARM

ert D. McIlwaine, where on the afternoon of April 2, 1865, General Lee ordered the evacuation of Richmond and Petersburg by the Confederates and the westward march which ended at Appomattox. *Dinwiddie County: Route 1 at s. limits of Petersburg.*

S-45   SCOTT'S LAW OFFICE

Just to the west stands the law office occupied in early life by Lieutenant-General Winfield Scott, commander of the United States Army, 1841–1861. Scott, born here, June 13, 1786 was admitted to the bar in 1806 and entered the army in 1808. He died, May 29, 1866. *Dinwiddie County: Route 1, at Dinwiddie.*

S-46*   RACELAND

Six miles east is Raceland, where the famous race horse, Timoleon, was born. The oldest part of the house was built in 1707. A museum, cotton gin and slave quarters are there. *Dinwiddie County: Route 1, n. entrance of Dinwiddie.*

S-47   EDGE HILL

To the right stood the Turnbull House, headquarters of General Robert E. Lee from November 23, 1864, until April 2, 1865. After Lee's departure to Cottage Farm, Federal artillery destroyed the house. The present residence was one of the detached buildings. *Dinwiddie County: Route 1 at s. limits of Petersburg.*

S-48   THE CATTLE (BEEFSTEAK) RAID

In a field here were penned the cattle herd captured near City Point September 16, 1864 by Confederate Cavalry under General Wade Hampton. The herd was penned here after Hampton's return within his own lines. *Dinwiddie County: Route 1 and 613, 5 miles s. of Petersburg.*

S-49 WHERE HILL FELL

In the field a short distance north of this road, the Confederate General A. P. Hill was killed, April 2, 1865. Hill, not knowing that Lee's lines had been broken, rode into a party of Union soldiers advancing on Petersburg. *Dinwiddie County: Route 1, 2.8 miles s. of Petersburg.*

S-50 HATCHER'S RUN

Lee's right wing was defended by earthworks on this stream, here and to the east. These works were unsuccessfully attacked by Union forces, February 5–7, 1865. On the morning of April 2, 1865, they were stormed by Union troops. *Dinwiddie County: Route 1, 6.4 miles s. of Petersburg.*

S-51 BURGESS MILL

An old mill stood here, with earthworks. On October 27, 1864, General Hancock, coming from the south, attempted to cross the run here and reach the Southside Railroad. He was supported on the east by Warren's (Fifth) Corps. The Confederates, crossing the run from the north side, intervened between the two Union forces and drove them back. *Dinwiddie County: Route 1, 6.4 miles s. of Petersburg.*

S-52 WHITE OAK ROAD

The extreme right of Lee's line rested on this road, which was entrenched. General Warren, advancing against Lee's works here, March 31, 1865, was driven back. Reinforced, Warren advanced again, forcing the Confederates to retire to the road. On it, six miles west, the battle of Five Forks was fought next day, April 1, 1865. *Dinwiddie County: Route 1, 6.8 miles s. of Petersburg.*

S-53* ACTION OF MARCH 29, 1865

Just south of the junction here of the Boydton Plank Road and Quaker Road, General Warren, moving northward, came into conflict with Anderson's Corps of Lee's army. After a sharp action, Anderson fell back to the trenches on the White Oak Road, March 29, 1865. *Dinwiddie County: Route 1, 7.7 miles s. of Petersburg.*

S-54 DINWIDDIE COURTHOUSE

Sheridan advanced to this place on March 29, 1865, while Warren was attacking Anderson about three miles north. On March 31 Sheridan moved south but was checked by Pickett and driven back to the courthouse. That night Pickett withdrew to Five Forks. *Dinwiddie County: Route 1, at Dinwiddie.*

S-55   VAUGHAN ROAD

Hancock moved by it to his defeat at Burgess Mill, October 27, 1864, and in 1865, Grant moved his forces on it from the east to attack Lee's right wing. On March 29, 1865, Sheridan came to Dinwiddie Court House over it in the operations preceding the Battle of Five Forks. *Dinwiddie County: Route 1, at Dinwiddie.*

S-56   CHAMBERLAIN'S BED

That stream flows into Stony Creek a mile west. On March 31, 1865, Pickett and W. H. F. Lee, coming from Five Forks, forced a passage of Chamberlain's Bed in the face of Sheridan's troops, who were driven back to Dinwiddie Courthouse. *Dinwiddie County: Route 1, 1.1 miles s. of Dinwiddie.*

S-57   BIRCH'S BRIDGE

At Birch's Bridge (very near this bridge) the second William Byrd and his party crossed the river, in September, 1733, on their way to inspect Byrd's land holdings in North Carolina. Byrd wrote an account of this trip which he called "A Journey to the Land of Eden." On his return, he "laid the foundation" of Richmond and Petersburg. *Brunswick County: Route 1, 2.8 miles s. of McKenney.*

S-58   EBENEZER ACADEMY

A few hundred yards east is the site of Ebenezer Academy, founded in 1793 by Bishop Asbury, the first Methodist school established in Virginia. It passed out of the hands of the church but remained a noted school for many years. *Brunswick County: Route 1, 6.8 miles n. of Cochran.*

S-60   STURGEON CREEK

A branch of the Nottoway, named for the huge fish once caught in it. William Byrd, returning from the expedition to survey the Virginia–North Carolina boundary line, camped on this stream in November, 1729. *Brunswick County: Route 1, 5.7 miles n. of Cochran.*

S-62   CAMPAIGN OF 1781

The British cavalryman Tarleton, returning to Cornwallis from a raid to Bedford, passed near here, July, 1781. *Dinwiddie County: Route 1, 1.5 miles s. of Dinwiddie.*

S-65   OLD BRUNSWICK COURTHOUSE

Here the first courthouse of Brunswick County was built about 1732. In 1746, when the county was divided, the county seat was moved east near Thomasburg. In 1783, after Greensville County had been formed, the courthouse was moved to Lawrenceville. *Brunswick County: Route 1, at Cochran.*

S-66   FORT CHRISTANNA

Nine miles south is the site of Fort Christanna, built in 1714 by Governor Alexander Spotswood as a protection to settlers and tributary Indians. Under its shelter several tribes dwelt and an Indian school was established there. When settlements spread beyond it to the west, the fort was abandoned. *Brunswick County: Route 1, at Cochran.*

S-70   SALEM CHAPEL

A mile south is the site of Salem Chapel, one of the pioneer Methodist churches of the state. Of it Francis Asbury wrote, "the best house we have in the country part of Virginia." There he held four sessions of the Virginia Annual conference: November, 1795; April, 1798; March, 1802; April, 1804. The building was burned about 1870. *Mecklenburg County: Route 1, at South Hill.*

S-72*   MEHERRIN HISTORY

Meherrin River was named for an Iroquoian tribe of Indians that long dwelt in this region. In 1669, there were about 200 of them. William Byrd, on his "Journey to the Land of Eden," crossed the river near here, September 13, 1733. *Brunswick County: Route 1, 7.3 miles s. of Cochran.*

S-76   EARLY EXPLORATION

Near here Edward Bland and Abraham Wood passed, August, 1650, going westward on an exploring expedition. They reached the site of Clarksville. *Mecklenburg County: Route 1, 1.6 miles n. of South Hill.*

S-79*   CAMPAIGN OF 1865

Sheridan, raiding to South Boston, crossed this river at the old bridge, April 24, 1865. *Brunswick County: Route 1, 7.3 miles s. of Cochran.*

SA-5   ELK HILL

Two miles south is Elk Hill, once owned by Thomas Jefferson. Lord Cornwallis made his headquarters there, June 7–15, 1781; this was the western limit of his invasion. On June 15 he turned eastward, leaving the place pillaged and carrying off slaves. *Goochland County: Route 6, 1 mile w. of George's Tavern.*

SA-10   GOOCHLAND COURTHOUSE

Near here the ancient trail used by the Iroquois Indians in their raids crossed James River. This trail later became the main north-south road through Virginia. In 1781, Lord Cornwallis, in his invasion of Virginia, marched by this point and his cavalry, under Simcoe, passed here going to Point of Fork. A cavalry skirmish took place here, March 11, 1865. *Goochland County: Route 6, at Goochland.*

SA-11   DUNGENESS

Seven miles south once stood Dungeness, built about 1730 by Isham Randolph (1685–1742), who was the grandfather of Thomas Jefferson, President of the United States, and of James Pleasants, Governor of Virginia. Sea captain, merchant and planter, Randolph also served as Virginia's agent in London and Adjutant General of the Colony. *Goochland County: Route 6 at the courthouse.*

SA-14 DAHLGREN'S RAID

Here Colonel Ulric Dahlgren, Union cavalryman, coming from the north, turned east. Dahlgren, who acted in concert with Kilpatrick, left Stevensburg, Culpeper County, on February 28, 1864, and moved toward the James River, tearing up the Virginia Central Railroad near Frederick's Hall. He went on toward Richmond, burning mills and barns. *Goochland County: Route 6, 2.1 miles e. of Crozier.*

SA-18 SABOT HILL

This is Sabot Hill, home of James A. Seddon, member of Congress and Confederate Secretary of War, 1862–65, who built the house in 1855. On March 1, 1864, the Union cavalryman, Colonel Ulric Dahlgren, raiding to Richmond, burned the barn and plundered the place. *Goochland County: Route 6, 2.6 miles e. of Crozier.*

SA-20 THE HUGUENOT SETTLEMENT

In this vicinity, though mainly on the south side of James River, Huguenot refugees from France settled, 1699–1701 and later. These industrious settlers left an enduring mark on the community. Manakin is a corruption of the name of the Monacan Indian tribe, which once occupied this region. *Goochland County: Route 6, 5.9 miles e. of Crozier.*

SA-22 WILLIAM WEBBER

Three miles north are the home site and grave of William Webber, pastor of Dover Baptist Church, 1773–1808. As an early Baptist leader before the Revolution, he was imprisoned in the jails of Chesterfield and Middlesex. He aided in organizing the Baptist General Association of Virginia; he was moderator in 1778. He was moderator of the Dover Association, 1783–1806; of the Baptist General Committee and of the General Meeting of Correspondence until his death in 1808. *Goochland County: Route 6, 6 miles e. of Crozier at Manakin.*

SA-24 TUCKAHOE

Perhaps the oldest frame residence on James River west of Richmond, Tuckahoe was begun about 1715 by Thomas Randolph. The little schoolhouse still stands here where Thomas Jefferson began his childhood studies. Famous guests here have included William Byrd of Westover, Lord Cornwallis and George Washington. Virginia's Governor Thomas Mann Randolph was born here. *Goochland County: Route 650, w. of Henrico County line.*

SA-27 DAHLGREN'S RAID

Here Colonel Ulric Dahlgren, Union cavalryman, raiding to Richmond, hanged a Negro on a tree beside the road, March 1, 1864. Dahlgren planned to cross the James River in this vicinity and enter Richmond from the south. A Negro guided the raiders to a ford but the water was too high for crossing. Dahlgren thought the guide had deceived him. *Goochland County: Route 650, 9 miles w. of Richmond.*

SA-29 WILTON

A short distance south is Wilton, built by William Randolph and completed in 1753. The house, which originally stood on the north side of James River below Richmond, was removed to this place by the Virginia Society of Colonial Dames, 1934. *Richmond: Cary Street Road and Wilton Road.*

SA-30 AMPTHILL

A short distance south is Ampthill House, built by Henry Cary about 1730 on the south side of James River. It was the home of Colonel Archibald Cary, Revolutionary leader, and was removed to its present site by a member of the Cary family. *Richmond: Cary Street Road and Ampthill Road.*

SA-31* DAHLGREN'S RAID

In this vicinity Colonel Ulric Dahlgren, Union cavalryman, raiding to Richmond, fought an action with the force defending the city in the early evening of March 1, 1864. Dahlgren, unable to cross to the southside of the river as planned, attempted to break through the defenses on this road but was repulsed. He then turned off to the east and was killed. *Henrico County: Route 650, 1.25 miles w. of Richmond.*

SM-2 UNION ACADEMY

Near here stood Union Academy, conducted by Hardy and Crenshaw from 1861 to about 1869. Dr. Walter Reed, who discovered the carrier of yellow fever, and Dr. Robert E. Blackwell, long President of Randolph-Macon College, attended school here. Nearby was an iron foundry, established in 1855 by Captain Richard Irby. *Nottoway County: Route 42, at s. entrance of Blackstone.*

SN-45 CRAIG'S MILL

Two miles south of Kenbridge stood Craig's Mill on Flat Rock Creek. There flour was ground and supplies were stored for the Revolutionary army. Tarleton, the British cavalryman, burned the mill in July, 1781, when raiding through the Southside. Rev. James Craig, the owner, is said to have been forced to help kill hogs for the troopers. *Lunenburg County: Route 40, .3 mile n. of Kenbridge.*

SN-60 MASON'S CHAPEL

Near here stood Mason's Chapel, one of the earliest Methodist churches in southern Virginia. The first Virginia conference, May, 1785, was held here or nearby; Bishop Asbury presided. The conference of 1801 was held here. The present Olive Branch church is four miles west. *Brunswick County: Route 46, 8 miles s. of Brunswick.*

T-1 CARTER HALL

The house was completed about 1792 by Nathaniel Burwell. Edmund Randolph, Governor of Virginia and Secretary of State, died here. General Stonewall Jackson had his headquarters here, October, 1862. *Clarke County: Route 255, just n. of Millwood.*

T-2 OLD CHAPEL

This place was called "Old Chapel" in 1773. The present building was erected in 1796. Bishop Meade was minister here. Edmund Randolph, Governor of Virginia and Secretary of State, was buried here. *Clarke County: Route 255, 3.2 miles s. of Berryville.*

T-3 GREENWAY COURT

Three miles south is Greenway Court, residence of Thomas, sixth Lord Fairfax, proprietor of the vast Northern Neck grant, which he inherited. Born in Leeds Castle, England, in 1693, Fairfax settled in Virginia, in 1747, for the rest of his life. He made Greenway Court his home in 1751. George Washington, employed as a surveyor on this grant, was there frequently in his youth. Fairfax died there, December 9, 1781. *Clarke County: Route 340, 2 miles n.w. of Millwood.*

T-4 AUDLEY

The house to the north is the home of Nellie Parke Custis, George Washington's ward, who married his nephew, Major Lawrence Lewis. After her husband's death in 1839, Nellie Custis Lewis settled here, and here she died in 1852. *Clarke County: Route 7, .7 mile e. of Berryville.*

T-5 MOTHER OF THE WRIGHT BROTHERS

Six miles north, at Hillsboro, was born in 1831 Susan Koerner, mother of Wilbur and Orville Wright, inventors of the airplane. *Loudoun County: Route 7, at Purcellville.*

T-6 THE BURWELL-MORGAN MILL

This grist mill, built in 1782–85 by General Daniel Morgan of Saratoga and Colonel Nathaniel Burwell of Carter Hall, was in continuous operation until 1943. Now owned by the Clarke County Historical Association. *Clarke County: Route 255, at Millwood.*

T-7* WHITE POST

The original white post on this spot was erected by Lord Fairfax as a guide post to Greenway Court, about 1760. *Clarke County: Route 255, at White Post.*

T-8 COLONIAL HIGHWAY

This is one of the oldest roads leading from the east to the Shenandoah Valley; it crosses the Blue Ridge at Snicker's Gap. The ferry right over the Shenandoah River was granted, 1766. Washington used this road many times. Some distance to the east the first aerial telegraph signals were sent from the roadside, 1868. *Clarke County: Route 7, 3.7 miles e. of Berryville.*

T-9   CASTLEMAN'S FERRY FIGHT

Three miles north in July 1864, General Jubal Early's Army, returning from his raid on Washington, was attacked by Federal units which forced a passage of the river. On July 18, Colonel Joseph Thoburn led his troops against the Confederates but was driven back across the river. Rutherford B. Hayes, 19th President of the United States, commanded a Federal brigade in the action. *Clarke County: Route 7, at intersection with Route 603.*

T-9*   CASTLEMAN'S FERRY FIGHT

Near here General Early, in July, 1864, returning from his Washington raid, was attacked by Crook, who forced a passage of the Shenandoah. Early, counterattacking, drove the Unionists back across the river. Rutherford B. Hayes, later President of the United States, commanded a brigade of Union troops. *Clarke County: Route 7, 4.5 miles e. of Berryville.*

T-10   CROOK AND EARLY

Early, while passing through this gap on his return from his Washington raid, was attacked by Crook's cavalry, July 16, 1864. Crook destroyed a few wagons. Early captured a cannon. *Clarke County: Route 7, 7.7 miles e. of Berryville.*

T-11   FORERUNNER OF WIRELESS TELEGRAPHY

From nearby Bear's Den Mountain to the Catoctin Ridge, a distance of fourteen miles, Dr. Mahlon Loomis, dentist, sent the first aerial wireless signals, 1866–73, using kites flown by copper wires. Loomis received a patent in 1872 and his company was chartered by Congress in 1873, but lack of capital frustrated his experiments. He died in 1886. *Clarke County: Route 7, 7.7 miles e. of Berryville.*

T-22   EARLY'S WASHINGTON CAMPAIGN

Jubal A. Early passed over this road on his return to the Shenandoah Valley, July 16, 1864. After leaving Lee before Richmond, June 13, Early traveled 450 miles, defeating Hunter at Lynchburg and Wallace on the Monocacy River, and threatening the city of Washington. On the approach of large Union forces he withdrew this way. *Loudoun County: Route 7, 2.1 miles w. of Leesburg.*

T-30   BELMONT

Belmont was patented early in the eighteenth century by Thomas Lee, of Stratford. About 1800, Ludwell Lee, an officer in the Revolutionary army, built the house and he lived here until his death in 1836. Here he entertained Lafayette in 1825. In 1931, Belmont became the home of Patrick J. Hurley, Secretary of War, 1929–1933. *Loudoun County: Route 7, 4.3 miles e. of Leesburg.*

T-36   ACTION AT DRANESVILLE

Near here two foraging expeditions came in conflict, December 20, 1861. The Union force was commanded by General Ord, the Confederate by J.E.B. Stuart. Stuart attacked in order to protect his foraging parties, but was forced to retire after a sharp fight. The next day he returned, reinforced, and carried off his wounded. *Fairfax County: Route 7, at Dranesville.*

T-37   SHARPSBURG (ANTIETAM) CAMPAIGN

Here Lee entered this road from Ox Hill, September 3, 1862, and turned west toward Leesburg. Crossing the Potomac at White's Ford, the army entered Maryland, September 5–6, 1862. *Fairfax County: Route 7, at Dranesville.*

T-38   GETTYSBURG CAMPAIGN

J.E.B. Stuart, operating on Lee's right, passed here on his way to the fords of the Potomac north of Dranesville, June 27, 1863. Crossing the river, he became separated from Lee's army and did not rejoin it until July 2, at Gettysburg. *Loudoun County: Route 7, 2.6 miles w. of Dranesville.*

T-44   VIRGINIA THEOLOGICAL SEMINARY—FOUNDED 1823

Half mile to the southeast. The idea for such an institution was conceived by a group of Alexandria and Washington clergymen in 1818. Among those interested was Francis Scott Key, author of the Star Spangled Banner. Originally at corner of Washington and King Streets in Alexandria, moved to present location in 1827. Closed in 1861 when occupied as a hospital for Union troops. *Alexandria: Route 7, w. of Quaker Lane.*

T-45*   EPISCOPAL HIGH SCHOOL— FOUNDED 1839

On the hill to the Southwest. One of the oldest preparatory schools for boys in the South. Taken over by Union Troops in 1861 for use as a Military Hospital. Reopened in 1866, the School was a pioneer in establishing the Honor Code in Education. *Alexandria: Route 7, w. of Quaker Lane.*

U-22   INDEPENDENCE

This place became the county seat of Grayson County in 1850; the first case was tried in the newly erected courthouse in 1851. The present courthouse was built in 1908. Independence was incorporated in 1934. *Grayson County: Route 58, at Independence.*

U-23 PEYTON GUYN HALE

Born in Elk Creek, Virginia, June 29, 1821, Member of the House of Delegates, 1874–1877. Member State Senate, 1879–1882. One of the "Big Four," a group which resisted many of the proposals of the Readjusters. Died in Elk Creek, December 25, 1885. *Grayson County: Route 21, at Elks Creek.*

U-25 FIRST COUNTY SEAT

Here at Old Tavern, in 1794, was built the first courthouse of Grayson County. The land was donated by Flower Swift. A second courthouse was built in 1838. The county seat was removed to Independence about 1850. *Grayson County: Route 640, 3 miles w. of Galax.*

U-26 GALAX

The town is on the dividing line between Grayson and Carroll counties. Its original name was Bonaparte, which was changed to Galax, the name of a mountain shrub abundant in the vicinity. In 1904 a spur of the Norfolk and Western Railroad came here, bringing the town into existence. It was incorporated in 1906. *Grayson County: Route 89 (Main Street), in Galax.*

U-28 BLUE RIDGE MISSION SCHOOL

The Blue Ridge Mission School was established by the Virginia Baptist General Convention in 1916 at a site just to the southeast. It provided general education and religious training, on both the elementary and secondary level, to day and boarding students. Its program was increasingly coordinated with, and in 1941 superseded by, that of the newly-developed public school system. *Patrick County: Route 8, at Route 613.*

U-30 STUART

This place, first known as Taylorsville for George Taylor, early settler, was established in 1792 after the formation of Patrick County. In 1849 it contained about fifty dwellings. The name was changed to Stuart for General J.E.B. Stuart, C.S.A., who was born in the county. The courthouse was built in 1852 and remodeled in 1928. *Patrick County: Route 58, at Stuart.*

U-32 FRONTIER FORT

About three miles north stood Fort Mayo, commanded by Captain Samuel Harris in 1756 and visited in that year by Washington. This fort was the southernmost of the line of stockade forts built from the Potomac River to North Carolina as a frontier defense in the French and Indian War. *Patrick County: Route 58, 14 miles e. of Stuart.*

U-34 REYNOLDS HOMESTEAD

Four miles to the north is Rock Spring Plantation, the boyhood home of Industrialist R. J. Reynolds. The land was settled in 1814 by Abram Reynolds and his wife Mary Harbour. About 1843 their son Hardin William Reynolds built the present brick house for his bride Nancy Jane Cox. The couple had 16 children, including Richard Joshua Reynolds, who founded R. J. Reynolds Tobacco Company. In 1970 the house was restored by Hardin's granddaughter, Nancy Susan Reynolds. *Patrick County: Route 58, at Critz.*

U-36 WILLIAM BYRD'S SURVEY OF 1728

This was the westernmost point of the survey of the Virginia–North Carolina border run in 1728 by a Joint Commission from both colonies led by Col. William Byrd II of Westover. The exact end of the line was marked on October 16, 1728, by a blazed red oak tree on the east bank of Peter's Creek. *Patrick County: Route 660, 4 miles s. of Route 8, at state line.*

U-40 BERRY HILL

Berry Hill is situated 7 miles to the south on the Dan River. The original portion of the main house was built in 1745 and there have been several additions. The property was used as a hospital for General Nathaniel Greene's army during the spring of 1781, following the Revolutionary War battle of Guilford Court House. *Pittsylvania County: Intersection of Routes 58 and 863.*

U-40 PATRICK HENRY'S LEATHERWOOD HOME

Leatherwood, ¼ mile to the south, was the home plantation of Patrick Henry from June 1779 until December 1784, when he left to serve his fourth term as governor of Virginia. Henry was one of the largest landowners of the area and served five terms as a member of the House of Delegates from Henry County. *Henry County: Route 57, .1 mile e. of Route 628.*

U-47 CARTERS TAVERN

Samuel and Elizabeth Carter operated an ordinary here from about 1808 until the 1840s. It is one of many historic buildings remaining along River Road, which, as the then principal roadway between Halifax Court House and Danville, formed a link in the main stage road between New York and New Orleans. The smaller and earliest section of Carter's Tavern was built by Joseph Dodson, who died in 1773. *Halifax County: Route 659, 3.3 miles e. of Halifax/Pittsylvania line.*

U-48 STAUNTON RIVER STATE PARK

This park was developed by the National Park Service, Interior Department, through the Civilian Conservation Commission in conjunction with the Virginia Conservation Commission. It covers 1200 acres and was opened, June 15, 1936. Nearby is Occaneechee Island where Nathaniel Bacon defeated the Indians in 1676. *Halifax County: Route 360, 7.1 miles e. of Halifax.*

U-50 NATHANIEL TERRY'S GRAVE

A short distance south is the grave of Nathaniel Terry, colonial soldier and statesman. Terry served as sheriff of Halifax County, 1752, and captain of Rangers, 1755. He was a member of the House of Burgesses, 1755–1765, 1771–1775, and also sat in the convention of 1776 that framed the Constitution of Virginia. Terry died in 1780. *Halifax County: Route 304, 6 miles n.e. of South Boston.*

U-60* OCCANEECHEE INDIANS

Nearby, on an island now inundated by the lake, the Occaneechee Indians lived and traded furs. About 1672 the Saponi and Tutelo moved to neighboring islands. Nathaniel Bacon, the rebel, killed many of them in 1676 and broke their power. *Mecklenburg County: Route 58, 1.5 miles e. of Clarkesville.*

U-80 A REVOLUTIONARY SOLDIER

Richard Kennon of Mecklenburg served as an officer in the 5th Virginia Regiment, 1776–1778 and later in the State Militia. He served in both houses of the General Assembly and was Presiding Officer of the Senate, 1800–1802. He died in 1805. *Mecklenburg County: Route 58, at Boydton.*

U-90* FORT CHRISTANNA

Three miles south is the site of Fort Christanna, which was built in 1714 by Governor Alexander Spotswood for the protection of friendly Indians from hostile tribes. A school for Indian children was also established there. *Brunswick County: Route 58, w. of Lawrenceville.*

U-102 TARLETON'S MOVEMENTS

Near this point Tarleton, the British cavalryman, entered the road from the south and moved westward to clear the fords for Cornwallis's army, May 14, 1781. Cornwallis was moving north on Petersburg. *Southampton County: Route 58, 8.2 miles e. of Emporia.*

U-105 JOHN Y. MASON'S HOME

Four miles west stood the home of John Y. Mason, statesman. Mason was a member of the House of Representatives; United States district judge; twice Secretary of the Navy; United States Attorney General, and Minister to France. He took part in the famous "Ostend Manifesto," 1854. Mason died in Paris, October 3, 1859. *Southampton County: Route 58, 8.2 miles e. of Emporia.*

U-115 BUCKHORN QUARTERS

One mile north was the estate of Major Thomas Ridley. In the servile [*sic*] insurrection of August, 1831, the houses were fortified by faithful slaves and made a place of refuge for fugitive whites. In this vicinity Nat Turner, the leader of the insurrection, spent the night after his defeat near Courtland, August 28, 1831. *Southampton County: Route 58, 4.5 miles w. of Courtland.*

U-120   GENERAL THOMAS'S BIRTHPLACE

General George H. Thomas, "The Rock of Chickamauga," was born on July 31, 1816, about five miles to the south. A graduate of West Point, Thomas sided with the Union during the Civil War and won distinction in the campaigns in Tennessee. *Southampton County: Route 58, 1.7 miles s.e. of Courtland.*

U-120*   GENERAL THOMAS'S BIRTHPLACE

Five miles southwest George H. Thomas was born, July 31, 1816. A graduate of West Point, Thomas served in the Mexican War and remained in the United States service in 1861. In saving Rosecrans' army from destruction, September 20, 1863, he won the name of "The Rock of Chickamauga." Commanding in Tennessee, he defeated Hood at Nashville, December 16, 1864. *Southampton County: Route 58, 1.7 miles s.e. of Courtland.*

U-122   SOUTHAMPTON INSURRECTION

Seven miles southwest Nat Turner, a Negro, inaugurated, August 21, 1831, a slave insurrection that lasted two days and cost the lives of about sixty whites. The slaves began the massacre near Cross Keys and moved eastward toward Courtland (Jerusalem). In meeting resistance, the insurrection speedily collapsed. *Southampton County: Route 58, 2 miles w. of Courtland.*

U-123   MAJOR JOSEPH E. GILLETTE

The "Southampton Cavalry" was formed just north of this site in May, 1861 at what was the Gillette Farm, Cedar Lawn. Joseph E. Gillette was elected captain. The Company eventually became Company A of the 13th Virginia Cavalry. Gillette was promoted to major in the regiment. He died here November 1, 1863, after being wounded at Brandy Station. The company served gallantly until the end of the Civil War as part of General J.E.B. Stuart's cavalry in General Robert E. Lee's Army of Northern Virginia. *Southampton County: Route 58, .9 mile w. of Franklin.*

U-124   OLD INDIAN RESERVATION

Just to the north was the Nottoway Indian Reservation. William Byrd, while running the boundary line between Virginia and North Carolina, visited these Indians, April 7, 1729. Indians were living here as late as 1825. *Southampton County: Route 58, .8 mile w. of Courtland.*

U-127   FIRST RURITAN CLUB

The first Ruritan Club was founded here in Holland, Va. on May 21, 1928. Ruritan is an organization of rural leaders striving through community service, fellowship and good will to make the rural community a better place in which to live. *Suffolk ("old" Nansemond County): Route 58, at Holland.*

U-130 DISMAL SWAMP

This swamp was visited by William Byrd in 1728. In 1763, George Washington made explorations in it and organized a company to drain it for farm land. Lake Drummond is in its midst. *Suffolk ("old" Nansemond County): Route 58, 4.7 miles e. of Suffolk.*

UC-5 STATE FISH HATCHERY

This fish cultural [*sic*] station was established in 1930 for hatching and rearing trout for the trout waters of Virginia. *Smyth County: Route 16, 5 miles s.e. of Marion.*

UE-2 FRIES

Center of early recorded country music. On March 1, 1923, in New York City Henry Whitter of Fries, Virginia recorded two songs "The Wreck of the Old 97" and "Lonesome Road Blues." These were among the first successful country recordings by a country artist. His recordings inspired many other local artists to record, including E. V. "Pop" Stoneman and Kelly Harrell. All three men were employees of the Fries Textile Plant. *Grayson County: Route 94 at Carroll County line.*

UE-5 FIRST COURT OF GRAYSON COUNTY

Near here, in the barn of William Bourne, was held the first court of this county, May 21, 1793. *Grayson County: Route 805, 5 miles s.w. of Fries.*

UE-6 FRIES—CENTER OF EARLY RECORDED COUNTRY MUSIC

On March 1, 1928, in New York City Henry Whitter of Fries, Virginia recorded two songs "The Wreck of the Old Southern 97" and "Lonesome Road Blues." These were among the first successful country recordings by a country artist. His records inspired many other local artists to record, including E. V. "Pop" Stoneman and Kelly Harrell. All three men were employees of the Fries Textile Plant. *Grayson County: Route 94, at Fries.*

UK-4 OLD NOTTOWAY MEETING HOUSE

This is the site of the Old Nottoway Meeting House, built in 1769, the second Baptist church established south of James River. Jeremiah Walker was the first minister. *Nottoway County: Route 723, 2 miles s. of Burkeville.*

UL-2 CAMPAIGN OF 1781

Boyd's and Irwin's ferries to the north were used by Nathanael Greene in his passage of Dan River, in mid-February, 1781, while Cornwallis was in close pursuit. Edward Carrington collected the boats for the crossing. *Halifax County: Route 501, .4 mile s. of South Boston.*

UL-4 OLD RANDOLPH-MACON COLLEGE

The large building to the north is old Randolph-Macon College, one of the first Methodist colleges in America. It was named for John Randolph of Roanoke and Nathaniel Macon, and was opened for instruction on October 9, 1832. The college was moved to Ashland in 1868. *Mecklenburg County: Route 58, .3 mile w. of Boydton.*

UL-5 TAYLOR'S FERRY

Seven miles south. There a detachment of Virginia militia crossed the Roanoke River in February, 1781, on the way to join Greene in North Carolina. There Baron Steuben, commanding the forces in Virginia, had a depot of supplies. *Mecklenburg County: Route 58, .3 mile w. of Boydton.*

UM-12* JARRATT'S STATION

Half a mile south is Jarratt's Station, a depot on the old Weldon Railroad. The Union cavalryman, Kautz, acting with Butler's Army of the James, burned the place, May 8, 1864. The Union General Wilson, retreating from Reams Station, camped here, June 29, 1864. Warren on his raid to destroy the Weldon Railroad camped here in December, 1864. *Sussex County: Route 301, at Jarratt.*

UM-14 OLD HALIFAX ROAD

Here the highway merges with the Halifax Road, the ancient road from Petersburg to Halifax, North Carolina. Over this road Cornwallis marched in May, 1781, from Halifax to Petersburg in his invasion of Virginia. Over this road the Confederates hauled supplies during the siege of Petersburg, 1864–65, and over it parts of the Union and Confederate armies constantly passed. *Sussex County: Route 301, at Jarratt.*

UM-16* NOTTOWAY RIVER

Near here the British cavalryman, Simcoe, crossed the river going south to join Cornwallis, May 11, 1781. Here Cornwallis, moving northward, was met by Benedict Arnold, coming from Petersburg, May 19, 1781. Here the Union General Wilson crossed the river, June 28, 1864, and recrossed, June 29, 1864. *Sussex County: Route 301, 3.4 miles s. of Stony Creek.*

UM-18 HISTORY AT STONY CREEK

In 1864, supplies for Lee's army were carted from the Weldon railroad here to Petersburg. Here the Union cavalryman, Wilson, returning from his raid to Burkeville, fought an action with Lee's cavalry, June 28–29, 1864. The place was raided by the Union cavalryman, Gregg, on December 1, 1864. *Sussex County: Route 301, at Stony Creek.*

UM-20 REAMS STATION

Three miles north. There, the Union cavalryman, Kautz, in Wilson's raid, destroyed the station, June 22, 1864. Returning from Burkeville, Kautz reached there again June 29, and was joined by Wilson. Attacked by Hampton, Wilson and Kautz hastily retreated to Grant's army. Hancock, while destroying the Weldon railroad, was attacked at Reams Station by A. P. Hill and Hampton, August 25, 1864, and driven back to Grant's army. *Prince George County: Route 301, 12.6 miles S. of Petersburg.*

UM-40 TARLETON'S MOVEMENTS

At this point Tarleton, the British cavalryman, crossed the Meherrin River, May 14, 1781. Sent ahead of Cornwallis's army, he had raided through Southampton and Greensville counties. *Greensville County: Route 301, at Emporia.*

UM-41 SITE OF "HOMESTEAD"

Near this site stood "Homestead," home of James Mason (1744–1784), officer in the continental army. Here was located the first clerk's office of Greensville County. This was the home of Edmunds Mason, county clerk 1807–1834, and birthplace of his sons John Y. Mason, statesman, and Dr. George Mason whose school, Homestead Seminary, occupied the house. *Greensville County: Route 58 and Chapman's Ford Road.*

UO-5 THE CATTLE (BEEFSTEAK) RAID

One mile southwest, on September 16, 1864, General Wade Hampton's Confederate Cavalry herded about 2,500 head of captured cattle across the Nottoway River, while two miles northwest, at Belsches' Mill, Federal troops sent to recapture the cattle were intercepted and repulsed. *Sussex County: Route 35, at 626.*

US-3 WILLIAM MAHONE'S BIRTHPLACE

Three and a half miles southwest, at Monroe, Major-General William Mahone was born, December 1, 1826. He served brilliantly in the Confederate army throughout the war, and won the title, "Hero of the Crater," at Petersburg, July 30, 1864. He was United States Senator, 1881–1887. Mahone died in Washington, October 8, 1895. *Southampton County: Route 258, 2.2 miles s. of Franklin.*

US-6* SOUTH QUAY

Two miles southeast is South Quay on the Blackwater, a port into which supplies and military stores were brought from Europe in the Revolution. A British force from Portsmouth burned stores there, July 16, 1781. At the ferry there, Confederates fought a skirmish with Union raiders, March 10, 1865. *Southampton County: Route 258, 4.8 miles s. of Franklin.*

UT-20 SUFFOLK CAMPAIGN

Longstreet crossed the river here and advanced on Suffolk, held by a Union garrison, April 10, 1863. The siege of Suffolk followed. *Isle of Wight County: Route 460, 6.3 miles n.w. of Windsor.*

UT-28* CAVALRY SKIRMISH

Near here, December 28, 1862, Confederate cavalry attacked Union vedettes and drove them in. The Unionists, reinforced, repulsed the attack. *Suffolk, ("old" Nansemond County): Route 460, 4.6 miles n.w. of Suffolk.*

V-1   WILTON

Five miles southwest. The house was built by William Randolph, son of William Randolph of Turkey Island, early in the eighteenth century. It was Lafayette's headquarters, May 15–20, 1781, just before Cornwallis crossed the James in pursuit of him. *Henrico County: Route 5, 2 miles s.e. of Richmond.*

V-2   VARINA AND FORT HARRISON

At Varina, a short distance south, John Rolfe and Pocahontas lived after their marriage in 1614. The place became the first county seat of Henrico County, and here also was the glebe house of Rev. James Blair, founder of William and Mary College. Under the name of Aiken's Landing, Varina was a point of exchange for prisoners in 1862. Fort Harrison near by was one of the principal works in the Richmond defenses, 1862–64. It was captured on September 29, 1864. *Henrico County: Route 5, 4.5 miles s.e. of Richmond.*

V-3*   CURLES NECK AND BREMO

Named for the curves made here by James River, Curles Neck was patented in 1617. It was the home of Nathaniel Bacon, the Rebel, in 1676. In 1698, William Randolph of Turkey Island obtained the estate, which he left to his son, Richard Randolph, grandfather of John Randolph of Roanoke. Just beyond is Bremo, patented by Richard Cocke in 1639. *Henrico County: Route 5, 9.3 miles s.e. of Richmond.*

V-4   MALVERN HILL

A colonial dwelling of the Cocke famly was here. Lafayette camped here in July-August, 1781, watching Cornwallis. Here McClellan's army retiring from Richmond was attacked by Lee on July 1, 1862. Lee did not storm the hill, but that night McClellan fell back to James River at Harrison's Landing. *Henrico County: Route 5, 13.3 miles s.e. of Richmond.*

V-5*   TURKEY ISLAND

So named in 1607 by Captain Christopher Newport on his voyage of discovery up James River. In 1684 it became the property of William Randolph, founder of the Randolph family in Virginia and ancestor of Jefferson, Marshall and Lee. The colonial house was destroyed by Union gunboats in 1862. An action took place near the creek between Union and Confederate forces, June 30, 1862. *Henrico County: Route 5, 12.3 miles s.e. of Richmond.*

V-6   SHIRLEY

The house is a short distance south. Shirley was first occupied in 1613 and was known as West-and-Shirley Hundred. In 1664, Edward Hill patented the place, which was left by the third Edward Hill to his sister, Elizabeth Carter, in 1720. Here was born Anne Hill Carter, mother of Robert E. Lee, who often visited Shirley. The present house was built about 1740. *Charles City County: Route 5, 17.1 miles s.e. of Richmond.*

V-7 BERKELEY AND HARRISON'S LANDING

A short distance south. The place was first settled in 1619 but was abandoned. It was repatented in 1636. Benjamin Harrison, signer of the Declaration of Independence, lived here; his son, William Henry Harrison, President of the United States, was born here, 1773. In July-August, 1862, General McClellan had his headquarters at Berkeley while the Army of the Potomac was here. *Charles City County: Route 5, 7.2 miles w. of Charles City.*

V-8 WESTOVER

Two miles southeast. In 1619 the first settlement was made there; settlers were killed there in the Indian massacre of 1622. In 1666, Theodoric Bland bought Westover; in 1688 it passed to William Byrd. His son, Colonel William Byrd, built the present house about 1730. In January, 1781, Cornwallis crossed the river there in pursuit of Lafayette. *Charles City County: Route 5, 7.2 miles w. of Charles City.*

V-9 GRANT'S CROSSING

A mile south, at Wilcox's Wharf, a part of Grant's army going to Petersburg was ferried over James River to Windmill Point, June 14–16, 1864. The rest of the army crossed a little lower on a pontoon bridge. *Charles City County: Route 5, 2.4 miles w. of Charles City.*

V-10 GREENWAY

This was the home of John Tyler, Governor of Virginia, 1808–1811. His son, John Tyler, President of the United States, was born here, March 29, 1790. *Charles City County: Route 5, .7 mile w. of Charles City.*

V-11 CHARLES CITY COURTHOUSE

In 1702 Charles City County, which then included both sides of James River, was divided; the courthouse here was built about 1730. Here Simcoe's British cavalry surprised a party of militia, January 8, 1781. Here Grant's army passed on its way to the river, June, 1864. *Charles City County: Route 5, at Charles City.*

V-12 UPPER WEYANOKE

Five miles due south. In 1617, the Indian chief, Opechancanough, gave Governor Yeardley land there. In 1665, the place passed to Joseph Harwood, whose descendants, the Douthats, still own it. In June, 1864, most of Grant's army crossed the James River at Weyanoke on a pontoon bridge nearly half a mile long. *Charles City County: Route 5, at Charles City.*

V-13 SALEM CHURCH

This church, four miles north, was used as a field hospital, June, 1864, following the action at Nance's Shop, where the Union cavalryman Gregg, guarding a wagon train, was attacked by Wade Hampton. Gregg was driven from the field but saved the wagons. Wounded soldiers were brought to the church and some of the dead were buried there. *Charles City County: Route 5, 5.9 miles w. of Charles City.*

V-14   WESTOVER CHURCH

A short distance south is Westover Church. It was first built on the James River near Westover House early in the eighteenth century. About 1730 the site was changed and the present building erected. Defaced in the Campaign of 1862, the church was re-opened for worship in 1867. *Charles City County: Route 5, 6.5 miles w. of Charles City.*

V-15   SCENE OF JEFFERSON'S WEDDING

Two miles east is the site of "The Forest," home of Martha Wayles Skelton, widow of Bathurst Skelton. There she was married to Thomas Jefferson, January 1, 1772. The bridal couple drove in the snow to Jefferson's home, "Monticello." *Charles City County: Route 5, 15.1 miles s.e. of Richmond.*

V-16   CAMPAIGN OF 1781

Tarleton, British cavalryman, moving eastward to join Cornwallis at Richmond, passed near here, June 15, 1781. *Henrico County: Route 250, 8.5 miles w. of Richmond.*

V-17*   OUTER DEFENSES

The outer line of Richmond defenses, 1862–65, here crossed the road. To the east were the intermediate defenses; the inner line lay well within the limits of the present city. *Henrico County: Route 250, 1.9 miles w. of Richmond.*

V-18   REUBEN FORD

A mile north are the home and grave of Reuben Ford, pastor of Goochland Baptist Church, 1771–1823. He was an advocate of equal religious rights for all, a leader in securing separation of church and state in Virginia. *Goochland County: Route 250, 1.9 miles e. of Oilville.*

V-19   PROVIDENCE CHURCH

Half a mile northeast stands Providence Presbyterian church, built probably in 1749 and little altered since. John Todd, Senior, a founder of Hampden-Sydney College, was pastor for forty years (1753–1793). Hanover Presbytery met there in October, 1762. *Louisa County: Route 250, .4 mile n.w. of Gum Spring.*

V-20   CAMPAIGN OF 1781

Here Lafayette, moving west to protect a supply depot in Albemarle from Cornwallis, entered this road, June 13, 1781. *Louisa County: Route 250, at Ferncliff.*

V-21   PRESIDENT TYLER'S HOME

Just to the south is Sherwood Forest, where President John Tyler lived after his retirement form the presidency until his death in 1862. He bought the place in 1842 and came to it as his home in March, 1845. Here Tyler, with his young second wife, entertained much and raised another large family. The house, well-furnished, was damaged in the war period. 1862–65. *Charles City County: Route 5, 3.5 miles e. of Charles City.*

W-1* TO FRAZIER'S FARM

Over this road Longstreet's and A. P. Hill's divisions moved, on June 29, 1862, to attack McClellan at Frazier's Farm. *Henrico County: Route 60, Williamsburg Avenue at Darbytown Road.*

W-2 WILLIAMSBURG ROAD

Over the road here D. H. Hill's and Longstreet's divisions moved, on May 31, 1862, to the battle of Seven Pines and over it, on June 29, 1862, Magruder moved to the battle of Savage's Station. *Henrico County: Route 60, .4 mile e. of Richmond.*

W-3* CHARLES CITY ROAD

Over this road Ruger's division moved, on June 29, 1862, to attack McClellan at Frazier's Farm. *Henrico County: Route 60, one mile e. of Richmond.*

W-4 McCLELLAN'S PICKET LINE

The picket line of McClellan's army crossed the road here on the morning of May 31, 1862. *Henrico County: Route 60, at Sandston.*

W-5 McCLELLAN'S FIRST LINE

Here was McClellan's first line of defense, held by Casey. The Confederates, advancing eastward on May 31, 1862, stormed the earthworks. *Henrico County: Route 60, at Sandston.*

W-6* MUNITIONS PLANT

Here stood a large munitions plant of the World War, 1918. *Henrico County: Route 60, e. entrance of Sandston.*

W-7* FAIR OAKS BATTLE

At Fair Oaks Station, a mile north, McClellan's right wing stayed the advance of the Confederates on May 31, 1862. *Henrico County: Route 60, .5 mile e. of Sandston.*

W-8 McCLELLAN'S WITHDRAWAL

In this vicinity a part of McClellan's army remained for several weeks after the battle of Seven Pines. The part of his army north of the Chickahominy was attacked by Lee, June 26–27, 1862. McClellan then began to withdraw to the James, June 28–29, 1862. *Henrico County: Route 60, 3.6 miles e. of Seven Pines.*

W 9 McCLELLAN'S SECOND LINE

Here, at Seven Pines, was McClellan's second and main line of defense. The Confederates under D. H. Hill, having taken the first line, attacked this position, held by Casey and Couch reinforced by Kearny, May 31, 1862. The battle was bitterly contested until Longstreet sent in fresh troops. The Union line was broken; the Unionists fell back a mile and a half east. *Henrico County: Route 60, at Seven Pines.*

W-10* SECOND DAY AT SEVEN PINES

The Confederates attacked Mc-Clellan's army along the railroad north of this road but soon withdrew, ending the battle, June 1, 1862. On the same day Robert E. Lee assumed command of the Army of Northern Virginia, replacing Johnston. *Henrico County: Route 60, .3 mile e. of Seven Pines.*

W-11 McCLELLAN'S THIRD LINE

Here ran McClellan's third line of defense, May 31–June 1, 1862. The Confederates, taking the first and second lines on this road, did not reach the third. *Henrico County: Route 60, 1.3 miles e. of Seven Pines.*

W-12* BATTLE OF SAVAGE'S STATION

Near here, on June 29, 1862, Magruder attacked the rear of McClellan's army withdrawing to the James and fought an indecisive action. McClellan continued his withdrawal. *Henrico County: Route 60, 2 miles e. of Seven Pines.*

W-13* TO WHITE OAK SWAMP AND MALVERN HILL

This road was used, on June 29, 1862, by McClellan's army moving to the James, and by Stonewall Jackson, following, on June 30. *Henrico County: Route 60, 2 miles e. of Sandston.*

W-14 McCLELLAN'S CROSSING

Here a part of McClellan's army crossed the Chickahominy on May 23, 1862, advancing on Richmond. It was attacked by the Confederates at Seven Pines. *New Kent County: Route 60, at Bottoms Bridge.*

W-15* CAMP BOTTOM'S BRIDGE

Here, in 1814, was a large camp of militia mustered to resist British invasion. *Henrico County: Route 60, 15 miles e. of Richmond.*

W-16 LAFAYETTE AND CORNWALLIS

Lafayette camped near here, on May 4, 1781. On May 28, 1781, Cornwallis camped here in pursuit of Lafayette and camped here again on June 21, 1781, while retiring eastward before Lafayette and Wayne. *New Kent County: Route 60, at Bottoms Bridge.*

W-17 NEW KENT ROAD

This was the main road to Williamsburg in early days. Cornwallis, retiring eastward, used this road in June, 1781. The Confederates, retreating westward, passed over it in May, 1862. *New Kent County: Route 60, at Bottoms Bridge.*

W-18 LONG BRIDGE

One mile south is Long Bridge over the Chickahominy River. Benedict Arnold sent Simcoe there in the British invasion of 1781. Longstreet crossed there in the Peninsular Campaign, May, 1862. Grant's Fifth and Second Corps crossed there, in June, 1864, on the way to Petersburg. *New Kent County: Route 60, 4.9 miles s.e. of Bottoms Bridge.*

W-19* SOANE'S BRIDGE

Half a mile south is Soane's Bridge over the Chickahominy. Here Stuart crossed, on June 14, 1862, in his famous ride around McClellan; here the Ninth and Sixth Corps of Grant's army crossed, June 13–14, 1864. *New Kent County: Route 60, at Bottoms Bridge.*

W-20   PROVIDENCE FORGE

Here about 1770, Charles Jeffery Smith, a Presbyterian minister, settled and, with William Holt, built a forge for making farm implements. Francis Jerdone became a partner in 1771. A militia camp was established here in 1781, and Lafayette was here in July and August, 1781. *New Kent County: Route 60, at Providence Forge.*

W-21   STATE GAME FARM

Established, 1920, for breeding partridges in captivity on a large scale. The first institution of the kind in the world. Game sanctuaries are stocked from this plant. *New Kent County: Route 60, 2.8 miles s.e. of Providence Forge.*

W-21   STATE GAME FARM

Established, 1920, for breeding partridges in captivity on a large scale. The first institution of the kind in the world. Game sanctuaries are stocked from this plant. *Cumberland County: Route 45, 6 miles s. of Cartersville at Route 615.*

W-22   CHICKAHOMINY INDIANS

One mile south is the home of descendants of the Chickahominy Indians, a powerful tribe at the time of the settlement of Jamestown. Chickahominies were among the Indians who took Captain John Smith prisoner in December, 1607. *New Kent County: Route 60, 4.2 miles s.e. of Providence Forge.*

W-23   FORT JAMES

A mile and a half south stood Moysonec, an Indian village occupied in 1607. This was the region of the Chickahominy tribe, members of which took part, in 1607, in the capture of Captain John Smith. There Fort James was established in 1645 after the great Indian massacre of 1644 in which several hundred colonists perished. *New Kent County: Route 60, 7.6 miles s.e. of Providence Forge.*

W-24   DIASCUND BRIDGE

Naval stores for the Virginia navy were destroyed here by British troops, April 22, 1781. *New Kent County: Route 60, 6.7 miles n.w. of Toano.*

W-25*   COOPER'S MILL

One-half mile north up Diascund Creek stood Cooper's Mill at which Cornwallis obtained supplies, June 23–24, 1781. *New Kent County: Route 60, 7.25 miles e. of Providence Forge.*

W-26*   NEW KENT ROAD

Cornwallis camped about a mile north of this point on June 24, 1781. A part of Lafayette's army, following, camped at the same place on June 27, 1781. *James City County: Route 60, 3 miles n.w. of Toano.*

W-27   WHITE HALL TAVERN

This was a station on the old stage road between Williamsburg and Richmond, before 1860. *James City County: Route 60, 1.3 miles n.w. of Toano.*

W-28*   OLIVE BRANCH CHRISTIAN CHURCH

This church was built in 1835 on land granted to Leonard Henley in 1661, and is one of the oldest churches of the Disciples of Christ in this part of the State. In 1862–65, it was occupied by Union soldiers; with that exception the church has been continuously in use since its erection. *James City County: Route 60, .9 mile s.e. of Toano.*

W-29   TYREE'S PLANTATION

North of the road was Tyree's Plantation, Lafayette's headquarters, June 28–July 5, 1781, in his campaign against Cornwallis. *New Kent County: Route 60, 6.7 miles n.w. of Toano.*

W-30   HICKORY NECK CHURCH

Hickory Neck Church was built about 1740. Militia opposing the British camped here on April 21, 1781. A few miles north is the foundation of an ancient stone house, dating possibly from about 1650. *James City County: Route 60, .8 mile n.w. of Toano.*

W-31   STATE SHIPYARD

On this road five miles west was the State shipyard on Chickahominy River, burned by the British General Phillips on April 21–22, 1781. *James City County: Route 60, at Toano.*

W-32   CHICKAHOMINY CHURCH

Two miles south is the site of the colonial Chickahominy Church, now destroyed. Lafayette's forces camped there, July 6–8, 1781. The church was used as a hospital after the battle of Green Spring, July 6, 1781. *James City County: Route 60, at Toano.*

W-33*   BURNT ORDINARY

Here was a colonial tavern which, after its destruction by fire, was known as "Burnt Ordinary." Cornwallis passed here on his way to Williamsburg, June 25, 1781. *James City County: Route 60, at Toano.*

W-34*   SIX-MILE ORDINARY

Near this spot was Allen's Ordinary, sometimes called "Six-Mile Ordinary." An early settlement of Quakers was east of this point, near Scimino Creek. Militia under Colonel James Innes camped here on April 20, 1781. Colonel Thomas Mathews and his militia were attacked here by Tarleton, August 22, 1781. *James City County: Route 60, 4.3 miles s.e. of Toano.*

W-35   SPENCER'S ORDINARY

On this road, four miles south, the action of Spencer's Ordinary was fought, June 24, 1781, between detachments from Lafayette's and Cornwallis's armies. *James City County: Route 60, 4.3 miles s.e. of Toano.*

W-36 GREEN SPRING

On this road, five miles south, is Green Spring, home of Governor Sir William Berkeley. Bacon, the Rebel, occupied it in 1676. Cornwallis, after moving from Williamsburg by this road on July 4, 1781, was attacked by Lafayette at Green Spring on July 6, 1781. Anthony Wayne was the hero of this fight. *James City County: Route 60, 4.3 miles s.e. of Toano.*

W-37* PENINSULAR CAMPAIGN

In the Peninsular Campaign, Johnston's army marched over this road toward Richmond, May 4–6, 1862. McClellan's army followed May 6–10, 1862. *James City County: Route 60, n.w. entrance of Williamsburg.*

W-38* IRON-BOUND ROAD

The Iron-Bound Road, the oldest road between Williamsburg and Jamestown, dates from the seventeenth century. *James City County: Route 60, 3 miles n.w. of Williamsburg.*

W-40 FIRST BALLOON FLIGHT IN VIRGINIA

On May 7, 1801, J. S. Watson, a student at William and Mary, wrote a letter detailing attempts at flying hot air balloons on the Court House Green. The third balloon, decorated with sixteen stars, one for each of the existing states, and fueled with spirits of wine, was successful. Watson wrote, "I never saw so great and so universal delight as it gave to the spectators." This is the earliest recorded evidence of aeronautics in the Commonwealth. *Williamsburg: Route 162, at entrance to Cary Field.*

W-42* QUARTER PATH

The first quarter mile of this side road was known as the "Quarter Path," a colonial race track. *James City County: Route 60, s.e. entrance of Williamsburg.*

W-43 BATTLE OF WILLIAMSBURG

To the east of the road here, centering at Fort Magruder, was fought the battle of Williamsburg on May 5, 1862. The Union General McClellan was pursuing General Johnston's retiring army, the rearguard of which was commanded by General Longstreet. Johnston ordered Longstreet to hold off McClellan's attacking forces until the Confederate wagon trains, bogged down in mud, were out of danger. This mission was accomplished and Johnston continued his retirement. *James City County: Route 60, .3 mile s.e. of Williamsburg.*

W-44 MAGRUDER'S DEFENSES

Here is a redoubt in the Line of Confederate defenses, built across the James-York peninsula in 1861–62 by General John B. Magruder. *James City County: Route 60, .3 mile s.e. of Williamsburg.*

W-45 WHITAKER'S HOUSE

A mile north of the road is Whitaker's House, headquarters of General W. F. Smith, battle of Williamsburg, May 5, 1862. *James City County: Route 60, 1.4 miles s.e. of Williamsburg.*

W-46   VINEYARD TRACT

One mile north of the highway, an experimental farm for the culture of grapes was established by the Virginia government in 1769. On this tract stood a hospital of the French-American army, 1781. *York County: Route 641, 1.4 miles e. of Williamsburg, on secondary road.*

W-47*   KINGSMILL

Kingsmill Plantation is two miles south. Burwell's Ferry, a river landing, was there. In January, 1781, General Thomas Nelson, with militia, prevented Benedict Arnold from landing at the ferry. On April 20, 1781, Arnold and Phillips landed there and marched to Williamsburg. *James City County: Route, 2.4 miles s.e. of Williamsburg.*

W-48*   LITTLETOWN

Here was Littletown, the plantation of George Menefie, occupied by him as early as 1633. Camp Wallace, an artillery camp of the World War, 1917–1918, was here. *James City County: Route 60, 2.8 miles s.e. of Williamsburg.*

W-49*   TREBELL'S LANDING

At Trebell's Landing, one mile southwest, the artillery and stores of the French and American armies for the siege of Yorktown were landed, September, 1781. These were conveyed by land (six miles) to Yorktown. The troops disembarked at the landings near Williamsburg. *James City County: Route 60, 5.1 miles s.e. of Williamsburg.*

W-50*   CARTER'S GROVE

Carter's Grove was owned by the Burwell family. Carter Burwell, who built the mansion in 1751, was the grandson of Robert ("King") Carter. *James City County: Route 60, 3.25 miles s.e. of Williamsburg.*

W-51   MARTIN'S HUNDRED

On both sides of this road and extending west was the plantation known as Martin's Hundred, originally of 80,000 acres. Settled in 1619, this hundred sent delegates to the first legislative assembly in America, 1619. In the Indian massacre of 1622, seventy-eight persons were slain here. *James City County: Route 60, 6.7 miles s.e. of Williamsburg.*

W-52   MARTIN'S HUNDRED CHURCH

A mile south is the site of the early colonial church of Martin's Hundred. *James City County: Route 60, 6.7 miles s.e. of Williamsburg.*

W-53*   SKIFFES CREEK

Skiffes, or Keith's Creek was named for Rev. George Keith, minister of Martin's Hundred parish in 1624. *Newport News ("old" Warwick County): Route 60, 1 mile n.w. of Lee Hall.*

W-54*   LEE HALL

Lee Hall was the headquarters of John B. Magruder, Confederate general, in April and May, 1862. *Newport News ("old" Warwick County): Route 60, at Lee Hall.*

W-55* TO YORKTOWN

On this road, seven miles north, is Yorktown, where Cornwallis surrendered to Washington and Rochambeau on October 19, 1781. *Newport News ("Old" Warwick County): Route 60, at Lee Hall*

W-56* FORT EUSTIS

Fort Eustis, half a mile south, was a cantonment of the World War and is now an artillery post. Within the fort grounds are the Jones House, built about 1660 and rebuilt in 1727; and Fort Crawford, a Confederate work. Here also was Stanley Hundred, granted to Sir George Yeardley in 1626. *Newport News ("old" Warwick County): Route 337, 1 mile s. of Lee Hall.*

W-57* MULBERRY POINT

Five miles through Fort Eustis grounds is Mulberry Point on James River. Near this spot, on June 8, 1610, the starving colonists, who had abandoned Jamestown, met a messenger bearing tidings of relief and returned to the settlement. *Newport News ("old" Warwick County): Route 337, 1 mile s. of Lee Hall.*

W-58* LEE'S MILL

A short distance north of this road across the reservoir is the site of the ancient Lee's Mill. The side road leads to the Miles Curtis farm, where, in April and May, 1862, officers of McClellan's army made balloon observations. *Newport News ("old" Warwick County): Route 337, 2 miles s.e. of Lee Hall.*

W-59* BATTLE OF DAM NO. 1

One mile east of this road is the battlefield of Dam No. 1 (or Lee's Mill), fought April 16, 1862, the opening engagement of the Peninsular Campaign. *Newport News ("old" Warwick County): Route 60, 1.9 miles s.e. of Lee Hall.*

W-60 WARWICK COURTHOUSE

The clerk's office was built in 1810, when Warwick Courthouse was moved here. *Newport News ("old" Warwick County): Route 60, at Denbigh (14421 Old Courthouse Way).*

W-61 DENBIGH PLANTATION

Two miles to the southwest was Denbigh, plantation of Samuel Matthews, who came to Virginia in 1622 and was governor in 1658. A public storehouse was built there in 1633 and Warwick Courthouse in 1691. *Newport News ("old" Warwick County): Route 60, 2.2 miles s.e. of Denbigh, at Menchville Road.*

W-62* WARWICK RIVER

A short distance west of this road is Warwick River, on the west side of which, extending to Yorktown, John B. Magruder built fortifications in January and February, 1862. *Newport News ("old" Warwick County): Route 337, 4 miles s.e. of Denbigh.*

W-63* YOUNG'S MILL

Here ran a line of Confederate fortifications, built in 1861 to oppose the Union advance from Fortress Monroe. *Newport News ("old" Warwick County): Route 337, .75 mile s.e. of Denbigh.*

W-64*   WATERS CREEK

In 1624 Captain Edward Waters obtained a patent on this creek. He was living here in 1625. *Newport News ("old" Warwick County): Route 60, 6.5 miles s.e. of Denbigh.*

W-65*   DENBIGH BAPTIST CHURCH

This church is near the site of the colonial church of Upper Denbigh Parish. *Newport News ("old" Warwick County): Route 60, 2.6 miles s.e. of Denbigh.*

W-66*   BATTLE OF BIG BETHEL

Five miles east is Big Bethel, where a battle was fought on June 10, 1861. *Newport News ("old" Warwick County): Route 60, at Morrison.*

W-66*   BATTLE OF BIG BETHEL

Five miles east was Big Bethel Church. On June 10, 1861, General Ebenezer W. Peirce attacked a numerically inferior confederate force under Colonel John B. Magruder. The assault was repulsed, and Peirce withdrew to Hampton and Newport News. *Newport News ("old" Warwick County): Route 60, at Route 306.*

W-67*   MARY'S MOUNT

Two and one-half miles east is Mary's Mount (present Merry Point), settled by Daniel Gookin, Jr., before 1630. *Newport News: Route 337, 1 mile n.w. of Hilton Village.*

W-68*   CAMP HILL

This was a World War Aeration camp, 1918. *Newport News: Route 337, near Hilton Village.*

W-69*   BLUNT POINT

Four miles south on James River is Blunt Point, named for Humphrey Blount, who was killed by the Indians in 1610. *Newport News: Route 337, 1 mile n.w. of Hilton Village.*

W-70*   NEWPORT NEWS

This community was known to Captain John Smith as Point Hope, but it was called "Newportes Newes" as early as 1619. The name may commemorate Captain Christopher Newport, Commander of five expeditions to Jamestown during 1606–1612. *Newport News: Twenty-seventh Street at the water front.*

W-70*   NEWPORT NEWS

Daniel Gookin, Sr., settled a colony of eighty people here in November, 1621. The place was named for Sir William Newce. *Newport News: Route 337, w. entrance of Newport News.*

W-70*   SETTLEMENT OF NEWPORT NEWS

The place appears on Captain John Smith's map as Point Hope. In 1621, Sir William Newce, marshal of Virginia, his brother, Captain Thomas Newce, and Daniel Gookin came here from Newcestown, Ireland, and made a settlement. It was known as Newport Newce, later Newport News. *Newport News: s. end of Twenty-sixth Street.*

W-79   LAST INDIAN RAID

Near this spot, in 1764, John Trimble was killed by Indians in the last raid in Augusta County. *Augusta County: Route 250, 4 miles w. of Staunton.*

W-84   FIRST BATTLE OF IRONCLADS

In Hampton Roads, southward and a mile or two offshore, the Virginia (Merrimac) and the Monitor fought their engagement, March 9, 1862. The day before the Virginia destroyed the Cumberland and Congress, wooden ships of the Union navy. *Hampton ("old" Elizabeth City County): Chesapeake Avenue between La Salle and East avenues.*

W-85   WYTHE'S BIRTHPLACE

Eight miles north George Wythe, Revolutionary leader and Signer of the Declaration of Independence, was born, 1726. *Hampton ("old" Elizabeth City County): Route 60, .5 mile west of Hampton.*

W-86*   FORTS HENRY AND CHARLES

A short distance to the east are the sites of Fort Henry and Fort Charles, built in 1610 by Sir Thomas Gates after the expulsion of the Indians living here. In 1637, Fort Henry was abandoned. *Hampton ("old" Elizabeth City County): Route 60, .5 mile s.w. of Hampton proper.*

W-87   HISTORIC HAMPTON

The Indian village of Kecoughtan stood here in 1607. An English village was built on its site in 1610. In 1630 William Claiborne set up a trading post here. The town of Hampton was established by law in 1680 and named for the Earl of Southampton. The first Revolutionary engagement in Virginia took place here, October 25, 1775. British sacked the town in June, 1813. Confederates burned it in August, 1861, to prevent its use by Union troops. *Hampton ("old" Elizabeth City County): corner of (Sunset and Kecoughtan roads).*

W-88   EMANCIPATION OAK

To the west, on the grounds of Hampton Institute, is the tree under which Mrs. Mary Peake, a Freedwoman, taught children of former slaves in 1861. Nearby stood the Butler School, a free school established in 1863 for colored children. *Hampton: East Tyler Street and ramp to Interstate 64.*

W-88*   LITTLE ENGLAND

This point, patented by William Capps about 1634, was known for a century as Capps Point. In June, 1813, a small militia garrison here was forced to retreat before a British invasion. *Hampton: Route 60, at Hampton/Newport News line.*

W-89 FORT ALGERNOURNE

Near here Captain John Ratcliffe built Fort Algernourne, 1609. In 1614, it was a stockade containing fifty people and seven cannon. In 1632, the fort was rebuilt. It was discontinued after 1667. In 1727, a new fort, Fort George, was ordered built here. This fort was destroyed by a hurricane in 1749. *Hampton ("old" Elizabeth City County): Route 60 at Fortress Monroe, near Old Point Comfort.*

W-90 FORT MONROE

The fort was begun in 1819 and named for President James Monroe. It remained in possession of the Union forces, 1861–65, and from it as a base McClellan began the Peninsular Campaign, 1862. Jefferson Davis was imprisoned here, 1865–67. *Hampton ("old" Elizabeth City County): Route 60, at Fortress Monroe, near Old Point Comfort.*

W-91 THE ZERO MILE POST

This zero mile post is a replica of the original post that stood here at the end of the track on the Chesapeake and Ohio Railway, from which point all main line distances have been measured for the 664.9 miles to Cincinnati, Ohio, since 1889. The Fort Monroe (Old Point Comfort) station located here ceased operation in December, 1939. *Hampton ("old" Elizabeth City County): Route 258 at Fort Monroe.*

W-92 CONFINEMENT OF JEFFERSON DAVIS

In this casemate Jefferson Davis, President of the Confederate States, was confined, May 22–October 2, 1865. As his health suffered in the casemate, he was removed to Carroll Hall in the fortress, where he remained from October, 1865, until May, 1867, when he was released on bail. He was never brought to trial. *Hampton ("old" Elizabeth City County): Route 60, at Fort Monroe, near Old Point Comfort.*

W-149* FORT EDWARD JOHNSON

This earthwork was made by the Confederate General Edward Johnson about April 1, 1862. He withdrew from it to occupy Shenandoah Mountain near Staunton, where he prepared to resist invasion from the west. *Highland County: Route 250, 5 miles w. of West Augusta.*

W-150 BATTLE OF McDOWELL

Stonewall Jackson, to prevent a junction of Fremont and Banks, took position on the hills just to the south and beat off the attacks of Fremont's advance under Milroy, May 8, 1862. Milroy retreated that night. *Highland County: Route 250, 1 mile e. of McDowell.*

W-155 TINKLING SPRING CHURCH

This was first the southern branch of the "Triple Forks of Shenandoah" congregation, which called John Craig as pastor in 1741. A church was completed here about 1748; two other buildings have succeeded it. Beginning with 1777, James Waddel, the noted blind preacher, was supply for some years. R. L. Dabney, of Stonewall Jackson's staff, was the minister here, 1847–1852. *Augusta County: Route 608, 4 miles w. of Staunton.*

W-159 FIRST SETTLERS' GRAVE

One mile north is the grave of John Lewis, first settler in this region, who came here in 1732 and died in 1762. He chose the site of the town of Staunton. His four sons, Thomas, Andrew, William and Charles, took an important part in the Indian and Revolutionary wars. *Augusta County: Route 250 at e. entrance of Staunton.*

W-160* EARLY'S LAST BATTLE

Sheridan attacked Early on the ridge west of this city, driving him from his position and capturing many of his men, March 2, 1865. This was the last important battle in northern Virginia. *Augusta County: Route 250, at w. entrance of Waynesboro.*

W-161 BIRTHPLACE OF MERIWETHER LEWIS

Half a mile north was born, 1774, Meriwether Lewis, of the Lewis and Clark Expedition, sent by Jefferson to explore the Far West, 1804–1806. The expedition reached the mouth of the Columbia River, November 15, 1805. *Albemarle County: Route 250, 5 miles w. of Charlottesville.*

W-162 JACKSON'S VALLEY CAMPAIGN

Near here, Stonewall Jackson's troops entrained, May 4, 1862, to go west to Staunton in the move that led to the battle of McDowell, May 8, 1862. *Albemarle County: Route 250, at Mechums River.*

W-163 REVOLUTIONARY SOLDIERS GRAVES

Jesse Pitman Lewis (d. March 8, 1849), of the Virginia Militia, and Taliaferro Lewis (d. July 12, 1810), of the Continental Line, two of several brothers who fought in the war for independence, are buried in the Lewis family cemetery 100 yards south of this marker. *Albemarle County: Route 250, w. entrance to Charlottesville.*

W-173 CROZET

The town grew around a rail stop established on Wayland's farm in 1876. It was named for Col. B. Claudius Crozet, (1789–1864)—Napoleonic army officer, and the state's engineer and cartographer. He built this pioneer railway through the Blue Ridge. The 4273' tunnel through the rocksolid mountain below Rockfish Gap carried traffic from 1858–1944. His talents were tested in solving safety, drainage and ventilation problems posed by the construction of this tunnel. *Albemarle County: Route 240, in Crozet.*

W-198 SHADWELL—THOMAS JEFFERSON'S BIRTHPLACE

To the south stands a representation of the house in which Thomas Jefferson was born. It stands on the original foundations, which were identified in 1955. It was completed in 1960. *Albemarle County: Route 250, 3 miles e. of Charlottesville.*

W-199 CLARK'S BIRTHPLACE

A mile north was born George Rogers Clark, defender of Kentucky and conqueror of the Northwest, November 19, 1752. *Albemarle County: Route 250, .2 mile e. of Charlottesville.*

W-200 MONTICELLO

Three miles to the southeast. Thomas Jefferson began the house in 1770 and finished it in 1802. He brought his bride to it in 1772. Lafayette visited it in 1825. Jefferson spent his last years there and died there, July 4, 1826. His tomb is there. The place was raided by British cavalry, June 4, 1781. *Charlottesville: at courthouse.*

W-201 COLLE

The house was built about 1770 by workmen engaged in building Monticello. Mazzei, an Italian, lived here for some years adapting grape culture to Virginia. Baron de Reidesel, captured at Saratoga in 1777, lived here with his family, 1779–1780. Scenes in Ford's novel, Janice Meredith, are laid here. *Albemarle County: Route 250, 4.2 miles e. of Charlottesville.*

W-202 SHADWELL ESTATE

Peter Jefferson acquired the land in 1735, and built the house about 1737. Thomas Jefferson was born here, April 13, 1743. He lived here, 1743–1745, and 1752–1770. The house burned in 1770, and Jefferson then moved to Monticello. *Albemarle County: Route 250, 2.9 miles e. of Charlottesville.*

W-203 EDGEHILL

The land was patented in 1735. The old house was built in 1790; the new in 1828. Here lived Thomas Mann Randolph, Governor of Virginia, 1819–1822, who married Martha, daughter of Thomas Jefferson. *Albemarle County: Route 250, 4.2 miles e. of Charlottesville.*

W-204 CASTLE HILL

The original house was built in 1765 by Doctor Thomas Walker, explorer and pioneer. Tarleton, raiding to Charlottesville to capture Jefferson and the legislature, stopped here for breakfast, June 4, 1781. This delay aided the patriots to escape. Castle Hill was long the home of Senator William Cabell Rives, who built the present house. *Albemarle County: Route 231, e. of Shadwell.*

W-205* MECHUNK CREEK

Two miles south of this place Lafayette camped, June 13–14, 1781. He had come from the Rapidan River to throw himself between Cornwallis on the east and military stores in Albemarle County. *Albemarle County: Route 22, 6 miles e. of Shadwell.*

W-206 THE MARQUIS ROAD

Lafayette reopened this road in June, 1781, when moving south to intervene between Cornwallis and military stores in Albemarle County. The road has ever since been known as "The Marquis Road." *Louisa County: Route 22, at Boswell's Tavern.*

W-207 BOSWELL'S TAVERN

At this old tavern Lafayette camped, on June 12, 1781, while moving southward to intervene between Cornwallis and military stores in Albemarle County. *Louisa County: Route 22, at Boswell's Tavern.*

W-208 GREEN SPRINGS

Near here Wade Hampton's Confederate cavalry camped the night of June 10, 1864, just before the battle of Trevilians. *Louisa County: Route 33, 7 miles w. of Louisa.*

W-209 BATTLE OF TREVILIANS

Here, on June 12, 1864, Sheridan's cavalry, coming from Trevilians, attacked Wade Hampton, who had taken position across the road. A bloody engagement followed. Fitz Lee joined Hampton, and the Union cavalry was driven back. That night Sheridan retired eastward. *Louisa County: Route 33, 4.5 miles w. of Louisa.*

W-210* BATTLE OF TREVILIANS

Near here Custer of Sheridan's cavalry, raiding westward, got between Fitz Lee's division and the rest of Wade Hampton's cavalry, capturing wagons. The Confederates recaptured the wagons but withdrew to the west after a fierce conflict, June 11, 1864. *Louisa County: Route 33, 4.5 miles w. of Louisa.*

W-211 PATRICK HENRY'S HOME

At Roundabout Plantation, eight miles southwest, Patrick Henry lived from 1765 to 1768, when he sat for Louisa County in the House of Burgesses. This was the beginning of his political career. *Louisa County: Route 33, at Louisa.*

W-212 HISTORIC LOUISA

Here the county seat was established in 1742. The British Cavalryman, Tarleton, stopped here on his raid to Charlottesville, June 3, 1781. Stoneman raided the place and destroyed the railroad, May 2, 1863. Near here Fitz Lee camped, June 10, 1864, just before the Battle of Trevilians. *Louisa: Routes 33 and 22, e. of Louisa.*

W-213 JACK JOUETT'S RIDE

From the tavern that stood here, Jack Jouett rode to Charlottesville, by the Old Mountain Road, in time to warn the members of the Virginia government of the coming of Tarleton's British cavalry, June 3, 1781. *Louisa County: Route 33, at Cuckoo.*

W-214 SCOTCHTOWN

A mile north is Scotchtown, Patrick Henry's home, 1771–1777. Dolly Madison, President James Madison's wife, lived here in her girlhood. Lafayette was here in May, 1781, retreating northward before Cornwallis. Cornwallis passed here in June, 1781, moving westward. *Hanover County: Route 54, 8 miles n.w. of Ashland.*

W-218 ROCKFISH GAP MEETING

In the tavern near here the commission appointed to select a site for the University of Virginia met, August 1–4, 1818. Ex-Presidents Thomas Jefferson and James Monroe and Judge Spencer Roane were the most distinguished members. After considering several places, Charlottesville was chosen. *Nelson County: Route 250, 2 miles n.w. of Afton.*

W-219 FLIGHT OF RICHARD C. DUPONT

Near this site on September 21, 1933, Richard C. duPont was launched from Afton Mountain in his Bowlus sailplane, Albatross. Four hours and fifty minutes later he landed at Frederick, Maryland, establishing a United States distance record for sail planing of 121.6 miles, almost double the previous U. S. Record of 66 miles. *Nelson County: Interstate 64 overlook on Afton Mountain.*

WO-12 THE WHITE HOUSE

This place, six miles northeast, was the home of Martha Custis. According to tradition, George Washington first met her at Poplar Grove, near by, in 1758. On January 6, 1759, Washington and Martha Custis were married, it is believed at the White House. The house was burned by Union troops when McClellan made the White House his base of operations in May, 1862. *New Kent County: Route 249, at Talleysville.*

WO-13 ST. PETER'S CHURCH

Two miles northeast is St. Peter's Church, built in 1703 in English bond. David Mossom, rector there for forty years, was the minister who married George Washington. According to one tradition, the wedding took place at St. Peter's Church. *New Kent County: Route 249, at Talleysville.*

WO-14 STUART'S RIDE AROUND McCLELLAN

J.E.B. Stuart, on his famous ride around McClellan's army, June 12–15, 1862, arrived here in the early night of June 13, coming from Hanover Courthouse. He rested here several hours and then pressed on to the Chickahominy River, rejoining Lee's army on June 15. *New Kent County: Route 33, at Talleysville.*

WO-16 NEW KENT COURTHOUSE

Lord Cornwallis's army was here, moving eastward, June 22, 1781; Lafayette, in pursuit, June 25; Washington, Rochambeau and Chastellux, on their way to Yorktown, September 14, 1781. A part of Joseph E. Johnston's army, retiring to Richmond, passed through, May, 1862. *New Kent County: Route 249, at New Kent.*

W0-18 MARTHA WASHINGTON'S BIRTHPLACE

About two miles northeast is the site of Chestnut Grove. Here Martha Dandridge was born June 2, 1731. The house here burned in 1927. Her first marriage was to Daniel Parke Custis in 1749, her second to George Washington on January 6, 1769. They honeymooned at the White House, her plantation in this county, later moving to Mount Vernon. *New Kent County: Route 249, 7 miles e. of New Kent.*

WO-30 ELTHAM

Eltham, a mile north, was long the home of the Bassett family and one of the largest and finest colonial houses in Virginia. Burwell Bassett, the owner at the time of the Revolution, was a patriot leader. Washington was a frequent visitor at Eltham and was there in November, 1781, at the death-bed of his stepson, John Parke Custis, a soldier of Yorktown. The old house was burned in 1875; the foundation remains. *New Kent County: Route 33, 1.9 miles w. of West Point.*

WO-31 PENINSULAR CAMPAIGN

A mile north, at Eltham Landing on the Pamunkey River, Franklin's division of McClellan's army disembarked on May 6, 1862. The next morning the Union troops came in contact with the Confederates retiring toward Richmond. The Confederate wagon trains were in danger; but Gustavus W. Smith drove Franklin back to the river. The action occurred in this vicinity, May 7, 1862. *New Kent County: Route 33, 1.5 miles w. of West Point.*

WO-33 THE BRICK HOUSE

A short distance south stood the Brick House. In 1677, at the end of Bacon's Rebellion, the rebel leaders, Drummond and Lawrence, were at Brick House when West Point surrendered to Berkeley. They fled, Drummond to be caught and executed, Lawrence never to be heard of again. In August, 1716, Governor Alexander Spotswood crossed the river there on his western expedition. *New Kent County: Route 33, 1.5 miles w. of West Point.*

WO-37 SCOTTISH FACTORS STORE

Two miles to the north, in the colonial port of entry of Urbanna, is a restored eighteenth century storehouse. Scottish merchants became active commercial factors in the colony subsequent to the Act of Union of England and Scotland. Urbanna was established as a town in 1706. *Middlesex County: Route 33, 1.5 miles e. of Saluda.*

WP-5*   GREAT BRIDGE CHAPEL

Here stood the second Southern Branch Chapel, or Great Bridge Chapel. It was built in 1701 as a Chapel of Ease for Elizabeth River Parish and in 1761 became a Chapel of St. Bride's Parish. The building was torn down about 1845. *Chesapeake ("old" Norfolk County): Route 168 in Great Bridge.*

WP-7*   NORFOLK COUNTY COURTHOUSE

One-half mile west is the last courthouse of Norfolk County. It was built in 1962 and is now the Courthouse of the City of Chesapeake. Continuous court records beginning in 1637 are preserved here. *Chesapeake ("old" Norfolk County): Route 168 in Great Bridge.*

WP-10   ST. BRIDE'S CHURCH

At this point stood St. Bride's Church, the Parish Church of St. Bride's Parish which was established in 1761. The church, sometimes known as Northwest Church, was built in 1762 and survived until 1853. *Chesapeake ("old" Norfolk County): Route 168, 4 miles n. of state line.*

WY-3   SALEM METHODIST CHURCH

1.8 miles east of here stood Salem Methodist Church (1836–1918) scene of the initial violence resulting from the schism between northern and southern Methodists in 1846. A northern circuit preacher was dragged from the pulpit by members of the congregation. The building burned in 1870 and was replaced. Salem was the mother church of congregations at Cheriton and Oyster and five Eastern Shore Methodist ministers. *Northampton County: Route 13, at Route 636.*

WY-5   ARLINGTON

Two miles west stood Arlington, original home of the Custis Family, built by John Custis. The family tombs are still preserved there. Governor William Berkeley made his headquarters there during Bacon's Rebellion in 1676. Arlington on the Potomac was named for this Arlington. *Northampton County: Route 13, 3 miles n. of Cape Charles.*

WY-5*   ARLINGTON

Five miles southeast, on the south side of Old Plantation Creek, is Arlington, built by John Custis before 1680. There Sir William Berkeley, when driven from Jamestown by Bacon in 1676, made his headquarters and thence he sailed back to Jamestown. *Northampton County: Route 13, 3 miles n. of Cape Charles.*

WY-6* OLD PLACES

Two miles south is Stratton Manor, built by Thomas Stratton about 1657 and remodeled in 1764. Five and a half miles south, on the east side of Old Plantation Creek, is the site of Magothy Bay Church, built about 1690. *Northampton County: Route 13, 3 miles n. of Cape Charles.*

WY-7 TOWNE FIELDS

This site, two and a half miles west was the first seat of local government on the Eastern Shore. Francis Bolton preached there in 1623, and the first church was built before 1632. The oldest continuous county records in the English Colonies began there in 1632. The first courthouse (built for that purpose) on the Eastern Shore was erected in 1664 and used until Court moved to the Eastville area in 1677. *Northampton County: Route 13, at Cheriton.*

WY-7* FIRST COURTHOUSE

Two and a half miles west, at Town Fields, the first courthouse on the Eastern Shore was built, 1664. Court was held here until 1677, when the courthouse was moved to Eastville. In the Revolution a fort stood at Town Fields. *Northampton County: Route 13, at Cheriton.*

WY-8 HOME OF FIRST SETTLER

Here, in Savages Neck, was the home of Ensign Thomas Savage, who came to Virginia in 1608. Granted a tract of land by Debedeavon, the "Laughing King" of the Indians, in 1619, Savage became the first permanent English settler on the Eastern Shore. A mile west is Old Castle, built in 1721. *Northampton County: Route 13, 1 mile s. of Eastville.*

WY-9 INDIAN VILLAGE

Three miles east, on Pocahontas farm, was the main village of the Gingaskin Indians, one of the largest tribes on the Eastern Shore. Survivors of this tribe were found here as late as 1860. *Northampton County: Route 13, at Eastville.*

WY-10 OLD COURTHOUSE

The courthouse was moved to Eastville in 1677, and court has been held here ever since. The old courthouse was built about 1731; from its door the Declaration of Independence was read, August 13, 1776. Militia Barracks were here during the Revolution. Just behind the courthouse is the debtors' prison. *Northampton County: Route 13, at Eastville.*

WY-11* HUNGARS CHURCH AND VAUCLUSE

Three miles west is Hungars Church, built by 1742. Two and a half miles west of the church is the Glebe farm, which was church property until 1840. Four and a half miles south of the Glebe is Vaucluse, birthplace of Abel Parker Upshur, Secretary of State, killed in the explosion on the Princeton, 1844. *Northampton County: Route 13, 2.8 miles s. of Nassawadox.*

WY-12* BATTLE OF PUNGOTEAGUE

Seven miles west. On May 30, 1814, the British Admiral Cockburn landed at Pungoteague Creek with 500 marines and fought a battle with the Eastern Shore militia under Major Finney. Cockburn, seeing that he would be surrounded, withdrew to Tangier Island, where the British had landed on April 5, 1814. *Accomack County: Route 13, at Melfa.*

WY-13 OCCAHANNOCK

Five miles west is "Hedra Cottage," site of the home of Colonel Edmund Scarborough (Scarburgh), Surveyor General of the Colony. Beyond, at the end of Scarborough's Neck, was the village of the Occahannock Indians, the seat of Debedeavon, the "Laughing King." *Accomack County: Route 13, at Belle Haven.*

WY-14 ONANCOCK

Two miles west is Onancock, founded in 1680. A courthouse was then built and used for a few years. Militia barracks were there in the Revolution. From Onancock, Colonel John Cropper went to the aid of Commodore Whaley in the last naval action of the Revolution, November 30, 1782. Near by is Onley, home of Henry A. Wise, Governor of Virginia, 1856–60. *Accomack County: Route 13, 2 miles s. of Accomac.*

WY-15* FOUNDER OF PRESBYTERIANISM

Five miles west was the home of Rev. Francis Makemie, founder of Presbyterianism in the United States. About 1684, Makemie established in Maryland the first Presbyterian church. Later he moved to Accomac and married. He died here in 1708. *Accomack County: Route 13, at Temperanceville.*

WY-16 OAK GROVE METHODIST CHURCH

Two miles east, on Route 600, meets what is possibly the nation's oldest continuous Sunday School. Begun by William Elliott in his home in 1785, it was moved in 1818 to Burton's Chapel and in 1870 to the present church. *Accomack County: Route 13, in Keller.*

WY-17 THE BEAR AND THE CUB

This first play recorded in the United States was presented August 27, 1665. The Accomack County Court at Pungoteague heard charges against three men "For Acting a Play," ordered inspection of costumes and script, but found men "Not Guilty." *Accomack County: Route 13, at Keller.*

WY-18 "THE BEAR AND THE CUB"

Probable site of Fowkes' Tavern where the first recorded play in English America was performed August 27, 1665. *Accomack County: Route 178, .5 mile n. of Pungoteague.*

WY-19 DEBTOR'S PRISON

Built in 1783 in one corner of the jail yard wall to serve as residence for the jailer. Iron bars, oak batten doors and locks were added in 1824 when the building was converted into a debtor's prison, the purpose it served until 1849. *Accomack County: Route 764, in town of Accomac.*

WY-88 THIRD ELIZABETH CITY PARISH CHURCH

Here is the site of "the New Church of Kecoughtan," built before 1667 on Pembroke Farm as the third church of Elizabeth City Parish, established in 1610. It was a frame building and its brick foundation and some early colonial tombstones remain. When the town of Hampton was founded in 1691, this church lay outside it, and in 1727 was ordered to be replaced by a fourth parish church within the town, the existing St. John's Church, Hampton. *Hampton: Route 351 (Pembroke Avenue and Parkdale Street).*

WY-89 SECOND CHURCH AT KECOUGHTAN

Nearby a monument marks the site of the second church at Kecoughtan (later Hampton), built in 1624 for Elizabeth City Parish, established 1610 and now the oldest Protestant parish in continuous existence in America. This building was replaced before 1667 by a third parish church west of the town and was pulled down in 1698. *Hampton: Tyler Street, exit 5 of Interstate 64.*

WY-90 FIRST CHURCH AT KECOUGHTAN

Near here on the church creek stood the first church at Kecoughtan (later Hampton). Built on the Parish Glebe Farm about 1616, as the first church of the oldest continuous settlement of English origin in America, William Mease was the first known minister of the Parish from 1613 until about 1620. *Hampton: corner of LaSalle and Kenmore streets.*

WY-91 CAMP HAMILTON

In this vicinity was situated Camp Hamilton, a large camp of Union troops first occupied in May, 1861. A great military hospital, Hampton Hospital, was here. *Hampton: corner of College Place and e. Queen Street.*

WY-92 BUCKROE

In 1620, Frenchmen sent over to plant mulberry trees and grape vines settled here. The name was taken from a place in England. *Hampton ("old" Elizabeth City County): at Buckroe Beach (Atlantic Avenue and Mallory Street).*

WY-93 PHOEBUS

Settled as Mill Creek and Strawberry Banks by English Colonists, the Town of Phoebus was "Roseland Farm" until 1871 when it was divided into lots and became known as Chesapeake City. When the town was incorporated in 1900, it was named PHOEBUS in honor of its leading citizen, Harrison Phoebus. *Hampton: County Street and Woodland Road.*

WY-94 PHOEBUS

Settled as Mill Creek and Strawberry Banks by English Colonists, the Town of Phoebus was "Roseland Farm" until 1871 when it was divided into lots and became known as Chesapeake City. When the town was incorporated in 1900, it was named PHOEBUS in honor of its leading citizen, Harrison Phoebus. *Hampton: Mallory Street and off ramp of Interstate 64.*

X-5 EARLY SETTLERS IN RUSSELL COUNTY

In 1787, Isaiah Salyer (1752–1818), son of Zachariah Salyer (1730–1789) of North Carolina, settled on Copper Creek, two miles southeast of here. Isaiah's brothers John Benjamin, and Zachariah, and sisters Sarah, wife of Solomon Saylor, and Rebecca, wife of Stephen Kilgore, settled on nearby land. The Salyer land was officially surveyed in 1790. The Salyers intermarried with other Virginia pioneer families—Castle, Isaacs, Nickels, Stapleton, Vicars, and Byerley. *Russell County: Route 71, at Grassy Creek Church.*

X-6 RUSSELL COURTHOUSE

The county government was organized at Russell's Fort, May 9, 1786, with the following officers: Alexander Barnett, County Lieutenant; David Ward, Sheriff; Henry Dickenson, Clerk. Justices: Alexander Barnett, Thomas Carter, Henry Smith, Henry Dickenson, David Ward, John Thompson, Samuel Ritchie. The present courthouse was built in 1874. *Russell County: Route 19, at Lebanon.*

X-7 RUSSELL'S FORT

On the hill to the north stood Russell's Fort, an important link in the chain of forts built to protect settlers on Clinch River in the Indian War of 1774. William Russell, who established it, was a prominent soldier of the Revolution. *Russell County: Route 615, at Castlewood.*

X-8 GLADE HOLLOW FORT

A short distance south stood Glade Hollow Fort, garrisoned by twenty-one men in 1774. From Witten's to Blackmore's these Clinch Valley forts were the frontier defenses in Dunmore's War, 1774. *Russell County: Route 71, 2 miles w. of Lebanon.*

X-9* ELK GARDEN FORT

A short distance south stood the fort commanded by John Kinkead, 1774. It was then the center of Elk Garden community, later the homestead of William A. Stuart. The house was built near the site of the fort. *Russell County: Route 19, 8 miles e. of Lebanon.*

X-10   WILLIAM WYNNE'S FORT

On the hillside to the north stood Wynne's Fort. A settlement was made here as early as 1752. Some years later William Wynne obtained land here and built a neighborhood fort. After 1776 the State government built a fort and garrisoned it. *Tazewell County: Route 19 (business), 2 miles e. of Tazewell.*

X-11   TAZEWELL

The town was laid off as the county seat in 1800, when Tazewell County was formed, on land given by William Peery and Samuel Ferguson. First known as Jeffersonville, the name was changed to Tazewell, for Senator Henry Tazewell. Averell was here in May, 1864, and the town was occupied in other raids. It was incorporated in 1866. *Tazewell County: Route 19 (business) at Tazewell.*

X-12   BURKE'S GARDEN

Eight miles east is Burke's Garden, discovered by James Burke in 1749. Major Lewis's expedition against the Indians, 1756, camped there, and Burke's fort was there in 1774. In 1781 Indians raided into Burke's Garden, carrying off the wife and children of Thomas Ingles. *Tazewell County: Route 19 (business), 2 miles e. of Tazewell.*

X-12-a   BURKE'S GARDEN

Burke's Garden was first settled about 1754 by James Burke who had been hunting in the area during the previous decade. Burke lived here until 1774 when he and his wife were killed by the Indians. Two years later a fort was erected here as a defense from the Indians. The area around Burke's Garden is known for its great natural beauty. *Tazewell County: Routes 666 and 623.*

X-13   MAIDEN SPRINGS FORT

On the hillside to the west stood Maiden Springs Fort, also known as Reese Bowen's Fort. It was garrisoned in Dunmore's War, 1774. Reese Bowen, the founder, fought at Point Pleasant, 1774, and was killed at King's Mountain, 1780. *Tazewell County: Route 91, 12 miles s.w. of Tazewell.*

X-14   BIG CRAB ORCHARD OR WITTEN'S FORT

On the hillside to the south stood Big Crab Orchard Fort, also known as Witten's Fort. Thomas Witten obtained land here in 1771 and built the fort as a neighborhood place of refuge. It was garrisoned in Dunmore's War, 1774. *Tazewell County: Route 19 (business) through town of Tazewell.*

X-15   BLUEFIELD, VIRGINIA

The place was first known as "Pin Hook." In 1883 the New River branch of the N. & W. Railroad was completed here and the first coal shipped from the Pocahontas mines. The town of Graham was incorporated in 1884 and named for Thomas Graham of Philadelphia. The town was reincorporated and the name changed to Bluefield, 1924, to conform to its sister city. *Tazewell County: Route 19, at Bluefield.*

X-16   INDIAN OUTRAGES

Four miles south the first Indian attack in the Upper Clinch Valley took place, September 8, 1774. John Henry was wounded and his wife and children were carried ito captivity. In 1781, Indians attacked the house of Robert Maxwell, near here, and killed two girls. *Tazewell County: Route 19 (business), 2 miles w. of Tazewell.*

X-17   SMITH'S FORT

Near here, in 1774, stood Daniel Smith's Fort, also known as Fort Christian. The fort was named for Smith, who was a surveyor and captain of the military company on upper Clinch River. *Russell County: Route 19, 17.5 miles e. of Lebanon.*

X-18*   MOORE'S FORT

Near here, on Clinch River, stood Moore's Fort. Daniel Boone, on his way to Kentucky with a party of settlers, stopped here for some time. On September 29, 1774, Indians made an attack here from ambush, killing John Duncan. *Russell County: Alternate 58, e. entrance of St. Paul.*

X-20   COEBURN

The town stands on the site of one of Christopher Gist's camps when he was returning from his exploration of the Ohio Valley about 1750. Big Tom and Little Tom creeks are named for him and his son. The name of the town comes from W. W. Coe, chief engineer of the N. & W. Railroad, and Judge W. E. Burns of Lebanon. Coeburn was incorporated in 1894. *Wise County: Route 58, at intersection with Route 72 in Coeburn.*

X-21   NORTON

As early as 1750 Christopher Gist explored in this vicinity. The first house here was built about 1785 by William Prince, for whom the settlement was called Prince's Flat. It was later named Norton for Eckstein Norton, president of the Louisville and Nashville Railroad, and was incorporated in 1894. Norton is the center of a bituminous coal region. High Knob, National Forest area, is nearby. *Wise County: Route 23, at Norton.*

X-22   BENGE'S GAP

The pass to the south was a secret route named Benge's Gap for an Indian half-breed who used it in making surprise attacks on settlers. The latter discovered the gap. When Benge was returning to it after his last raid, 1794, his party was attacked by settlers and exterminated. *Wise County: Alternate Route 58, at Norton.*

X-23 APPALACHIA

The town sprang up after the Louis-ville and Nashville Railroad and Southern Railroad made a junction here in 1890. Named for the Appala-chian Mountains, in the heart of which it stands, it was incorporated in 1906; the streets were laid out in 1907. Appalachia, in the Jefferson National Forest area, is the trading center of the Wise coal fields. *Wise County: Alternate Route 58, at Appa-lachia.*

X-24 SEMINARY METHODIST CHURCH

The foundation of this Methodist Church was laid in 1851 and built from brick made near the church. The first Board of Trustees: Henry C. Slemp, W.N.G. Barron, James F. Jones, John W. Slemp, John Snod-grass. First Circuit Rider: W. W. Far-thing. *Lee County: Alternate Route 58, 5 miles s.w. of Big Stone Gap.*

X-26* MEMBERS OF CONGRESS

Within one mile of this point three men were born who afterwards be-came members of Congress: James B. Richmond, 46th Congress, March 4, 1879–March 4, 1881. Campbell Slemp, 58th, 59th and 60th Con-gresses, March 4, 1903–October 13, 1907. Campbell Bascom Slemp, 61st–67th Congresses, October 13, 1907–March 3, 1923. Also: Jonathan Richmond (1805–1871), Brigadier-General Virginia Militia. *Lee County: Alternate Routd 58, 6 miles s.w. of Big Stone Gap.*

X-30 PENNINGTON GAP

Pennington Gap is a mountain pa named for an early settler. The tow came into existence with the exten sion of the Louisville and Nashvill Railroad, 1890. It was incorporated in 1891. Standing on a short-cut high-way to eastern Kentucky, it is a center for an extensive coal-mining region. *Lee County: Alternate Route 58, at Pennington Gap.*

XB-4 WISE

This town, one of the highest in Vir-ginia, was built on land first owned by Pierre de Tarbeau, French nobleman. Originally known as Big Glades, it became Gladesville in 1856. A first courthouse, built in 1858, was burned by Union troops. An action was fought here, July 7, 1863, between Confederates and Union raiders. The name was changed to Wise when the town was rechartered in 1928. *Wise County: Route 23 (Business), Main Street at Wise.*

XB-7* POUND GAP

Christopher Gist, returning from the Ohio River, crossed this gap in 1751. James A. Garfield (afterward Presi-dent) with Union troops forced this gap in March, 1862. In June, 1864, John H. Morgan, on his Kentucky raid, forced it from the Virginia side, capturing and destroying much prop-erty. *Wise County: Route 23, 4 miles n. of Pound.*

XB-10   OLD BUFFALO SCHOOL

Established in 1875 on land given by Simpson Dyer, the Old Buffalo School became the first free school of Dickenson County in 1880. Alexander Johnson Skeen served as first teacher. The school remained in operation for twenty-five years. During which time it educated many future leaders in the area. *Dickenson County: Route 63, at Nora.*

XB-11   CLINTWOOD

The name originally was Holly Creek. In 1882 the county seat of Dickenson County was moved from Ervington to this place, which was named Clintwood for Major Henry Clinton Wood. The town was incorporated in 1894. With the coming of the railroad to the county in 1915, the population rapidly increased as the mineral and timber resources were opened. *Dickenson County: Route 83, at Clintwood.*

XB-12*   EARLY SETTLER

Near here, on Holly Creek, John Mullins settled in 1829; becoming the second settler in this county. The county seat was moved from Nora to Clintwood in 1882. *Dickenson County: Route 83, at Clintwood.*

XB-13   JOHN MULLINS

Near here on Holly Creek, John Mullins settled in 1829, becoming the second settler in Dickenson County. His father John Mullins, the only known Revolutionary War soldier resting in this county, spent his last years here with his son. He died in 1849 and is buried nearby. *Dickenson County: Route 83, at Clintwood.*

XB-20*   FIRST SETTLER

Near here "Fighting" Dick Colley, from Clinch River, built, in 1816, his three-walled cabin and became the first permanent settler in this section. *Dickenson County: Route 83, at Haysi.*

XB-23   INDIAN OUTRAGE

In 1792, Indians attacked the home of David Musick, near Honaker, Russell County, killing him and capturing his wife and five children. Near here the Indians were overtaken by pursuing settlers and the captives were retaken. *Dickenson County: Route 83, at Haysi.*

XB-24   COLLEY'S CABIN

Near here stood the cabin of Richard "Fighting Dick" Colley who was one of the earliest settlers in what is now Dickenson County. *Dickenson County: Route 80, .3 mile s. of Haysi.*

XB-25   GRUNDY

This place became the county seat when Buchanan County was formed, in 1858, and was probably named for Felix Grundy of Tennessee, statesman. In October, 1864, the Union General Burbridge passed through Grundy on his raid to Saltville. The town was incorporated in 1876. *Buchanan County: Route 83, at Grundy.*

XC-4*   DORTOR'S FORT

The old building just to the east is Dortor's Fort, built as a protection for the early settlers from Indian attacks. Robin Kilgore lived here. *Scott County: Route 71, 1.5 miles w. of Nickelsville.*

XH-1   MOLLY TYNES' RIDE

To the north was "Rocky Dell," the home of Samuel Tynes. From here on July 17, 1863, his daughter Molly rode across the mountains to Wytheville to warn the town of an attack by Federal forces under Colonel J. T. Toland. *Tazewell County: Route 61, 3 miles e. of Tazewell.*

XL-4   RICHLANDS

This fertile region was known as Richlands from an early period. In 1782 and later Richlands was a militia station for frontier defense. The town was laid off in 1890, with the coming of the Norfolk and Western Railroad, and was incorporated in 1891. It is the center of an agricultural section. *Tazewell County: Route 460, at Richlands.*

XP-4   POCAHONTAS

This region was visited by the explorer, Dr. Thomas Walker, in 1750. Following a report by Captain I. A. Welch in 1873, the first coal mine was opened here in 1882. Shipment of coal followed in 1883, when the Norfolk and Western Railroad reached this point from Radford. First known as "Powell's Bottom," the town was incorporated in 1884 and named for the Indian princess Pocahontas. *Tazewell County: Route 102, just e. of Pocahontas.*

XP-5   ABB'S VALLEY

Five miles southwest is Abb's Valley, discovered by Absalom Looney. James Moore and Robert Poage were the first settlers, about 1770. In July, 1786, Shawnee Indians raided the valley, killing or carrying into captivity the Moore family. Mary (Polly) Moore, Martha Evans and James Moore (captured earlier) finally returned. They are known as "The Captives of Abb's Valley." *Tazewell County: Route 102, just e. of Pocahontas.*

The markers that follow were never assigned a letter and number designation and are therefore listed in alphabetical order.

BATTLE OF SEAWELL'S POINT

Confederate batteries at Seawall's Point were located near here. These batteries mounting twenty 32-pounders, three 42-pounder carronades, and six 9-inch rifles, successfully repulsed an attack by the Federal fleet, May 19, 1861. This was the first engagement fought in Virginia in the War between the States. These batteries, under fire many times, were never silenced or captured. They were abandoned when Norfolk was evacuated May 10, 1862. *Norfolk: Inside Naval Base Grounds.*

BUCKINGHAM COURTHOUSE

Designed by Thomas Jefferson in 1821, burned in 1869, rebuilt in 1873. The exterior follows Jefferson's plan with the interior redesigned. Copy of original plan and specifications on display in courthouse. Registered in 1969 as a National and Virginia historic landmark. Renovated in 1976. *Buckingham County: Route 60, at Buckingham Court House.*

THE BURNING OF NORFOLK

Lord Dunmore's fleet of seven vessels, extending in line of battle in the Elizabeth River from the eastern to the western end of Main Street, bombarded the Borough of Norfolk January 1, 1776. H.M.S. Liverpool lay off the end of Church Street. Much damage was done and many houses were burned. Nearly all remaining houses were later destroyed by the Virginia militia to prevent Dunmore's return. *Norfolk: St. Paul's Boulevard and City Hall Avenue.*

CAMP TALBOT

Half a mile west is site of Confederate Camp. Georgia and Virginia troops defending Norfolk were encamped there from April, 1861, until the evacuation of the city, May 10, 1862. *Norfolk: Corner Oak Grove Road and Granby Street.*

CRANEY ISLAND

is two miles down, and across the Elizabeth River from this point. There on June 22, 1813, the Virginia militia under General Robert B. Taylor of Norfolk, without losing a man, defeated 4,000 British troops. They had come to destroy Norfolk and Portsmouth. Repulsed at Craney Island, they wreaked their vengeance on Hampton, which was taken, pillaged, and well-nigh destroyed. *Norfolk: Norfolk-Southern R.R. Piers, Old Dominion Wharf.*

EASTERN TOWN LIMIT

The eastern limit of the fifty acres constituting the original town of Norfolk, established by Act of June, 1680, is a few feet east of this point. The land was purchased as a port for Lower Norfolk County from Nicholas Wise, Jr., for "Tenn thousand pounds of tobacco and caske." It was deeded by him August 16, 1682, to Capt. William Robinson and Lt. Col. Anthony Lawson feoffees in trust for Lower Norfolk County. *Norfolk: East Main Street.*

FATHER RYAN'S HOME

On Chapel Street south of this point stood the home of Father Abram J. Ryan, beloved poet of the Confederacy.

"But their memories e'er shall remain for us
And their names, bright names, without stain for us;
The glory they won shall not wane for us,
In legend and lay—our heroes in Gray
Shall forever live over again for us."

Norfolk: Tidewater Drive and Lafayette Boulevard.

THE FIRST CONFEDERATE FLAG

flown in the City of Norfolk was unfurled from a house-top about a block and a half east of this corner, April 2, 1861, two weeks before the secession of Virginia from the Union. *Norfolk: on Market Street at Monticello Avenue.*

FORT BARBOUR

This is the site of Fort Barbour, which, with Forts Tar, Norfolk, and Nelson, constituted the outer defenses of Norfolk and Portsmouth against the British in the War of 1812. Fort Barbour guarded against hostile advances from the north and east. *Norfolk: Corner Princess Anne Road and Church Street.*

FORT FARTHING OR TOWN POINT

Here at a cedar tree was the western limit of the fifty acres constituting the original town of Norfolk. The land was bought in 1682 as a port for Lower Norfolk County from Nicholas Wise, Jr., for "tenn thousand pounds of tobacco and caske." It was deeded to Capt. Wm. Robinson and Lt. Col. Anthony Lawson as feoffees in trust for the county. *Norfolk: near end of West Main Street.*

FORT TAR

This is the site of Fort Tar, built to guard the approach to the city from the west. Situated on the outskirts of Norfolk, near Armistead's Bridge, which spanned Glebe Creek near by, it served with Forts Barbour, Norfolk, and Nelson to protect Norfolk and Portsmouth from invasion by the British in the War of 1812. *Norfolk: Monticello Avenue n. of Virginia Beach Boulevard.*

INDIAN POOL BRIDGE*

A bridge has spanned Tanner's Creek (now called Lafayette River) at this—the ancient Indian Pool Point—since 1851. The bridge was burned by the Confederates to retard the advance of the Federal forces upon Norfolk, May 10, 1862. *Norfolk: New Granby Street Bridge.*

JOHN HUNTER HOLT

Norfolk's first newspaper, The Virginia Gazette or Norfolk Intelligencer, was put out of business when its press was seized by British troops near this spot on September 30, 1775. The editor, John Hunter Holt, who had defied Governor Dunmore, then volunteered for service in the Revolutionary Army. He died in Richmond June 8, 1787. *Norfolk: Main Street, s. of Commercial Place.*

MAIN STREET

This street followed a ridge of high land in the original town site, which was almost an island. It was laid out in the division of the fifty acres of Town Lands in 1682, and the angles in it were made to avoid the two creeks. Dunmore's ships lay along Main Street when they bombarded Norfolk, January 1, 1776. *Norfolk: Main Street facing Granby Street.*

THE NATIONAL HOTEL

originally French's, stood on this site. In it were entertained Prince Louis Napoleon (later Napoleon III) of France, 1837; General Winfield Scott, 1858; G.P.R. James, 1863; and President Tyler, 1859. It was later known as the Purcell House. *Norfolk: St. Paul's Boulevard opposite Courts Building.*

NORTHERN LIMIT OF OLD NORFOLK

This marks the northern limit of the fifty acres constituting the original town of Norfolk. It was bounded on the north by Town Back Creek and Dun-in-the-Mire Creek. The land was purchased as a port for Lower Norfolk County for "tenn thousand pounds of tobacco and caske," being deeded to feoffees in trust for the county in 1682. It was divided into streets and sold in half-acre lots. *Norfolk: Corner of City Hall Avenue and St. Paul's Boulevard.*

OLD ACADEMIC BUILDING SITE

On this site September 21, 1930, the first classes for 206 students were held at the Norfolk Division of the College of William and Mary, now Old Dominion University. That year the Norfolk School Board gave the building, constructed in 1912 as the Larchmont Elementary School, to William and Mary to establish the Division. The building served the institution until 1975 when it was razed. *Norfolk: On grounds of Old Dominion University.*

OLD NORFOLK COUNTY COURT HOUSE

The red brick house one block east was the courthouse of Norfolk County from 1784 to 1858. In the latter year the court was transferred to Portsmouth. *Norfolk: Northeast corner Chestnut and Pine streets.*

SALISBURY

Only a few yards from here stood Salisbury. Here Patrick Henry lived during his fourth and fifth terms as Governor of Virginia, 1784–1786. The Confederate Major General Edward Johnson lived here in his later years and died here. *Chesterfield County: Route 902, on Salisbury Road.*

SELDEN'S HOME

This house was built in 1807 as the country residence of Dr. William B. Selden. During the Federal occupation of Norfolk (1862–1865) it was seized and occupied as the headquarters of the Federal commanders. On his last visit to Norfolk, April, 1870, General Robert E. Lee was the guest here of his friend, Dr. William Selden, Surgeon, C.S.A. *Norfolk: Southeast corner Freemason and Botetourt streets.*

SITE OF LOWER NORFOLK COUNTY COURT

This was the site of the courthouse from 1689–1776. A debtor's prison, jail, ducking stool and pillory were in the rear. The Hustings Court of the Borough of Norfolk, erected on adjoining property in 1752, was moved in 1799 to Main and Nebraska streets, and in 1850 to the present courthouse on Bank Street. *Norfolk: Main Street facing Commercial Place.*

TAZEWELL'S HOME

On this site stood the residence of Littleton Waller Tazewell (1774–1860), Lawyer, Congressman, United States Senator, Governor of Virginia. His life was spent in the service of his native Virginia. *Norfolk: Tazewell Street near Granby Street.*

TRIPOLI STREET

Monticello Avenue, south of Market Street, was formerly Tripoli Street. It was named in honor of Commodore Stephen Decatur's victory over the Barbary pirates, after he had requested that his own name should not be used. *Norfolk: n.e. corner, City Hall Avenue and Monticello Avenue.*

VIRGINIA AND MONITOR

Across Hampton Roads from this point the C.S.S. Virginia (Merrimac) and the U.S.S. Monitor fought, March 9, 1862. This was the first combat between iron-clad vessels in the history of the world. After a severe engagement in which each vessel failed to pierce the other's armour, the Monitor retired. On the previous day, the Virginia had destroyed the U.S.S. Congress and the U.S.S. Cumberland, and dispersed the remainder of the Federal fleet. *Norfolk: West Ocean View Avenue between Thirteenth View and Fourteenth View streets.*

WHITTLE HOME

This house was built about 1791 and bought in 1803 by Richard Taylor, whose descendants still occupy it (1931). It was the home of Richard Lucien Page, Lieut. U.S.N., Capt. C.S.N., Brig.-Gen. C.S.A.; of William Conway Whittle, Jr., executive officer of the C.S.S. Shenandoah; the birthplace of Walter H. Taylor, Lt. Col. C.S.A., who served on Lee's staff for the whole period of the war. *Norfolk: 227 West Freemason Street, at s.e. corner of Duke Street.*

YOUEL—CONDON HOUSE

Built in 1819 by William Youel, Scottish immigrant who fought in the American Revolution. William, who died in 1834 at age 100, and his wife are buried in the family cemetery up the hill. The house, later owned by William's son and grandson, was bought by David Condon in 1863 and has been owned since then by the Condon family. *Rockbridge County: Route 39, 3.5 miles e. of Goshen.*

The following markers were a special gift from the French Government, Committee of the Bicentennial, to the Commonwealth of Virginia in 1976. Although not numbered in the state's marker system, they are the property of the Commonwealth and carry significant and interesting historical information.

WASHINGTON-ROCHAMBEAU ROUTE

Generals Washington and Rochambeau slept here the night of September 12, 1781. Having learned that Admiral de Grasse had put to sea to fight the British fleet under Admiral Graves, Washington and Rochambeau with their staffs hastened to Williamsburg. *Spotsylvania County: Route 17 (business), 200 ft. from Route 1.*

WASHINGTON-ROCHAMBEAU ROUTE

General Washington, in 1781, rode 60 miles in one day from Baltimore to Mount Vernon which he had not visited for over 6 years. General Rochambeau arrived the next day with his and Washington's staff. They spent September 10 and 11 at Mount Vernon before going on to Fredericksburg. *Fairfax County: Route 235, 800 ft. from Mount Vernon entrance.*

WASHINGTON-ROCHAMBEAU ROUTE

General Washington and General Rochambeau passed here on September 13, 1781 on their way to victory at Yorktown. One mile south, they turned east on State Route 605. *Hanover County: Route 301 at Hanover Courthouse.*

WASHINGTON-ROCHAMBEAU
ROUTE

Generals Washington and Rochambeau and their staffs arrived in Williamsburg on September 14, 1781.
Here they gathered their troops and
supplies prior to laying siege to Cornwallis at Yorktown 12 miles away on
September 28, 1781. *James City
County: Route 60, .4 mile w. of Williamsburg town limits.*

WASHINGTON-ROCHAMBEAU
ROUTE

General Washington, in 1781, rode 60
miles in one day from Baltimore to
Mount Vernon which he had not visited for over 6 years. General Rochambeau arrived the next day with
his and Washington's staff. They
spent September 10 and 11 at Mount
Vernon before going on to Fredericksburg. *Fairfax County: Route 235,
800 ft. from Mount Vernon entrance.*

Appendix: Historic Districts and Virginia's State Parks

HISTORIC DISTRICTS with Walking
Tours

Since 1968, a number of historic districts in Virginia have been recognized through listing on the Virginia Landmarks Register and the National Register of Historic Places. Communities so recognized have designed both guided and self-guided walking tours for tourists who are interested in seeing firsthand these important cultural resources of Virginia. Listed below are those localities that sponsor such programs, along with addresses and phone numbers of the sponsoring organizations.

ABINGDON

A self-guided walking tour of Abingdon's historic Main Street; attractions include the Barter Theatre and the Martha Washington Inn.
Washington County Chamber of Commerce
304 Depot Square
Abingdon, Va. 23210
(703) 628–8141

ALEXANDRIA

Self-guided walking tour of Old Town, encompassing historic residential and commercial structures in the historic district. Free *Walking Tour* guide to Old Town.
Alexandria Tourist Council
221 King Street
Alexandria, Va. 22314
(703) 549–0205

CHARLOTTESVILLE

Self-guided and guided walking tours. During academic year, five guided tours daily of the University of Virginia's buildings and grounds. Self-guided walking tours of downtown Charlottesville historic districts.
Thomas Jefferson Visitors Bureau
P.O. Box 161
Charlottesville, Va. 22902
(804) 977–1783

DANVILLE

Self-guided walking tour of "Millionaires' Row" Historic District on Danville's Main Street, including the last capital of the Confederacy. Tours from August 1 to November 1 of the fall tobacco-auction markets. Tours of National Tobacco Textile Museum located in a tobacco warehouse in the Tobacco Warehouse Historic District.
Visitors Center, City of Danville
P.O. Box 3300
Danville, Va. 24543
(804) 799–5149

EASTERN SHORE

A driving/walking tour of the Eastern Shore of Virginia featuring historic sites and structures. Publication Virginia's *Eastern Shore Tour* available.
Eastern Shore of Virginia Chamber of Commerce
P.O. Box 147
Accomac, Va. 23301
(804) 787–2460

FREDERICKSBURG

Self-guided tours or tours with costumed guides of attractions in the Fredericksburg Historic District. Guided driving tours to Civil War landmarks and national battlefields available. Block tickets, brochures, and map available. Some fees.
Fredericksburg Visitors Center
706 Caroline Street
Fredericksburg, Va. 22401
(703) 373–1776

HAMPTON

Self-guided walking tours of historic sites in Hampton.
Hampton Center for the Arts and Humanities
22 Wine Street
Hampton, Va. 23669
(804) 723–1776

Self-guided driving tours of landmarks in the Hampton area.
Conventions and Tourism
413 West Mercury Boulevard
Hampton, Va. 23666
(804) 727–6108

HOPEWELL

Self-guided tour of historic sites and structures in Hopewell; illustrated brochure.
Hopewell Chamber of Commerce
110 North Second Street
Hopewell, Va. 23860
(804) 458–5536

LEESBURG

Self-guided walking tours with illustrated booklet free. Historic district includes commercial and residential Federal-style buildings and late nineteenth-century structures.
Loudoun Museum/Information Center
16 West Loudoun Street
Leesburg, Va. 22075
(703) 777–0519

LEXINGTON

Self-guided walking tours of residential areas, commercial district, V.M.I. and Marshall Museum, and Lexington Historic District.
Chamber of Commerce
107 East Washington Street
Lexington, Va. 24450
(703) 463–3777

LYNCHBURG

Self-guided walking tours available for historic districts in Lynchburg. Included are Diamond Hill, Rivermont, Daniels Hill, Garland Hill, and Courthouse Hill.
Lynchburg Museum
P.O. Box 60
Lynchburg, Va. 24505
(804) 847–1459

MANASSAS

Self-guided walking tour of Manassas featuring late nineteenth-century commercial buildings and Victorian residences.
Manassas Museum
9406 Main Street
Manassas, Va. 22110
(703) 368–1873

NEWPORT NEWS

Self-guided driving tours of historic and military sites.
Deer Park Information Center
11523 Jefferson Avenue
Newport News, Va. 23601
(804) 595–2351

NORFOLK

Self-guided walking/driving tours of major attractions in Norfolk; blue and gold signs mark the tour. Attractions include St. Paul's Church, Monticello Arcade, and the MacArthur Memorial.
Norfolk Convention and Visitors Bureau
Monticello Arcade
Norfolk, Va. 23510
(804) 441–5266 Outside Virginia, toll free 1–800–368–3097

OCCOQUAN

Self-guided walking tour of Occoquan Historic District; map and brochure available.
Visitors Center
201 Union Street
Occoquan, Va. 22125
(703) 491–6550

ORANGE COUNTY

For information on historic sites and the Gordonsville Historic District, contact:
Orange County Historical Society
Box 591
Orange, Va. 22960
(703) 672–5366

PETERSBURG

Self-guided walking and driving tours of downtown Petersburg, the Petersburg National Battlefield Park, and Blandford Church.
Historic Petersburg Tourist Information Center
19 Bollingbrook Street
Petersburg, Va. 23803
(804) 861–8080

PORTSMOUTH

Self-guided Olde Towne Lantern Tour of Olde Towne Historic District.
Portsmouth Council of the Hampton Roads Chamber of Commerce
P.O. Box 70
Portsmouth, Va. 23705
(804) 397–3453

RICHMOND

Self-guided walking tour of downtown Richmond including the historic Capitol Square area, the John Marshall House, the White House of the Confederacy, and the James River and Kanawha Canal Historic District. Free brochure with map. Some fees.
Richmond Convention and Visitors Bureau
201 East Franklin Street
Richmond, Va. 23219
(804) 648–1234

Guided walking tours to a number of Richmond's historic districts including Shockoe Slip, Jackson Ward, Monument Avenue, West Franklin Street, Hollywood Cemetery. Schedules vary with season. Fee.
Richmond-on-the-James
104 Shockoe Slip
Bowers Brothers Coffee Building
Richmond, Va, 23219
(804) 780–0170

ROANOKE

Self-guided walking tour of Roanoke including the Market Square Historic District.
Roanoke Valley Historical Society
One Market Square
Center in the Square
Roanoke, Va. 24011
(703) 342–5770

STAUNTON

Self-guided walking tours of Staunton's historic districts, including the Woodrow Wilson Birthplace and both commercial and residential areas.
Historic Staunton Foundation
120 S. Augusta Street
Staunton, Va. 22401
(703) 885–7676

STRASBURG

Self-guided walking tours of Strasburg Historic District.
Strasburg Museum
West Main Street
Strasburg, Va. 22657
(703) 465–3175

WARRENTON

Self-guided walking tour of historic district in Warrenton; many eighteenth- and nineteenth-century residential and commercial buildings; Fauquier County Courthouse square area.
Warrenton/Fauquier Chamber of Commerce
P.O. Box 127
Warrenton, Va. 22186
(703) 347–4414

WILLIAMSBURG

Nine guided tours with costumed guides. Fee. Self-guided tour with admission ticket to buildings and shops of Colonial Williamsburg.
Colonial Williamsburg Foundation
Williamsburg, Va. 23187
(804) 229–1000

WINCHESTER

Self-guided walking tour of Winchester Historic District. Map available. Booklet available for fee.
Preservation of Historic Winchester, Inc.
8 East Cork Street
Winchester, Va. 22601
(703) 667–3577

VIRGINIA'S STATE PARKS

For General Information:
Division of State Parks
1201 Washington Building
Richmond, Va. 23219
(804) 786–2132

Bear Creek Lake
Route 1, Box 253
Cumberland, Va. 23040
(804) 492–4410

Breaks Interstate Park
Breaks, Va. 24607
(703) 865–4414

Chippokes Plantation
Route 2, Box 213
Surry, Va. 23883
(804) 294–3625

Claytor Lake
Dublin, Va. 24080
(703) 674–5492

Douthat
Box 212
Milboro, Va. 24460
(703) 862–0612

Stuart, Va. 24171
(703) 930–2424

False Cape
4001 Sandpiper Rd.
Virginia Beach, Va. 23456
(804) 426–7128

George Washington's Grist Mill
5514 Mt. Vernon Memorial Highway
Alexandria, Va. 22309
(703) 780–3383

Goodwin Lake-Prince Edward
Route 2, Box 70
Green Bay, Va. 23942
(804) 392–3435

Grayson Highlands
Route 2, Box 141
Mouth of Wilson, Va. 24363
(703) 579–7092

Holliday Lake
Route 2, Box 230
Appomattox, Va. 24522
(804) 248–6308

Hungry Mother
Route 5, Box 109
Marion, Va. 24354
(703) 783–3422

Lake Anna
Route 3, Box 215
Spotsylvania, Va. 22553
(703) 854–5503

Natural Tunnel
Route 3, Box 250
Clinchport, Va. 24244
(703) 940–2674

Occoneechee
Box 818
Clarksville, Va. 23927
(804) 374–2210

Pocahontas
10300 Beach Road
Chesterfield, Va. 23832
(804) 748–5929

Seashore
2500 Shore Drive
Virginia Beach, Va. 23451
(804) 481–2131

Sky Meadows
Box 219
Upperville, Va. 22176
(703) 592–3585

Smith Mountain Lake
Route 1, Box 181
Huddleston, Va. 14104
(703) 297–6606

Southwest Virginia Museum
Big Stone Gap, Va. 24219
(703) 523–1322

Staunton River
Route 2, Box 295
Scottsburg, Va. 24589
(804) 572–4623

Westmoreland
Route 1, Box 600
Montross, Va. 22520
(804) 493–8821

York River
Route 4, Box 329-F
Williamsburg, Va. 23185
(804) 564–9057

ALPHABETICAL INDEX

CHURCHES AND OTHER RELIGIOUS BUILDINGS AND SITES

The church has played a major role in Virginia's history since the settlement period. The great majority of markers note the sites of church buildings and cemeteries; many markers point out church buildings that are still standing. A few deal with the history and leaders of Virginia's religious institutions.

Many significant battles and campaigns in the American Civil War, 1861–65 were fought in Virginia, with few areas of the Commonwealth escaping its scars. The first group of markers includes information on Lee and his lieutenants. The next four groups are divided geographically: Fredericksburg and the campaign in northern Virginia; the Valley campaign and southwest Virginia; Richmond and the campaign in southeastern Virginia, and place names in the Richmond theater. The final group of markers follow Lee's retreat to Appomattox. Today these markers are often the only visible sign of the military strategy and maneuvers of the Civil War.

LEE AND HIS LIEUTENANTS

Cavalry Engagement, E-9*
Edge Hill, S-47
Jackson's Amputation, J-37
Jackson's Headquarters, N-11
Jackson's Headquarters, Q-4-F
Jackson, Stonewall, Home of (Q-11-a*)
Jackson, Stonewall, Mother of, F-15*
Wounding of Jackson, J-39
Lee's Headquarters, E-38
Lee's Headquarters, JJ-2*
Lee's Headquarters, S-23*
Lee's Headquarters, S-27
General Lee's Headquarters, QA-7
Lee's Stopping Place, JE-35
Longstreet's Headquarters, E-41*
Moomaw's Landing, L-11
Stuart, E-8
Stuart's Escape, JJ-12*
Stuart's Ride around McClellan, WO-14
Stuart's Ride around Pope, C-8

FREDERICKSBURG AND THE CAMPAIGN IN NORTHERN VIRGINIA

Ball's Bluff, Battle of, F-1
Brandy Station, Battle of, F-11
Bull Run Battlefields, C-19, C-31
Burke's Station Raid, BW-2
A Camp of Stonewall Jackson's, JE-15
Cavalry Affairs, N-5
Cavalry Engagement, C-4, G-11*
Cedar Mountain, Battle of, F-19*, F-20
Chancellorsville, Battle of, J-40
Confederate Defenses, C-21
Defenses of Washington, E-81*
Delaplane, B-21
Dranesville, Action at, T-36
Early's Line of Battle, E-42*
Ely's Ford, J-38
Fort Lowry, N-24, N-29
Fredericksburg, Battles of, E-44*
Fredericksburg Campaign, C-56*, N-4
Gettysburg Campaign, B-32*, FF-4*, J-14*, J-25, T-38
Gettysburg Campaign, Opening of, F-13
Grant's Supply Line, E-40*
Groveton, Battle of, C-26*
Jackson's Bivouac, B-20
Jackson's Crossing, F-22
Jackson's March to Fredericksburg, JE-1
Henry House, G-15
Lee and Pope, F-16
Lee's Escape, FF-5*
Lee's Position, E-43*
McClellan Relieved from Command, FF-8
McClellan's Farewell, C-5*
Manassas, First Battle of, C-20, C-34, C-42, C-44
Manassas, Second Battle of, B-11, C-6, C-22, C-27, C-33*, C-28, C-40, C-46, C-48, C-54*, C-58*, C-60, C-61, CB-1, F-9, F-32, FA-1, FB-4, G-9, JJ-6
Military Movements, B-22*
Mine Run Campaign, JJ-10
Mosby's Midnight Raid, B-26
Mosby's Rangers, B-25
The Mud March, N-6*
Ox Hill, Action of, B-13*

VALLEY CAMPAIGN AND SOUTHWEST VIRGINIA

RICHMOND AND THE CAMPAIGN IN SOUTHEASTERN VIRGINIA

PLACE NAMES IN THE RICHMOND THEATER

COURTHOUSES AND OTHER PUBLIC
    BUILDINGS

The courthouse served as the center of
Virginia's political life in the colonial
period; throughout the nineteenth century and to the present day, the county
courthouses have remained significant
local landmarks. Other markers note
the sites of institutional structures that
have contributed to Virginia's history.

EARLY SETTLEMENTS IN VIRGINIA'S
    TIDEWATER AND MOUNTAIN
    REGIONS

Early Settlements include building,
sites, and events associated with Virginia's early European settlers. Many
of the seventeenth-century sites are
located in the Tidewater region; a
number of the eighteenth-century

FORTS

Forts played a major role in the defense of colonial Virginia. Many forts, particularly in the mountain regions of the state, were designed to protect settlements from Indians attacks. Few colonial fort structures exist today.

Russell's Fort, X-7
Site of Black's Fort, K-48
Smith's Fort, X-17
White House, C-30
William Wynne's Fort, X-10

HOMES AND HOMESITES OF COLONIAL VIRGINIA

Homes and Homesites of Colonial Virginia include residential structures and plantations dating from before the American Revolution. Virginia as the earliest and one of the largest of the British colonies boasts a large number of such sites. Although the texts of these markers are basically accurate, more recent research has assigned later building dates to a number of these homes. Many of the plantations are associated with Virginia's colonial leadership.

Ampthill, SA-30
Ampthill Estate, S-3
Anchor and Hope Plantation, K-36
Arlington, WY-5, WY-5*
Bacon's Castle, K-235
Battersea, QA-9*
Bellefont, A-62*
Belleview, A-135
Bell Farm (Colonel Michael Blow), K-230
Belvoir (Fort Humphreys), E-64*
Bennett's Home, K-257
Berkeley and Harrison's Landing, V-7
Berry Hill, U-40
Bewdley, J-81
Bizarre, MJ-1
Bloomsbury, JJ-4
Brandon, K-218
The Brick House, WO-33
Bushfield, JT-5
Carter's Grove, W-50*
Castle Hill, W-204
Chantilly, J-74*, J-76
Chatham, J-60
Chericoke, OC-26
Chestnut Hill, K-146*
Chippokes Plantation, K-279

Chrisman's Spring, A-42*
Claremont, K-225*
Clark Home, O-20
Clayspring (Clay's Birthplace), ND-6
Clement Hill, L-32
Clifton, JE-36
Colle, W-201
Colonial Home, F-8, FR-8*
Colonial Mansion Site, K-74
A Colonial Soldier's Home, K-23
Corotoman, J-85
Curles Neck and Bremo, V-3*
Dale Point, K-264*
Ditchley and Cobbs, J-88
Dungeness, SA-11
Early, Joseph, Home, G-12
East Hill, QA-13
Edgehill (Charlotte County), FR-6, W-203
Edmundsbury (Edmund Pendleton's Home), ND-5
Elk Hill, SA-5
Eltham, WO-30
Epping Forest (Birthplace of Washington's Mother), J-80, J-80*
"Fall Hill", E-49-A, E-49-B
Flowerdew Hundred, K-214
Folly Castle, QA-1
Fort Bowman, A-55*
"Fotheringay", K-67
Frontier Fort, A-20
Gouldborough Plantation (later Goldberry), N-27
Greenfield (Botetourt County), D-30*
Greenfield (Charlotte County), FR-7
Green Spring, W-36
Greenway, V-10
Greenway Court, T-3
Gunston Hall, E-65
Hackwood Park, A-38*
Hewick, N-45
Hillsboro, OB-5
Home of First Settler, WY-8
Kingsmill, W-47*
Laneville, OB-16
Leeton Forest, G-2
Level Green (Thomas Massie), OQ-4*
Littletown, W-48*
Macclesfield, K-247*
The McKay Home, J-7
Malvern Hill, V-4

HOMES OF FAMOUS VIRGINIANS IN THE NINETEENTH CENTURY

This section includes birthplaces as well as major residences associated with notable citizens of the Commonwealth. All structures date from after the American Revolution.

INDIANS

Landmarks associated with Virginia's native population are scattered throughout the state. Important sites include towns, burial grounds, and locations of Indian trails.

INDUSTRY AND AGRICULTURE IN VIRGINIA

"Industry and Agriculture in Virginia" includes markers pointing out sites of early industrial efforts in Virginia, such as grist mills, mines, and furnaces. Several markers explain aspects of Virginia's agricultural history.

NATURAL FEATURES

"Natural Features" include creeks, capes, islands, points, rivers, mountains, and fords in Virginia. Many of these features are associated with events in Virginia history.

NOTABLE PERSONS IN VIRGINIA

Markers for "Notable Persons in Virginia" include biographical data on many of Virginia's leading sons and citizens.

SITES OF SOME NOTABLE EVENTS IN VIRGINIA'S HISTORY

A small group of markers in the Virginia system notes certain interesting events in Virginia's history.

TRANSPORTATION AND COMMUNICATION

Markers for Transportation and Communication point out sites in Virginia associated with travel and commerce, including taverns, ordinaries, roads, ferries, railroads, and sites of significant aeronautical accomplishments.

TWENTIETH CENTURY

Twentieth-century markers note events and people of recognized importance in the century. Included are a number of Virginia's state parks.

VIRGINIA'S CITIES AND TOWNS

Markers for Virginia's cities and towns include information on the founding of these towns, together with significant historical events associated with them. Several towns noted no longer exist. Some markers indicate original boundaries of cities that have long since expanded.

VIRGINIA'S EDUCATIONAL INSTITUTIONS AND EDUCATORS

Markers in this section relate to Virginia's colleges and universities together with secondary and primary schools dating from the nineteenth century. Several markers commemorate noted Virginia educators.

WARS WITH THE BRITISH—THE REVOLUTION AND THE WAR OF 1812

Two major wars were fought against the British on Virginia soil: the American Revolution and the War of 1812, both of which assured American independence. Markers note the leaders, events, and battles of the wars.

GEOGRAPHIC INDEX

COUNTIES

ACCOMACK COUNTY
Area: 502 square miles

The Eastern Shore was called Accomack, the Indian name meaning the "across-the-water-place." It was one of the original shires formed in 1634. The name was changed to Northampton in 1643. In 1663 the present Accomack county was made from Northampton.

Birthplace of Governor Wise, EP-21 — Route 13 business town of Accomac
Tangier Island, Q-7-a — On Tangier Island
Battle of Pungoteague, WY-12* — Route 13, at Melfa
Occahannock, WY-13 — Route 13, at Belle Haven
Onancock, WY-14 — Route 13, 2 miles s. of Accomac
Founder of Presbyterianism, WY-15* — Route 13, at Temperanceville
Oak Grove Methodist Church, WY-16 — Route 13, in Keller
The Bear and the Cub, WY-17 — Route 13, at Keller
"The Bear and the Cub," WY-18 — Route 178, 0.5 mile n. of Pungoteague
Debtor's Prison, WY-19 — Route 764, in town of Accomac

ALBEMARLE COUNTY
Area: 751 square miles

Formed in 1744 from Goochland and named for the Earl of Albemarle, titular governor of Virginia, 1734–54. In 1761 Albemarle was divided and Buckingham and Amherst formed, and a part of Louisa was added to Albemarle. Thomas Jefferson was born in this county and lived in it.

Ash Lawn, FL-8, — Route 695, 4 miles s. of Charlottesville
General Sumter's Boyhood, G-25* — Route 29, 5 miles s. of Ruckersville
Barclay House and Scottsville Museum, GA-35 — Route 6, at Scottsville
Historic Scottsville, GA-36 — Route 20, Int. Route 6 in Scottsville
Maury's School, JE-6 — Route 231, 4.5 miles s.e. of Gordonsville
Birthplace of Meriwether Lewis, W-161 — Route 250, 5 miles w. of Charlottesville
Jackson's Valley Campaign, W-162 — Route 250, at Mechums River
Revolutionary Soldiers Graves, W-163 — Route 250, w. entrance to Charlottesville
Crozet, W-173 — Route 240, in Crozet
Shadwell—Thomas Jefferson's Birthplace, W-198 — Route 250, 3 miles e. of Charlottesville
Clark's Birthplace, W-199 — Route 250, .2 mile e. of Charlottesville
Monticello, W-200 — Route 250, at courthouse in Charlottesville
Colle, W-201 — Route 250, 4.2 miles e. of Charlottesville
Shadwell Estate, W-202 — Route 250, 2.9 miles e. of Charlottesville
Edgehill, W-203 — Route 250, 4.2 miles e. of Charlottesville
Castle Hill, W-204 — Route 231, e. of Shadwell
Mechunk Creek, W-205* — Route 22, 6 miles e. of Shadwell

ALLEGHANY COUNTY
Area: 458 square miles

Formed in 1822 from Bath, Botetourt, and Monroe, and named for the Alleghany Mountains. At Fort Mann in this county a battle took place between settlers and Indians led by Cornstalk, 1763.

Fort Breckenbrudge, D-26	Route 220, 3 miles n. of Covington
Governor Floyd's Grave, KH-1	Route 311, just s. of Sweet Chalybeate
Douthat State Park, L-3	Route 60, 1.5 miles e. of Clifton Forge
Lucy Selina Furnace, L-5	Route 60, at Longdale

AMELIA COUNTY
Area: 371 square miles

Formed in 1734 from Prince George and Brunswick, and named for Princess Amelia, daughter of King George II. William B. Giles, Governor of Virginia 1827–30, lived in this county.

Lee's Retreat, M-11	Route 360, at Amelia
Lee's Retreat, M-12	Route 360, 4.8 miles s.w. of Amelia
Lee's Retreat, M-13	Route 360, 5.3 miles s.w. of Amelia
Lee's Retreat, M-14	Route 360, 0.7 miles s.w. of Jetersville
Lee's Retreat, M-15	Route 360, at Jetersville
Lee's Retreat, M-19	Route 360, at Jetersville
Battle of Sailors (Sayler's) Creek, M-26	Route 617, 5 miles n.e. of Rice
Lee's Retreat, OL-10	Route 38, 7 miles e. of Mannboro

AMHERST COUNTY
Area: 470 square miles

Formed in 1761 from Albemarle, and named for Jeffrey, Lord Amherst, British commander in the French and Indian War. Balcony Falls are in this county.

State Colony, I-5*	Route 29, 1 mile n. of Lynchburg
Lynchburg Defenses, R-4*	Route 29, 1 mile n. of Lynchburg
Sweet Briar College Chartered 1901, R-20	Route 29, 2 miles s. of Amherst
Grave of Patrick Henry's Mother, R-60	Route 151, just s. of Clifford
Action at Tye River, R-61	Route 29, s. of Tye River Bridge

APPOMATTOX COUNTY
Area: 342 square miles

Formed in 1845 from Buckingham, Prince Edward, Charlotte, and Campbell, and named for an Indian tribe. This county was the scene of Lee's surrender, April 9, 1865.

The Last Fight, K-156	Route 460 at Route 131 in Appomattox
Surrender at Appomattox, D-157	Route 460 at Route 131 in Appomattox
Appomattox Court House, New and Old, K-158*	Route 131, at town of Appomattox
Battle of Appomattox Station—1865, K-159	At the corner of Main and Church streets in town of Appomattox

Inventor of the Banjo, M-66
Eldon, M-66
Eldon, M-66*
Clay Smoking Pipes, M-67
Appomattox Court House Confederate
    Cemetery, MG-1
The Last Positions, MG-2*
Wildway, MG-3

Route 24, 3.2 miles e. of Appomattox
Route 460 at 131, in Appomattox
Route 24, 1.1 miles n. of Appomattox
Route 460, at Pamplin
Route 24, .2 mile e. of Appomattox

Route 24, 2 miles n. of Appomattox
Route 24, at Vera

ARLINGTON COUNTY
Area: 31 square miles

This county, formerly Alexandria County, was formed in 1847 from the part of the District of Columbia retroceded to Virginia. It was renamed Arlington in 1920 for Arlington estate.

Clay and Randolph Duel, C-1*
World's First Public Passenger Flight, C-2
First Heavier-than-Air Flight in Virginia,
    C-7

Route 123, near Fairfax County line
Route 50 and Pershing Drive, at Fort Myer
Route 50, at entrance to Fort Myer

AUGUSTA COUNTY
Area: 1,006 square miles

Formed in 1738 from Orange, and named for Augusta, Princess of Wales and mother of King George III. Originally it included a large part of the Middle West. President Woodrow Wilson was born in Staunton.

Old Providence Church, A-31
New Providence Church, A-39
First Settler's Camp, A-40*
Virginia Inventors, A-51
Bethel Church, A-53
Bellefont, A-62*
Glebe Burying Ground, AL-5
Roanoke College, I-11-a
Jarman's Gap, JD-14
Walnut Grove, JF-15

Last Indian Raid, W-79
Tinkling Spring Church, W-155
First Settler's Grave, W-159
Early's Last Battle, W-160*

Route 340, 1.4 miles n. of Steeles Tavern
Route 340, at Steeles Tavern
Route 340, at Steeles Tavern
Route 340, at Steeles Tavern
Route 340, 2.1 miles n. of Greenville
Route 254, 1 mile w. of Route 11
Route 876, 12 miles s.w. of Staunton
Route 340, 2.1 miles n. of Greenville
Route 340, 1.2 miles n. of Waynesboro
Route 340, .3 mile s. of Waynesboro city
    limits
Route 250, 4 miles w. of Staunton
Route 608, 4 miles w. of Staunton
Route 250, at e. entrance of Staunton
Route 250, at w. entrance of Staunton

BATH COUNTY
Area: 545 square miles

Formed in 1790 from Augusta, Greenbrier, and Botetourt, and probably named for the town of Bath in England. The Warm Springs and Hot Springs are in this county.

Fort Lewis, D-24
Fort Dickinston, KB-75
Fort Dinwiddie, Q-5

Route 220, 11 miles n. of Warm Springs
Route 42, 3 miles s.e. of Milboro Springs
Route 39, 5 miles w. of Warm Springs

BEDFORD COUNTY
Area: 790 square miles

Formed in 1753 from Lunenburg and Albemarle, and named for the fourth Duke of Bedford, English statesman. The Peaks of Otter are in this county.

Indian Remains, K-119	Route 460, 12 miles w. of Bedford
Colonial Fort, K-121	Route 460, 11 miles w. of Bedford
Hunter's Bivouac, K-130	Route 460, 3 miles w. of Bedford
Home of John Goode, K-132	Route 460, at Bedford
Bedford, K-134	Route 460, at Bedford
Peaks of Otter Road, K-136	Route 460, at Bedford
Poplar Forest, K-138	Route 460, 6.5 miles w. of Lynchburg
St. Stephen's Church, K-140	Route 460, 8 miles w. of Lynchburg
New London Academy, K-141	Route 460, at New London Academy
Quaker Baptist Church, KM-5	Route 24, 3.0 miles e. of intersection of Routes 122 and 24

BLAND COUNTY
Area: 360 square miles

Formed in 1861 from Wythe, Tazewell, and Giles. Named for Richard Bland, Revolutionary leader. This county is rich in coal.

Bland, KC-1	Route 52, .35 mile s. of intersection with Route 98
A Great Preacher, KC-2*	Route 52, 2 miles s. of Rocky Gap
One of the "Big Four," KC-3	Route 42, 7 miles s. of Bland

BOTETOURT COUNTY
Area: 360 square miles

Formed in 1769 from Augusta, and named for Lord Botetourt, Governor of Virginia 1768–70. Buchanan was the western terminus of the noted James River and Kanawha Canal.

Audley Paul's Fort, A-48	Route 11, 4.5 miles s. of Natural Bridge
Indian Massacre, A-50	Route 11, .9 mile n. of Buchanan
Buchanan, A-58	Route 11, at Buchanan
Coming of the Railroad, A-80	Route 11, 4.2 miles n. of Troutville
Old Carolina Road, A-81	Route 11, 8 miles n. of Roanoke
Cloverdale Furnace, A-82	Route 11, 8.2 miles n. of Roanoke
Looney's Ferry, A-91	Route 11, .7 mile s. of Buchanan
Cartmill's Gap, A-92	Route 11, 1.4 miles n. of Buchanan
Fincastle, D-28	Route 220, at Fincastle
Fort William, D-29	Route 220, 3 miles s. Fincastle
Greenfield, D-30*	Route 220, 5 miles s. of Fincastle

BRUNSWICK COUNTY
Area: 557 square miles

Formed in 1720 from Prince George, Surry, and Isle of Wight. Named for the House of Brunswick, which came to the throne of England in 1714, when George I was crowned king. Colonial Fort Christanna was in this county.

Ebenezer Academy, S-58

Birch's Bridge, S-57

Sturgeon Creek, S-60

Old Brunswick Courthouse, S-65

Fort Christanna, S-66

Meherrin History, S-72*

Campaign of 1865, S-79*

Mason's Chapel, SN-60

Fort Christanna, U-90*

Route 1, 6.8 miles n. of Cochran

Route 1, 2.8 miles s. of McKenney

Route 1, 5.7 miles n. of Cochran

Route 1, at Cochran

Route 1, at Cochran

Route 1, 7.3 miles s. of Cochran

Route 1, 7.3 miles s. of Cochran

Route 46, 8 miles s. of Brunswick

Route 58, w. of Lawrenceville

BUCHANAN COUNTY
Area: 514 square miles

Formed in 1858 from Tazewell and Russell and named for James Buchanan, President of the United States 1857–61.

Grundy, XB-25

Route 83, at Grundy

BUCKINGHAM COUNTY
Area: 584 square miles

Formed in 1761 from Albermarle, and named for Buckinghamshire, England. Peter Francisco, noted Revolutionary soldier, lived in this county.

Carter G. Woodson, F-53

Female Collegiate Institute, F-54

Gold Mines, F-55

Old Buckingham Church, F-56

March to Appomattox, F-59

Eve of Appomattox, F-60

New Store Village, F-61

Geographical Center of Virginia, O-39

After Appomattox, O-42

Buckingham Courthouse, p. 182

Route 15, 10 miles n. of Dillwyn

Route 15, 5 miles n. of Dillwyn

Route 15, at Dillwyn

Route 15, .75 mile sw of Route 610

Route 15, 8.8 miles s. of Sprouses

Route 15, 11.3 miles s. of Sprouses

Route 15, 11.3 miles s. of Sprouses

Routes 60 and 24 at Mount Rush

Route 60, 1.1 miles e. of Buckingham

Route 60, at Buckingham Court House

CAMPBELL COUNTY
Area: 557 square miles

Formed in 1781 from Bedford, and named for General William Campbell, hero of the battle of King's Mountain, 1780. Tarleton passed through the county in 1781. The Union General Hunter was defeated near Lynchburg, 1864.

Hat Creek Church, FR-16

Patrick Henry's Grave, FR-25

Birthplace of General Pick, FR-27

New London (K-139; front and back of
marker)

Mount Athos, K-148*

Oxford Furnace, K-140

Concord Station, K-152

Shady Grove, L-12

Route 40, 2.1 miles e. of Brookneal

Route 40, 2.5 miles e. of Brookneal

Route 40, in Brookneal

Route 858, 4 miles w. of Lynchburg

Route 460, 6 miles e. of Lynchburg

Route 460, 2.5 miles e. of Lynchburg

Route 460, at Concord

Route 501, at Gladys

Origin of Lynch Law, L-30*
Patrick Henry's Grave, R-15*
Old Rustburg, R-62

Route 29, 1 mile n. of Alta Vista
Route 501, at Brookneal
Route 501, at Rustburg

CAROLINE COUNTY
Area: 529 square miles

Formed in 1727 from Essex, King and Queen, and King William. Named for Queen Caroline, wife of King George II. George Rogers Clark, conqueror of the Northwest, passed his youth in this county.

Lee and Grant, E-23
Long Creek Action, E-24
Grant's Operations, E-25
Dickinson's Mill, E-26
Bull Church, E-27*
Nancy Wright's, E-28
Doctor Flippo's, E-29*
John Wilkes Booth, EP-20

Jackson's Headquarters, N-11
Lederer Expedition, N-8
Windsor, N-12
Skinker's Neck, N-13
Hazelwood, N-14
Rappahannock Academy, N-15
Where Booth Died, N-16
Old Port Royal, N-17
Edmund Pendleton's Home, ND-5
Campaign of 1781, ND-7

Route 1, 2.8 miles s. of Carmel Church
Route 1, 2.4 miles s. of Carmel Church
Route 1, at Carmel Church
Route 1, 2.2 miles s. of Ladysmith
U.S. 1 at Ladysmith
Route 1, 5.1 miles n. of Ladysmith
Route 1, 1.6 miles n. of Ladysmith
Route 301, 9.1 miles n.e. of Bowling Green
Route 17, 5.7 miles s.e. of New Post
Route 17, 12.5 miles s.e. of Fredericksburg
Route 17, 6.9 miles s.e. of New Post
Route 17, 6.9 miles s.e. of New Post
Route 17, 12.7 miles s.e. of New Post
Route 17, 10 miles s.e. of New Post
Route 301, at Port Royal Cross Roads
Route 301, at Port Royal Cross Roads
Route 2, 2.5 miles s. of Bowling Green
Route 2, at Bowling Green

CARROLL COUNTY
Area: 458 square miles

Formed in 1842 from Grayson, and named for Charles Carroll of Carrollton, signer of the Declaration of Independence. New River runs through this county.

Hillsville, KD-12

Route 52, at Hillsville

CHARLES CITY COUNTY
Area: 188 square miles

One of the original eight shires formed in 1634, and named for Charles City at Bermuda Hundred. William Henry Harrison and John Tyler, presidents of the United States, were born in this county.

Benjamin Harrison Bridge, PA-250
Action of Nance's Shop, PH-6
Shirley, V-6
Berkeley and Harrison's Landing, V-7
Westover, V-8

Route 156, at bridge
Route 603, 13.4 miles s.e. of Seven Pines
Route 5, 17.1 miles s.e. of Richmond
Route 5, 7.2 miles w. of Charles City
Route 5, 7.2 miles w. of Charles City

Grant's Crossing, V-9 — Route 5, 2.4 miles w. of Charles City
Greenway, V-10 — Route 5, .7 mile w. of Charles City
Charles City Courthouse, V-11 — Route 5, at Charles City
Upper Weyanoke, V-12 — Route 5, at Charles City
Salem Church, V-13 — Route 5, 5.9 miles w. of Charles City
Westover Church, V-14 — Route 5, 6.5 miles w. of Charles City
Scene of Jefferson's Wedding, V-15 — Route 5, 15.1 miles s.e. of Richmond
President Tyler's Home, V-21 — Route 5, 3.5 miles e. of Charles City

CHARLOTTE COUNTY
Area: 496 square miles

Formed in 1764 from Lunenburg, and named for Queen Charlotte, wife of King George III. Patrick Henry and John Randolph of Roanoke lived in this county, and Henry is buried here.

Colonial Home, F-8 — Route 15, 2.4 miles n. of Keysville
Early Exploration, F-77 — Route 15, .2 mile n. of Keysville
Campaign of 1781, F-78 — Route 15, at s. entrance of Keysville
Roanoke Plantation, F-80 — Route 15, Wyliesburg
Staunton Bridge Action, F-82 — Route 15, at Wyliesburg
Red House, FR-3 — Route 727, at Red House
Edgehill, FR-6 — Route 40, 2 miles e. of Charlotte
Greenfield, FR-7 — Route 40, 2 miles e. of Charlotte
Colonial Home, FR-8* — Route 40, 2 miles e. of Charlotte Court-house

Henry and Randolph's Debate, FR-10 — Route 40, at Charlotte
Campaign of 1781, FR-12 — Route 40, at Charlotte
Cub Creek Church, FR-14 — Route 40, 2 miles e. of Phenix
Rough Creek Church, FR-15 — Route 727, n. of Phenix
Paul Carrington, M-9 — Route 360, at Route 607 in Wylliesburg

CHESTERFIELD COUNTY
Area: 468 square miles

Formed in 1748 from Henrico, and named for the Earl of Chesterfield, noted courtier. The first iron furnace in America, 1619, was in this county. The battle of Drewry's Bluff, 1864, took place here.

Ettrick, K-204 — Route 36, .2 mile w. of Petersburg
Bethlehem Baptist Church, O-27* — Route 60, 5.4 miles w. of Richmond
Huguenot Settlement, O-28 — Route 60, 1.7 miles e. of Midlothian
Salisbury, O-29 — Route 60, at Midlothian
Black Heath, O-34 — Route 60, 1.7 miles e. of Midlothian
Midlothian Coal Mines, O-35* — Route 60, at Midlothian
Bellona Arsenal, O-40* — Route 60, 5.7 miles w. of Richmond
Eppington, M-8* — Route 677, .5 miles e. of Amelia
Goode's Bridge, M-10 — Route 360, 7.8 miles e. of Amelia
Arnold at Warwick, S-2* — Route 1, 1.5 miles s. of Richmond
Ampthill Estate, S-3 — Route 1, .7 mile s. of Richmond
First Iron Furnace, S-4 — Route 1, 1.5 miles s. of Richmond

Drewry's Bluff, S-5

Main Confederate Line, S-6*
Chesterfield Courthouse, S-7*
Battle of Drewry's Bluff, S-8
Battle of Drewry's Bluff, S-9*
Half-Way House, S-10
Proctor's Creek Fight, S-11*
Into the Bottle, S-12
Into the "Bottle," S-12*
Dutch Gap, S-13
Osborne's Wharf, S-14*
Drewry's Bluff, S-15

Pocahontas State Park, S-16
Redwater Creek, S-16*
Chester Station Fight, S-17
The "Bottle," S-18*
Feeling Out Fight, S-19*
A Railroad Raid, S-20*
Bermuda Hundred, S-21
Port Walthall Junction, S-22*
Lee's Headquarters, S-23*
Advance on Petersburg, S-24*
Union Army Checked, S-25
Lafayette at Petersburg, S-26
Lee's Headquarters, S-27
Salisbury, p. 185

Route 1, 2.5 miles s. of Richmond on
   northbound lane
Route 1, 8 miles s. of Richmond
Route 1, 2.9 miles s. of Richmond
Route 1, 3.9 miles s. of Richmond
Route 1, 4.5 miles s. of Richmond
Route 1, 5.4 miles s. of Richmond
Route 301 at Proctors Creek
Route 1, 6.5 miles s. of Richmond
Route 1, 6 miles s. of Richmond
Route 1, 6.7 miles s. of Richmond
Route 1, 6.7 miles s. of Richmond
Route 1, 2.5 miles s. of Richmond on
   southbound lane
Route 655, 4.1 miles w. of Chesterfield
Route 1, 4.5 miles n. of Petersburg
Route 1, 7.8 miles s. of Richmond
Route 1, 6.2 miles n. of Petersburg
Route 1, 6.9 miles n. of Petersburg
Route 1, 4.25 miles n. of Petersburg
Route 1, 7.8 miles s. of Richmond
Route 1, 5.4 miles n. of Petersburg
Route 1, 7.5 miles n. of Petersburg
Route 1, 4.1 miles n. of Petersburg
Route 1, 3.4 miles n. of Petersburg
Route 1, at Colonial Heights
Route 1 at Colonial Heights
Route 902, on Salisbury Rd.

CLARKE COUNTY
Area: 171 square miles

Formed in 1836 from Frederick, and added to from Warren. Named for George Rogers Clark, conqueror of the Northwest. Lord Fairfax and General Daniel Morgan, Revolutionary hero, lived in this county.

The Briars, B-2*
Saratoga, B-4*
Signal Station, B-7
Ashby's Tavern, B-23*
A Raid of Mosby's, J-1*
Buck March Baptist Church, J-1-a
Buck Marsh, J-2*
Gettyburg Campaign, J-14*
Anderson and Crook, J-30*
Carter Hall, T-1
Old Chapel, T-2
Greenway Court, T-3
Audley, T-4
The Burwell-Morgan Mill, T-6

Route 50, 3 miles n.w. of Boyce
Route 50, at Boyce
Route 50, .7 mile w. of Paris
Route 50, 2 miles n.w. of Paris
Route 340, 1 mile n. of Berryville
Route 340, n. of Berryville
Route 340, 1.5 miles n. of Berryville
Route 340, 1 mile n. of Berryville
Route 7, .7 mile w. of Berryville
Route 255, just n. of Millwood
Route 255, 3.2 miles s. of Berryville
Route 340, 2 miles n.w. of Millwood
Route 7, 0.7 mile e. of Berryville
Route 255, at Millwood

White Post, T-7*   Route 255, at White Post
Colonial Highway, T-8   Route 7, 3.7 miles e. of Berryville
Castleman's Ferry Fight, T-9   Route 7, at intersection with Route 603
Castleman's Ferry Fight, T-9*   Route 7, 4.5 miles e. of Berryville
Crook and Early, T-10   Route 7, 7.7 miles e. of Berryville
Forerunner of Wireless Telegraphy, T-11   Route 7, 7.7 miles e. of Berryville
Berryville, Q-3-a-b-c-d*   *a* and *c*: e. and w. entrances on Route 7; *b*: n. entrance on Route 340; *d*: s. entrance on Route 12

CRAIG COUNTY

Area: 333 square miles

Formed in 1851 from Botetourt, Roanoke, Giles, and Monroe. Named for Robert Craig, member of Congress. Craig Healing Springs are in this county.

New Castle, KH-4   Route 311, at Newcastle

CULPEPER COUNTY

Area: 384 square miles

Formed in 1748 from Orange, and named for Lord Culpeper, Governor of Virginia 1680–83. The battle of Cedar Mountain, 1862, was fought in this county.

Stuart's Ride around Pope, C-8   Route 613, 6 miles w. of Warrenton
Greenwood, F-3   Route 15, .8 mile s. of Culpeper
Where Pelham Fell, F-10   Route 15, at Elkwood
Battle of Brandy Station, F-11   Route 29, 1 mile n. of Brandy
Battle of Brandy Station, F-11   Routes 15 and 29, .7 mile n.e. of Brandy
Betty Washington, F-12*   Route 15, 3.1 miles n.e. of Culpeper
Opening of Gettysburg Campaign, F-13   Route 15, .5 mile s.w. of Brandy
Signal Station, F-15*   Route 15, 2 miles s. of Culpeper
Lee and Pope, F-16   Route 15, 4.7 miles s. of Culpeper
Battle of Cedar Mountain, F-19*   Route 15, 3 miles s. of Culpeper
Battle of Cedar Mountain, F-20   Route 15, 6.1 miles s. of Culpeper
Crooked Run Baptist Church, F-21*   Route 15, 9.7 miles s. of Culpeper
Campaign of Second Manassas, G-9   Route 211, 7 miles n.w. of Warrenton
Little Fork Church, G-9   Route 229, 6 miles s. of Route 211
General Edward Stevens, G-10   Route 229, at n. entrance of Culpeper
John S. Barbour's Birthplace, J-6*   Route 522, at w. entrance of Culpeper
Culpeper Minute Men, J-10   Route 522, at w. entrance of Culpeper
Signal Stations, J-15   Route 3, 3.6 miles e. of Culpeper
Opening of the Wilderness Campaign, J-33   Route 3, at Stevensburg

CUMBERLAND COUNTY

Area: 293 square miles

Formed in 1748 from Goochland, and named for the Duke of Cumberland, second son of King George II. The earliest call for independence came from this county, April 22, 1776.

Lee's Stopping Place, JE-35

Clifton, JE-36

Bizarre, MJ-1
Campaign of 1781, O-44
Campaign of 1781, ON-7
State Game Farm, W-21
Campaign of 1781, ON-5

Route 690 at Route 612, 8.8 miles s. of Columbia
Route 690, at Route 605, 11 miles s. of Columbia
Route 45, at n. entrance of Farmville
Route 60, 1.8 miles w. of Cumberland
Route 45, 1.8 miles s. of Cartersville
Route 45, at Route 615
Route 45, at Cartersville

DICKENSON COUNTY
Area: 325 square miles

Formed in 1880 from Russell, Wise, and Buchanan, and named for W. J. Dickenson, prominent public man.

Old Buffalo School, XB-10
Clintwood, XB-11
Early Settler, XB-12
John Mullins, XB-13
First Settler, XB-20*
Indian Outrage, XB-23
Colley's Cabin, XB-24

Route 63, at Nora
Route 83, at Clintwood
Route 83, at Clintwood
Route 83, in Clintwood
Route 83, at Haysi
Route 83, at Haysi
Route 80, .3 miles s. of Haysi

DINWIDDIE COUNTY
Area: 521 square miles

Formed in 1752 from Prince George, and named for Robert Dinwiddie, Governor of Virginia 1751–56. General Winfield Scott was born in this county, and in it took place the battle of Five Forks, 1865.

Central State Hospital, I-6
Lee's Retreat, K-305
Battle of Five Forks, K-307
Saponey Church, S-40
Dinwiddie Tavern, S-41*
Quaker Settlement, S-42*
Cottage Farm, S-43
Scott's Law Office, S-45
Raceland, S-46*
Edge Hill, S-47
The Cattle (Beefsteak Raid), S-48
Where Hill Fell, S-49
Hatcher's Run, S-50
Burgess Mill, S-51
White Oak Road, S-52
Action of March 29, 1865, S-53*
Dinwiddie Courthouse, S-54
Vaughan Road, S-55
Chamberlain's Bed, S-56
Campaign of 1781, S-62

Route 1, .4mile w. of Petersburg
Route 460, .2 mile e. of Sutherland
Route 460, 4.9 miles w. of Sutherland
Route 1, at Dewitt
Route 1, at Dinwiddie
Route 1, 6 miles s.w. of Petersburg
Route 1, at s. limits of Petersburg
Route 1, at Dinwiddie
Route 1, n. entrance of Dinwiddie
Route 1 at s. limits of Petersburg
Routes 1 and 613, 5 miles s. of Petersburg
Route 1, 2.8 miles s. of Petersburg
Route 1, 6.4 miles s. of Petersburg
Route 1, 6.4 miles s. of Petersburg
Route 1, 6.8 miles s. of Petersburg
Route 1, 7.7 miles s. of Petersburg
Route 1, at Dinwiddie
Route 1, at Dinwiddie
Route 1, 1.1 miles s. of Dinwiddie
Route 1, 1.5 miles s. of Dinwiddie

ESSEX COUNTY
Area: 258 square miles

Formed in 1691 from Old Rappahannock County, and named for Essex County, England. R.M.T. Hunter, United States Senator and Confederate Secretary of State, lived in this county.

Early Settlement, N-9	Route 17, 7 miles n.w. of Caret
Old Rappahannock Courthouse, N-18	Route 17, at Caret
Portobago Indian Towns, N-19	Route 17, 11.8 miles n.w. of Caret
Fonthill, N-20	Route 17, 3 miles n.w. of Caret
Historic Tappahannock, N-21	Route 360, at Tappahannock
Ritchie's Birthplace, N-22	Route 17, at Tappahannock
Vauter's Church, N-23	Route 17, 10.7 miles n.w. of Caret
Fort Lowry—Camp Byron, N-24	Route 17, at Route 611
Ancient Indian Town, N-25	Route 17, 1.75 miles w. of Tappahannock
Mann Meeting House, N-26	Route 17, 12.4 miles s.e. of Tappahannock
Gouldborough Plantation, N-27	Route 17, 2.27 miles s. of Caret
Departure of the Indians, N-28	Route 17, 2.8 miles n.w. of Tappahannock
Fort Lowry, N-29	Route 646, at Fort Site
Mattapony Indian Town, O-22	Route 360, at Millers Tavern
Bacon's Northern Force, O-23	Route 360, at Millers Tavern

FAIRFAX COUNTY
Area: 417 square miles

Formed in 1742 from Prince William and Loudoun, and named for Lord Fairfax, proprietor of the Northern Neck. Mount Vernon, George Washington's home, is in this county.

Campaign of Second Manassas, B-11	Route 50, 2.8 miles w. of Fairfax
Action of Ox Hill, B-13*	Route 50, 6.9 miles w. of Fairfax
First Battle of Manassas, C-20	Route 211, at Centreville
Confederate Defenses, C-21	Route 211, at Centreville
Second Battle of Manassas, C-22	Route 211, at Centreville
Campaign of Second Manassas, C-40	Route 211, at Centreville
First Battle of Manassas, C-42*	Route 211, 1.8 miles w. of Centreville
The Falls Church, C-90	Route 211, at Falls Church, s. of Route 7
Events On Pohick Creek, E-60*	Route 1, 3.2 miles n. of Woodbridge
Occoquan Workhouse, E-61	Route 123, at Lorton Penitentiary Youth Center
Old Telegraph Line, E-62	Route 1, 4.1 miles n. of Woodbridge
Early Land Patents, E-63*	Route 1, 5.6 miles n. of Woodbridge
Fort Humphreys, E-64*	Route 1, .7 mile n. of Woodbridge
Gunston Hall, E-65	Route 1, 2.4 miles n. of Woodbridge
Woodlawn, E-66*	Route 1, 7.4 miles s. of Alexandria
History On Dogue Run, E-67*	Route 1, 7.1 miles s. of Alexandria
Mount Vernon Estate, E-68*	Route 1, 4.5 miles s. of Alexandria
Little Hunting Creek, E-69*	Route 1, 4.5 miles s. of Alexandria
Colonial Fort, E-70*	Route 1, at Alexandria
Pohick Church, E-72	Route 1, 4.3 miles n. of Woodbridge
Old Road to West, E-72*	Route 50, at n. entrance of Alexandria

Washington's Mill, E-73

Indian Massacre, E-80*
Defenses of Washington, E-81*
Action at Dranesville, T-36
Sharpsburg (Antietam) Campaign, T-37

Route 1, 7.4 miles s. of Alexandria at
  Route 235
Route 1, 8.25 miles s. of Alexandria
Route 1, .8 mile s. of Alexandria
Route 7, at Dranesville
Route 7, at Dranesville

FAUQUIER COUNTY
Area: 666 square miles

Formed in 1759 from Prince William, and named for Francis Fauquier, Governor of Virginia,
1758–1768. Chief Justice John Marshall was born in this county.

Jackson's Bivouac, B-20
Delaplane, B-21
Ancient Highway, B-24*
Mosby's Rangers, B-25
Stuart and Gregg, B-31
Stuart and Mosby, B-36

Brent Town, BX-2*
Neavil's Ordinary, BX-7
McClellan's Farewell, C-5*
Colonial Road, C-29
Campaign of Second Manassas, C-54*
Fredericksburg Campaign, C-56*
Campaign of Second Manassas, C-58*
Campaign of Second Manassas, C-60
Campaign of Second Manassas, CB-1
John Marshall's Birthplace, CL-3
Campaign of Second Manassas, F-9
Goldvein, F-18
John Marshall's Home, FB-2
Campaign of Second Manassas, FB-4
Gettysburg Campaign, FF-4*
Lee's Escape, FF-5*
McClellan Relieved from Command, FF-8
Leeton Forest, G-2
Warrenton, Q-9

Routes 50 and 17 at Paris
Route 17, 6.5 miles s. of Paris—Route 50
Route 17, 1 mile s. of Paris
Route 50, 4 miles w. of Middleburg
Route 50, .4 mile e. of Upperville
Route 28, 3.1 miles w. of Prince William
  County line
Route 806, 5 miles s. of Catlett
Route 670, 6.1 miles e. of Warrenton
Route 211, 3 miles w. of Buckland
Route 211, 2.6 miles e. of Warrenton
Route 211, 4.5 miles w. of Gainesville
Route 211, 2.6 miles e. of Warrenton
Route 211, 4 miles w. of Warrenton
Route 211, 5.1 miles w. of Warrenton
Route 688, 12 miles w. of Warrenton
Route 28, .8 mile e. of Midland
Route 55, at The Plains
Route 17 at Goldvein
Route 55, 4 miles w. of Marshall
Route 55, at Marshall
Route 55, at Markham
Route 55, 2 miles w. of Marshall
Route 55, at Marshall
Route 802, 0.5 miles s. of Warrenton
Route 802, at Warrenton

FLOYD COUNTY
Area: 376 square miles

Formed in 1831 from Montgomery, and added to from Franklin. Named for John Floyd,
Governor of Virginia 1830–34. Buffalo Knob is in this county.

Floyd, KG-5

Route 8, at Floyd

FLUVANNA COUNTY
Area: 285 square miles

Formed in 1777 from Albemarle. Named (in Latin) Anne's River, the early name of the Upper James given in honor of Queen Anne. Point of Fork was an important supply depot in 1781.

Point of Fork, F-50	Route 15, at Dixie
Bremo, F-52	Route 15, 3.2 miles s. of Fork Union
Point of Fork, GA-32	Route 6, .8 mile w. of Columbia
Fork Union Academy, GA-33	Route 6, .8 mile w. of Columbia
Rassawek, GA-34	Route 6, at Route 15 in Fork Union

FRANKLIN COUNTY
Area: 697 square miles

Formed in 1785 from Henry and Bedford and added to from Patrick. Named for Benjamin Franklin. General Jubal A. Early lived in this county.

Rocky Mount, A-60	Route 220, at Rocky Mount
Fort Blackwater, A-93	Route 220, 3 miles n. of Rocky Mount
Booker Washington's Birthplace, KP-4	Route 122, just w. of Hales Ford Church

FREDERICK COUNTY
Area: 435 square miles

Formed in 1738 from Orange, and named for Frederick, Prince of Wales, father of King George III. Several battles were fought in the vicinity of Winchester, 1862–64.

Action at Stephenson's Depot, A-1*	Route 11, 4 miles n. of Winchester
Action of Carter's Farm, A-2*	Route 11, 2.75 miles n. of Winchester
Capture of Star Fort, A-3	Route 11, .8 mile n. of Winchester
Fort Collier, A-4*	Route 11, .4 mile n. of Winchester
First Battle of Winchester, A-6*	Route 11, s. of Winchester
First Battle of Winchester, A-7	Route 11, .6 mile s. of Winchester
Second Battle of Winchester, A-8*	Route 11, .6 mile s. of Winchester
Battle of Kernstown, A-9	Route 11, 5.3 miles n. of Stephens City
Early and Crook, A-10	Route 11, 1 mile n. of Kernstown
First Battle of Winchester, A-11	Route 11, 3.2 miles n. of Stephens City
House of First Settler, A-12	Route 11, 2.3 miles n. of Stephens City
Stephens City, A-13*	Route 11, center of Stephens City
End of Sheridan's Ride, A-14	Route 11, 3.2 miles s. of Stephens City
Battle of Cedar Creek, A-15	Route 11, .2 mile n. of Middletown
Engagement of Middletown, A-16	Route 11, at Middletown
Tomb of an Unknown Soldier, A-17	Route 11, 1 mile s. of Middletown
Old Stone Fort, A-37	Route 11, at Middletown
Hackwood Park, A-38*	Route 11, 1.7 miles n. of Winchester
Chrisman's Spring, A-42*	Route 11, 2 miles s. of Stephens City
Battle of Cedar Creek, A-56	Route 11, 1.3 miles s. of Middletown
Willa Cather Birthplace, B-18	Route 50, at Gore
Second Battle of Winchester, B-19	Route 50, 2.5 miles w. of Winchester
Third Battle of Winchester, J-3*	Route 522, at e. entrance to Winchester

Third Battle of Winchester, J-13* Route 50, at Winchester
Defenses of Winchester, J-16 Route 522, 4 miles s. of Winchester

GILES COUNTY
Area: 369 square miles

Formed in 1806 from Montgomery, Tazewell, and Monroe, and named for William B. Giles, United States Senator and Governor of Virginia 1827–30. Mountain Lake is in this county.

Eggleston's Springs, KB-56 Route 730, at Eggleston
Mountain Evangelist, KG-15 Route 100, at Route 730
Old-Fashioned Camp Meeting, KG-16 Route 100, .6 mile n. of Route 659
Snidow's Ferry, KG-17 Route 460, 3 miles e. of Pearisburg
Discovery of New River, KG-19 Route 460, 3 miles e. of Pearisburg
First Court of Giles County, KG-20 Route 460, 1 mile n. of Pearisburg
Pearisburg, KG-21 Route 460, at Pearisburg
Narrows, KG-22 Route 460, at Narrows

GLOUCESTER COUNTY
Area: 223 square miles

Formed in 1651 from York, and named for Gloucester County, England. Bacon the Rebel died in this county, 1676. Gloucester Point was the outpost of Cornwallis at Yorktown, 1781.

Poplar Spring Church, N-61 Route 17, 5 miles n.w. of Gloucester
Marlfield, N-66* Route 17, 4.5 miles n.w. of Gloucester
Gloucester Courthouse, NW-1 Route 17, at Gloucester
Ware Church, NW-2 Route 17, at eastern entrance of Gloucester
To Gwynn's Island, NW-3 Route 17, at eastern entrance of Gloucester
Warner Hall, NW-4 Route 17, 4.2 miles s. of Gloucester
Abingdon Church, NE-5 Route 17, 6.2 miles s. of Gloucester
White Marsh and Reed's Birthplace, NW-6 Route 17, 5.3 miles s. of Gloucester
Tarleton's Last Fight, NW-7 Route 1216, 2.1 miles n. of Gloucester
 Point
Rosewell and Werowocomoco, NW-8 Route 17, 5.3 miles s. of Gloucester
Gloucester Point, NW-9 Route 17, at Gloucester Point
Early Land Patent, NW-10 Route 17, at Gloucester Point
Cappahosic, Q-10-a Route 17, at Gloucester

GOOCHLAND COUNTY
Area: 287 square miles

Formed in 1727 from Henrico, and named for William Gooch, Governor of Virginia 1727–49. Cornwallis and Lafayette passed through this county in 1781.

Elk Hill, SA-5 Route 6, 1 mile w. of George's Tavern
Goochland Courthouse, SA-10 Route 6, at Goochland
Dungeness, SA-11 Route 6, at the court house
Dahlgren's Raid, SA-14 Route 6, 2.1 miles e. of Crozier
Sabot Hill, SA-18 Route 6, 2.6 miles s. of Crozier
The Huguenot Settlement, SA-20 Route 6, 5.9 miles e. of Crozier

William Webber, SA-22
Tuckahoe, SA-24
Dahlgren's Raid, SA-27
Reuben Ford, V-18

Route 6, 6 miles e. of Crozier at Manakin
Route 650, w. of Henrico County Line
Route 650, 9 miles w. of Richmond
Route 250, 1.9 miles e. of Oilville

GRAYSON COUNTY
Area: 425 square miles

Formed in 1792 from Wythe, named for William Grayson, one of the first two United States Senators from Virginia. Headwaters of New River are in this county.

Caty Sage, KC-10
Independence, U-22
Peyton Guyn Hale, U-23
First County Seat, U-25
Galax, U-26
Fries, UE-2
First Court of Grayson County, UE-5
Fries—Center of Early Recorded Country
     Music, UE-6

Route 21, 4 miles s. of Wythe County line
Route 58, at Independence
Route 21, at Elks Creek
Route 640, 3 miles w. of Galax
Route 89 (Main Street
Route 94 at Carroll County line
Route 805, 5 miles s.w. of Fries
Route 94, at Fries

GREENE COUNTY
Area: 155 square miles

Formed in 1838 from Orange, and named for General Nathanael Greene, commander of the Army of the South in the Revolutionary War.

No markers except county marker.

GREENSVILLE COUNTY
Area: 307 square miles

Formed in 1780 from Brunswick, and probably named for Sir Richard Grenville, leader of the settlement on Roanoke Island, 1585. Cornwallis passed through this county in 1781.

Tarleton's Movements, UM-40
Site of "Homestead," UM-41

Route 301, at Emporia
Route 58 and Chapman's Ford Road

HALIFAX COUNTY
Area: 814 square miles

Formed in 1752 from Lunenburg, and named for George Montague Dunk, Earl of Halifax, British statesman. Berry Hill, old home, is in this county.

History at Halifax, R-77*
Green's Folly, R-79
Minister Who Married Lincoln, R-80
Carters Tavern, U-47
Staunton River State Park, U-48
Nathaniel Terry's Grave, U-50
Campaign of 1781, UL-2

Route 360, at Halifax
Route 501, 2 miles s. of Halifax
Route 501, 2 miles s. of Halifax
Route 659, 3.3 miles e. of Halifax
Route 360, 7.1 miles e. of Halifax
Route 304, 6 miles n.e. of South Boston
Route 501, .4 mile s. of South Boston

HANOVER COUNTY
Area: 512 square miles

Formed in 1720 from New Kent, and named for the Electorate of Hanover. Patrick Henry and Henry Clay were born in this county. In it were fought the battles of Gaines's Mill, 1862, and Cold Harbor, 1864.

Fork Church, E-5	Route 738, 4.5 miles w. of Route 1
Battles on the Chickahominy, E-11*	Route 1, 4.9 miles s. of Ashland
Smith and Lafayette, E-12*	Route 1, 4.9 miles s. of Ashland
Lee's Turn to Cold Harbor, E-13	Route 1, 4.5 miles s. of Ashland
Jackson's March to Gaines's Mill, E-14*	Route 1, .4 mile south of Ashland
Cavalry Skirmish, E-14*	Route 1, 1 mile s. of Ashland
Henry at Hanover Courthouse, E-15	Route 1, at Ashland
Ashland, E-16*	Route 1, at Ashland
Ellett's Bridge, E-17*	Route 1, 3 miles n. of Ashland
Lafayette and Cornwallis, E-18	Route 1, 3.6 miles n. of Ashland
Lee's Left Wing, E-19	Route 1, 5.2 miles n. of Ashland
Lee's Movements, E-20	Route 1, 6.2 miles n. of Ashland
Hanover Junction, E-21*	Route 1, 7.6 miles n. of Ashland
Lafayette and Cornwallis, E-22*	Route 1, 3 miles s. of Carmel Church
Stuart's Ride around McClellan, E-74	Route 1, 1.9 miles n. of Ashland
Randolph-Macon College, I-10-b	Route 54, at Ashland
Randolph-Macon College, I-10-a	Route 1, at Ashland
Patrick Henry's Birthplace, ND-4	Route 2, 8.9 miles s. of Hanover
Clay's Birthplace, ND-6	Route 2, 4.5 miles s. of Hanover
Cornwallis's Route, ND-9	Route 2, 1.3 miles s. of Hanover
Seven Days' Battles, O-6	Route 360 at Hanover / Henrico line
Seven Days' Battles, O-7*	Route 156, .5 mile s. of Mechanicsville
Sheridan's Raid, O-8*	Route 360, e. entrance of Mechanicsville
Seven Days' Battles, O-9	Route 360, .2 mile n.e. of Mechanicsville
Battle of Cold Harbor, O-11	Route 360, 3.6 miles n.e. of Mechanicsville
Bethesda Church, O-12*	Route 360, 4.6 miles n.e. of Mechanicsville
Cornwallis's Route, O-13*	Route 360, 10.6 miles n.e. of Mechanicsville
Grant's Crossing, O-14*	Route 360, 11.8 miles n.e. of Mechanicsville
Henry's Call to Arms, O-15	Route 360, 11.8 miles n.e. of Mechanicsville
Edmund Ruffin's Grave, O-24	Route 360, 8.9 miles n.e. of Mechanicsville
Seven Days' Battles, Merchanicsville, PA-2	Route 360, at Mechanicsville
Seven Days' Battles, Mechanicsville, PA-4	Route 156, .8 mile s. of Mechanicsville
Seven Days' Battles, Mechanicsville, PA-6	Route 156, 1.2 miles s. of Mechanicsville
Seven Days' Battles, Porter's Withdrawal, PA-8	Route 156, 1.7 miles s. of Mechanicsville
Seven Days' Battles, Gaines's Mill, PA-9*	Route 360, 1.8 miles n.e. of Mechanicsville

Seven Days' Battles, Gaines's Mill, PA-10   Route 156, 2.7 miles s. of Mechanicsville
Seven Days' Battles, New Bridge, PA-12*   Route 156, 4.3 miles s. of Mechanicsville
Seven Days' Battles, Gaines's Mill, PA-16   Route 156, 5 miles s. of Mechanicsville
Seven Days' Battles, Gaines's Mill, PA-   Route 156, 5.7 miles s. of Mechanicsville
   20*
Seven Days' Battles, Gaines's Mill, PA-   Route 156, 6.3 miles s. of Mechanicsville
   23*
Seven Days' Battles, Gaines's Mill, PA-25   Route 718, 6.5 miles s. of Mechanicsville
Seven Days' Battles, Gaines's Mill, PA-60   Route 156, 7.8 miles s. of Mechanicsville
Seven Days' Battles, Gaines's Mill, PA-70   Route 156, 8.2 miles s. of Mechanicsville
Seven Days' Battles, Gaines's Mill, PA-80   Route 156, 8.5 miles s. of Mechanicsville
Grape Vine Bridge, PA-105   Route 156, 11.1 miles s. of Mechanicsville
Scotchtown, W-214   Route 54, 8 miles n.w. of Ashland

HENRICO COUNTY
Area: 280 square miles

An original shire formed in 1634. Named for Henrico Town, founded in 1611, which was named for Henry, Prince of Wales. The battles of Seven Pines, Savage's Station, Glendale, and Malvern Hill took place in this county in 1862.

Intermediate Defenses, E-2*   At Laburnum and Chamberlayne avenues
Where Sheridan Moved East, E-3*   Chamberlayne and Azalea avenues
Outer Fortifications, E-6   Route 1, .7 mile n. of Richmond
Yellow Tavern, E-7   Route 1, 2.5 miles n. of Richmond
Stuart's Mortal Wound, E-9   Route 1, at Route 677, Francis Road
Cavalry Engagement, E-9*   Route 1, 6.25 miles n. of Richmond
Outer Fortifications, O-5   Route 360, 1.4 miles s.w. of Mechanics-
                            ville

Seven Days' Battles, Golding's Farm, PA-   Route 156, 12.8 miles s. of Mechanicsville
   125
Seven Days' Battles, Allen's Farm, PA-140 Route 156, at Seven Pines
Seven Days' Battles, Savage's Station, PA- Route 60, 3.6 miles e. of Seven Pines
   142
Seven Days' Battles, Savage's Station, PA- Route 60, 3.6 miles e. of Seven Pines
   144
Seven Days' Battles, White Oak Swamp,   Route 156, 6.7 miles s.e. of Seven Pines
   PA-148
Seven Days' Battles, White Oak Swamp,   Route 156, 7.1 miles s. of Seven Pines
   PA-152
Seven Days' Battles, Glendale (Frayser's   Route 156, on Darbytown Road, 10.2
   Farm), PA-159*   miles s. of Seven Pines
Seven Days' Battles, Glendale (Frayser's   Route 156, on Darbytown Road, 10.5
   Farm), PA-163   miles s. of Seven Pines
Seven Days' Battles, Glendale (Frayser's   Route 156, 10 miles s. of Seven Pines
   Farm), PA-175
Seven Days' Battles, Malvern Hill, PA-180 Route 156, 10.6 miles s. of Seven Pines
Seven Days' Battles, Glendale (Frayser's   Route 156, 11.1 miles s. of Seven Pines
   Farm), PA-190
Seven Days' Battles, Malvern Hill, PA-195 Route 156, 12.3 miles s. of Seven Pines

Seven Days' Battles, Malvern Hill, PA-220
Seven Days' Battles, Malvern Hill, PA-230
Seven Days' Battles, Malvern Hill, PA-235
Seven Days' Battles, Malvern Hill, PA-240*

Dahlgren's Raid, SA-31*
Wilton, V-1
Varina and Fort Harrison, V-2
Curles Neck and Bremo, V-3*
Malvern Hill, V-4
Turkey Island, V-5*
Campaign of 1781, V-16
Outer Defenses, V-17*
To Frazier's Farm, W-1*

Williamsburg Road, W-2
Charles City Road, W-3*
McClellan's Picket Line, W-4
McClellan's First Line, W-5
Munitions Plant, W-6*
Fair Oaks Battle, W-7*
McClellan's Withdrawal, W-8
McClellan's Second Line, W-9
Second Day at Seven Pines, W-10*
McClellan's Third Line, W-11
Battle of Savage's Station, W-12*
To White Oak Swamp and Malvern Hill, W-13*
Camp Bottom's Bridge, W-15*

Route 156, 12.5 miles s. of Seven Pines
Route 156, 12.6 miles s. of Seven Pines
Route 156, 12.7 miles s. of Seven Pines
Route 156, 13.8 miles s. of Seven Pines

Route 650, 1.25 miles w. of Richmond
Route 5, 2 miles s.e. of Richmond
Route 5, 4.5 miles s.e. of Richmond
Route 5, 9.3 miles s.e. of Richmond
Route 5, 13.3 miles s.e. of Richmond
Route 5, 12.3 miles s.e. of Richmond
Route 250, 8.5 miles w. of Richmond
Route 250, 1.9 miles w. of Richmond
Route 60, Williamsburg Avenue at Darbytown Road
Route 60, .4 mile e. of Richmond
Route 60, 1 mile e. of Richmond
Route 60, at Sandston
Route 60, at Sandston
Route 60, e. entrance of Sandston
Route 60, .5 mile e. of Sandston
Route 60, 3.6 miles e. of Seven Pines
Route 60, at Seven Pines
Route 60, .3 mile e. of Seven Pines
Route 60, 1.3 miles e. of Seven Pines
Route 60, 2 miles e. of Seven Pines
Route 60, 2 miles e. of Sandston

Route 60, 15 miles e. of Richmond

HENRY COUNTY
Area: 444 square miles

Formed in 1776 from Pittsylvania, and named for Patrick Henry, Governor of Virginia. Henry lived in this county, 1779–84.

Fort Trial, A-54
William Byrd's Camp, A-57
Belleview, A-135
Patrick Henry's Leatherwood Home, U-40

Route 57, 6 miles n. of Martinsville
Route 220, 3.5 miles s.w. of Ridgeway
Route 220, 4 miles s. of Martinsville
Route 57, .1 mile e. of 628

HIGHLAND COUNTY
Area: 422 square miles

Formed in 1847 from Pendleton and Bath, and given its name because of its mountains. The battle of McDowell, 1862, was fought in this county.

Fort Edward Johnson, W-149*
Battle of McDowell, W-150

Route 250, 5 miles w. of West Augusta
Route 250, 1 mile e. of McDowell

ISLE OF WIGHT COUNTY
Area: 314 square miles

One of the original shires formed in 1634. Its name was at first Warrascoyack, changed in 1637 to Isle of Wight. One of the oldest churches in the United States is in this county.

Old Town, K-238	Route 621, .1 mile e. of Route 10
Lawne's Creek, K-239	Route 10, 8.1 miles n.w. of Smithfield
Wrenn's Mill Site, K-240*	Route 10, 4.5 miles n.w. of Smithfield
Wrenn's Mill (K-240-b)	Route 10, 4.5 miles w. of Smithfield
Bennett's Plantation, K-241*	Route 10, 2 miles n.w. of Smithfield
Basse's Choice, K-242*	Route 10, 2 miles n.w. of Smithfield
Smithfield, K-243	Route 10, at Smithfield
Pagan Point, K-244	Route 10, .4 mile w. of Smithfield
Saint Luke's Church, K-245	Route 10, 4.25 miles s.e. of Smithfield
Saint Luke's Church, K-245*	Route 10, .25 mile n.w. of Benn's Church
Benn's Church, K-246	Route 10, 4.2 miles s.e. of Smithfield
Macclesfield, K-247	Route 10, 4.2 miles s.e. of Smithfield
Suffolk Campaign, UT-20	Route 460, 6.3 miles n.w. of Windsor

JAMES CITY COUNTY
Area: 164 square miles

One of the original shires formed in 1634, and named for Jamestown, the first settlement in Virginia, 1607. Williamsburg is in this county.

New Kent Road, W-26*	Route 60, 3 miles n.w. of Toano
White Hall Tavern, W-27	Route 60, 1.3 miles n.w. of Toano
Olive Branch Christian Church, W-28*	Route 60, .9 mile s.e. of Toano
Hickory Neck Church, W-30	Route 60, .8 mile n.w. of Toano
State Shipyard, W-31	Route 60, at Toano
Chickahominy Church, W-32	Route 60, at Toano
Burnt Ordinary, W-33*	Route 60, at Toano
Six-Mile Ordinary, W-34*	Route 60, 4.3 miles s.e. of Toano
Spencer's Ordinary, W-35	Route 60, 4.3 miles s.e. of Toano
Green Spring, W-36	Route 60, 4.3 miles s.e. of Toano
Peninsular Campaign, W-37*	Route 60, n.w. entrance of Williamsburg
Iron-Bound Road, W-38*	Route 60, 3 miles n.w. of Williamsburg
Quarter Path, W-42*	Route 60, s.e. entrance of Williamsburg
Battle of Williamsburg, W-43	Route 60, .3 mile s.e. of Williamsburg
Magruder's Defenses, W-44	Route 60, .3 mile s.e. of Williamsburg
Whitaker's House, W-45	Route 60, 1.4 miles s.e. of Williamsburg
Kingsmill, W-47*	Route 60, 2.4 miles s.e. of Williamsburg
Littletown, W-48*	Route 60, 2.8 miles s.e. of Williamsburg
Trebell's Landing, W-49*	Route 60, 5.1 miles s.e. of Williamsburg
Carter's Grove, W-50*	Route 60, 3.25 miles s.e. of Williamsburg
Martin's Hundred, W-51	Route 60, 6.7 miles s.e. of Williamsburg
Martin's Hundred Church, W-52	Route 60, 6.7 miles s.e. of Williamsburg

KING AND QUEEN COUNTY
Area: 320 square miles

Formed in 1691 from New Kent, and named for King William III and Queen Mary. The family of George Rogers Clark long lived in this county.

The Servants' Plot, N-58*	Route 14, 1.1 miles w. of Adner
Old Places, O-17*	Route 631, two miles n. of Manquin
Clark Home, O-20	Route 360 at Saint Stephens Church
Where Dahlgren Died, O-21*	Route 360 at Saint Stephens Church
Piscataway Church, O-41*	Route 360, 1.6 miles s.w. of Millers Tavern
Bruington Church, OB-2	Route 14, 6.2 miles n.w. of Stevensville
Mattapony Church, OB-3	Route 14, 4.1 miles n.w. of King and Queen Courthouse
Hillsboro, OB-5	Route 14, 4.7 miles n.w. of Stevensville
Where Dahlgren Died, OB-6	Route 631, 2.5 miles n.w. of King and Queen Courthouse
Newton, OB-9	Route 625 and 721
Newington, OB-10	Route 14, 1 mile n.w. of King and Queen Courthouse
Laneville, OB-16	Route 14, 10 miles s.e. of King and Queen Courthouse
Colonial Church, OB-18	Route 14, 8.5 miles s.e. of King and Queen Courthouse
Poropotank Creek, OB-50	Route 14, 1.1 miles w. of Adner
State Fish Hatchery, PB-4	Route 14, 1 mile n.w. of Stevensville

KING GEORGE COUNTY
Area: 180 square miles

Formed in 1720 from Richmond, and named for King George I. James Madison, "Father of the American Constitution" and President of the United States, was born in this county.

Birthplace of Madison, EP-8	Route 301, .4 mile n. of Port Royal
Lamb's Creek Church, J-62	Route 3, 5.5 miles w. of King George
Marmion, J-63	Route 3, 2.3 miles w. of King George
St. Paul's Church, J-65	Route 3, 1.5 miles w. of King George
Historic Port Conway, J-66*	Route 3, 2.7 miles e. of King George

KING WILLIAM COUNTY
Area: 263 square miles

Formed in 1701 from King and Queen, and named for King William III. Here lived Carter Braxton, signer of the Declaration of Independence.

Rumford Academy, O-16	Route 360, at Central Garage
Cavalry Raids, O-18	Route 360 at Aylett
Montville Estate, O-25*	Route U.S. 360, 1 mile s.w. of Aylett
Pamunkey Reservation, OC-14	Route 30, .6 mile s.e. of King William
Mattapony Reservation, OC-15	Route 30, 4.9 miles s.e. of King William
Campaign of 1781, OC-22*	Route 30, 6.6 miles n.w. of West Point
Campaign of 1781, OC-25	Route 30, 3.4 miles n.w. of West Point

St. John's Church, OC-18

Home of Signer, OC-26

Route 30, 8.9 miles n.w. of West Point

Route 33, at West Point

LANCASTER COUNTY
Area: 130 square miles

Formed in 1652, and named for Lancaster, England. Ancient Christ Church and Epping Forest, birthplace of Washington's mother, are in this county.

Birthplace of Washington's Mother, J-80

Epping Forest, J-80*

Bewdley, J-81

St. Mary's White Chapel, J-82

White Marsh Church, J-83

Corotoman, J-85

Christ Church, J-86

Windmill Point, J-87

Ditchley and Cobbs, J-88

First American Woman Missionary to China, J-89

Route 3, 9.3 miles e. of Farnham

Route 3, 12 miles e. of Warsaw

Route 354, 2.13 miles e. of Route 3

Route 3, at Lively

Route 3, 3.6 miles n.w. of Kilmarnock

Route 646, .66 mile w. of Route 3

Route 646, .66 mile w. of Route 3

Route 695, 6.50 miles e. of Route 3 in Whitestone

Route 3, at Kilmarnock

Route 3, at Kilmarnock

LEE COUNTY
Area: 446 square miles

Formed in 1792 from Russell, and named for Henry (Light-Horse Harry) Lee, Revolutionary soldier and Governor of Virginia 1791–94. Daniel Boone's son was killed by Indians here.

Cumberland Gap, K-1

Indian Mound, K-3

Colonial Fort, K-4

Indian Massacre, K-5

Thompson Settlement Church, K-6

Hanging Rock, K-7

Doctor Still's Birthplace, K-8

Jonesville Methodist Camp Ground, K-9

Jonesville, K-10

Death of Boone's Son, K-32*

Donelson's Indian Line, KA-8

Seminary Methodist Church, X-24

Members of Congress, X-26*

Pennington Gap, X-30

Route 58, at Cumberland Gap

Route 58, 2 miles w. of Rose Hill

Route 58, at Rose Hill

Route 58, at Stickleyville

Route 758, 10.2 miles s.w. of Jonesville

Route 58, .25 mile w. of Ewing

Route 58, at western entrance of Jonesville

Route 58, 2 miles w. of Jonesville

Route 58, at Jonesville

Route 58, 1 mile e. of Stickleyville

Route 23, 5 miles s. of Big Stone Gap

Alternate Route 58, 5 miles s.w. of Big Stone Gap

Alternate Route 58, 6 miles s.w. of Big Stone Gap

Alternate Route 58, at Pennington Gap

LOUDOUN COUNTY
Area: 519 square miles

Formed in 1757 from Fairfax, and named for Lord Loudoun, titular governor of Virginia, and head of the British forces in America, 1756–58. Oak Hill, President James Monroe's home, is in this county.

Military Movements, B-22*

Braddock Road, B-27*

Mercer's Home, B-28

Stuart and Bayard, B-30*

Gettysburg Campaign, B-32*

A Revolutionary Hero, B-33

Battle of Ball's Bluff, F-1

Potomac Crossings, F-2

Oak Hill, F-4

Wayne's Crossing, F-5

Sharpsburg (Antietam Campaign), F-6

Goose Creek Chapel, F-7

Mother of Stonewall Jackson, F-15*

Mother of the Wright Brothers, T-5

Early's Washington Campaign, T-22

Belmont, T-30

Gettysburg Campaign, T-38

Route 50, at Middleburg

Route 50, at Aldie

Route 50, at Aldie

Route 50, at Aldie

Route 50, at e. entrance of Middleburg

Route 50, 1.1 miles w. of Aldie

Route 15, .9 mile n. of Leesburg

Route 15, 6.9 miles n. of Leesburg

Route 15, 3 miles n. of Aldie

Route 15, 7.2 miles n. of Leesburg

Route 15, 2.7 miles n. of Leesburg

Route 15, 2 miles n. of Leesburg

Route 15, .9 mile s. of Gilberts Corner

Route 7, at Purcellville

Route 7, 2.1 miles w. of Leesburg

Route 7, 4.3 miles e. of Leesburg

Route 7, 2.6 miles w. of Dranesville

LOUISA COUNTY
Area: 516 square miles

Formed in 1742 from Hanover, and named for the queen of Denmark, daughter of King George II. Patrick Henry lived in this county for some years. In it was fought the cavalry battle of Trevillians, 1864.

Campaign of 1781, F-40

Providence Church, V-19

Campaign of 1781, V-20

The Marquis Road, W-206

Boswell's Tavern, W-207

Green Springs, W-208

Battle of Trevilians, W-209

Battle of Trevilians, W-210*

Patrick Henry's Home, W-211

Historic Louisa, W-212

Jack Jouett's Ride, W-213

Route 15, 3.3 miles s. of Boswell's Tavern

Route 250, .4 mile n.w. of Gum Spring

Route 250, at Ferncliff

Route 22, at Boswell's Tavern

Route 22, at Boswell's Tavern

Route 33, 7 miles w. of Louisa

Route 33, 4.5 miles w. of Louisa

Route 33, 4.5 miles w. of Louisa

Route 33, at Louisa

Routes 33 and 22, e. of Louisa

Route 33, at Cuckoo

LUNENBURG COUNTY
Area: 430 square miles

Formed in 1746 from Brunswick. Named for King George II, who was also duke of Brunswick-Lunenburg. Tarleton passed through the county in 1781.

Craig's Mill, SN-45   Route 40, .3 mile n. of Kenbridge

MADISON COUNTY
Area: 324 square miles

Formed in 1792 from Culpeper, and named for James Madison, "Father of the American Constitution" and President of the United States. Governor Spotswood's exploring expedition passed here, 1716.

Jackson's Crossing, F-22   Route 15, 7.6 miles n. of Orange
Cavalry Engagement, G-11*   Route 231, 5.5 miles s. of Madison
Joseph Early Home, G-12   Route 29, 3 miles s. of Madison
Jackson's March to Fredericksburg, JE-1   Route 231, at Madison
Knights of the Golden Horseshoe, JE-2   Route 15, 3.3 miles n. of Orange
Hebron Church, JE-4   Route 231, 9.5 miles n. of Madison
A Camp of Stonewall Jackson's, JE-15   Route 670, 1 mile n. of Criglersville

MATHEWS COUNTY
Area: 94 square miles

Formed in 1790 from Gloucester, and named for Colonel Thomas Mathews, Revolutionary soldier. Gwynn's Island, from which Dunmore was driven in 1776, is here.

Battle of Cricket Hill, N-85   Route 223, 4 miles n. of Mathews
Fitchett's Wharf, N-86   Route 642, at Moon Post Office
John Clayton, Botanist, NN-3   Route 14, e. of Gloucester County line

MECKLENBURG COUNTY
Area: 669 square miles

Formed in 1764 from Lunenburg, and named for Princess Charlotte, of Mecklenburg-Strelitz, queen of George III. Bacon the Rebel defeated the Indians near the present town of Clarksville, 1676.

Prestwould Plantation, F-95   Route 15, 3 miles n. of Clarksville
Occaneechee Island, F-98*   Route 15, near state line
Salem Chapel, S-70   Route 1, at South Hill
Early Exploration, S-76   Route 1, 1.6 miles n. of South Hill
Occaneechee Indians, U-60*   Route 58, 1.5 miles e. of Clarksville
A Revolutionary Soldier, U-80   Route 58, at Boydton
Old Randolph-Macon College, UL-4   Route 58, .3 mile w. of Boydton
Taylor's Ferry, UL-5   Route 58, .3 mile w. of Boydton

MIDDLESEX COUNTY
Area: 146 square miles

Formed in 1673 from Lancaster, and named for an English county. Rosegill, frequented by colonial governors, is here.

Glebe Landing Church, N-40   Route 17, 12.1 miles n.w. of Saluda
Hewick, N-45   Route 17, 3.1 miles n.w. of Saluda
Christ Church, N-48   Route 33, 2.4 miles s. of Urbanna
Tomb of Puller, N-49   Route 33, 3 miles e. of Saluda
Lower Methodist Church, N-50   Route 33, 9.3 miles s.e. of Saluda
Stingray Point, N-77   8.6 miles w. of Deltaville
Rosegill, OC-35   Route 227, .7 mile s. of Urbanna
Urbanna Creek, OC-40*   Route 227, at Urbanna
Scottish Factors Store, WO-37   Route 33, 1.5 miles e. of Saluda

MONTGOMERY COUNTY
Area: 401 square miles

Formed in 1776 from Fincastle, and named for General Richard Montgomery, killed at Quebec, 1775. The Virginia Polytechnic Institute is in this county.

Virginia Polytechnic Institute, I-2-a	Route 11, .6 mile e. of Christianburg
Virginia Polytechnic Institute, I-2-b	Route 11, at w. entrance of Christiansburg
Virginia Polytechnic Institute, I-2-c	Route 460, at Blacksburg
"Fotheringay", K-67	Route 11, 4.5 miles w. of Roanoke County
Ingles Ferry Road, K-70	Route 11, 1.4 miles e. of Radford
Lewis-McHenry Duel, K-71	Routes 11 and 460, at Christiansburg
Christiansburg, K-72	Route 11, .6 mile e. of Christiansburg
Fort Vause, K-73	Route 11, .3 mile w. of Shawsville
Colonel William Preston, KG-8	Route 460 at Blacksburg
Draper's Meadow Massacre, KG-10	Route 460, at s. entrance of Blacksburg
Montgomery White Sulphur Springs, KG-12	Interstate 81, .75 mile n. of exit 38 at rest area, northbound lane

NELSON COUNTY
Area: 473 square miles

Formed in 1807 from Amherst, and named for General Thomas Nelson, Governor of Virginia, 1781. Oak Ridge, an old home, is in this county.

Thomas Massie, OQ-44*	Routes 56 and 666 at Massie's Mill
William Cabell, OQ-5	Route 56, at Wingina
Boyhood Home of Colonel Mosby, R-50*	Route 6, 3 miles n. of Woods Mill
Hurricane Camille, R-51	Route 29 at Woods Mill Wayside
Lovingston, R-56	Route 250, at Lovingston
Birthplace of Rives, R-58	Route 29, 4 miles s. of Lovingston
Rockfish Church, RA-4	Route 151, 10.6 miles s. of Afton
William H. Crawford, RA-6	Route 151, 12.7 miles s. of Afton
Rockfish Gap Meeting, W-218	Route 250, 2 miles n.w. of Afton
Flight of Richard C. duPont, W-219	Interstate 64 overlook on Afton Mountain

NEW KENT COUNTY
Area: 191 square miles

Formed in 1654 from York, and named for an English county. The White House, where Washington's wife lived, was in this county, and here he married her.

McClellan's Crossing, W-14	Route 60, at Bottoms Bridge
Lafayette and Cornwallis, W-16	Route 60, at Bottoms Bridge
New Kent Road, W-17	Route 60, at Bottoms Bridge
Long Bridge, W-18	Route 60, 4.9 miles s.e. of Bottoms Bridge
Soane's Bridge, W-19*	Route 60, at Providence Forge
Providence Forge, W-20	Route 60, at Providence Forge
State Game Farm, W-21	Route 60, 2.8 miles s.e. of Providence Forge
Chickahominy Indians, W-22	Route 60, 4.2 miles s.e. of Providence Forge

Fort James, W-23	Route 60, 7.6 miles s.e. of Providence Forge
Diascund Bridge, W-24	Route 60, 6.7 miles n.w. of Toano
Cooper's Mill, W-25*	Route 60, 7.25 miles e. of Providence Forge
Tyree's Plantation, W-29	Route 60, 6.7 miles n.w. of Toano
The White House, WO-12	Route 249, at Talleysville
St. Peter's Church, WO-13	Route 249, at Talleysville
Stuart's Ride around McClellan, WO-14	Route 249, at Talleysville
New Kent Courthouse, WO-16	Route 249, at New Kent
Martha Washington's Birthplace, WO-18	Route 249, 7 miles e. of New Kent
Eltham, WO-30	Route 33, 1.9 miles w. of West Point
Peninsular Campaign, WO-31	Route 33, 1.5 miles w. of West Point
The Brick House, WO-33	Route 33, 1.5 miles w. of West Point

NORTHAMPTON COUNTY
Area: 239 square miles

One of the original shires formed in 1634 and named Accomac. In 1643 the name was changed to Northampton for an English county. This county was Governor Berkeley's stronghold in the rebellion of 1676.

Salem Methodist Church, WY-3	Route 13 at Route 636
Arlington, WY-5	Route 13, 3 miles n. of Cape Charles
Arlington, Wy-5*	Route 13, 3 miles n. of Cape Charles
Old Places, WY-6*	Route 13, 3 miles n. of Cape Charles
Towne Fields, WY-7	Route 13, at Cheriton
First Courthouse, WH-7*	Route 13, at Cheriton
Home of First Settler, WY-8	Route 13, 1 mile s. of Eastville
Indian Village, WY-9	Route 13, at Eastville
Old Courthouse, WY-10	Route 13, at Eastville
Hungars Church and Vaucluse, WY-11*	Route 13, 2.8 miles s. of Nassawadox

NORTHUMBERLAND COUNTY
Area: 205 square miles

Originally an Indian district called Chickacoan. In 1648 it became Northumberland County, named for an English county. The mouth of the Potomac River is here.

Coan River, JT-9*	Route 360, 2.2 miles w. of Heathsville
Northumberland House and Mantua, JT-12	Route 360, 1 mile e. of Heathsville
Morattico Baptist Church, JX-5	Route 200, 2.8 miles n. of Kilmarnock
St. Stephen's parish, O-49	Route 360 at Heathsville

NOTTOWAY COUNTY
Area: 310 square miles

Formed in 1788 from Amelia, and named for an Indian tribe. Tarleton passed through this county in 1781. Here lived William Hodges Mann, Governor of Virginia 1910–14.

Nottoway Courthouse, K-170,   Route 460, .2 mile w. of Nottoway
Blackstone, K-172,   Route 460, at Blackstone
Lee's Retreat, M-16,   Route 360, at Burkeville
Historic Burkeville, M-17,   Route 360, at Burkeville
Francisco's Fight, M-18,   Route 360, 6 miles n.w. of Burkeville
T. O. Sandy (First Co. Agent) M-20)   Route 460, 2.1 miles e. Burkeville
Union Academy, SM-2   Route 40, at s. entrance of Blackstone
Old Nottoway Meeting House, WK-4   Route 723, 2 miles s. of Burkeville

ORANGE COUNTY
Area: 359 square miles

Formed in 1734 from Spotsylvania, and named for the prince of Orange, who in that year married Princess Anne, daughter of King George II. President James Madison lived in this county and President Zachary Taylor was born here.

Montebello, D-20   Route 33, 3 miles w. of Gordonsville
Barboursville, D-22   Route 33, at Barboursville
Kemper's Grave, F-17   Route 15, 2.7 miles n. of Orange
Church of the Blind Preacher, F-23   Route 15, .5 mile n. of Gordonsville
Woodberry Forest School, F-24   1.5 miles n. of Orange
Montpelier and Madison's Tomb, F-26   Route 15, at Orange
Campaign of Second Manassas, F-32   Route 15, 3.2 miles s. of Orange
Germanna, J-34*   Route 3, 4.8 miles w. of Wilderness
Germanna Ford, J-35   Route 3, 4.8 miles w. of Wilderness
Lee's Headquarters, JJ-22*   Route 20, 1.6 miles e. of Orange
Bloomsbury, JJ-4   Route 20, 3.3 miles e. of Orange
Campaign of Second Manassas, JJ-6   Route 20, 5.7 miles e. of Orange
Mine Run Campaign, JJ-10   Route 20, 6.6 miles e. of Unionville
Stuart's Escape, JJ-12*   4.1 miles e. of Unionville
Robinson's Tavern, JJ-15   Route 20, at Locust Grove
Battle of the Wilderness, JJ-20   Route 20, 2.9 miles e. of Locust Grove
Campaign of 1781, JJ-24   Route 20, 2.6 miles e. of Unionville (at Rhodesville)

PAGE COUNTY
Area: 322 square miles

Formed in 1831 from Shenandoah and Rockingham, and named for John Page, Governor of Virginia 1802–5. Luray Cave is in this county.

Cavalry Engagement, C-3*   Route 211 at Luray
White House, C-30   Route 211, 4 miles w. of Luray
Fort Long, C-31*   Route 211, 2 miles w. of Luray
William Randolph Barbee, C-56   Route Skyline Drive and U.S. 211

PATRICK COUNTY
Area: 485 square miles

Formed in 1790 from Henry, and named for Patrick Henry, who thus had two counties named for him. General J.E.B. Stuart was born in this county.

Fairy Stone State Park, AS-1

Colonel Abram Penn, HD-1

Stuart's Birthplace, KG-2
Blue Ridge Mission School, U-28
Stuart, U-30
Frontier Fort, U-32
Reynolds Homestead, U-34
William Byrd's Survey of 1728, U-36

Intersection of Routes 346 and 623, 6 miles
s. of Franklin County line
Route 58, 1.86 miles s.e. of Henry County
line
Route 103, 4 miles s. of Friends Mission
Route 8, at intersection with Route 613
Route 58, at Stuart
Route 58, 14 miles e. of Stuart
Route 58, at Critz
Route 660, 4 miles s. of Route 8, at state
line

PITTSYLVANIA COUNTY
Area: 1,015 square miles

Formed in 1766 from Halifax, and named for William Pitt, Earl of Chatham, British
statesman. This is the largest county in Virginia. The home of Claude A. Swanson, Governor
of Virginia 1806–10.

Pittsylvania Court House, KG-23

Clement Hill, L-32
Peytonsburg, L-50*
Markham, L-52
Beavers Tavern, L-61
Callands, LT-1
Clerk's Office, Q-12-a
John Weatherford's Grave, RG-5*
Berry Hill, U-40

Route 29, in front of Court House, at
Chatham
Route 29, 1 mile s. of Alta Vista
Route 29, at Chatham
Route 29, at Chatham
Route 29, 5 miles n. of Danville
Route 57, at Callands
Route 969, at Callands
Route 29, 9 miles s.e. of Chatham
Intersection of Routes 58 and 863 south

POWHATAN COUNTY
Area: 273 square miles

Formed in 1777 from Cumberland and Chesterfield and named for Powhatan, the noted
Indian ruler. Many Huguenots settled in this county, 1699–1700. Here Robert E. Lee spent
the summer of 1865.

Dunlora Academy, O-25
Derwent, O-30
Giles's Home, O-31
Powhatan Courthouse, O-32
Lee's Last Camp, OH-10*

Route 60, 5.7 miles w. of Powhatan
Route 13, 2 miles e. of Tobaccoville
Route 60, 1.7 miles w. of Powhatan
Route 13, at Powhatan
Route 711, 9.5 miles n. of Powhatan

PRINCE EDWARD COUNTY
Area: 356 square miles

Formed in 1753 from Amelia, and named for Prince Edward, son of Frederick, prince of
Wales, and younger brother of King George III. General Joseph E. Johnston was born in this
county; Hampden-Sydney College is in it.

Old Worsham, F-65	Route 15, 5.6 miles s. of Farmville
Slate Hill Plantation, F-66*	Route 15, 6.5 miles s. of Farmville
Randolph-Macon Medical School, F-69	Route 15, 5 miles s. of Farmville
Kingsville, F-70	Route 15, 4.5 miles s. of Farmville
Providence, F-71	Route 15, 5.6 miles s. of Farmville
Campaign of 1781, F-72	Route 15, 5.6 miles s. of Farmville
Old Briery Church, F-75	Route 15, 2.4 miles n. of Keysville
Hampden-Sydney College, I-9*	Route 133, at Hampden-Sydney
State Teachers College at Farmville, I-15*	Route 15, at Farmville
Longwood College (I-15-a*)	Route 460, at Farmville
Robert Russa Moton High School, M-1	Route 15 and Ely Street in Farmville
Lee's Retreat, M-24*	Route 307, 3 miles e. of Rice
Battle of Sailor's Creek, M-25	Route 460, at Rice
Action of High Bridge, M-30*	Route 460, at Rice
Longwood Estate, M-33*	Route 460, at Farmville

PRINCE GEORGE COUNTY

Area: 294 square miles

Formed in 1702 from Charles City, and named for Prince George of Denmark, husband of Queen Anne. The battles of the crater, 1864, and Fort Steadman, 1865, took place in this county.

City Point and Hopewell, K-205	Route 36, .7 mile e. of Petersburg
Bailey's Creek, K-206*	Route 106, 5.5 miles e. of Petersburg
History at Prince George Courthouse, K-207	Route 106, at Prince George
Jordan's Point, K-208,	Route 106, 2.9 miles e. of Prince George
Merchant's Hope Church, K-209	Route 10, 8.3 miles n.w. of Burrowsville
Coggins's Point, K-210,	Route 10, 8.3 miles n.w. of Burrowsville
The Cattle Raid, K-211	Route 106, 6.8 miles e. of Prince George
Powell's Creek, K-212,	Route 10, 5.3 miles n.w. of Burrowsville
Maycock's Plantation, K-213	Route 10, 5.3 miles n.w. of Burrowsville
Flowerdew Hundred, K-214,	Route 10, 5.3 miles n.w. of Burrowsville
Ward's Creek, K-216,	Route 10, at Burrowsville
Hood's, K-215	Route 10, at Burrowsville
Brandon, K-218	Route 10, at Burrowsville
Reams Station, UM-20	Route 301, 12.6 miles s. of Petersburg

PRINCE WILLIAM COUNTY

Area: 345 square miles

Formed in 1730 from Stafford and King George, and named for William Augustus, Duke of Cumberland, second son of King George II. The first and second battles of Manassas took place in this county.

The Stone Bridge, C-23	Route 211, 6 miles e. of Gainesville
Battle of Groveton, C-26*	Route 211, 3.5 miles e. of Gainesville
Second Battle of Manassas, C-27	Route 211, 1.6 miles e. of Gainesville
Campaign of Second Manassas, C-28*	Route 211, at Gainesville

Bull Run Battlefields, C-31 — Route 211, .4 mile e. of Gainesville
Second Battle of Manassas, C-33* — Route 211, 3 miles e. of Gainesville
First Battle of Manassas, C-34 — Route 211, 4.7 miles e. of Gainesville
First Battle of Manassas, C-44 — Route 211, 4.7 miles e. of Gainesville
Second Battle of Manassas, C-46 — Route 211, 4.7 miles e. of Gainesville
Campaign of Second Manassas, C-48 — Route 211, 4.7 miles e. of Gainesville
Thoroughfare Gap (C-50, — Route 55, at Gainesville
Chopawamsic, E-52 — Route 1, 4.3 miles s. of Dumfries
Campaign of 1781 (E-53, — Route 1, at northern entrance of Dumfries
Early Land Patents, E-53* — Route 1, s. of Dumfries
Ancient Road to Valley, E-54* — Route 1, s. of Dumfries
History at Dumfries, E-55 — Route 1, at Dumfries
Early Land Patents, E-56* — Route 1, 1.1 miles s. of Woodbridge
Early Land Patents, E-57* — Route 1, 4 miles n. of Dumfries
Early Iron Furnace, E-58* — Route 1, 3.2 miles n. of Dumfries
The Occoquan, E-59 — Route 1, at Woodbridge
Simon Kenton's Birthplace, F-14 — Route 15, 6.9 miles s. of Gilberts Corner
Campaign of Second Manassas, FA-1 — Route 55, 5 miles s.e. of The Plains
Henry House, G-15 — Route 234, 5.1 miles n.w. of Manasas

PULASKI COUNTY
Area: 333 square miles

Formed in 1839 from Wythe and Montgomery, and named for Count Casimir Pulaski, killed at the siege of Savannah, 1779. New River flows through this county.

New River, K-25 — Route 11, .6 miles n.w. of Radford
First Settlement, K-29 — Route 11, 1.9 miles w. of Radford
Battle of Cloyd's Mountain, K-38* — Route 100, at Dublin
Draper's Valley, K-40 — Route 11, 1.9 miles s. of Pulaski
Pulaski, K-41 — Route 11, at Pulaski
Page's Meeting House, K-45 — Route 11, 1.25 miles w. of Radford
Battle of Cloyd's Mountain, KE-5 — Route 100, 5 miles n. of Dublin

RAPPAHANNOCK COUNTY
Area: 274 square miles

Formed in 1833 from Culpeper, and named for the Rappahnnock River, headwaters of which are in this county.

Cavalry Engagement, C-4 — Route 211, at Sperryville
Washington, Virginia, the First of Them All, C-5 — Route 211, at Washington
Campaign of Second Manassas, C-6 — Route 211, 7.2 miles e. of Massies Corner
William Randolph Barbee, C-56 — Route 211 and Skyline Drive, at Panoramo
Campaign of Second Manassas, C-61 — Route 211, 9.5 miles e. of Massies Corner
Gettysburg Campaign, J-25 — Route 522, 5 miles s. of Front Royal
Albert Gallatin Willis, J-26 — Route 522, 5.5 miles n. of Flint Hill
Pope's Army of Virginia, J-29* — Route 522, at Sperryville

RICHMOND COUNTY
Area: 204 square miles

Formed in 1692 from Old Rappahannock County, and named for the town of Richmond, Surrey, England. Sabine Hall and Mount Airy, noted old homes, are in this county.

Menokin, J-73 — Route 690, 4.1 miles n. of Warsaw
North Farnham Church, J-77 — Route 692, at Farnham
Cyrus Griffin's Birthplace, J-78 — Route 2, 2.8 miles s.e. of Farnham
Sabine Hall, O-45 — Route 360, .3 mile w. of Warsaw
Warsaw, O-46 — Route 360, at Warsaw

ROANOKE COUNTY
Area: 305 square miles

Formed in 1838 from Botetourt and Montgomery, and probably named for the Roanoke River. General Andrew Lewis lived here. The city of Roanoke is known as the Magic City of the South.

Hollins College, A-79 — Route 11, 5.8 miles n. of Roanoke
Catawba Sanatorium, I-4 — Route 311 at Catawba
Roanoke College, I-11-b — Route 11, .2 mile w. of Salem
Colonial Mansion Site, K-74 — Route 11, 2.5 miles w. of Salem
Old Lutheran Church, K-76 — Route 11, .8 mile w. of Roanoke
Old Salem Inns, K-88 — Route 11, .2 mile w. of Salem
Hanging Rock, KH-7 — Route 311, n. of Salem at Route 116

ROCKBRIDGE COUNTY
Area: 616 square miles

Formed in 1778 from Augusta and Botetourt, and named for the Natural Bridge. Samuel Houston and Cyrus H. McCormick were born in this county. Robert E. Lee and Stonewall Jackson are buried in Lexington. Washington and Lee University and the Virginia Military Institute are there.

Ruffner's Home, A-42* — Route 11, at Lexington
McDowell's Grave, A-43 — Route 11, 1.1 miles s. of Fairfield
Liberty Hall Academy, A-44 — Route 11, 5.3 miles n. of Lexington
Red House Estate, A-45* — Route 11, 1.1 miles s. of Fairfield
Timber Ridge Church, A-46 — Route 11, 5.3 miles n. of Lexington (at Sam Houston Wayside)

Cherry Grove Estate, A-47 — Route 11, .3 mile s. of Fairfield
Thorn Hill Estate, A-39 — Route 251, .6 mile n. of Lexington
Birthplace of Sam Houston, A-52 — Route 11, 5.3 miles n. of Lexington
Natural Bridge of Virginia, A-72 — Route 11, at Natural Bridge
Virginia Military Institute, I-1 — Route 11, at Lexington
Washington and Lee University, I-8 — Route 11, at Lexington
New Monmouth Church and Morrison's Birthplace, L-8 — Route 60, 2 miles w. of Lexington

First Indian Fight, L-10 — Route 130, at Glasgow
Moomaw's Landing, L-11 — Route 60, west end of Buena Vista
Falling Spring Presbyterian Church, R-63 — Route 11, 7 miles s. of Lexington
Youel-Condon House, p. 186 — Route 39, 3.5 miles e. of Goshen

ROCKINGHAM COUNTY
Area: 876 square miles

Formed in 1778 from Augusta, and named for the Marquis of Rockingham, British statesman. John Sevier, of Tennessee, was born in this county. In it took place the battles of Cross Keys and Port Republic, 1862.

Abraham Lincoln's Father, A-18	Route 11, at Lacey Spring
Cavalry Engagement, A-29	Route 11, 7.5 miles n. of Harrisonburg
Where Ashby Fell, A-30	Route 11, 1.5 miles s. of Harrisonburg
Sheridan's Last Raid, A-32	Route 11, .3 mile s. of Mount Crawford
Dr. Jessee Bennett, A-59	Route 42, at Edom
Battle of Cross Keys, D-6	Route 33, 5 miles e. of Harrisonburg
Knights of the Golden Horseshoe, D-10	Route Route 33, 7 miles s.e. of Elkton
Bridgewater College, I-13	Route 11, at Va. 257 (Mount Crawford)
Bridgewater College, I-13-A	Routes 613 and 748, at Spring Creek
First Settler, Green Meadow, JD-8	Route 340, .5 mile n. of Elkton
Battle of Port Republic, JD-10	Route 340, 3 miles n. of Grottoes
Lincoln's Virginia Ancestors, KB-65	Route 42, 2.5 miles n. of Edom

RUSSELL COUNTY
Area: 496 square miles

Formed in 1786 from Washington, and named for General William Russell, pioneer and Revolutionary soldier. Clinch River runs through the county.

Early Settlers in Russell County, X-5	Route 71 at Grassy Creek Church
Russell Courthouse, X-6	Route 19, at Lebanon
Russell's Fort, X-7	Route 615, at Castlewood
Glade Hollow Fort, X-8	Route 71, 2 miles w. of Lebanon
Elk Garden Fort, X-9*	Route 19, 8 miles e. of Lebanon
Smith's Fort, X-17	Route 19, 17.5 miles e. of Lebanon
Moore's Fort, X-18*	Alternate 58, e. entrance of St. Paul

SCOTT COUNTY
Area: 543 square miles

Formed in 1814 from Lee, Washington, and Russell. Named for General Winfield Scott, later commander of the American army. The Natural Tunnel is in this county.

Gate City, K-11	Route 71, at Gate City
Faris Station, K-12	Route 71, at Gate City
Fort Blackmore, K-13	Route 71, at Gate City
McConnell's Birthplace, K-14	Route 58, 2 miles e. of Gate City
Big Moccasin Gap, K-15	Route 58, 2.1 miles e. of Gate City
Donelson's Indian Line, K-16	Route 58, 2.1 miles e. of Gate City
Houston's Fort, K-17	Route 613, 6.8 miles s. of Route 71
Carter's Fort, KA-10	Route 871, 1 mile e. of Sunbright
First Court of Scott County, KA-15	Route 23, 2.1 miles e. of Gate City
Dortor's Fort, XC-4*	Route 71, 1.5 miles w. of Nickelsville

SHENANDOAH COUNTY
Area: 510 square miles

Formed in 1772 from Frederick, and first named Dunmore for Lord Dunmore, Governor of Virginia 1771–75. In 1778 the county was renamed for the Shenandoah River.

Trenches on Hupp's Hill, A-19	Route 11, .8 mile n. of Strasburg
Frontier Fort, A-20	Route 11, at Strasburg
Battle of Cedar Creek, A-21	Route 11, at Strasburg
Battle of Fisher's Hill, A-22*	Route 11, 1.9 miles s. of Strasburg
Battle of Fisher's Hill, A-23	Route 11, 3.1 miles s. of Strasburg
Banks' Fort, A-24	Route 11, at Strasburg
Action of Tom's Brook, A-25	Route 11, .1 mile s. of Tom's Brook
Cavalry Engagement, A-26*	Route 11, 1 mile s. of Mount Jackson
Rude's Hill Action, A-27	Route 11, 3.7 miles n. of New Market
Battle of New Market, A-28	Route 11, .6 mile n. of New Market
Sevier's Birthplace, A-34	Route 11, .7 mile s. of New Market
Fairfax Line, A-36	Route 11, .7 mile s. of New Market
Last Indian Outrage, A-41	Route 11, 1.9 miles s. of Woodstock
Fort Bowman, A-55*	Route 11, 1.9 miles n. of Strasburg

SMYTH COUNTY
Area: 435 square miles

Formed in 1832 from Washington and Wythe, and named for General Alexander Smyth, member of Congress for many years. Saltworks here were operated at an early date, and at Saltville a battle was fought in 1864.

Seven Mile Ford, K-19	Route 11, 2.9 miles e. of Chilhowie
William Campbell's Grave, K-20	Route 11, 2 miles e. of Chilhowie
Chilhowie, K-22	Route 11, at Chilhowie
Farthest West, 1750, K-21	Route 11, at Chilhowie
Early Church, K-24*	Route 11, .6 mile e. of Marion
Battle of Marion, K-26	Route 11, at Marion e. corporate limits
Site of Colonial Home, K-27	Route 11, at intersection with Route 16 in Marion
Early Settlers, K-30	Route 11, 8.5 miles e. of Marion
Hungry Mother State Park, K-33	Route 11, at intersection with Route 16 in Marion
Marion, K-34	Route 11, at Marion
Sherwood Anderson, K-46	Route 11, at e. corporate limits of Marion
Saltville, KB-6	Route 91, at Saltville
State Fish Hatchery, UC-5	Route 16, 5 miles s.e. of Marion

SOUTHAMPTON COUNTY
Area: 604 square miles

Formed in 1748 from Isle of Wight and Nansemond. Named for a locality that was originally named for the Earl of Southampton, active in the first settlement. General William Mahone was born in this county.

Tarleton's Movements, U-102
Route 58, 8.2 miles e. of Emporia

John Y. Mason's Home, U-105
Route 58, 8.2 miles e. of Emporia

Buckhorn Quarters, U-115
Route 58, 4.5 miles w. of Courtland

General Thomas' Birthplace, U-120
Route 58, 1.7 miles s.e. of Courtland

General Thomas's Birthplace, U-120*
Route 58, 1.7 miles s.e. of Courtland

Southampton Insurrection, U-122
Route 58, 2 miles w. of Courtland

Major Joseph E. Gillette, U-123
Route 58, .9 mile w. of Franklin

Old Indian Reservation, U-124
Route 58, .8 mile w. of Courtland

William Mahone's Birthplace, US-3
Route 258, 2.2 miles s. of Franklin

South Quay, US-6*
Route 258, 4.8 miles s. of Franklin

SPOTSYLVANIA COUNTY
Area: 413 square miles

Formed in 1720 from Essex, King and Queen, and King William, and named for Alexander Spotswood, Governor of Virginia 1710–22. The battles of Fredericksburg, Chancellorsville, the Wilderness, partly, and Spotsylvania were fought in this county.

Stuart, E-8
Route 1, 5.4 miles s. of Falmouth

Turn in Sheridan's Raid, E-30
Route 1, 1.8 miles s. of Thornburg

Jerrell's Mill, E-31
Route 1, 1.1 miles s. of Thornburg

Mud Tavern, E-32
Route 1, at Thornburg

A Raid's End, E-33*
Route 1, 2 miles n. of Thornburg

Where Burnside Turned, E-34*
Route 1, 1.3 miles n. of Thornburg

Where Burnside Crossed, E-35*
Route 1, 1.3 miles n. of Thornburg

Union Army Route, E-36
Route 1, 3.8 miles n. of Thornburg

Massaponax Church, E-37*
Route 1, 4.5 miles n. of Thornburg

Lee's Headquarters, E-38
Route 1, 5.4 miles s. of Falmouth

Start of Sheridan's Raid, E-39
Route 1, 5.3 miles s. of Falmouth

Grant's Supply Line, E-40*
Route 1, 4 miles s. of Fredericksburg

Longstreet's Headquarters, E-41*
Route 1, 3.5 miles s. of Fredericksburg

Early's Line of Battle, E-42*
Route 1, 3.5 miles s. of Fredericksburg

Lee's Position, E-43*
Route 1, 1 mile s. of Fredericksburg

Battles of Fredericksburg, E-44
Route 1, at s. entrance of Fredericksburg

Fredericksburg, E-45*
Route 1, at n. entrance of Fredericksburg

Colonial Fort, E-46*
Route 1, at n. entrance of Fredericksburg

Fredericksburg, E-46-a, (E-46-b*)
Route 1, 2 miles s. of Falmouth

Fall Hill, E-49-a, E-49-b)
Route 1, 2 miles s. of Stafford

Asbury's Deathplace, EH-8
Route 738, 5.5 miles s. of Spotsylvania Courthouse

Fredericksville Furnace, EM-1
Route 208, 100 yards s.w. of Furnace

Jackson's Amputation, J-37
Route 3, e. of Va. 20

Ely's Ford, J-38
Route 610, .54 mile e. of Culpeper County line

Wounding of Jackson, J-39
Route 3, .9 mile w. of Chancellorsville

Battle of Chancellorsville, J-40
Route 3, at Chancellorsville

Spotswood's Furnace, J-42
Route 3, 5.4 miles w. of Fredericksburg

Colonial Post Office, N-10
Route 17, .4 mile n.w. of New Post

STAFFORD COUNTY
Area: 274 square miles

Formed in 1664 from Westmoreland, and named for Staffordshire, England. The Army of the Potomac camped in this county, 1862–63.

Historic Aquia Creek, E-41	Route 1, 3.6 miles n. of Stafford
Historic Falmouth, E-47	Route 1, .95 mile n. of Route 17
Potomac Creek, E-48	Route 1, 3.8 miles n. of Falmouth
Potomac Creek, E-48*	Route 1, 3 miles n. of Falmouth
Smith and Pocahontas, 0-00	Route 1, 1.5 miles n. of Falmouth
Ancient Iron Furnace, E-49*	Route 1, 2 miles s. of Stafford Courthouse
Indian Trail, E-50*	Route 1, .3 mile n. of Stafford
Marlborough, E-75	Route 1, 3.8 miles n. of Falmouth
Peyton's Ordinary, E-79	Route 1, 1.8 miles n. of Stafford
Aquia Church, E-90	Route 1, 2.7 miles n. of Stafford
Chatham, J-60	Route 3, .2 mile east of Fredericksburg
Washington's Boyhood Home, J-61	Route 3, 1.1 miles e. of Fredericksburg
Fredericksburg Campaign, N-4	Route 17, 4.1 miles n.w. of Falmouth
Cavalry Affairs, N-5	Route 17, 8 miles n.w. of Falmouth
The Mud March, N-6*	Route 17, 4.1 miles n.w. of Falmouth

SURRY COUNTY
Area: 278 square miles

Formed in 1652 from James City, and named for an English county. Bacon's Castle, a fortress in the rebellion of 1676, is in this county.

Upper Chippokes Creek, K-211*	Route 10, 13.5 miles w. of Surry
Historic Cabin Point, K-222	Route 10, 4 miles n.w. of Spring Grove
Flying Point, K-223	Route 10, 4 miles n.w. of Spring Grove
Pace's Paines, K-224	Route 10, 3.5 miles w. of Surry
Claremont, K-255	Route 613 at corporate line of Claremont
Wakefield and Pipsico, K-226	Route 10, at Spring Grove
Pleasant Point, K-227	Route 10, 1.3 miles s.e. of Surry
Glebe House, K-228*	Route 10, 4.7 miles w. of Surry
Southwark Church, K-229	Route 10, 3.5 miles w. of Surry
Swann's Point, K-231	Route 10, at Spring Grove
Cypress Church, K-232*	Route 10, 1 mile s. of Surry
Smith's Fort Plantation, K-233	Route 10, at Surry
History on Crouch's Creek, K-234*	Route 10, at Surry
Bacon's Castle, K-235	Route 10, at Bacon's Castle
Organization of the Christian Church, K-236	Route 10, 1.5 miles w. of Surry
Hog Island, K-237	Route 10, at Bacon's Castle
Settlement on Gray's Creek, K-230*	Route 10, 2 miles n.w. of Surry
Historic Claremont, K-255*	Route 10, at Spring Grove
Chippokes Plantation, K-279	Route 10, 1.3 miles s.e. of Surry
Lawnes Creek Church, K-300	Route 10, 7.2 miles s.e. of Surry

SUSSEX COUNTY
Area: 515 square miles

Formed in 1753 from Surry, and named for an English county. Cornwallis passed through this county in 1781.

Colonel Michael Blow, K-230 — Route 460 at Route 628)
Route Early Peanut Crop, K-306 — Route 460, 4 miles s.e. of Waverly
Jarratt's Station, UM-12* — Route 301, at Jarratt
Old Halifax Road, UM-14 — Route 301, at Jarratt
Nottoway River, UM-16* — Route 301, 3.4 miles s. of Stony Creek
History at Stony Creek (UM-18, — Route 301, at Stony Creek
The Cattle, Beefsteak Raid, UO-5 — Route 35, at Route 626

TAZEWELL COUNTY
Area: 531 square miles

Formed in 1799 from Russell and Wythe, and named for Henry Tazewell, United States Senator 1794–99. Beautiful Burke's Garden is in this county.

William Wynne's Fort, X-19 — Route 19, business, 2 miles e. of Tazewell
Tazewell, X-11 — Route 19, business, at Tazewell
Burke's Garden, X-12 — Route 19, business, 2 miles e. of Tazewell
Burke's Garden, X-12-1 — Routes 666 and 623
Maiden Springs Fort, X-13 — Route 91, 12 miles s.w. of Tazewell
Big Crab Orchard or Witten's Fort, X-14 — Route 19, business, through town of Tazewell

Bluefield, Virginia, X-15 — Route 19, at Bluefield
Indian Outrages, X-16 — Route 19, business, 2 miles w. of Tazewell
Molly Tynes' Ride, XH-1 — Route 61, 3 miles e. of Tazewell
Richlands, XL-4 — Route 460, at Richlands
Pocahontas, XP-4 — Route 102, just e. of Pocahontas
Abb's Valley, XP-5 — Route 102, just e. of Pocahontas

WARREN COUNTY
Area: 216 square miles

Formed in 1836 from Frederick and Shenandoah, and named for General Joseph Warren, killed at Bunker Hill, 1775.

The McKay Home, J-7 — Route 340, at Cedarville
Capture of Front Royal, J-8 — Route 340, at Front Royal
Mosby's Men, J-9 — Route 340, .5 mile n. of Front Royal
Guard's Hill Affair, J-11* — Route 340, .2 mile n. of Riverton
Recreational Center of Front Royal, J-12 — Route 340, 1.1 miles n. of Riverton
Brother against Brother, J-17 — Route 340, at Front Royal
Belle Boyd and Jackson, JD-1 — Route 340, 3 miles s.w. of Front Royal
William E. Carson, JD-2 — Route 340, at Front Royal
State Fish Hatchery, FF-2 — Route 55, 5 miles w. of Riverton

WASHINGTON COUNTY
Area: 604 square miles

Formed in 1776 from Fincastle, and named for George Washington. This county was the first locality named for him. General William Campbell, hero of King's Mountain, lived in this county. Emory and Henry College is here.

Emory and Henry College, I-7	Route 11, 8.3 miles e. of Abingdon
Saltville History, K-28	Route 11, 4.1 miles w. of Chilhowie
King's Moutain Men, K-47*	Route 11, at w. entrance of Abingdon
Site of Black's Fort, K-48	Route 11, at Abingdon
Abingdon, K-49	Route 11, at Abingdon

WESTMORELAND COUNTY
Area: 252 square miles

Formed in 1653 from Northumberland and King George, and named for an English county. In it were born George Washington, James Monroe, and Robert E. Lee.

Bristol Iron Works, J-64	Route 3, 2.6 miles w. of Oak Grove
History at Oak Grove, J-67	Route 3, at Oak Grove
Westmoreland Association, J-68	Route 3, at Oak Grove
Leedstown, J-68*	Route 3, s. of Colonial Beach
The Washington Home, J-69*	Route 3, 2.8 miles s.e. of Oak Grove
Popes Creek Episcopal Church, J-69-a	Route 3, 4.8 miles s.e. of Oak Grove
Washington's Birthplace, J-69-b	Route 3, 2.8 miles s.e. of Oak Grove
Lee's Birthplace, J-70*	Route 3, 4 miles n.w. of Montross
Old Westmoreland Courthouse, J-71	Route 3, at Montross
Nomini Hall, J-72	Route 3, at Templeman's Cross Roads
Chantilly, J-74*	Route 3, 4 miles n.w. of Montross
Westmoreland State Park, J-75	Route 3, 4.7 miles n.w. of Montross
Stratford and Chantilly, J-76	Route 3, 4 miles n.w. of Montross
Birthplace of Monroe, JP-6	Route 205, 1.8 miles s. of Colonial Beach
Nominy Church, JT-2	Route 202, 3.7 miles e. of Templemans Cross Roads
The Glebe, JT-3	Route 202, 4.4 miles e. of Templemans Cross Roads
Washington's Mother, JT-4	Route 202, 4.8 miles n.w. of Callao
Bushfield, JT-5	Route 202, 4.4 miles east of Templemans Cross Roads
Richard Henry Lee's Grave, JT-6	Route 202, 8.8 miles s.e. of Templemans Cross Roads
Yeocomico Church, JT-7	Route 202, 8.1 miles n.e. of Callao
Kinsale, JT-8	Route 202, 4.8 miles n.w. of Callao
Leedstown, JT-15	Route 637, at Leedstown
Sandy Point, JT-16	Route 604, at Sandy Point

WISE COUNTY
Area: 420 square miles

Formed in 1856 from Lee, Scott, and Russell, and named for Henry A. Wise, Governor of Virginia 1856–60.

Southwest Virginia Museum, I-2
Big Stone Gap, KA-11
Coeburn, X-20

Norton, X-21
Benge's Gap, X-22
Appalachia, X-23
Wise, XB-4
Pound Gap, XB-7*

Alternate Route 58, at Big Stone Gap
Alternate Route 58, at Big Stone Gap
Route 58, at intersection with Route 72 in
 Coeburn
Route 23, at Norton
Alternate Route 58, at Norton
Alternate Route 58, at Appalachia
Route 23, business, Main Street, at Wise
Route 23, 4 miles n. of Pound

WYTHE COUNTY
Area: 479 square miles

Formed in 1789 from Montgomery, and named for George Wythe, signer of the Declaration of Independence. New River flows through this county.

St. John's Lutheran Church, FR-26
A Colonial Soldier's Home, K-23
Site of Mount Airy, K-31
Wytheville, K-35
Anchor and Hope Plantation, K-36
Ingleside, K-37
Lead Mines, K-39
Toland's Raid, KC-4
Seat of Fincastle County, KD-5
Jackson's Ferry and Old Shot Tower, KD-6
Austin's Birthplace, KD-8

Route 21, at Wytheville
Route 11, at e. entrance of Wytheville
Route 11, 12.9 miles w. of Wytheville
Route 11, at Wytheville
Route 52, at Fort Chiswell
Route 11, at e. entrance of Wytheville
Route 52, at Fort Chiswell
Route 52, at Bland-Wythe County line
Route 52, 5.5 miles s.e. of Fort Chiswell
Route 52, 7.7 miles s.e. of Fort Chiswell
Route 52, at Poplar Camp

York County
Area: 136 square miles

One of the eight original shires formed in 1634. First called Charles River, which was named for King Charles I. The name was changed in 1643 to York for Yorkshire, England. Cornwallis's surrender, October 19, 1781, took place at Yorktown.

Vineyard Tract, W-46
Charles Church, NP-1

Route 641, 1.4 miles e. of Williamsburg
Routes 134 and 17 at Tabb

INDEPENDENT CITIES

ALEXANDRIA

Land was first patented here in 1657. In 1731 a warehouse was built on Hunting Creek, about which grew up the village of Belhaven. The town of Alexandria was established in 1749 and became one of the main colonial trading centers. It was a part of the original District of Columbia but was returned to Virginia in 1847.

Historic Alexandria, E-71*	Route 1, at s. entrance of Alexandria
Lee's Boyhood Home, E-91	In front of 607 Oronoco Street
Virginia Theological Seminary, T-44	Route 7, w. of Quaker Lane
Episcopal High School, T-45*	Route 7, w. of Quaker Lane

BRISTOL

The Sapling Grove tract (Bristol) was surveyed for John Tayloe in 1749. It was owned by Isaac Baker and Evan Shelby, who built a post about 1770. The Virginia tract was bought by John Goodson, whose son founded the town of Goodson, incorporated as a city.

Bristol, Virginia, K-42*	Route 11, at Bristol
Historic Bristol, K-43*	Route 11, at Bristol

CHARLOTTESVILLE

The site was patented by William Taylor in 1737. The town was established by a law in 1762 and was named for Queen Charlotte, wife of George III. Burgoyne's army, captured at Saratoga in 1777, was long quartered near here. The legislature was in session here in June 1781, but retired westward to escape Tarleton's raid on the town. Jefferson, who lived at Monticello, founded the University of Virginia in 1819.

University of Virginia, I-3	Route 29, at Charlottesville:
Charlottesville, Q-1-a-b-d	a. High Street near Hazel Street intersection;
	b. Monticello Road at Henderson & Ervin factory;
	d. Route 29 near Piedmont Avenue
Tarleton's Oak, Q-1-1	intersection
	Intersection of High Street and Lexington Avenue

CHESAPEAKE
(Includes old Norfolk County)

Craney Island, K-262	Route 17, w. of Churchland bypass
Dismal Swamp Canal, NW-15*	Route 17, 1 mile s. of Va. 104
Craney Island, K-262*	Route 337, 2.8 miles w. of Portsmouth
Hodges Ferry, K-263*	Route 337, 2.3 miles w. of Portsmouth
Dale Point, K-264*	Route 460, 0.25 miles w. of Portsmouth
Fort Nelson, K-265*	Route 337, near w. city limits of Portsmouth
Great Bridge, K-275*	Route 17, 3 miles s. of Portsmouth

Battle of Great Bridge, KY-4*
Battle of Great Bridge, KY-5
Great Bridge Chapel, WP-5*
Norfolk County Courthouse, WP-7*
St. Bride's Church, WP-10

Route 170, at Great Bridge
Route 168, at Great Bridge
Route 168, at Great Bridge
Route 168, in Great Bridge
Route 168, 4 miles n. of state line

COVINGTON

Fort Young, D-27

City of Covington: Route 154, on Durant Road, n. of Jackson River

DANVILLE

Last Confederate Capitol, Q-5-a
Wreck of the Old 97, Q-5-b
The Gibson Girl, Q-5-c
Lady Astor, Q-5-c
Loyal Baptist Church, Q-5-c
Danville System, Q-5-d
Stratford College, Q-5-e
Cavalry United Methodist Church, Q-5-f
750 Main Street, Q-7-e

At Sutherlin Avenue and Main Street
Between Pickett and Farrar streets
Broad and Main Street
Main Street at Broad Street
400 block Loyal Street
126 N. Union Street
1125 W. Main Street
924 N. Main Street
750 Main Street

FAIRFAX CITY

Mosby's Midnight Raid, B-26
Sharpsburg, Antietam Campaign, B-29
Burke's Station Raid, BW-2
Bull Run Battlefields, C-19

Route 123, .34 mile s. of Route 236
Route 50, w. entrance of Fairfax City
Route 236, 1 mile e. of Route 123
At Fairfax, e. of Route 236

FREDERICKSBURG

Captain John Smith was here in 1608; Lederer, the explorer, in 1670. In May, 1671, John Buckner and Thomas Royster patented the Lease Land Grant. The town was established in 1727 and lots were laid out. It was named for Frederick, Prince of Wales, father of George III. The court for Spotsylvania County was moved here in 1732 and the town was enlarged in 1759 and 1769. Fredericksburg was incorporated as a town in 1781, as a city in 1879, and declared a city of the first class in 1941.

Fredericksburg, E-46-a, E-46-b

Alternate Route 1, at Fredericksburg

HAMPTON
(includes Old Elizabeth City County)

First Battle of Ironclads, W-84

Chesapeake Avenue between La Salle and East avenues

Wythe's Birthplace, W-85
Forts Henry and Charles, W-86*

Route 60, .5 mile w. of Hampton
Route 60, .5 mile s.w. of, then Hampton

Historic Hampton, W-87

Emancipation Oak, W-88
Little England, W-88*
Fort Algernourne, W-89

Fort Monroe, W-90

Confinement of Jefferson Davis, W-92

Third Elizabeth City Parish Church, WY-88
Second Church at Kecoughtan, WY-89
First Church at Kecoughtan, WY-90
Camp Hamilton, WY-91
Buckroe, WY-92

Phoebus, WY-93
Phoebus, WY-94
Zero Mile Post, W-91
John Baptist Pierce, S-28

Route 60, at w. entrance of Hampton (Sunset and Kecoughtan roads)
East Tyler Street and ramp to Interstate 64
Route 60, at Hampton/Newport News line
Route 60 at Fort Monroe, near Old Point Comfort
Route 60, at Fort Monroe, near Old Point Comfort
Route 60, at Fort Monroe, near Old Point Comfort
Route 351 (Pembroke Avenue and Parkdale Street)
Tyler Street, exit 5 of Interstate 64
LaSalle and Kenmore streets
College Place and e. Queen Street
At Buckroe Beach (Atlantic Avenue and Mallory Street)
County Street and Woodland Road
Mallory St. and off ramp of Interstate 64
Route 258 at Fort Monroe
Route 60 between Interstate 64 and Emancipation Drive

HARRISONBURG

Harrisonburg, A-33
End of the Campaign, A-35

Route 11, at Harrisonburg
Route 11, at Harrisonburg

LEXINGTON

Stonewall Jackson's Home, Q-11-a*

Lexington: Washington and Main streets

LYNCHBURG

In 1757 John Lynch opened a ferry here; in 1765 a church was built. In 1786 Lynchburg was established by act of assembly; in 1791 the first tobacco warehouse was built. Lynchburg was incorporated as a town in 1805. In 1840 the James River and Kanawha Canal, from Richmond to Lynchburg, was opened; the section to Buchanan, in 1851. Lynchburg became a city in 1852.

John Daniel's Home, K-142*
Chestnut Hill, K-146*
Quaker Meeting House, L-20
Sandusky, L-22
Lynchburg Defenses, M-60
Fort Early, Q-6-1
Fort McCausland, Q-6-2

Inner Defenses, 1864, Q-6-3

720 Court Street
Route 501, 4 miles e. of Lynchburg
Fort Avenue at Quaker Parkway
Fort Avenue at Quaker Parkway
Route 501, e. entrance of Lynchburg
Fort Avenue, near Early Monument
Langhorne Road, about 1200 feet w. of Clifton Street
Twelfth Street, between Fillmore and Floyd streets

Inner Defenses, Q-6-4

Defense Works, Q-6-5

Mustered and Disbanded, 1861–65, Q-6-6

Inner Defenses, 1864, Q-6-7

Inner Defenses, Q-6-8

Inner Defenses, Q-6-9*

Miller-Claytor House, Q-6-10

Lynchburg, Q-6-11—front and back of
marker

Carter Glass, Q-6-12

Lynchburg College, Q-6-13

Randolph-Macon Woman's College, Q-6-14

Virginia Seminary and College, Q-6-15

Allen Weir Freeman, M.D. 1881–1954, Q-6-16*

Douglas Southall Freeman, Ph.D., Q-6-17

Samuel D. Rockenbach, Q-6-18

The Anne Spencer House, Q-6-20

Corner Bedford Avenue and Holly Street

Rivermont Avenue and Langhorn Road

Between Rivermont Avenue and Monsview
Drive

Ninth and Polk streets

Between 9th and Polk streets

Between Wise and Floyd streets

Rivermont Avenue and Treasure Island
Road

Ninth and Church Street

829 Church Street

Lakeside Drive w. of Old Forest Road

Rivermont Avenue and Princeton Circle

Campbell Avenue and DeWitt Street

In front of 416 Main Street

South end of Rivermont Bridge

Eighth and Court streets

1313 Pierce Street

MANASSAS

Ruffner Public School Number 1, CL-2

Route 28, .1 mile s. of Route 334

MARTINSVILLE

Named for Joseph Martin, pioneer, who settled here in 1773. In 1793 the courthouse of Henry County was moved here and the town was established. Patrick Henry for whom the county was named, lived near here once. In 1865, Stoneman, moving south to join Sherman, captured Martinsville. It was incorporated as a town in 1873 and as a city in 1929.

Martinsville, A-94

Route 220 at Martinsville

NEWPORT NEWS
(includes old Warwick County)

This community was known to Captain John Smith as Point Hope, but it was called Newportes Newes as early as 1619. The name may commemorate Captain Christopher Newport, commander of five expeditions to Jamestown during 1606–12.

Skiffes Creek, W-53*

Lee Hall, W-54

To Yorktown, W-55*

Fort Eustis, W-56*

Mulberry Point, W-57*

Lee's Mill, W-58*

Battle of Dam No. 1, W-59*

Warwick Courthouse, W-60

Route 60, 1 mile n.w. of Lee Hall

Route 60, at Lee Hall

Route 60, at Lee Hall

Route 337, 1 mile s. of Lee Hall

Route 337, 1 mile s. of Lee Hall

Route 337, 2 miles s.e. of Lee Hall

Route 60, 1.9 miles s.e. of Lee Hall

Route 60, at Denbigh (14421 Old Courthouse Way)

NORFOLK

This marks the northern limit of the fifty acres constituting the original town of Norfolk. It was bounded on the north by Town Back Creek and Dun-in-the-Mire Creek. The land was purchased as a port for Lower Norfolk County for "tenn thousand pounds of tobacco and caske," being deeded to feoffees (sic) in trust for the county in 1682. It was divided into streets and sold in half-acre lots.

PETERSBURG

PORTSMOUTH

The site of this city was patented in 1659 by Captain William Carver. Established as a town in 1752 and named by its founder, Lt. Col. William Crawford. Chartered as a city in 1858, it has the country's oldest naval shipyard, established in 1767, the nation's oldest naval hospital, commenced in 1827, and is the birthplace of the world's largest naval installation.

Trinity Church, Q-8-a	High and Court streets
Monumental Methodist Church, Q-8-b	Dinwiddie Street near High Street
Watts House, Q-8-c	At 517 North Street
Ball House, Q-8-d	At 213 Middle Street
Benedict Arnold at Portsmouth, Q-8-e	Bayview and Maryland avenues
Cornwallis at Portsmouth, Q-8-f	Crawford Parkway e. of Court Street
Collier's Raid, *Q-8-g	Bayview and Maryland avenues
Portsmouth Naval Hospital, Q-8-h	On hospital grounds
Elizabeth River, Q-8-k	Crawford Parkway at Court Street
City of Portsmouth, Q-8-L	Route 17 at Churchland Bridge
Crawford House, Q-8-m	Corner of Crawford and Queen streets
Norfolk County Court House, Q-8-n	High and Court streets
Arnold's British Defense, 1781, Q-8-o	Corner of Washington Street and King streets
Arnold's British Defenses, 1781, Q-8-p	Crawford Parkway at Court Street
Arnold's British Defenses, 1781, Q-8-q*	Corner of Washington and Brighton streets

RADFORD

It originated as a railroad town in 1856 and was known as Central. In 1862–65 this section was in the range of Union raids; Confederates burned the bridge at Ingles Ferry to retard raiders. Incorporated in 1887 as a town, the place was incorporated as a city in 1892 and named Radford, for Dr. John B. Radford, prominent citizen. Radford State Teachers College was established here, 1913.

Radford, K-65	Route 11, at Radford
State Teachers College at Radford, K-66	Route 11, at Radford

RICHMOND

Bacon's Plantation, E-1*	Chamberlayne Avenue
Brook Road, E-4*	Intersection of Brook Road and Route 1
Steuben and Lafayette, S-1*	Route 1, at s. entrance to city
Wilton, SA-29	Cary Street Road and Wilton Road
Ampthill, SA-30	Cary Street Road and Ampthill Road
Windsor, SA-28	4601 Lilac Lane

ROANOKE

In June 1864, General Hunter passed here retreating from Lynchburg. In 1874 Big Lick was incorporated. In 1881, with the junction of the new Shenandoah Valley Railroad and the N. & W., rapid growth began. In 1882 the name was changed to Roanoke; in 1884 it was incorporated as a city. In 1909 the Virginian Railroad operated its first train. In recent years Roanoke became the third city of Virginia.

A Colonial Ford, K-116	Franklin Road s.w. between Naval Reserve and Brandon avenues
Roanoke, K-95—front and back of marker	East Bullit and south Jefferson streets

STAUNTON

SUFFOLK
(includes old Nansemond County)

VIRGINIA BEACH
(includes old Princess Anne County)

First Landing, KV-15

Oldest Brick House in Virginia, KW-16*

Route 60, at Cape Henry, .85 mile w. of
    Route 305
Route 500, 7 miles e. of Norfolk

WAYNESBORO

Here, on one of the first roads west of the Blue Ridge, a hamlet stood in colonial times. The Walker exploring expedition started from this vicinity in 1748. Here, in June, 1781, the Augusta militia assembled to join Lafayette in the east. A town was founded in 1797. It was established by law in 1801 and named for General Anthony Wayne.

Waynesboro, Q-2a, Q-2b

Route 250, at e. and w. entrances of
    Waynesboro

WILLIAMSBURG

First Balloon Flight in Virginia, W-40

Route 162, at entrance to Cary Field

WINCHESTER

At first called Frederickstown, it was founded in 1744, near a Shawnee Indian village, by Colonial James Wood, a native of the English city of Winchester. The town was situated in Lord Fairfax's proprietary of the Northern Neck. It was chartered in 1752.

Third Battle of Winchester, J-4

At National Cemetery, Route 422, Win-
    chester

General Daniel Morgan, Q-4-a
Winchester, Q-4-a
Joist Hite and Braddock, Q-4-b*
Winchester, Q-4-b*
George Washington, Q 4-c
Winchester, Q-4-c*
Lord Fairfax, Q-4-d*
Winchester, Q-4-d*
Colonel James Wood, Q-4-e
Winchester, Q-4-e
Jackson's Headquarters, Q-4-F

Route 50, at e. limits of Winchester
Route 50, at e. limits of Winchester
Route 7, at e. limits of Winchester
Route 7, at e. limits of Winchester
Route 11, at n. limits of Winchester
Route 11, at n. limits of Winchester
Route 522 at Winchester
Route 50, at w. limits of Winchester
Route 50, just w. of Route 11
Route 522, at s. limits of Winchester
415 North Braddock Street, at Winchester

COUNTIES THAT ARE NO LONGER IN

EXISTENCE AND IN BORDERING STATES

ELIZABETH CITY COUNTY

Area: 54 square miles

One of the eight original shires formed in 1634, and named for Elizabeth City, or Hampton. This is the oldest English-settled town in America.

See Hampton.

NANSEMOND COUNTY

Area: 423 square miles

Formed in 1637 from New Norfolk County. It was first called Upper Norfolk County, but in 1642 it was named Nansemond for an Indian tribe. Dismal Swamp is partly in this county.

See Suffolk.

NORFOLK COUNTY

Area: 415 square miles

Formed in 1637, when New Norfolk County was divided into Upper Norfolk and Lower Norfolk. The name is that of an English county. The battle of Great Bridge, 1775, took place in this county, and in the waters near its shores the warship *Merrimac* performed her exploits in 1862.

See Chesapeake.

PRINCESS ANNE COUNTY

Area: 279 square miles

Formed in 1691 by a division of Lower Norfolk County into Norfolk and Princess Anne. Named for Queen Anne (then Princess Anne). The first settlers first landed at Cape Henry, April 26, 1607.

See Virginia Beach.

WARWICK COUNTY

Area: 69 square miles

One of the original shires formed in 1634, it was given the name of the Warwick River. The river itself was named for the Earl of Warwick.

See Newport News.

KENTUCKY

This first permanent settlement was made at Harrodsburg in 1774. Kentucky County was established in 1776 and was represented in the Virginia legislature by Daniel Boone. Kentucky was admitted to the Union as the fifteenth state in 1792.

MARYLAND

Maryland was one of the original thirteen states. At first a part of Virginia, it became a separate colony under a charter granted Lord Baltimore, and was settled in 1634.

NORTH CAROLINA

North Carolina was one of the original thirteen states. The first settlement was made on Roanoke Island, 1585, but was not permanent. Settlers from Virginia occupied the Albemarle region before 1663, in which year the colony of Carolina was founded.

TENNESSEE

First permanently settled in 1769 and long a part of North Carolina. In 1785, settlers formed the state of Franklin, not recognized by Congress. Tennessee was admitted to the Union as the sixteenth state in 1796.

WEST VIRGINIA

West Virginia was long a part of Virginia. Morgan Morgan began the settlement of the region in 1727. A great battle with the Indians took place at Point Pleasant in 1774. West Virginia became a separate state of the Union in 1863.

The following map shows the boundaries of Virginia's counties and its independent cities. It also includes all
interstate highways and all primary
roads on which more than twelve
markers are located. For highways not
shown on this map, please consult the
official highway map of Virginia.

COUNTIES

Accomack	I-3
Albemarle	F-3
Alleghany	E-3
Amelia	G-4
Amherst	E-3, F-3
Appomattox	F-4
Arlington	G-2
Augusta	E-3, F-3
Bath	E-3
Bedford	E-4
Bland	C-4, D-4
Botetourt	E-3, E-4
Brunswick	G-4, G-5
Buchanan	B-4, C-4
Buckingham	F-3, F-4
Campbell	F-4
Caroline	G-3, H-3
Carroll	D-4, D-5
Charles City	H-4
Charlotte	F-4
Chesterfield	G-4
Clarke	G-2
Craig	D-4
Culpeper	G-2
Cumberland	G-3, G-4
Dickenson	B-4
Dinwiddie	G-4
Essex	H-3
Fairfax	G-2, H-2
Fauquier	G-2
Floyd	D-4
Fluvanna	F-3
Franklin	E-4
Frederick	F-1, F-2
Giles	D-4
Gloucester	H-3
Goochland	G-3
Grayson	C-5
Greene	F-2, F-3
Greensville	G-4, G-5
Halifax	F-4, F-5
Hanover	G-3
Henrico	G-3
Henry	E-5
Highland	E-2, E-3

Isle of Wight	H-4	Warren	F-2
James City	H-4	Washington	B-5, C-5
King and	H-3	Westmoreland	H-3
Queen		Wise	B-4
King George	H-3	Wythe	C-4, D-4
King William	H-3	York	H-4
Lancaster	H-3		
Lee	A-5		
Loudoun	G-2		
Louisa	G-3		

INDEPENDENT
CITIES WITH
HISTORICAL
MARKERS

Lunenburg	F-4, G-4	Alexandria	H-2
Madison	F-2	Bristol	B-5
Mathews	I-4	Charlottesville	F-3
Mecklenburg	F-5, G-5	Chesapeake	I-5
Middlesex	H-3	Covington	E-3
Montgomery	D-4	Danville	E-5
Nelson	F-3	Fairfax	G-2
New Kent	H-3	Hampton	I-4
Northampton	I-4	Harrisonburg	F-2
Northumber-	H-3	Lexington	E-3
land		Lynchburg	E-4
Nottoway	G-4	Manassas	G-2
Orange	G-3	Martinsville	E-5
Page	F-2	Newport News	H-4
Patrick	D-5	Norfolk	I-4
Pittsylvania	E-4, F-5	Petersburg	G-4
Powhatan	G-3	Portsmouth	I-4
Prince Edward	F-4	Radford	D-4
Prince George	H-4	Richmond	G-3
Prince William	G-2	Roanoke	E-4
Pulaski	D-4	Staunton	F-3
Rappahannock	F-2, G-2	Suffolk	H-4
Richmond	H-3	Virginia Beach	I-4
Roanoke	E-4	Waynesboro	F-3
Rockbridge	E-3	Williamsburg	H-4
Rockingham	F-2	Winchester	F-1
Russell	B-4, C-4		
Scott	B-5		
Shenandoah	F-2		
Smyth	C-4, C-5		
Southampton	H-4, H-5		
Spotsylvania	G-3		
Stafford	G-2		
Surry	H-4		
Sussex	G-4, H-4		
Tazewell	C-4		

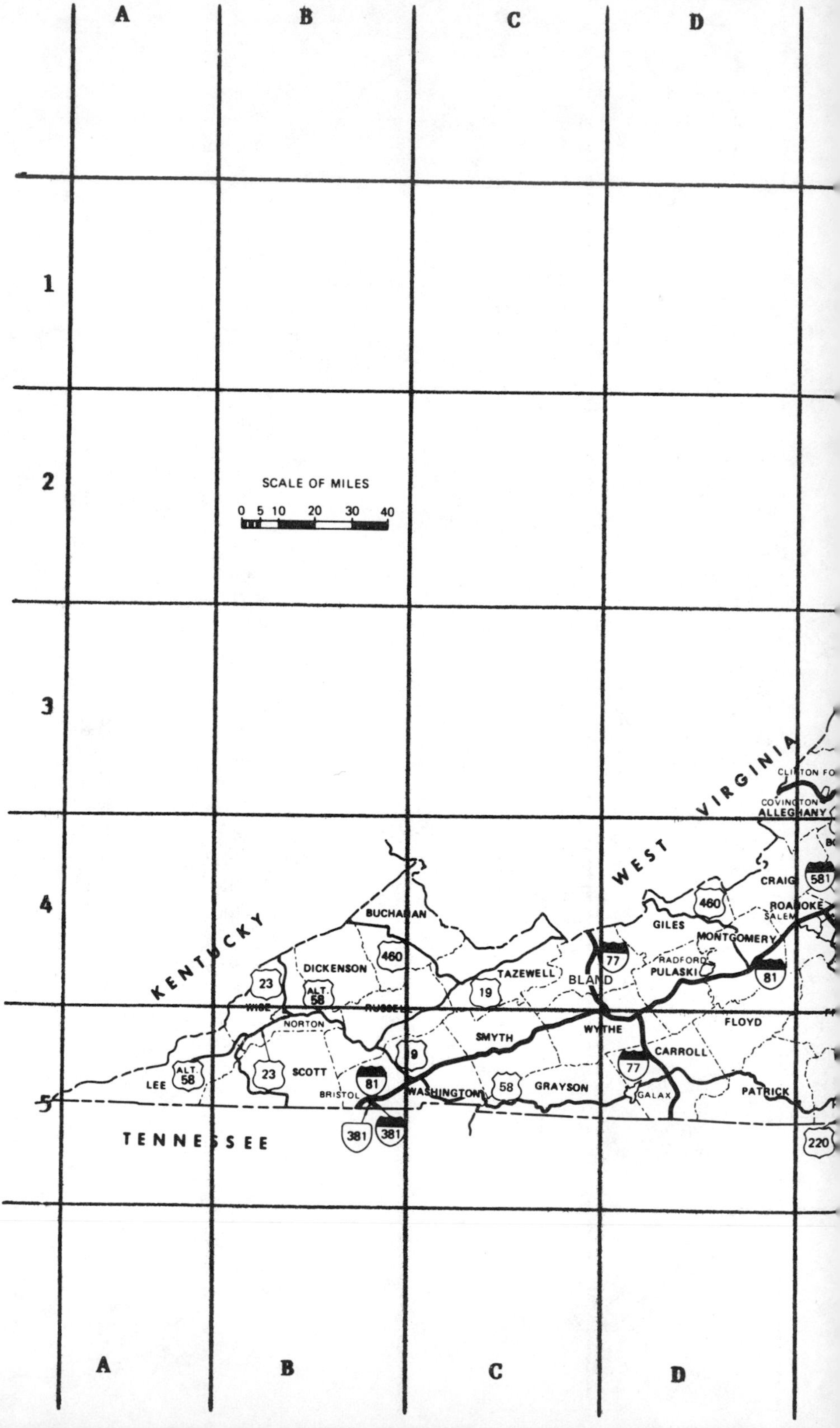
A
B
C
D
1
2
3
4
5
SCALE OF MILES
0 5 10 20 30 40
KENTUCKY
WEST VIRGINIA
TENNESSEE
BUCHANAN
DICKENSON
TAZEWELL
BLAND
GILES
MONTGOMERY
RADFORD
PULASKI
CRAIG
ROANOKE
SALEM
ALLEGHANY
COVINGTON
WISE
NORTON
RUSSELL
LEE
SCOTT
BRISTOL
WASHINGTON
SMYTH
WYTHE
GRAYSON
GALAX
CARROLL
FLOYD
PATRICK
23
ALT. 58
460
19
77
81
581
9
58
381
220

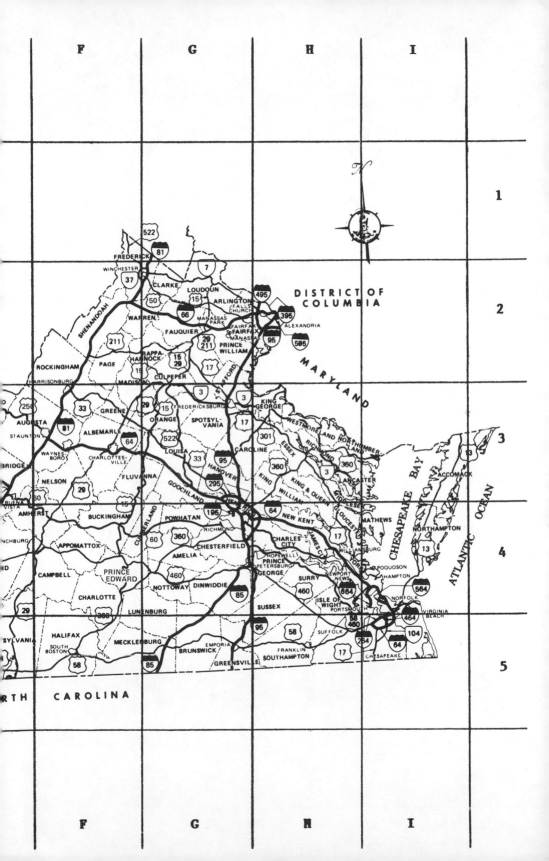